THE BIG BASICS BOOK OF THE INTERNET

by Joe Kraynak, Jennifer Fulton,
Sherry Kinkoph, and Aaron Weiss

A Division of Macmillan Computer Publishing
201 West 103rd Street, Indianapolis, Indiana 46290 USA

International Standard Book Number: 0-7897-0753-5

Library of Congress Catalog Card Number: 95-73288

98 97 96   8 7 6 5 4 3 2

Interpretation of the printing code: the rightmost double-digit number is the year of the book's first printing; the rightmost single-digit number is the number of the book's printing. For example, a printing code of 96-1 shows that this copy of the book was printed during the first printing of the book in 1996.

Screen reproductions in this book were created by means of the program Collage Complete from Inner Media, Inc, Hollis, NH.

Printed in the United States of America

Publisher
Roland Elgey

Vice President and Publisher
Marie Butler-Knight

Publishing Manager
Lynn E. Zingraf

Editorial Services Director
Elizabeth Keaffaber

Managing Editor
Michael Cunningham

Acquisitions Coordinator
Martha O'Sullivan

Product Development Specialists
Lori L. Cates, Melanie Palaisa

Production Editor
Audra Gable

Copy Editor
San Dee Phillips

Book Designer
Barbara Kordesh

Cover Designer
Jay Corpus

Production Team
Stephen Adams
Jason Carr
Jason Hand
Sonja Hart
Bill Hartman
Bob LaRoche
Glenn Larsen
Stephanie Layton
Michelle Lee
Julie Quinn
Kaylene Riemen
Bobbi Satterfield
Kelly Warner
Todd Wente
Jody York

Indexers
Bront Davis
Carol Sheehan

➤ *Special thanks to C. Herbert Feltner for ensuring the technical accuracy of this book.*

Contents

Part 1 How To...

Play Sound and Video Clips with Helper Applications   **161**

Search for Information on the Internet   **179**

Send and Receive Electronic Mail   **193**

Read and Post Messages in Newsgroups   **221**

Part 2   Do It Yourself...

Part 3   Quick Fixes...

Part 4   Handy Reference

Introduction

You can't avoid the Internet. An ad pops up on your TV screen, saying that you can find information about the movie *Toy Story* at www.toystory.com (pronounced dubayou-dubayou-dubayou-dot-toystory-dot-kahm). You flip to a page in *Time* magazine and find out that you can write to the editor at talktotime@time.timeinc.com. What do these odd bits of text and periods stand for? Where can you find out about all this hip '90s technology that's taking the country by storm? And once you find out about it, how can you tap into it and reap its benefits?

Welcome to *The Big Basics Book of the Internet*. This book doesn't assume that you're a computer wiz or a seasoned programmer. It provides instructions that tell and show you (the average computer user) how to connect to the Internet and make full use of its resources. In this book, you won't find a bunch of cryptic commands you need to memorize. And you won't find long-winded discussions about how the Internet was built.

Instead, *The Big Basics Book of the Internet* gives you complete information about the most commonly used Internet features. It weeds out all the high-tech fluff and offers you the practical instructions you need to survive and succeed on the Internet. Like those illustrated books you may have used to learn how to fix your plumbing or create a quilt, this book provides step-by-step instructions and is thoughtfully illustrated, to both tell and show you how to perform such tasks as:

- Setting up your modem (or using a network connection) to connect to the Internet from Windows 3.1 or Windows 95.

- Using an online service (such as America Online or CompuServe) as an easy way into the Internet.

- Connecting to the Internet in Windows 3.1 or Windows 95.

- Finding and setting up a Web browser to make it easy to move around the Internet. (You'll even learn what the Web and Web browsers are.)

- Sending and receiving mail electronically.

- Sharing common interests with other people in newsgroups (using electronic bulletin boards where you can post and read messages).

- Playing movie clips, animations, sound recordings, and other snippets that you will find as you wander the Internet.

- Chatting with other users (sort of like talking on the phone by using your keyboard).

- Finding specific information on the Internet.

- ...and much, much more.

How to Find What You Need in This Book

This *Big Basics Book* has four easy-to-use, distinct parts. Each part focuses on a particular type of information and presents that information in the best format for beginners. You don't need to read the book from cover to cover; you can just skip to the section you need.

Part 1: How to covers all the tasks that a new or casual Internet user needs. A brief introduction leads into each task, and complete step-by-step instructions show you just what to do. A clear illustration accompanies almost every step, and cross-references tell you where to look in the book for even more information.

Part 2: Do It Yourself also offers illustrated steps that explain how to perform specific tasks. However, this part covers practical projects you can use to hone your skills and become more productive on the Internet.

Part 3: Quick Fixes anticipates the inevitable: it identifies the problems that every Internet user will encounter and offers the simplest solutions for those problems. Scan the Quick-Finder Table at the beginning of this section to quickly locate your problem.

Part 4: Handy Reference is a list of lists, including lists of Internet sites where you can obtain files, chat with complete strangers, and write letters to famous people. You'll also find lists of commands that are just too boring to include anywhere else in the book.

How This Book Is Set Up

This book was specially designed to make it easy to use. Each task has a title that tells you what you'll be doing. Immediately following the title is a text section that gives you background information on the task. After that is a *Guided Tour*, which shows you step-by-step how to perform the task. Additional text tells you why you might want to perform the task and provides details on what to do. The following figure shows you how the pages are laid out.

Running heads help you find what you want to learn.

Tips provide shortcuts or reference other useful information.

Additional information answers all your questions.

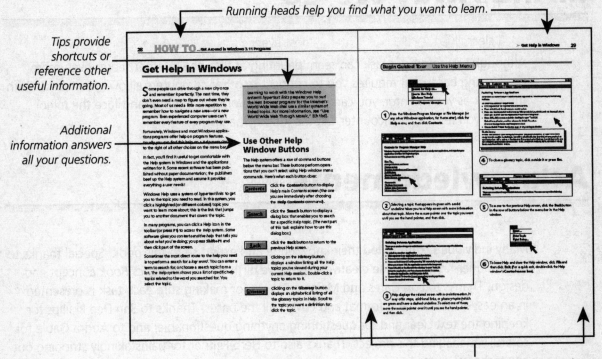

The Guided Tour shows you how to complete the task step by step.

To help you quickly figure out which buttons to press and which commands to enter, this book uses the following standard conventions:

- Text you are supposed to type and keyboard keys you have to press appear in bold. For example, if the step says, type **http://www.whitehouse.com** and press **Enter**, you type the text "http://www.whitehouse.com" and press the Enter key on your keyboard.

- If you have to press two keys at the same time to execute a command, the key combination appears as **Key1+Key2**, which means you hold down the first key and press the second key. For example, if you're told to press **Ctrl+B**, hold down the Ctrl key and press the B key.

- Menu names and commands are also bold, so if you're told to open the **File** menu and select **Save**, click on File in the menu bar at the top of the window, and then click on the Save command.

> Look to sidebars like this for tips, hints, references to other sections of the book, and additional information about how to perform a task.

...And Away We Go

Although any computer task can seem daunting at first, the Internet seems even more challenging because it requires you to connect to other computers all over the world. With this book as your mentor, you can confidently explore the Internet and face the minor glitches you're sure to encounter. Let the journey begin!

Acknowledgments

Many individuals contributed their knowledge and expertise to this book. Special thanks to Marie Butler-Knight, whose creative mind gave birth to the *Big Basics Book* concept and design. Thanks to Lori Cates and Melanie Palaisa for making sure each task is presented in an easy-to-understand format and covers all the bases. Thanks to San Dee Phillips for keeping the text clear and for questioning anything questionable; and to Audra Gable for carefully managing this project. Thanks also to Herb Feltner for painstakingly stripping out any technical errors.

Trademarks

Terms suspected of being trademarks or service marks have been appropriately capitalized throughout this book. Que Corporation cannot attest to the accuracy of this information. Use of a term in this book should not be regarded as affecting the validity of any trademark or service mark.

PART 1

How To...

The Internet has been touted as the ultimate tool of the information age—the pinnacle of "let your fingers do the walking." From a keyboard in your cozy home or office, you can connect to computers all over the world, shop at electronic malls, view video clips of yet-to-be-released films, listen to music clips, research topics of interest, invest your money, send and receive mail electronically, and even "talk" with other people.

Before you can take advantage of the Internet, you need to acquire and set up the tools required to tap its resources. In this part, you'll learn all you need to know to start: how to set up a modem, how to subscribe to an Internet service, and how to set up Windows 3.1 or Windows 95 to establish your Internet connection. You'll also learn how to set up and use the programs you need in order to take full advantage of all the Internet features.

What You Will Find in This Part

HOW TO...

What Is the Internet?

The Internet is a global collection of high-powered computers that are connected to each other with network cables, telephone cables, satellites, and any other electronic wizardry you can imagine. Think of it as an enormous phone system for computers.

As awesome as this appears, it really doesn't mean much until you start to look at what these interconnected computers can do for you. Each computer on the Internet stores vast resources, including documents, sound and video clips, program files, electronic shopping centers, animations, pictures, and anything else that can be stored and presented electronically. When you connect to the Internet, all these resources are available to you.

And because any person who's connected to the Internet is connected to you, you can communicate with anyone on the Internet by sending e-mail, posting messages in newsgroups (electronic bulletin boards), and typing messages back and forth in chat areas.

This section provides an overview of what's available on the Internet and what you can expect when you connect. Simply follow the *Guided Tours* throughout this section to take a glance at what the Internet has to offer.

What You Will Find in This Section

Find an Entrance Ramp to the Internet

Once you connect to the Internet, most tasks are fairly simple. You use specialized programs to access and explore the many Internet features that are available. But how do you connect to the Internet? Well, that depends a great deal on whether your computer is already connected to a network. If your computer is connected to a network (say, at the place where you work), and if this network is on the Internet, you can usually connect for free simply by having the person who acts as network administrator set up the connection.

If you're at home or you work at a place where the computers are not networked, you have to connect via a modem to a service provider's computer on the Internet. A *service provider* is a company that allows you to connect to and use its computer to connect to the Internet. First you call a service provider in your area and start an account, which will cost you about $15 per month. The service provider usually gives you the software and instructions you need to connect. This software enables your computer and modem to dial the phone number of the service provider's computer and establish a connection. Once you establish a connection, you can run other programs that make it easy to navigate the Internet.

The next three sections of this book provide detailed instructions on how to find a reliable service provider, set up your modem, and establish your Internet connection for the first time. The following *Guided Tour* provides an overview of these operations so you'll know what to expect.

Begin Guided Tour   Establish an Internet Connection

1 If your computer is on a network that is already connected to the Internet, ask the person who acts as your network administrator to help you establish a connection.

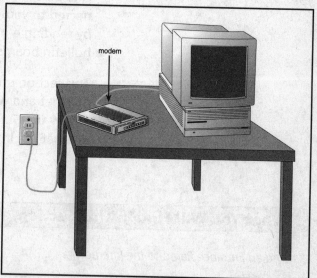

2 If your computer is not on a network, you need a modem. The modem will dial the phone number and handle the transfer of data between your computer and the Internet. See "Set Up Your Modem in Windows 95" on page 62 to learn how to install a modem.

Guided Tour Establish an Internet Connection

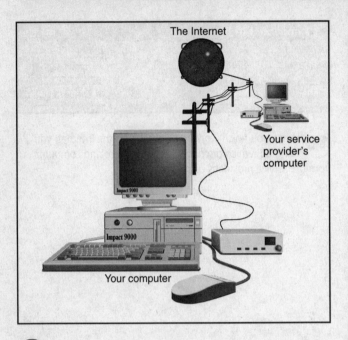

The Internet

Your service provider's computer

Your computer

3 You also need to subscribe to an Internet service provider. The service provider's computer acts as a middleman, transferring information between your computer and the Internet. The tasks in "Prepare to Connect to the Internet" (page 29) tell you how to shop for a service provider.

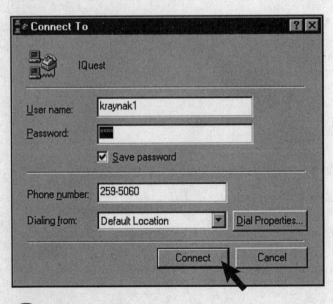

4 A special computer program tells the modem which phone number to dial and how to establish the connection between your computer and the service provider's computer. "Configure Your TCP/IP Software" on page 97 explains how to connect to the Internet using Windows.

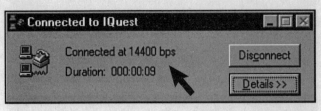

5 The specialized program dials and connects to the Internet but does not allow you to do much else. You need additional programs to use the Internet features.

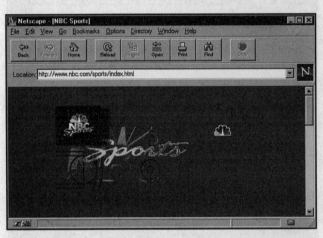

6 Once you connect your computer to the Internet, you use other programs that bring the Internet to your computer. The Web browser shown here allows you to access the World Wide Web, a graphical part of the Internet. You'll learn all about Web browsers later in this book.

7 E-mail programs such as Eudora (shown here) allow you to send and receive messages electronically. You can correspond with anyone in the world who is connected to the Internet. To send and receive e-mail, see "Send and Receive Electronic Mail" on page 193.

(continues)

Guided Tour   Establish an Internet Connection

(continued)

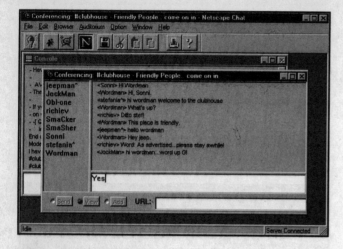

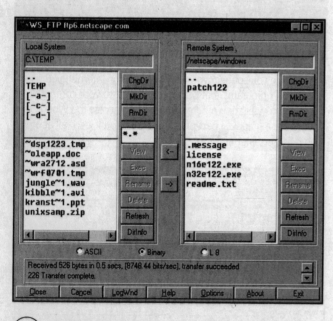

8 Chat programs such as Netscape Chat (shown here) allow you to carry on conversations with other users. Any message you type appears on the screens of all the other users in the "chat room" you're in. "Chat with People on the Internet" (page 243) tells you how to start.

9 Additional programs help you search for and find the information you need and copy files from the Internet to your computer.

10 When you finish working or playing on the Internet, you hang up, which disconnects your modem and computer from the service provider's computer.

Take a Quick Look at UNIX

UNIX (pronounced "You-nicks") comes from the words UNI (single user) and MULTICS (the multi-user operating system on which UNIX is based). Because UNIX enables many users to use one computer and perform several tasks at the same time, it is the primary operating system on many of the computers you will encounter on the Internet. Think of it as the "DOS of networks." It's the ugly face that stands behind many parts of the Internet and performs the basic operations that enable computers on the Internet to function.

Fortunately, you can usually avoid UNIX, just as you can avoid DOS by using Windows. However, you should be aware that UNIX does exist, and you should be able to recognize its ugly countenance when you see it. That will help keep you from going into shock if you happen upon a UNIX prompt (a bit of confusing text on the screen that signals you to type something). The following *Guided Tour* gives you a brief glimpse of UNIX, intended to prepare you for the off-chance that you encounter it.

Begin Guided Tour   Work at a UNIX Prompt

1 As you *surf* (move around) the Internet, you usually encounter screens something like this one. These screens provide a graphical way of touring the Internet.

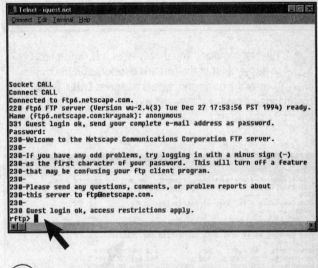

2 On rare occasions, you will happen across a UNIX prompt like the one shown here. In such a case, you have to know which commands to type and how to type them.

(continues)

Guided Tour   Work at a UNIX Prompt

(continued)

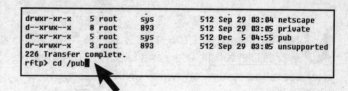

```
drwxr-xr-x    5 root      sys         512 Sep 29 03:04 netscape
d--xrwx---x   8 root      893         512 Sep 29 03:05 private
dr-xr-xr-x    5 root      sys         512 Dec  5 04:55 pub
dr-xrwxr-x    3 root      893         512 Sep 29 03:05 unsupported
226 Transfer complete.
rftp> cd /pub
```

6 To change to a directory, type **cd *directory name*** (where *directory name* is the name of the directory you want to change to) and press **Enter**. You can then enter the **ls** command to view a list of files and subdirectories in that directory.

3 UNIX organizes files in directories and subdirectories. So to use UNIX, you need to know how to display directory and subdirectory names, change to a directory, and display the names of the files in the current directory.

```
rftp> ls
```

4 The first command you usually enter is **ls**, which tells UNIX to display a list of the files and directories on the current drive. To enter the command, type **ls** and press **Enter**. (UNIX commands are case-sensitive, and you usually enter them in lowercase characters.)

```
rftp> cd /pub
250 CWD command successful.
rftp> cd ..
250 CWD command successful.
rftp>
```

7 To move back up to the previous directory in the directory tree, type **cd ..** and press **Enter.**

```
250 CWD command successful.
rftp> cd ..
250 CWD command successful.
rftp> exit
```

8 The most important UNIX command you'll learn is the command to exit the system. At the UNIX prompt, try entering **q**, **quit**, or **exit** and pressing **Enter**. If none of those commands work, try pressing **Ctrl+C** or **Ctrl+D**.

```
Telnet - iquest.net
Connect  Edit  Terminal  Help
230-Please send any questions, comments, or problem reports about
230-this server to ftp@netscape.com.
230-
230 Guest login ok, access restrictions apply.
rftp> ls
Socket CALL
200 PORT command successful.
150 Opening ASCII mode data connection for /bin/ls.
total 14
dr-xr-xr-x   14 root      sys         512 Dec  7 09:11 .
dr-xr-xr-x   14 root      sys         512 Dec  7 09:11 ..
drwxr-xr-x    6 root      sys         512 Nov 23 05:14 2.0b3
drwxr-xr-x    5 root      sys         512 Nov 23 05:14 2.0beta
drwxr-xr-x    5 root      sys         512 Sep 29 03:04 betas.obsolete
d--x--x--x    2 root      sys         512 Sep 29 03:04 bin
drwxr-xr-x    4 root      sys         512 Sep 29 03:04 collabra
dr-xr-xr-x    2 root      sys         512 Sep 29 03:04 dev
d--x--x--x    2 root      sys         512 Sep 29 03:04 etc
dr-xr-xr-x    2 root      sys         512 Sep 29 03:04 lib
drwxr-xr-x    5 root      sys         512 Sep 29 03:04 netscape
d--xrwx---x   8 root      893         512 Sep 29 03:05 private
dr-xr-xr-x    5 root      sys         512 Dec  5 04:55 pub
dr-xrwxr-x    3 root      893         512 Sep 29 03:05 unsupported
226 Transfer complete.
rftp>
```

You can enter **cal** at the UNIX prompt to display a calendar for the current month. You can enter **finger** to display a list of all the users who are currently using UNIX on this computer.

5 The list that appears shows both directory and file names. A directory name is preceded by a forward slash (/) instead of the backward slash used in DOS.

Make the Internet Graphical

If the Internet were nothing more than a collection of computers running UNIX, Internet traffic would be extremely light. No sane person wants to enter text commands at a text prompt to view nothing more than file lists.

Knowing this, programmers created other more graphical approaches to the Internet. The most popular of these offerings is the *World Wide Web* (or Web, for short). The Web is a collection of interconnected documents stored on computers all over the world. Each Web document contains text, usually some pictures, and, if you're lucky, some icons or highlighted text that you can click on to view pictures or play video and sound clips. Think of the Web as a huge multimedia encyclopedia like *Microsoft Encarta* or *Groliers*.

In addition, Web documents contain *links* to other Web documents, and it's the links that tie all the documents together. Suppose, for example, that you are reading an article that mentions Oprah Winfrey, and her name appears in blue or is underlined (both

of which are common ways to indicate that the text acts as a link to another document). You click on the highlighted text, and a page specially devoted to Oprah Winfrey pops up on your screen.

Links make it easy to wander the Web without really knowing what you're doing or where you're going. You simply click on link after link to aimlessly peruse all the documents you find interesting. The following *Guided Tour* gives you a brief overview of the World Wide Web and shows you what to expect. See "Find and Install a Web Browser" on page 123 to learn how to begin your own wanderings.

> Web browsers have recently become so sophisticated that they enable you to use most Internet features. Netscape Navigator, a popular Web browser, enables you to send and receive mail, copy files from the Internet, and even read and post messages in newsgroups (electronic bulletin boards).

Begin Guided Tour   Wander the World Wide Web

1 To tap into the Web, you need a special program called a *Web browser*. This program gives the Internet a pretty face and allows you to easily move around the Internet. Netscape Navigator (shown here) is the most popular Web browser.

(continues)

Guided Tour   Wander the World Wide Web   *(continued)*

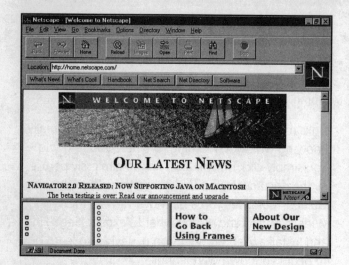

2 When you run the Web browser, it automatically loads a page that came with the browser or a page on the Web itself. You can click on links to bring up other Web documents or perform other tasks.

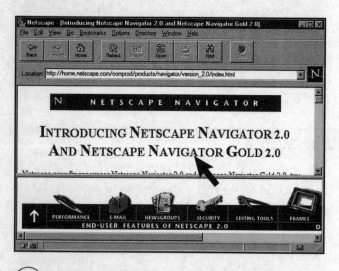

3 In most cases, when you click on a link, the Web browser automatically opens and displays the Web page to which the link points.

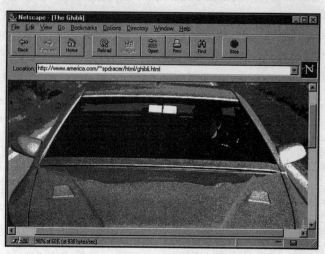

4 Some links point to pictures, video and sound clips, or files that the Web browser can "play." Netscape Navigator can display common graphic files like the one shown here.

5 For files that the Web browser cannot open, you can set up helper applications to open the files. When you click on a link for such a file, the Web browser transfers the file to your computer and opens the file in the helper application. See "Play Sound and Video Clips with Helper Applications" on page 161 for details.

Guided Tour   Wander the World Wide Web

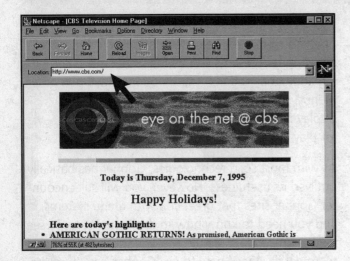

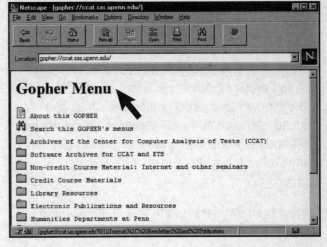

6 Every Web document has a unique address called a *URL* (pronounced "yew-are-ell" and short for Uniform Resource Locator). If you know a document's URL, you can enter it in the **Location** text box, and your Web browser opens the document. "Explore the World Wide Web" on page 143 explains how to use URLs to load Web documents.

8 Web browsers also enable you to go beyond the Web and use other Internet resources, such as the Gopher menu system that's shown here and covered next.

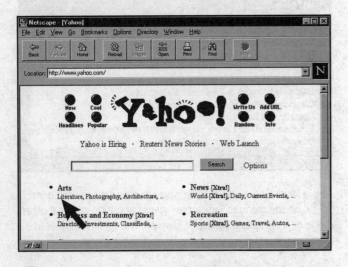

7 The Web has many sites where you can find the link you're looking for. The Yahoo Home Page (shown here) contains links to thousands of documents, grouped by category. "Search for Information on the Web" on page 180 explains Yahoo and other available search tools.

Use Menu Systems to Travel

As the Internet became more popular, but before the advent of the World Wide Web, Internet professionals scrambled to find better ways to organize and present Internet resources. In an attempt to find their own solution, a group of teachers and students gathered at the University of Minnesota in 1991 and developed a menu system called *Gopher* (named after the school's mascot, the Golden Gopher).

Gopher is an indexing system that enables you to access various Internet services through menus. Whenever you connect to a Gopher site (a computer that's running Gopher), it presents you with an opening menu. You select an option from the menu, and Gopher presents you with another menu containing additional options. These options may open other menus, shuffle you off to other Gopher sites, or display files that you can copy to your computer (or play, just as if you were on the Web).

As with most solid technologies, Gopher has basically outlived its usefulness. However, you will still encounter Gopher sites that greet you with menu systems, and you need to know how to deal with them. To see Gopher in action, take the following *Guided Tour*. For more details about how to use Gopher, see "Surf the Internet Using Gopher Menus" on page 281.

Begin Guided Tour   Access the Internet with Gopher

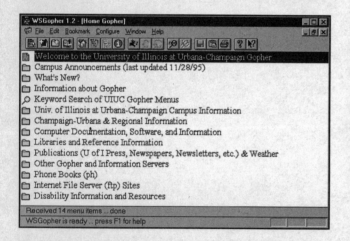

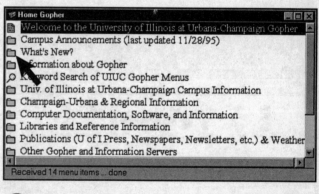

1 To use Gopher, you need a special Gopher program. This program translates the behind-the-scenes Gopher activity into a neat little menu system that you can navigate by pointing and clicking.

2 Most Gopher programs display an icon next to each item on the menu to indicate whether the option opens another menu or represents a particular file type. This folder icon means that if you select the option, you'll see another menu.

Guided Tour Access the Internet with Gopher

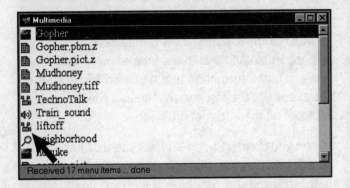

3 The movie camera icon represents a video clip that you can play; the speaker icon represents a sound file; and the page icons represent text files you can view. As you work with Gopher more, you'll gain a better understanding of what each icon represents.

5 Like a Web browser, a Gopher menu cannot handle all the files you might encounter. Again, you can set up helper applications to open the files; see "Play Sound and Video Clips with Helper Applications" on page 161).

4 To select an option from a Gopher menu, double-click on its text or on the icon next to it.

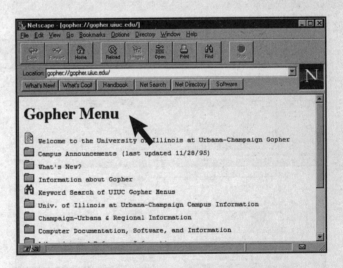

6 Any Web browser can connect to a Gopher site and provide you with the tools you need to move around at that site. Compare this figure with the one in step 1, and you can see that a Web browser gives Gopher a different look.

Search for Information

Sociologists commonly refer to the current era as the "Information Age." When you first hit the Internet, you may find yourself thinking that it's more like the Information Overload Age. You'll find sites that have electronic versions of classic literature, teasers for just about any magazine you can find in print, pages and pages of movie facts and trivia, stock quotes, collections of music, gobs of computer graphics, and mountains of additional information. At first, the enormity of the offerings will overwhelm you. And if you need specific information for a project you're working on, you may have trouble finding a place to start.

Fortunately, some companies on the Internet have built search tools (*search engines*) that can ferret out the information you need and tell you where to find

it. Most of these search tools (Web Crawler, Lycos, Yahoo, and WAIS) search the Internet on a regular basis to find information that has been added to the Internet since the last search. The tool then creates an index of all the information it finds.

When you connect to an Internet site that has a search tool, you usually see a form that asks what you want to search for. You type one or two words to look for, and then press Enter or click on a button to start the search. The search tool displays a list of locations that match your search instructions.

The following *Guided Tour* shows you some of the more useful search tools in action. In addition, "Search for Information on the Web" (page 180) provides the locations of popular search tools and gives detailed instructions on how to use them.

Begin Guided Tour   Use Internet Search Tools

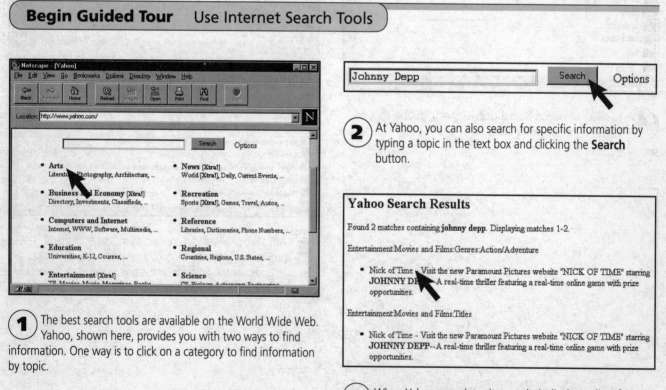

1 The best search tools are available on the World Wide Web. Yahoo, shown here, provides you with two ways to find information. One way is to click on a category to find information by topic.

2 At Yahoo, you can also search for specific information by typing a topic in the text box and clicking the **Search** button.

Yahoo Search Results

Found 2 matches containing **johnny depp**. Displaying matches 1-2.

Entertainment:Movies and Films:Genres:Action/Adventure

- Nick of Time - Visit the new Paramount Pictures website "NICK OF TIME" starring JOHNNY DEPP--A real-time thriller featuring a real-time online game with prize opportunities.

Entertainment:Movies and Films:Titles

- Nick of Time - Visit the new Paramount Pictures website "NICK OF TIME" starring JOHNNY DEPP--A real-time thriller featuring a real-time online game with prize opportunities.

3 When Yahoo completes its search, it displays a list of Internet sites that might have the information you're looking for. Simply click on a link to go to the desired site.

Guided Tour   Use Internet Search Tools

Other Search Engines
Open Text | Lycos | WebCrawler | InfoSeek | Inktomi | DejaNews | More...

4 Yahoo also contains links to other Internet search tools. If Yahoo doesn't find what you're looking for, you can use another search tool by clicking on its link.

5 The popular search tool WebCrawler is a *form-based* search tool. You complete the form by typing one or two words of the topic in which you're interested. Then click the **Search** button.

6 Lycos is also a form-based search tool. Again, you type a unique word or two, and then send Lycos off on the search. Lycos completes a typical search in seconds.

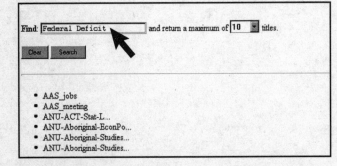

7 WAIS (which sounds like "ways") stands for Wide Area Information Server. You can search WAIS databases for specific articles.

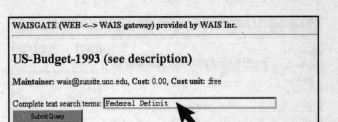

8 In WAIS, you pick the database you want to search and then enter one or two unique words you want to search for. For example, you can search a "Budget" database for "Federal Deficit."

- 422 -1 ecat-library.src
- 422 -1 usdacris.src
- 420 -1 USDACRIS.src
- 387 -1 National-Performance-Review.src
- 342 -1 eros-data-center.src
- 318 -1 Department-of-Education-Programs.src
- 279 -1 GCRIO-DIFs.src
- 260 -1 NPR-Library.src
- 260 -1 npr-library.src
- 253 -1 US-Budget-1993.src
- 248 -1 isoc.src
- 206 -1 USHOUSE_bill_status_today.src
- 195 -1 USHOUSE_bill_status_104th.src
- 190 -1 US-State-Department-Travel-Advisories.src
- 159 -1 Health-Security-Act.src
- 1 -1 Query Report for this Search

9 WAIS locates the articles for you and tells you where to find them.

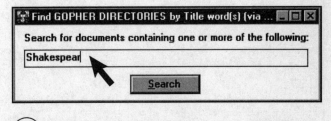

10 You can search for particular information in Gopher by using Gopher's search tools called Veronica and Jughead. Veronica searches all Gopher sites, while Jughead searches only the current Gopher site.

(continues)

Guided Tour Use Internet Search Tools

(continued)

11 To search for a specific *file* on the Internet, you use Archie. In Archie, you simply type the name of the file you're looking for. Archie searches can take several minutes.

12 When Archie is done searching, it displays a list of all the places where you can find the file. You can then copy the file to your computer.

Reading about Veronica, Archie, and Jughead may make you feel as though you just stepped into a comic book. Actually, Archie is short for "archive," which is a record of files on the Internet. Veronica and Jughead don't really stand for anything; the names are a play on the term "Archie."

Use Electronic Mail

One of the most often used features on the Internet is electronic mail (*e-mail* for short). With e-mail, you can type a message, address it, and send it without ever leaving your keyboard. The mail arrives in the recipient's electronic mailbox usually within seconds (although it can take several minutes). And, depending on the reliability of your friend, you can expect a response in a matter of minutes or hours instead of days.

When someone sends you an e-mail message, it's stored in your e-mail mailbox (on your service provider's computer). Using a special e-mail program, you connect to your service provider's computer and read your mail. You can then reply to the message if necessary.

As you can see, e-mail does away with the need for postage stamps, and greatly reduces the time you spend sending and receiving messages. As long as both you and your fellow correspondent check your mail several times a day, you can carry on e-mail conversations without having to wait for the mail carrier.

To see how easy it is to send and receive e-mail, take the following *Guided Tour*. To learn more about e-mail and how to address your e-mail messages, see "Send and Receive Electronic Mail" on page 193.

Begin Guided Tour   Send and Receive Mail

1 One of the most popular Internet e-mail programs is Eudora, shown here.

2 After you connect to your service provider's computer, you check your mail. Eudora displays a list of messages. Double-click on the description to read the message's contents.

(continues)

Guided Tour   Send and Receive Mail

(continued)

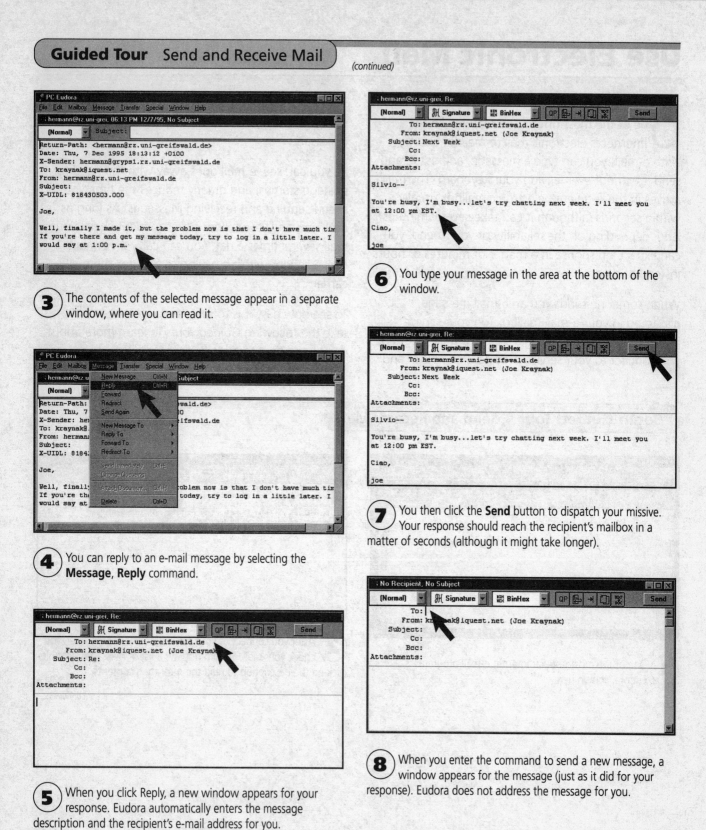

3 The contents of the selected message appear in a separate window, where you can read it.

4 You can reply to an e-mail message by selecting the **Message**, **Reply** command.

5 When you click Reply, a new window appears for your response. Eudora automatically enters the message description and the recipient's e-mail address for you.

6 You type your message in the area at the bottom of the window.

7 You then click the **Send** button to dispatch your missive. Your response should reach the recipient's mailbox in a matter of seconds (although it might take longer).

8 When you enter the command to send a new message, a window appears for the message (just as it did for your response). Eudora does not address the message for you.

Guided Tour Send and Receive Mail

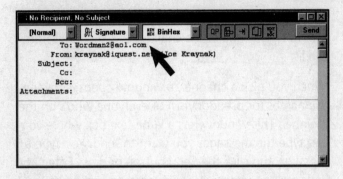

9 You type the person's e-mail address next to **To:**. An e-mail address usually consists of an abbreviated form of the person's name, followed by the at sign (@), followed by the address of the person's service provider's computer.

10 You must type a description of the message in the **Subject** line. This description will appear on the recipient's screen when he checks for mail.

11 You type your message in the blank area at the bottom of the window, and then click on the **Send** button.

Chat with Other People

If you like to talk to complete strangers and make new friends, there's no better place to do it than on the Internet. With a chat program, you can carry on conversations with groups of people (or just one or two others) by typing messages back and forth. You even have the option of signing on as yourself or using a nickname for anonymity.

Here's how it works. You connect to your service provider's computer and fire up your chat program. You enter the address (the Uniform Resource Locator) of a *chat server* (a computer on the Internet that allows people to gather and chat). These chat servers usually have more than one hundred channels, each devoted to a different topic of conversation. For example, you might find a channel called Friends where people are talking about the latest episode of *Friends*, or a channel called Newbies, where new Internet users are helping each other learn the

Internet. You tune into a channel by selecting it from the list.

When you pick a channel, a window opens, showing the names (or pseudonyms) of everyone who's on the channel. This window has a large text box where you can type the messages you want to send. You type a message and click the Send button or press Enter, and your message pops up on your screen and on the screen of everyone on the channel. Likewise, the messages that other people type pop up on your screen. As you can guess, this running conversation can be a bit difficult to follow. But once you get the hang of it, you'll become addicted to the frenetic banter.

The following *Guided Tour* shows a typical chat session in action. To learn more about where to find chat programs and places to chat, see "Chat with People on the Internet" on page 243.

Begin Guided Tour   Chat on the Internet

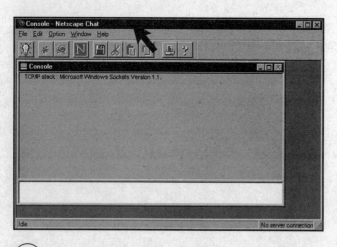

1 The easiest way to chat is to use a special chat program, such as Netscape Chat (shown here) or Internet Relay Chat (IRC).

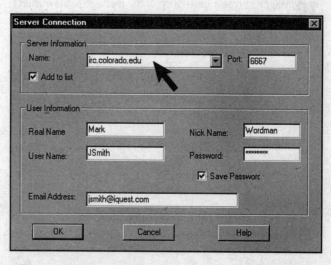

2 First, you enter the address of the chat server you want to use. You must also enter information about yourself, such as your name, the nickname you want to use, and (optionally) your e-mail address.

Guided Tour   Chat on the Internet

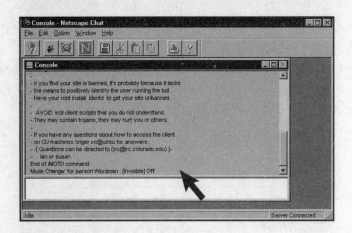

3 Once you enter the appropriate information, the chat program connects to the chat server. As you can see, not much is going on at this stage.

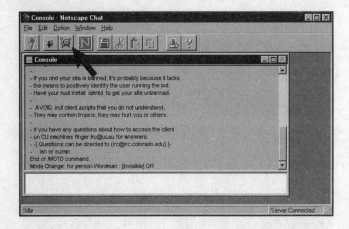

4 In some programs, you must enter a command to access a group conversation or a private conversation (a conversation by invitation only). In Netscape Chat, you can click the **Group** button to enter a group conversation.

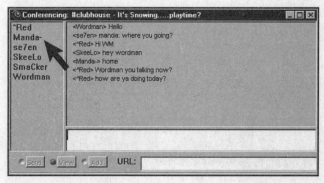

5 When you choose to enter a group conversation, a list of channels appears. Each channel represents a different conversation. The channel list usually tells how many people are currently on each channel. Click the desired channel, and then click **Join**.

6 In the next window, you can join the discussion. Usually, this window contains the names of all the people in the discussion and an area in which the messages appear as people enter them.

(continues)

Guided Tour   Chat on the Internet

(continued)

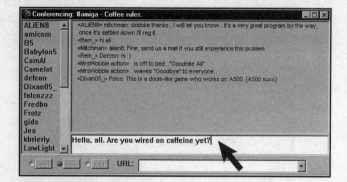

7 You enter your messages in a text box in this window. Type your message into the text box, and then press **Enter** or click on a button.

8 The message you enter appears in the discussion window and on the screen of each user who is on the channel.

One of the most difficult aspects of Internet chat is actually finding a chat server. Because chatting consumes computer power and time, few institutions offer chat areas, and the ones that do often shut down or limit access when they become too busy. In "Chat with People on the Internet" (page 243), you'll learn how to find a chat server that will let you in.

Copy Files from the Internet

As you've learned, you need a Web browser to wander the World Wide Web. Similarly, you need a special e-mail program to send and receive messages, a Gopher program to display Gopher menus, and a chat program to talk with people. Knowing all that, you're probably beginning to wonder where you can purchase all these programs and how much this Internet thing is going to cost you.

Fortunately, you can get all of the Internet programs you need from the Internet itself. Freeware or shareware (try before you buy) versions of these programs are stored on computers all across the Internet. You simply connect to a computer that has the program you want, and then you copy it. The program file is copied from the Internet to your hard drive, from which you can then install the program.

You can also copy other types of files from the Internet. For example, you can copy a file that has a list of current chat servers. Or, you can copy sound files, video clips, pictures, games, and many other types of files.

You copy files using a program called *FTP* (or by using your Web browser). FTP stands for File Transfer Protocol, which is a set of rules and regulations that govern how files are transferred across the Internet. With an FTP program, you can connect to an FTP site (a computer on the Internet where files are stored). Many FTP sites allow anonymous file transfers, which means that anyone can connect to the site and copy files. Other FTP sites are for "members only."

When you connect to an FTP site, a list of the available directories and files appears. You can move through the directory tree and display lists of files in much the same way you do in the Windows Explorer. You can then copy the file to your computer simply by clicking on its name or by copying it from one window to another using your FTP program.

This *Guided Tour* shows how easy it is to copy files from the Internet. For more information about how to connect to FTP sites and copy files, see "Find and Copy Files from the Internet" on page 263.

Begin Guided Tour   Copy Files from an FTP Site

1 The easiest way to copy files from the Internet is to use a Web browser like the one shown here. When you connect to an FTP site, you see a list of directories and files.

2 To access a particular directory, you click its link.

(continues)

Guided Tour Copy Files from an FTP Site

(continued)

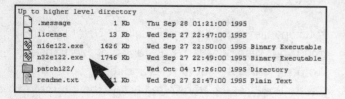

3 To copy a file from the directory to your computer, click on the name of the desired file. (In some Web browsers, you must hold down the **Shift** key while clicking on the file's name.)

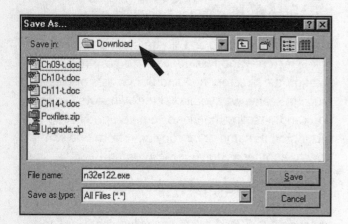

4 Your Web browser displays a dialog box, asking where you want the file stored on your computer. Select the drive and folder (directory), where you want the file placed.

5 As your Web browser downloads (copies) the file to your computer, a dialog box appears, showing the progress.

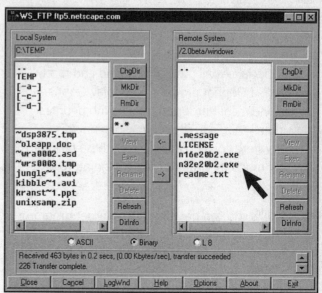

6 Another way to download files is to use a special FTP program. This figure shows the program WS_FTP, which displays two lists: one that shows the contents of your computer, and one that shows the directories and files at the FTP site.

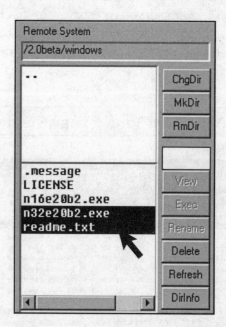

7 To copy a file (or files) to your computer, you first select the file you want to copy from the list of files and directories at the FTP site.

Guided Tour Copy Files from an FTP Site

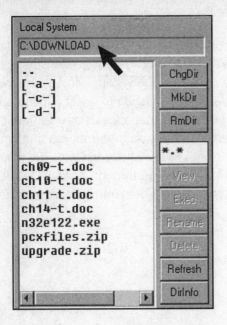

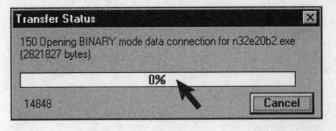

10 As your FTP program copies the selected file(s) to your computer, it displays a dialog box showing you the progress of the operation.

8 Then, in the list that shows the contents of your computer, change to the drive and directory where you want the copies stored.

Many files are stored on the Internet in a compressed form so they take up less storage space and travel through the phone lines faster. Before you can use these files, you have to decompress them using a special program. For instructions on how to decompress files, see "Find and Copy Files from the Internet" on page 263.

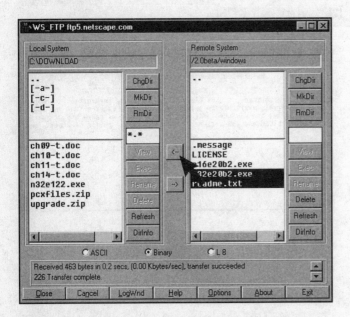

9 Click the **<-** button (the arrow that's pointing toward the contents of your hard drive) to copy the names of the files from the Internet site to the selected folder or directory on your computer.

Telnet to Other Computers

One of the most complex operations you can perform on the Internet is *telnetting* (short for "networking over the telephone"). With a Telnet program, you connect to another computer and use it as if you were sitting at its keyboard. For example, you can connect to the Washington University library's computerized card catalog and use its resources just as if you were sitting in front of a PC at that library.

> If you have Windows 95, you already have a Telnet program. It's called Telnet.exe, and it is in your Windows folder. You can run this program simply by changing to the Windows folder and then double-clicking on the **Telnet** icon. However, you must first establish your Internet connection.

Almost every Telnet site greets you with a rudimentary menu system and a set of on-screen instructions that explain how to use the system. Most of the menus you encounter require you to select a menu option by typing the number that appears next to the option. You select a series of options until you find what you need—or until you reach a dead end. The following *Guided Tour* leads you through a typical Telnet session, giving you a brief introduction to telnetting.

Begin Guided Tour   Use Another Computer with Telnet

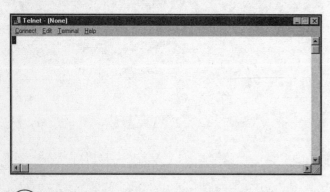

1 A Telnet program allows you to connect to another remote computer and use it just as if you were sitting at its keyboard.

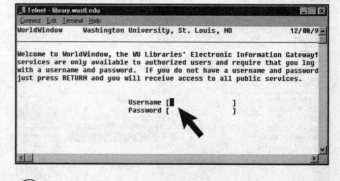

2 When the Telnet program connects your computer to the remote computer, the remote computer usually asks you to enter a username and a password. At Telnet sites that allow anonymous access, you can type **anonymous** as your username and your e-mail address as the password.

Guided Tour   Use Another Computer with Telnet

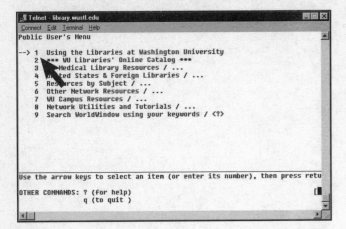

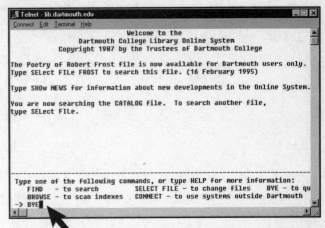

3 The remote computer usually displays a menu system at the top of the window. In most cases, you can select an option from the menu by typing the number that appears next to the option. Some systems have other ways of marking menu options, such as underlining one of the characters in the option's name.

5 When you first connect, look for the command to exit or quit the Telnet session. If you can't find a command, try typing **q** or **exit** and pressing **Enter**. You should exit the remote computer before you shut down your Telnet program.

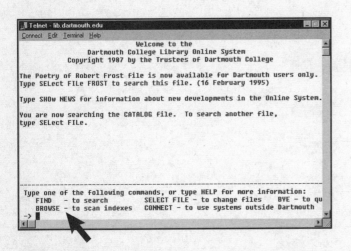

4 Some Telnet sites require that you type commands at a prompt. In such cases, instructions usually appear at the bottom of the screen telling you what to type. If no instructions appear, you can often view a list of commands or instructions by typing **help** or **?** at the prompt and pressing **Enter**.

HOW TO...

Prepare to Connect to the Internet

A s with any new adventure, you have to prepare for your journey on the Internet. You must make sure that you have all the right equipment, a service provider you can dial in order to connect to the Internet, and the software you need to make the most of your journey.

In this section, you'll find out what you need to venture into the Internet. In case you don't have a modem yet, this section tells you how to shop for a modem that's fast enough to handle the Internet. And for those of you who have older computers, this section tells what additional equipment you'll need in order to take advantage of all the Internet's features.

You will also learn how to locate an Internet service provider or use your existing online service (such as CompuServe or Prodigy) to connect to the Internet. Using the list of service providers in the Handy Reference section on page 425, you can contact a service provider in your area today and be up and running immediately.

What You Will Find in This Section

Find a Fast Modem

Before you can connect to the Internet, you should make sure you have all the right equipment. Obviously, the first thing you need is a fast modem (or a network connection). If you are going to connect to the Internet through a network at your school or business, you don't need (or want) a modem. The network connection transfers data to your computer much more quickly than any modem could.

Those of you who are less fortunate will need the fastest modem you can get your hands on (or afford). As you surf the Internet, you will encounter thousands of multimedia files, including computer graphics, sounds, video clips, and animations. All these files are large, and they take a long time to travel through the phone lines. Therefore, the faster the modem you have, the less time you'll be twiddling your thumbs waiting for data to reach your computer.

Modem speeds are commonly expressed in *bits per second* (bps), where the more bits per second, the faster the modem. Old 2,400 bps modems are way too slow to handle Internet data transfers. And although a 14,400 bps modem is sufficient, if you plan to spend much time on the Internet, you're better off to buy a 28,800 bps modem (or faster).

The *Guided Tour* shows you the type of modem you need, provides brief instructions on how to set up a modem in Windows 95, and shows you how to check the speed of your modem.

> Modem speed is the major concern when you're shopping for a modem, but you should also consider such other modem features as whether the modem can handle voice calls (so you can use your computer as an answering machine) and whether the modem is internal or external (whether it sits inside your PC or connects to your PC with a cable).

Begin Guided Tour   Install a Fast Modem

1 If you don't have a modem or a network cable connection, buy a 14,400 bps or faster modem. A 28,800 bps modem is fairly inexpensive and will pay for itself in the long run.

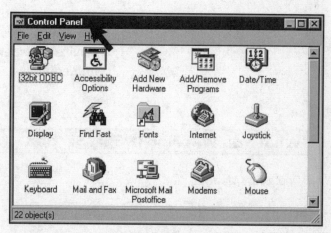

2 Follow the instructions that came with the modem to connect it to your computer, or see "Install a Modem" on page 58. Then open the Windows Control Panel.

Guided Tour Install a Fast Modem

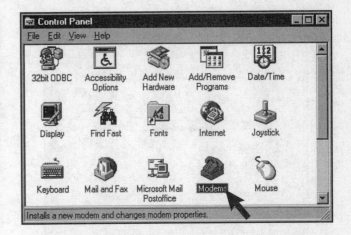

③ Double-click the **Add New Hardware** icon.

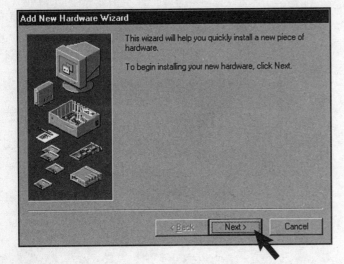

④ The Add New Hardware wizard leads you step by step through the modem installation. Respond to the dialog boxes that appear. See "Set Up Your Modem in Windows 95" (page 62) for details.

⑤ If you already have a modem installed but you're not sure how fast it is, open the Windows Control Panel and double-click the **Modems** icon.

⑥ A dialog box appears, showing information about your modem. Click the **Properties** button to see how fast your modem is.

(continues)

Guided Tour Install a Fast Modem *(continued)*

Gateway 2000 Telepath II 14400 Internal Properties ? X

General | Connection |

Gateway 2000 Telepath II 14400 Internal

Port: Communications Port (COM1) ▼

Speaker volume

Off ——|———— High

Maximum speed

38400 ▼

☐ Only connect at this speed

OK | Cancel

Gateway 2000 Telepath II 14400 Internal Properties ? X

General | Connection |

Gateway 2000 Telepath II 14400 Internal

Port: Communications Port (COM1) ▼

Speaker volume

Off ——|———— High

Maximum speed

38400 ▼

☐ Only connect at this speed

OK | Cancel

7 The Properties dialog box appears. At the bottom of the dialog box is the maximum speed at which the modem can transfer data. Because most modems use data compression, the speed you see is typically higher than the modem's speed rating.

8 Click the **OK** button to close the Properties dialog box, and then click the **Close** button to close the Modems Properties dialog box.

Acquire Additional Equipment

Although a network or modem connection is the essential element for connecting to the Internet, you need some high-powered equipment to get the most out of the Internet. For example, if you have anything less than an SVGA (Super Video Graphics Adapter) monitor, you will be sorely disappointed when you try to view pictures on the Internet. And if you want to hear the sounds of the Internet, you'll need a sound card and speakers. You might also need more memory, more disk space and …well, you get the idea.

The *Guided Tour* leads you through a check list of things you need in order to take full advantage of the Internet. In addition, the following sections go into more detail about the various types of hardware you'll need.

Shop for an SVGA Monitor

As you poke around on the Internet, you'll come across pictures and movie clips you will want to play. If you have an old VGA monitor, those pictures and movie clips will look fuzzy at best. At worst, you won't even be able to view an image you find. In order to view these images, you need an SVGA monitor that can display 256 colors or more.

Make Sure You Have Enough Memory

Most new computers come with 8 or 16 megabytes of RAM (random-access memory), which your programs use to store data while your computer is using that data. For most Internet programs, 8 megabytes is usually sufficient. However, if you plan to work with other programs while you're on the Internet, you may need to upgrade to 16 megabytes. The *Guided Tour* shows how to check your system's memory.

Check the Free Space on Your Hard Disk

Your computer is going to need some free disk space for the Internet. The Internet software you will use can take up several megabytes of disk space. In addition, Windows will undoubtedly use some of your disk space for memory, and some of the graphics and movie clips you will want to copy from the Internet can demand more than a megabyte of disk space apiece.

You should have at least 20 megabytes of free disk space before you begin. You can find out how much free space your hard disk has by using File Manager (in Windows 3.1) or the Windows Explorer (in Windows 95). Simply run File Manager or Explorer and look at the status bar (at the bottom of the window) for the Disk free space.

If you're low on disk space, you might consider installing a bigger hard disk or removing some of the programs and files that you no longer use. Whatever you do, be sure to back up all the files on your hard disk before you clean house—just in case you delete something by mistake.

In Windows 95, you can usually reclaim a great deal of hard disk space by emptying the Windows Recycle Bin. Before you do this, however, make sure you won't need any of the files it contains. To empty the Bin, double-click on the **Recycle Bin** icon, open the **File** menu, and select **Empty Recycle Bin**.

Wire Your Computer for Sound

The Indiana University School of Law has an Internet site that contains a large collection of recordings giving legal advice. You can click on a picture of a speaker and then listen to a presentation about the lemon law or renter's rights. Similarly, several record labels have sites where you can play portions of recordings, including some that haven't been released yet.

To take advantage of online recordings, you must equip your computer with a sound card and speakers. And don't go cheap. Purchase a 16-bit sound card with a couple of good speakers. A 16-bit sound card can play stereo recordings; an 8-bit sound card can't.

Begin Guided Tour Make Sure Your Computer Is Internet Ready

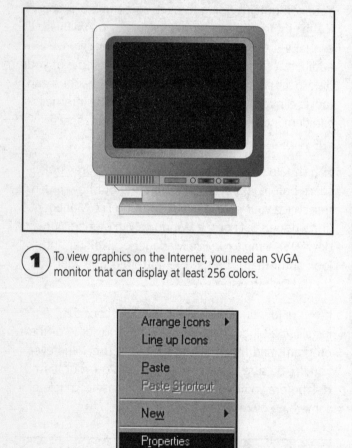

1 To view graphics on the Internet, you need an SVGA monitor that can display at least 256 colors.

2 Even if you have an SVGA monitor, it might not be set to a high-resolution. In Windows 95, you can find out about that by checking your monitor's properties. Right-click on a blank area of the Windows desktop, and a shortcut menu appears. Click **Properties**.

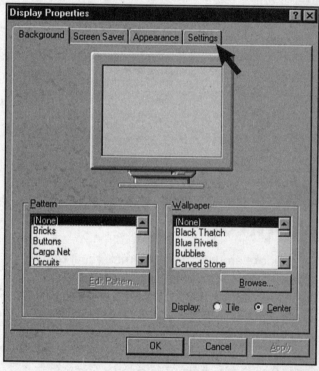

3 You can use the options in the Display Properties dialog box to turn the screen saver on or off, change the Windows colors, and check your monitor setup. Click the **Settings** tab.

Guided Tour Make Sure Your Computer Is Internet Ready

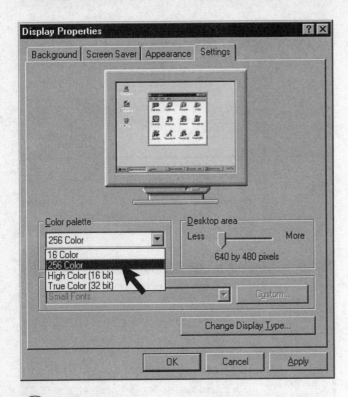

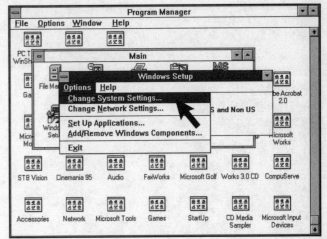

4 The Color palette setting should be 256 or more. If the setting is lower than that, click the drop-down arrow and select **256 Color**. If there isn't a setting of 256 or higher, check your monitor's documentation to learn how to change the setting.

6 The Windows Setup dialog box shows whether your monitor is set to VGA or SVGA. If the monitor is set to SVGA, open the **Options** menu and select **Change System Settings**.

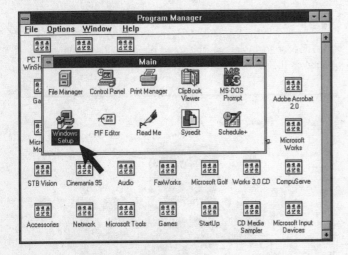

5 In Windows 3.1, you can check your monitor settings by opening the **Main** group window and double-clicking the **Windows Setup** icon.

7 Open the **Display** drop-down list and click the correct display type for your monitor. Then click **OK**.

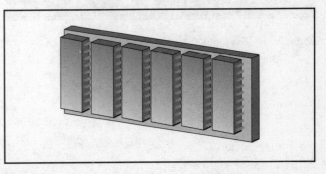

8 Your computer uses RAM to temporarily store the data it is processing. RAM consists of electronic chips like the one shown in this figure. Your computer should have at least 8 megabytes of RAM.

(continues)

Guided Tour Make Sure Your Computer Is Internet Ready

(continued)

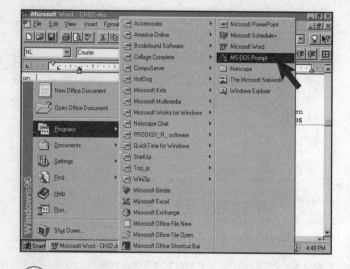

9 You can check the amount of memory from the DOS prompt. To go to the DOS prompt in Windows 95, open the **Start** menu, point to **Programs**, and click **MS-DOS Prompt**. In Windows 3.1, double-click the **MS-DOS Prompt** icon in the **Main** program group window.

10 At the DOS prompt, type **mem** and press **Enter**. DOS displays your computer's total amount of memory.

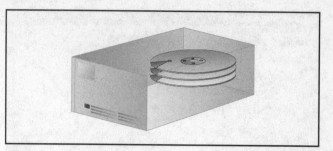

11 Your hard disk stores program files and data files. If your hard disk has fewer than 20 megabytes of free space, you might run into problems when you install an Internet program or copy (*download*) files from the Internet.

12 In Windows 95, you can check the amount of free disk space in the Windows Explorer; in Windows 3.1, look in the File Manager window. The status bar at the bottom of both windows shows the amount of free disk space.

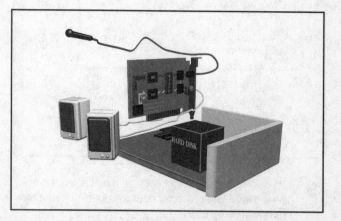

13 Many Internet sites have sound recordings that you can play. Although you can enjoy the Internet without listening to sounds, a stereo sound card and speakers will greatly enhance your Internet experience.

Use America Online's Internet Connection

By far, the simplest way to encounter the Internet for the first time is to use a commercial online service such as Prodigy, America Online, or Compu-Serve. For a monthly charge (and usually some connect time charges that are levied per hour of use), the online service provides you with the following things to get you started:

- *The program you need to connect to the service.* This program will dial into the service, connect, and provide a screen that lets you explore the service and access the Internet.

- *Easy setup.* The online service provides a disk that comes with a setup program. You simply run the setup program and follow the on-screen instructions. The program sets up your modem, helps you pick a local number to dial, and gets you up and running in no time.

- *A local service number.* If you live in or near a major city, you can dial a local number to connect, thereby avoiding long-distance charges.

- *A free trial membership.* All of the online services mentioned here provide a trial period of free membership (usually either a month or 10 hours of use). If you want to stop using the service, you simply call them and cancel your account.

The only drawback of using a commercial online service is the expense. Most services cost a mere ten bucks per month, but they give you only three to five hours of connect time each month at that rate. Every additional hour you spend on the service in a given month costs extra (usually more than three dollars per hour extra).

You can find free offers for most online services in computer magazines. Or, call one of the following toll-free numbers:

Prodigy: 1-800-PRODIGY

CompuServe: 1-800-487-0588

America Online: 1-800-827-6364

Take as many free offers as you can find, and try out the different services. You'll learn a great deal for free. Just be sure to cancel the service at the end of the trial period.

Begin Guided Tour   Connect to the Internet with America Online

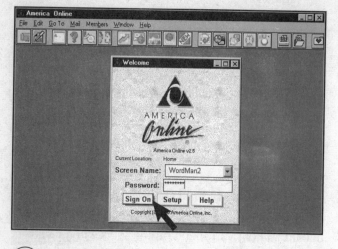

1 Connect to America Online as you normally do.

2 The Main Menu that appears when you sign on has a button called Internet Connection. Click the **Internet Connection** button to view a list of Internet features. (If you don't see the Main Menu, press **Ctrl+K**, type **internet**, and press **Enter**.)

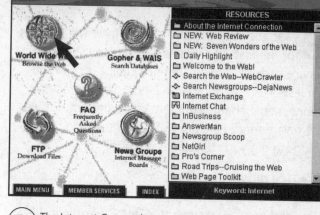

3 The Internet Connection appears, displaying links to the various Internet features. To wander the World Wide Web (as an example), click the **World Wide Web** icon.

4 America Online has its own Web browser, which allows you to navigate the World Wide Web. Click on any available links (buttons or highlighted text) to move around the Web. For more information on how to navigate the Web, see "Explore the World Wide Web" on page 143.

Guided Tour   Connect to the Internet with America Online

5 When you finish using the Web browser, click its **Close** button.

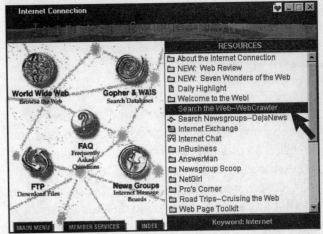

7 The panel on the right provides links to specific commonly used Internet features.

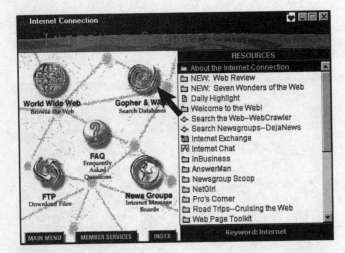

6 America Online closes the browser window and returns you to the Internet Connection window. You can use other icons in this window to explore Gopher, WAIS, or News Groups, or to use FTP to copy files from the Internet.

8 From the Internet Connection window, you can continue your exploration of the Internet. Be sure to disconnect from America Online when you're done.

Use CompuServe's Internet Connection

Unlike America Online, which requires you to access the Internet just as if you were using an America Online service, CompuServe provides a more direct, faster Internet connection.

Here's how it works. For any CompuServe services, you use CompuServe as you normally would, and you are billed accordingly. Whenever you choose to use an Internet feature, CompuServe starts its dialer (a built-in TCP/IP program), which connects you to the Internet just as if you were using an Internet service provider. The only difference is that CompuServe bills you according to its hourly rate, just as if you were using one of its basic services.

The following *Guided Tour* shows just how easy it is to connect to the Internet through CompuServe.

> If you plan to spend more than five hours per month on the Internet, you should use a local Internet service provider instead of an online service. Most service providers charge approximately $15 per month and give you more than one hundred hours of connect time. Some even offer unlimited connect time. To learn more about Internet service providers, see "Find a Service Provider" on page 52.

Begin Guided Tour   Connect to the Internet with CompuServe

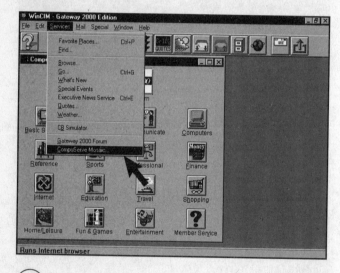

1 CompuServe is one of the few online services that requires you to select a feature before you connect. To wander the World Wide Web with CompuServe, open the **Services** menu and select **CompuServe Mosaic**.

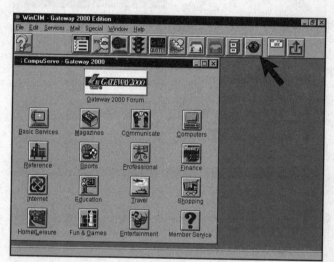

2 You can also go to CompuServe Mosaic by clicking the **CompuServe Mosaic** button in CompuServe's toolbar. CompuServe Mosaic is CompuServe's World Wide Web browser.

Guided Tour Connect to the Internet with CompuServe

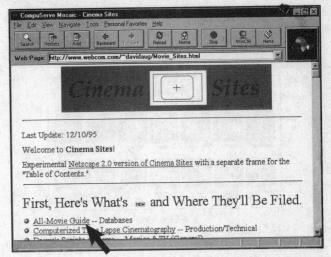

3 The CompuServe program dials into CompuServe, connects, and displays the Web browser window shown here. The Search link is a good starting point for your wanderings. Click **Search** now.

5 CompuServe's Web browser works like most Web browsers. You click highlighted text or icons called *links* to move from one Web page to another. For more information on how to wander the Web with a browser, see "Explore the World Wide Web" on page 143.

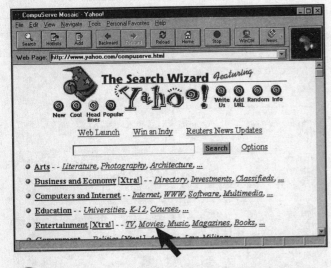

4 The Search button brings up Yahoo's search page. Here you can click a category link to view a list of links for the category in which you are interested.

6 As you click link after link, you move deeper into the Web. You can back up to previous pages by clicking the **Backward** button.

(continues)

Guided Tour Connect to the Internet with CompuServe (continued)

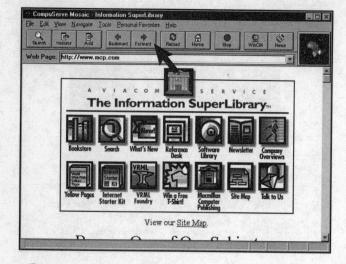

7 If you go back to a previous page, the Forward button becomes active. Click **Forward** to move ahead to a Web page you have already visited.

8 You can return to the main CompuServe screen at any time by clicking the **WinCIM** button in the toolbar. Or if you are done browsing the Web, click the **Close** button in the upper-right corner of the browser window.

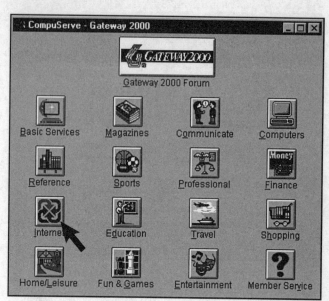

9 You can access almost all Internet features through CompuServe Mosaic. However, CompuServe offers additional ways to tap into other Internet features. From CompuServe's main menu, click the **Internet** icon.

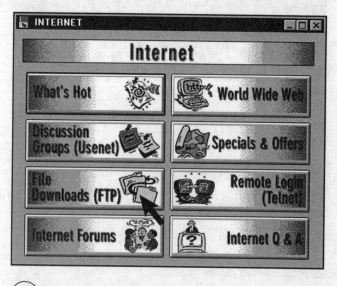

10 The Internet window contains several buttons you can click to access other Internet features. For example, you can click the File Downloads (FTP) button to look for and copy files from the Internet.

Guided Tour   Connect to the Internet with CompuServe

11 The Discussion Groups (Usenet) button lets you read and post messages in online bulletin boards called newsgroups. To learn more about newsgroups, see "Read and Post Messages in Newsgroups," on page 221.

13 For more information about connecting to and using the Internet through CompuServe, click the **Internet Q & A** button.

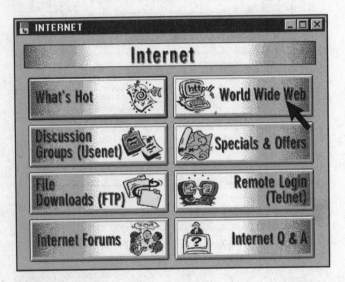

12 The World Wide Web button is misleading: it does not connect you to the World Wide Web. Instead, it displays a list of topics on how you can connect more directly to the Web. (If you want to connect to the Web, click the **CompuServe Mosaic** button, as explained earlier.)s

Use Prodigy's Internet Connection

If you used Prodigy more than a year ago, wipe any memories of it out of your mind. The new Prodigy is more like an Internet service provider than like an online service. Sure, Prodigy still offers bulletin boards, news services, and online shopping as it did in the past, but Prodigy now prides itself on its Internet access. Prodigy also has a new look and feel that is helping it compete with the giants—CompuServe and America Online.

Accessing the Internet with Prodigy is fairly simple. When you start Prodigy, the opening screen allows you to connect directly to the World Wide Web. You select **Web Browser** from the opening menu, enter your user ID and password, and then click the **Connect** button. The *Guided Tour* leads you step-by-step through the sign-on procedure.

Begin Guided Tour   Connect to the Internet with Prodigy

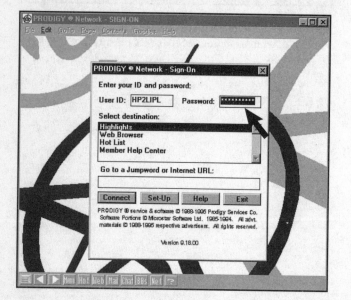

1 Anyone who has used Prodigy in the past will be surprised that Prodigy is now more like a Web browser than a standard online service. When you run Prodigy, you'll see the dialog box shown here. Enter your user ID and password.

2 Click the **Web Browser** option, and then click the **Connect** button. If this is your first time to use Prodigy's Web Browser, a window appears, warning you that some areas on the Web are for adults only and asking you to select which members of your family you want to give Web access to.

Guided Tour   Connect to the Internet with Prodigy

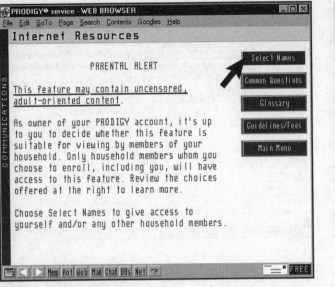

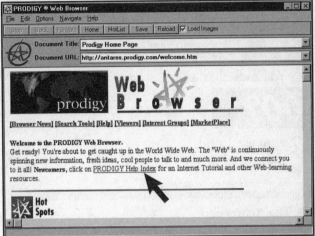

3 Respond to any warning screens as instructed. When you finish entering the requested information, Prodigy sends you the files you need to access the World Wide Web.

5 Like all Web browsers, Prodigy's browser displays an opening Web page that contains links to other pages. At the bottom of the opening Web page are links for various categories. Click a link to view the associated page.

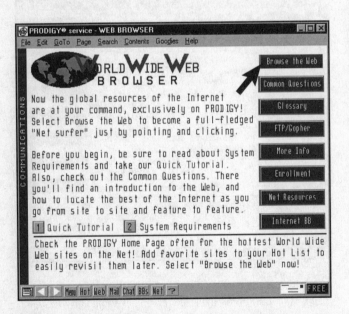

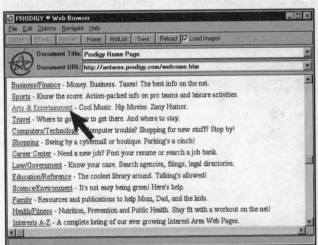

6 Continue clicking links to jump from one Web page to another.

(continues)

4 Now that you're ready to encounter the Web, click the **Browse the Web** button.

Guided Tour Connect to the Internet with Prodigy *(continued)*

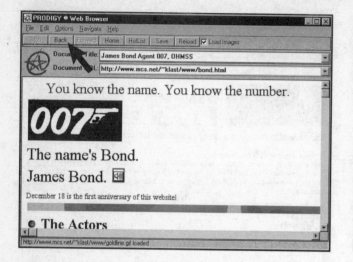

7 When you're moving forward through the Web pages, the Back button is active. To move back to a previous page, click the **Back** button.

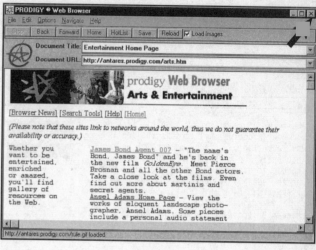

9 When you finish browsing the Web, you can return to the standard Prodigy service by closing the Web browser. To do so, click the **Close** button.

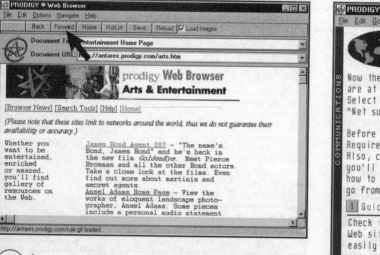

8 If you move back to a previous page, the Forward button becomes active. Click the **Forward** button to display a page you've already visited.

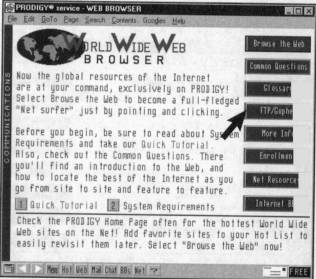

10 Back at the opening Prodigy menu, you can use any of the other buttons on the screen to obtain additional information about the Internet. The other buttons do not link you directly to an Internet resource; they merely teach you how to tap into other Internet resources.

Guided Tour   Connect to the Internet with Prodigy

Prodigy uses its Web browser as the sole tool for using the Internet. For example, instead of using a special Gopher or FTP program, Prodigy requires you to access Gopher menus and to download files by using the Web browser.

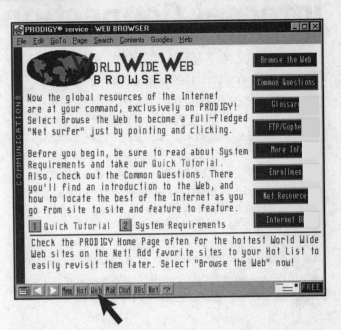

11 You can return to Prodigy's World Wide Web Browser page from anywhere in Prodigy by clicking the **Web** button at the bottom of the window. When you're done using Prodigy, click the **Close** button. Respond to the resulting dialog box to end the session.

Use The Microsoft Network's Internet Connection

The latest entry in the world of online services is The Microsoft Network (or MSN for short). With Windows 95, you got the software you need to connect to MSN, along with a free one-month membership. To sign on and start your MSN account, simply double-click the **MSN** icon on your Windows desktop. Then follow the on-screen instructions (and have your credit card handy) to sign on and start using the service.

Like the three major online services (America Online, CompuServe, and Prodigy), MSN offers e-mail, special services that you can access only through MSN,

forums where you can post questions and answers, online chat rooms, and much more. MSN also offers Internet access. During the writing of this book, Microsoft was developing a new way to access the Internet (similar to the way that CompuServe connects you to the Internet); MSN's previous Internet access was less than desirable.

This *Guided Tour* shows you how to sign on to The Microsoft Network and establish your Internet connection through this new online service. However, the steps may vary slightly depending on the changes MSN undergoes between the time of this writing and the time you sign on.

Begin Guided Tour   Connect to the Internet Through MSN

1 After you set up your MSN account, you can sign on at any time by double-clicking **The Microsoft Network** icon on your Windows desktop.

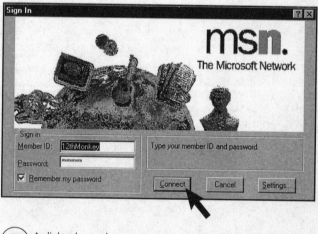

2 A dialog box asks you to enter your member ID and password. Enter the requested information and click the **Connect** button.

Guided Tour   Connect to the Internet Through MSN

3 Whenever you connect to MSN, you get the MSN Today window, which provides news about The Microsoft Network. Click the **Close** button to close this window.

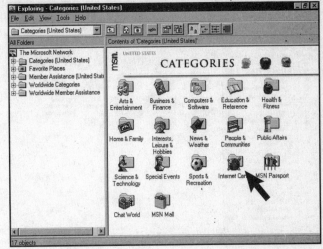

5 The Categories screen provides some areas of general interest on MSN, including an area for Internet information. Double-click the **Internet Center** icon.

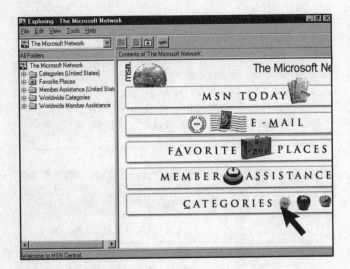

4 To access the Internet, you need a special phone number and the Internet Explorer (MSN's Web browser). Click the **Categories** button to access MSN's Internet tools.

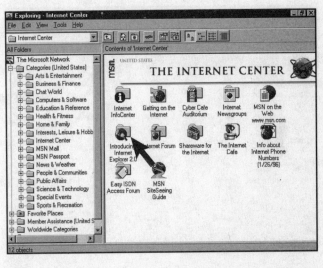

6 Another group of icons appears. Double-click the **Introducing Internet Explorer 2.0** icon.

(continues)

Guided Tour Connect to the Internet Through MSN

(continued)

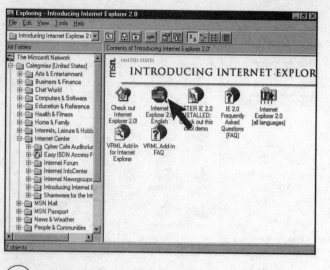

7 You download Internet Explorer by double-clicking the **Internet Explorer 2.0 English** icon. Then follow the on-screen instructions to install the program.

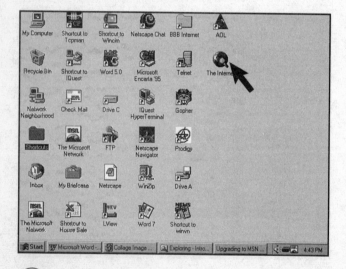

8 When you finish installing the program, you should have an icon called The Internet on your Windows desktop. Double-click **The Internet** icon.

9 The Internet program leads you through the process of picking a local MSN Internet access number and setting up your computer to access the Internet through MSN. Follow the on-screen instructions.

As this book was being written, MSN was in the process of adding Internet access phone numbers for many cities. If you don't live near a major city, you may have trouble finding a number. Look in the Internet Center for a list of the latest Internet access numbers.

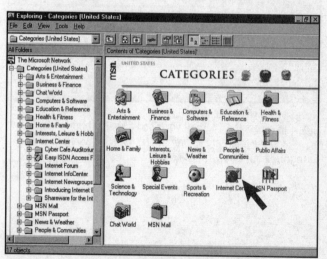

10 Once you are connected to MSN, you can use Internet Explorer to wander the World Wide Web. Click the **Categories** button in MSN's opening screen, and then double-click the **Internet Center** icon.

Guided Tour Connect to the Internet Through MSN

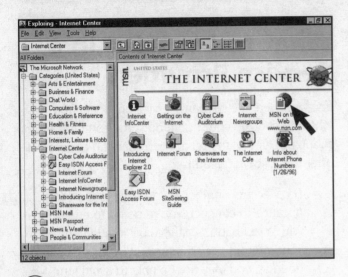

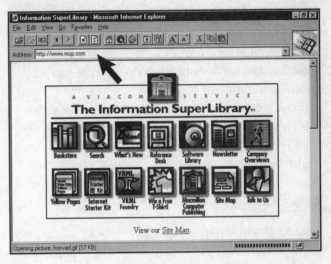

11 Double-click the **MSN on the Web** icon.

13 You can also go to a specific Web page by typing its URL in the **Address** text box and pressing **Enter**. To return to MSN's main screen, simply close the Internet Explorer window.

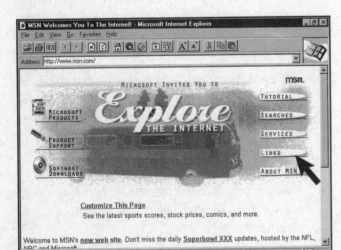

12 MSN automatically runs Internet Explorer and loads MSN's Web page. From this page, you can start exploring other Web pages by clicking on a link.

Find a Service Provider

The cheapest way to surf the Internet is to use an Internet service provider. Unlike online services, most Internet service providers do not give you a special program that connects to their computer and displays a pretty screen. They also don't offer all the features that an online service provides. For example, if you have America Online, you can check your mutual funds by connecting to Morningstar. Internet service providers don't offer these valuable commercial services.

Instead, the Internet service provider gives you access to the service provider's computer, which happens to be connected to the Internet. Because the service provider doesn't have to fork over part of its profits for commercial features, the service provider can offer very inexpensive Internet access. You pay a flat monthly fee (about 15 dollars) for virtually unlimited connect time.

In addition, a good service provider supplies generic software that's designed to make establishing a connection easy. Sections 4 ("Connect to Your Service Provider") and 5 ("Configure Your TCP/IP Software") outline the steps you need to follow to copy these files from your service provider, to install the files, and to connect to your service provider.

To find a local service provider, check with computer stores and user groups where you live, or ask your friends. Chances are good that somebody you know is already connected to the Internet. If you can't find anyone to recommend a service provider, flip to the Handy Reference section on page 425 to find a list of providers.

What to Look for in a Service Provider

Because there are so many service providers from which to choose, you should do some comparison shopping. Ideally, the service provider you choose will offer the following features:

- *Local access number.* If you have to dial long distance to connect, you're going to end up with a steep long-distance bill in addition to your Internet bill. Of course, if you live in the boonies, you may not be able to avoid long-distance charges.

- *Internet software and instructions.* Connecting to the Internet service provider for the first time is difficult. The Internet service provider should help you set up the connection for free.

- *PPP or SLIP service (preferably PPP).* PPP stands for Point-to-Point Protocol; SLIP stands for Serial Line Internet Protocol. Both PPP and SLIP enable you to connect directly to the Internet so that you can use programs on your own computer (instead of on the service provider's computer). Avoid anything called "terminal" or "dial-up" service, both of which give you an indirect Internet connection.

- *Reasonable startup fee.* Most service providers will not levy a startup fee. They want you to try their service in the hopes that you will become a regular user (and pay your monthly fee on time).

- *Unlimited connect time.* Many service providers charge a flat monthly rate for using the service. Beware of providers who charge by the hour or minute. Some service providers limit you to 100 or 200 hours of use per month, which is plenty.

- *A technical support number.* Occasionally, you might have to call for help. Make sure that the service provider is willing (and able) to give you the support for which you are paying.

You'll Need Some Information in Order to Connect

When you call your Internet service provider for the first time, make sure you have the following information handy:

> Your computer type: PC-compatible
>
> Your operating system: Windows 3.1 or Windows 95
>
> Your modem's maximum speed: _____bps
>
> The COM port of your modem: COM1, COM2, or COM3

COM stands for Communications, and a port is an outlet into which you plug a cable. Modems on most new computers are connected to COM1. To be sure which yours is, check the documentation that came with your computer or refer to "Install a Modem" on page 58 for instructions on how to determine which COM port your modem uses.

When you call, have pen and paper handy. The service provider will give you the information you need to connect: the phone number that your modem must dial, the modem speed setting, and your username and password. (A username is the name assigned to you by your service provider. It usually consists of the first letter of your first name, followed by your last name—such as jsmith.)

The service provider may give you additional information over the phone or may offer to send it to you as e-mail. If you choose to receive the information electronically, you will have to connect to your service provider (using Windows Terminal or HyperTerminal as explained in "Connect to Your Service Provider" on page 69) and check your mail. If you choose to take the information over the phone, be sure you get the following information:

- Connection type: SLIP or PPP

  To connect directly to the Internet, you need a SLIP or PPP connection. Circle the type of connection you have.

- Internet phone number: _____

  The most important piece of information is the number your modem must dial to connect to the service provider's computer. Write the phone number in this blank.

- Username or User ID: _____

  Although you might get to pick your username or user ID, often the service provider assigns it to you. Whenever you dial into the service, you will be asked to identify yourself. Write this information down so you will have it later.

- Password: ************

  Don't write down your password here. Instead, write it down on a piece of scrap paper and stick it in your sock drawer (or somewhere else where nobody dares to look). You'll need to enter this password whenever you connect to the service provider's computer.

- Terminal emulation: _____

  Write down the terminal emulation setting you need to use to connect to your service provider's computer. (It's usually VT100 or VT52.) In order to communicate with your service provider's computer, your computer must emulate (act like) a specific type of terminal.

- E-mail address: _____

  You'll use your e-mail address to tell other people how to address e-mail to you. You'll also need to enter your e-mail address in your Internet programs. This address consists of your username, followed by the at sign (@), followed by your Internet post office address (for example, jsmith@pop.iquest.net).

- Domain Name Server: _____

  This "address" consists of four numbers separated by periods (such as 012.345.678.9111). A domain name server is a tool that the service provider's computer uses to locate other computers on the Internet.

- Domain Name: _____

  A domain name identifies each computer on the Internet. Each service provider's computer has a domain name, which might look something like iquest.net. Write down the domain name of your service provider's computer.

- IP address: _____

  IP stands for Internet Protocol, a system that governs the transfer of data over the Internet. If your service provider assigns your computer a specific IP address, write it down. Some service providers automatically assign an IP address when you connect to the service.

- News server: _____

  In Section 11, "Read and Post Messages in Newsgroups," you will learn how to read and post messages in newsgroups (Internet bulletin boards). To do this, you need to know the name of your service provider's news server. This name usually looks something like news.iquest.net.

- Mail server: _____

  In Section 10, "Send and Receive Electronic Mail," you will learn how to send and receive e-mail. All mail must pass through your service provider's mail server. Write down the mail server's name for future reference. Mail server names usually look like mail.mcp.com or pop.mcp.com.

Use Your Office or School Network Connection

Most people connect to the Internet using a modem. However, if you are a college student, or if you work at a company where the computers are networked, it's likely that the network is already connected to the Internet. In fact, the computer you use at work or school may already be set up to connect to the Internet.

This type of connection (a direct network connection) is the best type of Internet connection you can have. Instead of using a modem to transfer data across the Internet, a network uses high-speed cables. Because of this, you get an almost immediate response to any request for data. Web pages pop up on your screen almost immediately, and your computer is rarely disconnected by a glitch in the phone lines.

If the network you're on is not connected to the Internet, there's not much you can do about it. A person called a *network administrator* is in charge of setting up and maintaining the network. You have to go through that person in order to establish your Internet connection. The network administrator takes care of signing you up, setting up your software, and teaching you the one or two steps you need to take to connect to the Internet.

> Don't attempt to set up a direct network connection by yourself. The network administrator has special training and knows the network settings you must enter to connect. If you enter the wrong settings, you risk fouling up the network and making the administrator's job more difficult.

Because the steps you take depend on how your network administrator has set up your system, no *Guided Tour* can show you how to do it. Check with your network administrator to determine how your system is set up, and be sure to ask which software you need to use to access the Internet.

HOW TO...

Set Up Your Modem

A modem is a device that changes digital information into analog beeps and buzzes that can be sent over a phone line. At the other end, a receiving modem converts the beeps and buzzes back into digital computer data. A communications program at each end controls the whole exchange.

As you learned in "Prepare to Connect to the Internet" on page 29, you need a modem in order to connect to an Internet site. With your modem, you can travel to the Internet cyberspace where you can jump from one location on the Net to another via various interconnected modems. And with the proper program, you can use your modem to receive (download) files from various Internet sites, called FTP (file transfer protocol) sites.

In this section, you'll learn how to install your modem under Windows 95. If you're a Windows 3.1 user, don't feel left out—there's just not a lot you have to do under Windows 3.1 (once you get the modem physically installed, that is) to get your modem to work. However, you'll see tips along the way for using Windows 3.1.

What You Will Find in This Section

Install a Modem

There are two types of modem: internal (which is inside the PC) and external (which is connected by a cable to the back of the PC). Of the two, external modems are easier to install.

Regardless of the type of modem you buy, before you can install it, you have to select the *COM port* the modem will use. You can think of a port in the same way the captain of a ship does—as a place to drop off and pick up supplies. In the case of a PC, a port is where a device such as a modem can drop off or pick up data. In other words, a port is a route through which a device such as a modem communicates with your PC.

Your PC has two kinds of ports: COM ports, also known as serial ports, and parallel ports, which are generally used for printers. When connecting a modem, you'll use one of the COM (serial) ports. Your PC has up to four of these COM ports, but it can use only two of them at any one time.

Serial devices such as your modem use these COM ports. Other devices that might use a COM port (and therefore cause a conflict by using the port your modem wants to use) include a mouse, scanner, or serial printer. (Most printers are parallel not serial, so this is usually not a problem.)

The COM port setting a modem uses depends on whether it's an external or internal modem. If your modem is external, its COM port number is based on the external port to which it is connected. For example, if you connect your external modem to the port marked COM1 on the back of your PC, the modem uses the COM port setting "COM1." If you connect it to the COM2 port instead (if there is one), the modem uses COM2.

If your modem is internal, its COM port setting is set either with a set of jumpers or DIP switches on the card itself, or through special software that came with your modem when you bought it. If your modem uses

jumpers, the settings for the various COM ports are probably printed on the card—so you shouldn't have to hunt down your manual just to set your jumpers.

When selecting a COM port for your modem, keep in mind that even an unused COM port can cause a conflict just by its very existence. How so? Well, most PCs come with at least one, if not two, COM port connectors accessible through the back of the PC. You can identify a COM port by looking at it: a COM (serial) port has pins—exactly 9 or 25 of them—instead of holes. If your PC has a COM1 connector and you insert an internal modem, you must set the modem's COM port to COM2 because even though nothing is cabled to the COM1 connector, the PC considers it "in use." If you want to use two internal serial devices, you can usually disable the COM1 connector (check your PC's manual for details).

If you use Windows 95, you'll need to perform some extra steps after you install your modem. Be sure to read "Set Up Your Modem in Windows 95" on page 62 for more information.

Before You Install an Internal Modem

Before you can insert your internal modem, you need to make sure that you set it to use the appropriate COM port. Usually you set the COM port by changing some DIP switches or jumpers on the modem card. DIP switches are kind of like light switches: they're either set on or off. By setting these switches to certain positions, you can select the COM port you want to use. Check the manual that came with the modem for details on which switch to change in order to select the COM port you want. If you want to use COM1, you usually don't have to do anything because your modem was probably preset for COM1 when it was shipped. Then, before you touch the modem itself, make sure that you've discharged any static by touching something metal (but do not touch your PC's case—that's not where you want the static to go).

> You can change the COM port settings for some modems using a software program included with the modem instead of a bunch of switches. Check the modem's manual for help.

Setting Communications Parameters

After you install your modem, you'll need to install a communications program, which you use to control each telecommunications session. For general modeming, you'll use a program such as Hyper-Terminal (or Terminal, if you use Windows 3.1), ProComm Plus, or CrossTalk. To connect to the Internet, you'll use TCP/IP software such as Trumpet Winsock or Dial-Up Networking. In any case, you'll need to use your particular program to set up your communications parameters before you're ready for business.

> If you plan to connect to the Internet directly through your network, you can forget this nonsense; the network itself handles everything.

Every telecommunication session has particular parameters under which it operates. There are four basic parameters involved: the speed of the transmission, the number of data bits, the number of stop bits, and the parity. The speed of the transmission is measured by *bits per second* or *bps* (sometimes called

the "baud rate," although that is technically incorrect). Most modems today transmit at a rate of either 28,800 or 14,400 bits per second, although 9,600, 4,800, and 2,400 bps modems are still used. The speed of the transmission is determined by the speed of the slowest of the two modems in the connection. For example, if you use a 28,800 bps modem and you connect to the Internet at 14,400 bps, 14,400 bps will be the speed of the transmission.

The number of data bits and stop bits and the parity of the transmission are used to determine whether the data being sent over the phone line is received correctly. Therefore, the data bits, stop bits, and parity settings that you choose at your end must match those of the modem on the other end. When you instruct your communications program to connect to an online service, the Internet, or some other modem, you select the parameters for the call. (You can save these parameters so that you don't have to enter them each time.) The communications program passes these parameters to the modem at the other end so that it knows exactly how to make the connection. Your Internet provider will tell you which parameters to use for your connection. The two most common sets of parameters are eight data bits, one stop bit, and no parity (8/1/none) or seven data bits, zero stop bits, and even parity (7/0/1).

> Parity is used to determine an error in data transmission. For example, suppose you're set up for seven data bits and even parity. In that case, seven bits make up a single character (such as the letter J). With even parity, your communications software adds an eighth bit to each seven-bit sequence.
>
> Now, a bit can be either a 1 or a 0. The letter J in a seven-bit pattern looks like 1001010. There are three 1 bits in the sequence. Because of the even parity setting, an extra 1 bit is added to the end, making a pattern that looks like 10010101. Now there are four 1 bits—an even number—in the eight-bit sequence. So if your modem receives a sequence such as 10010100 that results in an odd number of bits, the modem knows there has been an error.

Begin Guided Tour Install an Internal Modem

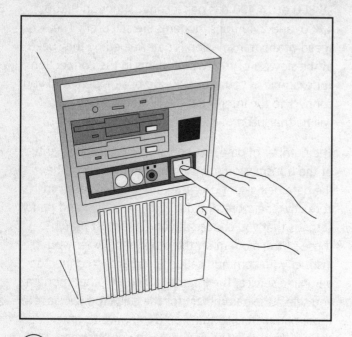

1 Turn off your PC and unplug it from the wall. Then disconnect anything else that plugs into your PC—such as your monitor, modem, or printer. (You'll probably have to unscrew them first.)

Before you touch anything inside your PC, touch a doorknob or something metal to eliminate static electricity. Do not touch the PC's metal case.

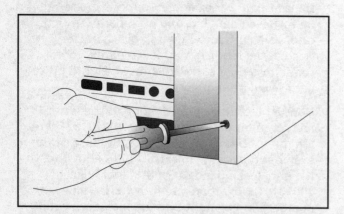

2 Unscrew the PC's cover. Remove the cover by sliding it forward or backward (depending on the cover's design) and then lifting it straight up.

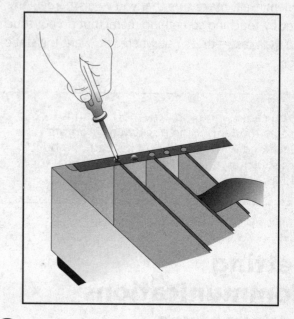

3 Locate an open slot and unscrew the retaining screw holding the slot cover in place. Remove the slot cover. (Don't throw the cover away; if you ever take the modem out, you'll need it.)

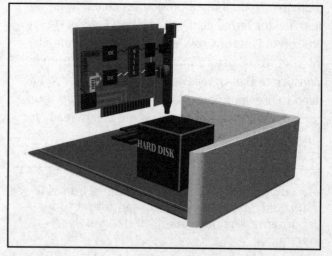

HARD DISK

4 Hold the modem at the top with both hands and carefully position the edge connectors on the bottom of the card over their slots. Gently rock the card until it slips into place.

Leave the PC open while you test the modem. You can correct problems more easily if you still have access to the modem.

Guided Tour   Install an Internal Modem

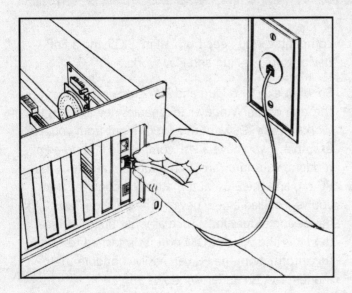

5 On the back of the modem, you'll see two connections. Plug the phone cord into the one marked "To Line" or "To Wall." Plug the other end of the phone cord into a regular telephone jack.

If you have only one phone line, you must disconnect your phone from the wall and plug it into the connector on the modem marked "To Phone." Then follow step five to connect the modem's phone cord. Note that with only one phone line, you can't use the modem and the phone at the same time.

Begin Guided Tour   Install an External Modem

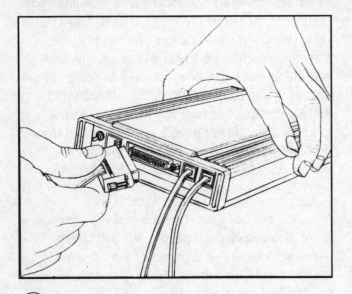

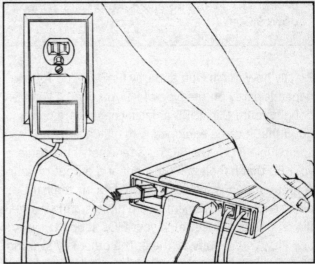

1 Connect the serial cable to the back of the modem. Connect the other end to a serial (COM) port on your PC.

2 Plug in the power cable.

3 On the back of the modem, you'll see two telephone jacks. Connect a phone cord to the one marked "To Line" or "To Wall." Then plug the other end of the phone line into a phone jack and turn on your modem.

If you have only one phone line, you must disconnect your phone from the wall and plug it into the other phone jack on the modem (the one marked "To Phone"). If you do this, you cannot use your phone and the modem at the same time.

Set Up Your Modem in Windows 95

Once you install your modem, you need to configure it in order for the modem to work correctly under Windows 95. Thankfully, Windows 95 includes Plug and Play technology that makes this process fairly painless.

> Unlike in Windows 95, you don't actually have to do much in Windows 3.1 to make your new modem work; you simply install it. That's because Windows 3.1, like DOS, leaves the problem of communicating with the modem to your communications program, such as Terminal. (Setting up the terminal communication program is discussed in "Use a Windows Telecommunications Program" on page 70.) Of course, this seeming simplicity is not without its own problems. If you set your modem to a COM port that conflicts with another device, Windows 3.1 can't do anything to help; Windows 95 can.

Exactly how much Plug and Play (PnP) will do for you depends partly on the type of PC you own. If you bought your PC in 1995 or later, chances are pretty good that it came equipped with a Plug and Play compatible *BIOS*. The BIOS is a series of chips inside your PC that handles all the input and output of your computer (things such as getting data off the hard disk, sending a document to the printer, and saving a file on a floppy diskette). If your BIOS supports Plug and Play, you're halfway there. The other key to using Plug and Play is that the new device you're installing—in this case, the modem—must be Plug and Play compatible. You need both a PnP BIOS and a PnP device to make Plug and Play work.

So what exactly is Plug and Play? It's a method through which Windows 95 enables new devices to work in your PC, without a lot of input from you. For example, if you have a PnP compatible PC and a PnP modem, you simply install the modem and turn the PC on, and the BIOS automatically recognizes that you've installed a new device. The PC then "asks" the device some questions, such as what brand of modem it is and which COM port it's attached to. With this information, the PC can easily configure the modem for use under Windows 95.

Even with Plug and Play, you will have to answer some questions. Sometime during the modem setup, Windows 95 will ask you for the area code and phone number of the telephone line your modem will be using. Windows 95 also asks if you need to dial something such as a 9 to get an outside line, and whether or not the phone line you'll be using has call waiting. If you do have call waiting, Windows 95 needs to disable it temporarily when you use the modem; if you do not disable call waiting and someone calls while you're connected to the Internet, the modem tries to answer the phone and disconnects you in the process.

If you did not buy your PC in the past year, it probably is not Plug and Play compatible. But don't worry. Windows 95 makes it super easy to install a modem, even without Plug and Play. Follow the steps in the *Guided Tour* to learn how.

Begin Guided Tour   Configure Your Modem for Windows 95

1 Open the **Start** menu, select **Settings**, and select **Control Panel**.

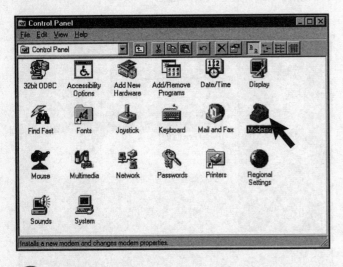

2 Double-click the **Modems** icon. The Modems Properties dialog box appears.

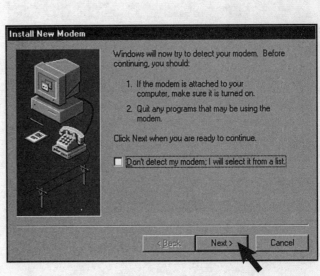

3 Click **Add**.

4 Even if you don't have Plug and Play, you should let Windows 95 try to detect your modem. Turn your modem on and click **Next>**.

(continues)

Guided Tour   Configure Your Modem for Windows 95   *(continued)*

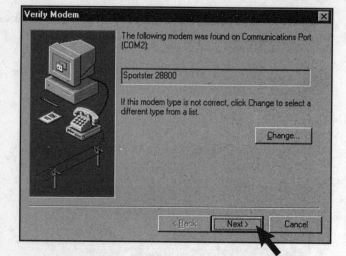

5 In the Verify Modem dialog box, Windows 95 tells you what kind of modem it found. If it identified your modem correctly, click **Next>** and skip to step 9.

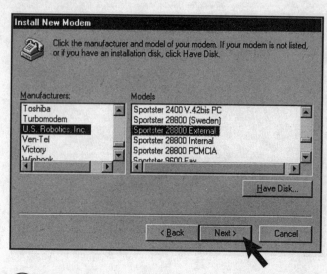

7 Click the brand and model names of your modem. (If the modem came with an installation diskette, insert it and click **Have Disk** instead.) Click **Next>**.

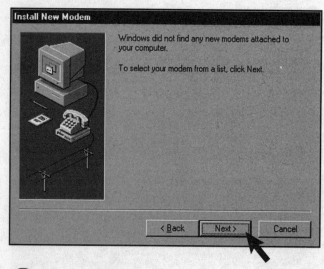

6 If Windows cannot identify your modem, you'll see this message. Click **Next>**.

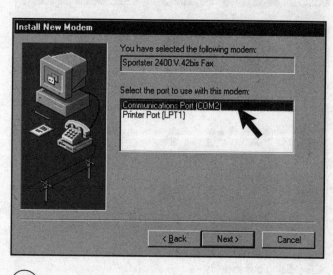

8 Select the COM port you want to use and click **Next>**.

Guided Tour   Configure Your Modem for Windows 95

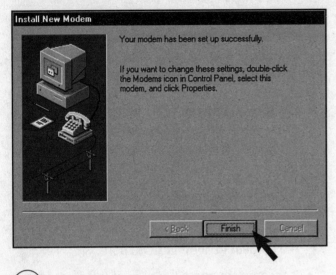

9 In the Install New Modem dialog box, click **Finish**.

10 Click **Close** to return to Windows.

If you want to change any of your choices later (if, for example, you want to change your modem's phone number), just repeat the process and make any necessary changes in the Modems Properties dialog box.

Find Out If Your Modem Works

Now that you've installed your modem, you're probably anxious to see if the thing is working. Some modems come with software you can use to test them. If yours did not and you don't have any other way to test the modem, take this *Guided Tour* to test it. If you're in Windows, you'll need to start a DOS window first.

If the test fails, consider each of these problems and try the possible solutions.

- If nothing seems to happen, first make sure that the modem is turned on and plugged in. If you're using an internal modem, try taking it out and reseating it.

- If you know it's on but it still doesn't work, make sure that your modem is connected to a phone jack. If it's a new phone jack and you haven't used it before, you need to make sure that it's working. To test a phone jack, plug a regular phone (not one of those digital read-out things) into it and see if you can hear a dial tone.

> If you can get only a digital phone to work in the phone jack, don't try to use that particular phone line for your modem. The phone line carries extra digital "stuff" that can interfere with modem communications.

- If you can't hear the modem dialing, check the preferences for your communications program to see if it is turning off your modem's internal speaker (or turning it down so low that you can't hear it).

- If you receive a write fault error when you test the modem using the *Guided Tour*, your computer is having trouble locating the modem. This usually happens when you select the wrong COM port during installation. Select a different one and try the modem again.

- If you have an older modem and it has a switch that sets the COM port, make sure that switch matches the setting you chose during installation. Check the modem's manual for help. Also, the communications program that you want to use (in this case, the TCP/IP software) needs to use the same COM port that the modem is on or they won't find each other.

- If your modem appears to be working but stops suddenly in the middle of transmission, you probably have a COM port conflict. Try setting the modem to another COM port.

- If the modem doesn't answer at the other end, make sure that the number you're trying to use is a valid one. Dial it using a regular phone to make sure the number is correct. Be sure that the modem is dialing a 9 if necessary to get an outside line. When typing the number, you enter the 9 followed by a comma, as in "9,5551212"; this tells the modem to pause a second to access the outside line.

- Make sure you've disabled call waiting. The modem will disconnect you if you have call waiting turned on and another call comes in. The best solution is to have separate phone and modem lines. If that's not possible, enter ***70** in front of the phone number you want to call (*70,355-9089). If you use an old-fashioned rotary (pulse) system, enter **1170** instead (1170,355-9089).

- If you're typing a message and you can't see what you're typing on-screen, you need to turn on local echo. To do so, stop your Internet session and choose the appropriate menu command in your TCP/IP program (such as Trumpet Winsock) to turn on local echo.

- If you're seeing double (two of everything you type), change to full duplex and turn off local echo in your TCP/IP program.

- If you can't get the modem to hang up after exiting your TCP/IP program, try turning off your modem if it's external. You can also try unplugging the phone line. As a final resort, restart your PC.

For further help with modem problems, check out the Quick-Finder table in Part 3 to quickly locate your problem and find its solution.

Begin Guided Tour   Test Your Modem

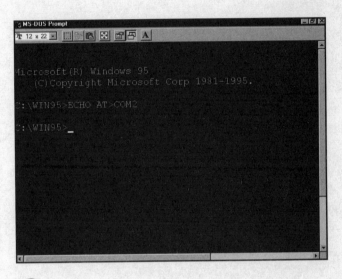

1 Power up the PC. If you have an external modem, turn it on. Open a DOS window and type **ECHO AT>COM1** if your modem is connected to COM1. If you connected your modem to COM2 instead, type **ECHO AT>COM2**. Press **Enter**.

To open a DOS window in Windows 95, click the **Start** button, select **Programs**, and select **MS-DOS Prompt**. To open a DOS window in Windows 3.1, open the **Main** window and double-click the **MS-DOS Prompt** icon.

2 If everything works right, you will be returned to a DOS prompt without incident. If you left the PC's case open during the testing phase, go ahead and close it up. You're done.

3 If something's not right (if the modem is connected—assigned—to the same COM port as another device, for example), you'll get the error message **Write fault error writing device COM1. Abort, Retry, Ignore, Fail?** Press **A** for abort and check out the text discussion for help determining what's wrong.

HOW TO...

Connect to Your Service Provider

In most cases, your service provider will place the files and instructions you need to start on the service provider's computer (called a server). You then have to use your modem and a telecommunications program (which controls the modem) to connect to the server and copy the files to your computer. This section explains how to do that.

If you've never used a telecommunications program (or you don't even know that you have one), this procedure can be a bit challenging. But don't panic. You'll learn how to use the telecommunications program that comes with Windows 3.1 or Windows 95 to connect to your service provider's computer and get your files.

In the off chance that the service provider mailed the files and instructions to you (through the postal service), you can skip this section. You can also skip this section if you purchased a special Internet program (such as Chameleon) at your local computer store. Such programs usually contain all the tools you need to establish a direct Internet connection without the help of your service provider.

What You Will Find in This Section

Use a Windows Telecommunications Program

If your service provider told you that you have to *download* (copy) the files and instructions from the service provider's computer, you have to connect to the service provider's computer to fetch the files you need. You do this by using a *telecommunications* program. This program tells your modem how to dial and how to transfer data between your computer and the service provider's computer. If you don't have a telecommunications program that you are accustomed to using, you can use Terminal (which comes with Windows 3.1) or HyperTerminal (which comes with Windows 95).

indirect connection. Be patient—you have to do this only once.

> With a *direct Internet connection*, you run programs on your computer. These programs give the Internet a graphical look and make it easy to navigate. With an *indirect connection*, you use a menu system on the service provider's computer to access the Internet. This menu system can be awkward to use.

Direct and Indirect Connections

When you connect to the service provider's computer using Terminal or HyperTerminal, your computer acts as a *terminal* of the service provider's computer and is said to be connected *indirectly* to the Internet. With an indirect (terminal) connection, you type at your keyboard, but your service provider's computer carries out your commands.

With a *direct* connection, you use programs on your computer to steer your way around the Internet. To use any of the nifty Internet programs you've previewed earlier in this book, you eventually need to establish a direct connection.

So why are you bothering with this indirect connection? Because you'll need some files from your service provider (and possibly from the Internet itself), and the only way to get these files is to use an archaic

Pick a Telecommunications Program

Fortunately, both Windows 95 and Windows 3.1 come with a telecommunications program you can use. In Windows 95, the telecommunications program is called HyperTerminal. Although the telecommunications program in Windows 3.1 (called Terminal) is less powerful, it works well enough. The *Guided Tour* shows you how to connect to your service provider's computer with either of these programs.

You may also have received a Windows telecommunications program with your modem. It's probably better than HyperTerminal or Terminal, so feel free to use it instead. Note, however, that the steps for using your program will vary from the steps in the *Guided Tour*.

Begin Guided Tour Connect Using Windows 95 HyperTerminal

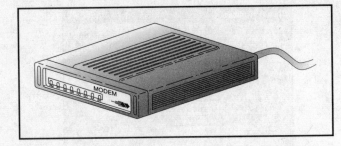

1 If you have an external modem, turn it on. (Internal modems receive power from the power supply in the system unit.)

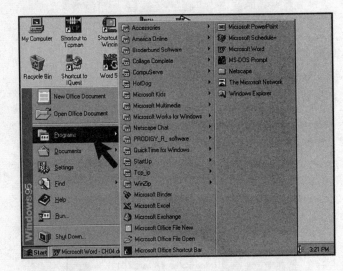

2 In Windows 95, you use the Start button to start all your programs. Click the **Start** button, and then point to **Programs**.

3 The Programs submenu appears, showing icons for programs and program groups. Point to **Accessories**, and then click **HyperTerminal**.

4 The HyperTerminal window appears. You will use this window to create an icon for dialing and connecting to your service provider. Double-click the **Hypertrm** icon.

(continues)

Guided Tour Connect Using Windows 95 HyperTerminal

(continued)

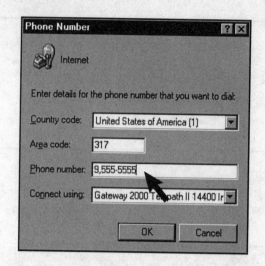

5 The Connection Description dialog box appears, asking you to type a description for the new connection. This description will appear below the icon you create. Type a name for the connection in the **Name** text box.

7 Click inside the **Phone number** text box and type the phone number of the service provider's computer. If you must dial a 9 to get an outside line, type **9** and a **,** before the phone number (the comma tells the program to pause before dialing the phone number). Don't forget to add 1-800 or an area code (respectively) for toll-free and long-distance calls.

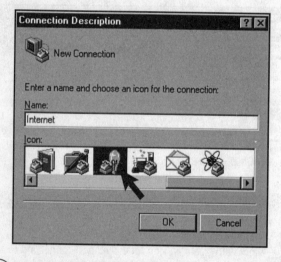

6 In the **Icon** box, click the icon you want to use to represent the connection. Then click **OK.**

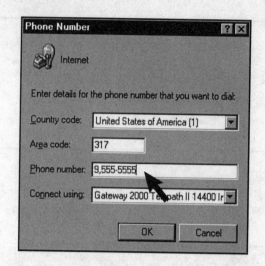

8 If you have call waiting and you get an incoming call while connected, it will automatically disconnect you from your service provider. You should disable it by typing a code in front of the phone number (or before 9,). In most areas, the code is ***70,**. Click **OK.**

Windows allows you to set dialing preferences for all your modem calls. Open the Control Panel, click **Modems,** and then click the **Dialing Properties** button. Enter the requested information, such as the number to dial for an outside line or before a long distance call, or the number to disable call waiting.

Guided Tour Connect Using Windows 95 HyperTerminal

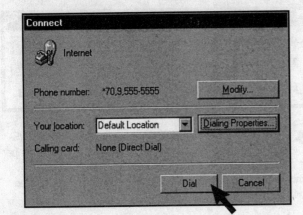

9 The Connect dialog box appears when you're ready to dial your service provider's computer. Click the **Dial** button.

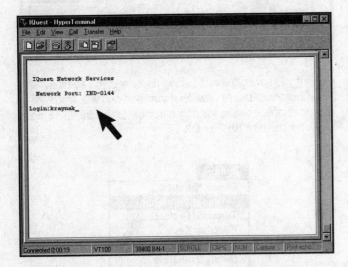

10 HyperTerminal dials the phone number you entered and connects with your service provider's computer. This computer is set up to ask for your login name (username) and password. Type your login name exactly as your service provider told you to type it (usually in lowercase letters) and press **Enter**.

```
IQuest Network Services

  Network Port: IND-0144

Login:kraynak
Password:
```

11 After you enter your login name, the service provider prompts you for your password. Type your password and press **Enter**. When you type, your password may not appear at all, or it may appear as a series of asterisks (********).

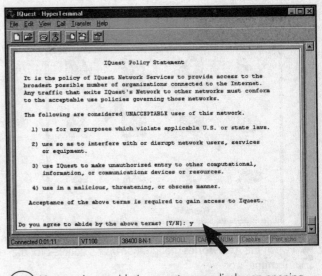

12 Your service provider's computer may display an opening screen asking you to agree to the terms of service. You can move on by typing **Y** for Yes.

```
Iquest Network Services
(You have mail.)
------------------------------------------------
Enter Command: Network
------------------------------------------------
HELP SCREEN
(I)nfo           Get Version and Copyright Information
(T)alk           Enter Talk Menu (Talk, Chat, Query, User List)
(N)etwork        News, Email, FTP, and other network Access
(F)iles          Enter File Transfer Menu
(C)hange         Vote, Change passwd, term type, sig file and plan
(E)xit           Leave This system
(H)elp           Get Help Screen
```

13 You should eventually see a menu like the one shown here. If you see a prompt instead, try typing **menu** at the prompt and pressing **Enter**. Skip ahead to the next section, "Use a UNIX Menu System," for details on how to proceed.

Begin Guided Tour   Connect with Windows 3.1 Terminal

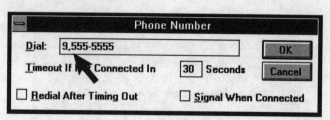

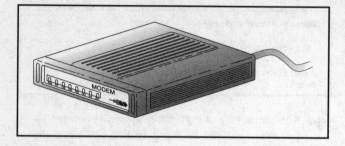

1 If you have an external modem, turn it on. Internal modems receive power from the power supply in the system unit.

4 Type your service provider's phone number. If you must dial a 9 to get an outside line, type **9,** before the phone number (the comma tells Terminal to pause before dialing the phone number). Don't forget to add 1-800 or an area code for toll-free and long-distance calls, respectively.

2 Open the **Accessories** group window, and double-click the **Terminal** icon.

5 If you have call waiting, it will disconnect you automatically from your service provider if someone calls you. Insert the code to disable it before the phone number (or before 9,). In most areas, the code is ***70**. Click **OK**.

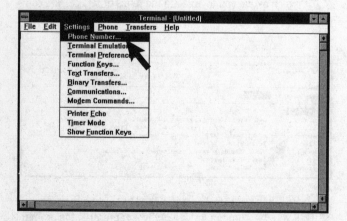

3 You will use the Terminal window to connect to your service provider. Open the **Settings** menu and click **Phone Number**.

6 You must now pick the type of terminal emulation required by your service provider. This tells terminal which "language" to speak. Open the **Settings** menu and click the **Terminal Emulation** command.

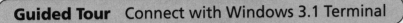

Guided Tour Connect with Windows 3.1 Terminal

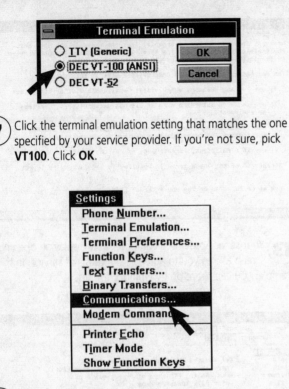

7 Click the terminal emulation setting that matches the one specified by your service provider. If you're not sure, pick **VT100**. Click **OK**.

8 Once you've picked a terminal emulation, you must enter the communications settings that govern the transfer of data over the connection. Open the **Settings** menu and click **Communications**.

If all the options are dimmed in the Communications dialog box, you haven't picked a port for your modem to use. In the Connector list, click on the port into which you plugged your modem (usually COM1 or COM2).

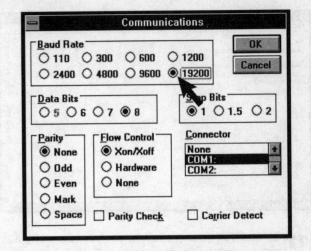

9 The baud rate specifies the speed at which your modem can transfer data. Click the fastest baud rate listed, and then click **OK**. Most modems will automatically adjust to a slower baud rate, if necessary, so pick the fastest baud rate. If you run into problems, you can try a slower baud rate later.

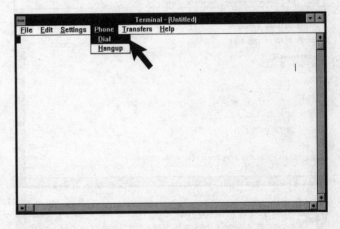

10 Terminal is ready to dial the phone number and establish the connection. Open the **Phone** menu and click **Dial.**

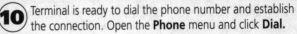

(continues)

Guided Tour Connect with Windows 3.1 Terminal *(continued)*

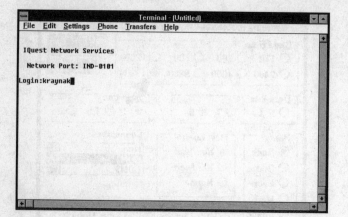

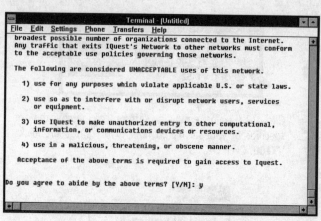

11 Terminal dials the phone number you entered and connects with your service provider's computer. This computer is set up to ask for your login name (username) and password. Type your login name exactly as your service provider told you to type it (usually in lowercase letters) and press **Enter**.

13 Your service provider's computer may display an opening screen asking you to agree to the terms of service. In this example, you can move on by typing **Y** for Yes.

12 After you've entered your login name, the service provider prompts you to type your password. Type your password and press **Enter**. As you type, your password may not appear, or it may appear as a series of asterisks (************).

14 You should eventually see a menu like the one shown here. If you see a prompt, instead, try typing **menu** at the prompt and pressing **Enter**. Skip ahead to "Use a UNIX Menu System" on page 77 for details on how to proceed.

Use a UNIX Menu System

When you connect to your service provider's computer and log in, you get a menu that allows you to run programs on your service provider's computer to access your e-mail, copy files, and even wander the Web. Compared to other tools you will use to navigate the Internet, this menu is fairly archaic; however, it does give you the basic access you need to start.

All menu systems sport a different look, provide different options, and have their own ways of asking you to select an option. Most menus have a high-lighted or underlined letter that you press (on your keyboard) to select the option. Other menus place a number next to each option, and you press a number to select one. Once you select a command, you press

Enter to execute it. Most commands you select open another menu from which you select additional options. Continue to select options until you find what you're looking for.

> When you first encounter the menu, look at the bottom of the screen for instructions that explain how to select and enter commands.

The following *Guided Tour* takes you on an Internet excursion with a typical UNIX menu. Later in this section, you will use this menu to check your e-mail (for instructions from your service provider) and to copy files from your service provider's computer.

Begin Guided Tour   Select Options from a UNIX Menu

```
Enter Command: Network

HELP SCREEN
(I)nfo        Get Version and Copyright Information
(T)alk        Enter Talk Menu (Talk, Chat, Query, User List)
(N)etwork     News, Email, FTP, and other network Access
(F)iles       Enter File Transfer Menu
(C)hange      Vote, Change passwd, term type, sig file and plan
(E)xit        Leave This system
(H)elp        Get Help Screen
```

1 When you connect to your service provider, you meet a UNIX menu system. In this case, you select an option from the menu by pressing the letter in parentheses. For example, press **N** for (N)etwork.

```
Enter Command: Network

HELP SCREEN
(I)nfo        Get Version and Copyright Information
(T)alk        Enter Talk Menu (Talk, Chat, Query, User List)
(N)etwork     News, Email, FTP, and other network Access
(F)iles       Enter File Transfer Menu
(C)hange      Vote, Change passwd, term type, sig file and plan
(E)xit        Leave This system
(H)elp        Get Help Screen
```

2 Notice that the command line above the menu displays the selected command. To enter the selected command, press **Enter**.

```
Enter Command: Help

Network Menu Help Screen
(F)tp          Obtain a file, via Interactive FTP
               into your personal file area
(T)elnet       Telnet to a host
(A)rchie       Locate files on the network via archie
(W)orld Web    Navigate the World Wide Web
(S)ervices     Access to misc. known good network services
(M)ail         Electronic mail access
(N)et-News     UseNet news access
(O)ffline      Offline Mail/News processing
(G)roup picker UseNet newsgroup picking program
(1)Gopher      Use gopher to navigate the network
(I)RC          Enter IRC Chat
(P)ersonal     Manipulate files in your personal area
(E)xit         Exit Network Menu
(H)elp         Get Help Screen
```

3 Entering the Network command brings up another menu displaying the network options. In this case, most of the network options provide access to the Internet. If your UNIX menu system offers a Help command, enter it now.

(continues)

Guided Tour   Select Options from a UNIX Menu

(continued)

```
(F)tp          Obtain a file, via Interactive FTP

This command will allow you to get files from remote systems, via
Unix FTP (File Transfer Protocol).  The files will then be stored in you
personal files area.  You can then download them to your local system by
using the (P)ersonal option below.  FTP is very easy to use, you will be
asked for a hostname.  You can either enter the full domain name or the
address of the site you wish to access.  A domain name looks like
"ftp.iquest.net", and an IP address would be 198.70.36.70.  You will the
be asked for a username and password.  On some systems, you can enter a
name of 'anonymous' and a password of 'username@iquest.net'.  On most
systems, you can abbreviate the password to 'username@' dropping off the
of your local system.  Once your connected, type 'help' and the system w
give you a list of commands.


(T)elnet          Telnet to a host

The Telnet command will allow you to login to a remote system on the
Internet.  Unlike FTP, Telnet allows you to connect to the remote system
a user, and run programs.  Some of the uses are to access other Archie a
--More-- (18%)
```

4 In this case, the Help command brings up a list of the other commands on the menu with a description of each command. If all of the help text does not fit on the screen, an indicator such as "—More—" appears at the bottom of the screen. You can usually move down the page by pressing the **Spacebar**.

```
the file.

(P)ersonal       Manipulate files in your personal area

This is your personal file area.  From this area, you can download
files you FTP'ed or saved from WWW or Gopher.  This is different then th
(F)iles option on the main menu, although it is possible to access your
area from the (F)iles option on the main menu.  You can save NewsGroup a

and Personal mail, and download them from this option.

(E)xit           Exit Network Menu

This option will take you back to the Main Menu.

(H)elp           Get Help Screen

        If you need further assistance, please feel free to send e-mail
        support@iquest.net or call IQuest Network Services at 722-4600.

Press [RETURN] to continue
```

5 When you reach the end of the file, you can go back to the menu by pressing **Enter** (Return).

```
--------------------------------------------------------------
Enter Command: Exit

Network Menu Help Screen
(F)tp          Obtain a file, via Interactive FTP
               into your personal file area
(T)elnet       Telnet to a host
(A)rchie       Locate files on the network via archie
(W)orld Web    Navigate the World Wide Web
(S)ervices     Access to misc. known good network services
(M)ail         Electronic mail access
(N)et-News     UseNet news access
(O)ffline      Offline Mail/News processing
(G)roup picker UseNet newsgroup picking program
(1)Gopher      Use gopher to navigate the network
(I)RC          Enter IRC Chat
(P)ersonal     Manipulate files in your personal area
(E)xit         Exit Network Menu
(H)elp         Get Help Screen
```

6 As you select commands, you move from one menu to another. To back up to a previous menu, enter the Exit command. For example, in the menu system shown here, you would press **E** to select Exit and then press **Enter**.

```
Galaxy Mall  The Scene SuperSearcher NanoLinks WWW Services

 [IMAGE]

WELCOME TO IQUEST NETWORK SERVICES

 Please select from the icons above or the following menu of choices:

WWW SERVICES AND HOME PAGES - EVERYTHING YOU WANTED TO KNOW ABOUT INTE
AND WWW SERVICES HERE AT IQUEST

GALAXY MALL - BROWSE AND PURCHASE SERVICES AND PRODUCTS AT OUR VARIOUS
CLIENTS SITES

THE SCENE - RELAX AT THE SCENE, THE COOLEST SPOT ON THE WEB FOR ART AN
-- press space for more, use arrow keys to move, '?' for help, 'q' to qu
 Arrow keys: Up and Down to move. Right to follow a link; Left to go ba
H)elp O)ptions P)rint G)o M)ain screen Q)uit /=search [delete]=history
```

7 Eventually, a command you enter will take you to a specific service screen. In this figure, the service provider has connected to the World Wide Web. (Notice how different the Web looks when you use a terminal connection; you get no fancy text or pictures.)

Guided Tour Select Options from a UNIX Menu

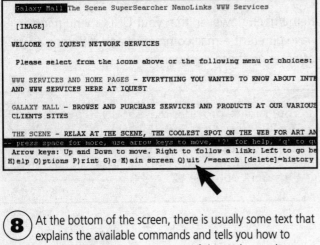

```
Galaxy Mall The Scene SuperSearcher NanoLinks WWW Services

 [IMAGE]

WELCOME TO IQUEST NETWORK SERVICES

 Please select from the icons above or the following menu of choices:

WWW SERVICES AND HOME PAGES - EVERYTHING YOU WANTED TO KNOW ABOUT INTE
AND WWW SERVICES HERE AT IQUEST

GALAXY MALL - BROWSE AND PURCHASE SERVICES AND PRODUCTS AT OUR VARIOUS
CLIENTS SITES

THE SCENE - RELAX AT THE SCENE, THE COOLEST SPOT ON THE WEB FOR ART AN
-- press space for more, use arrow keys to move, '?' for help, 'q' to qu
 Arrow keys: Up and Down to move. Right to follow a link; Left to go be
H)elp O)ptions P)rint G)o M)ain screen Q)uit /=search [delete]=history
```

```
Enter Command: Exit

HELP SCREEN
(I)nfo         Get Version and Copyright Information
(T)alk         Enter Talk Menu (Talk, Chat, Query, User List)
(N)etwork      News, Email, FTP, and other network Access
(F)iles        Enter File Transfer Menu
(C)hange       Vote, Change passwd, term type, sig file and plan
(E)xit         Leave This system
(H)elp         Get Help Screen
```

10 For now, remain connected to your service provider so you can check your e-mail and get your files. However, when you do finish an Internet session, you enter the **Quit** or **Exit** command to return to the opening menu. Then select **Quit** or **Exit** and press **Enter** to log out and disconnect.

8 At the bottom of the screen, there is usually some text that explains the available commands and tells you how to proceed. In this case, you can see more of this Web page by pressing the **Spacebar**.

```
Commands: Use arrow keys to move, '?' for help, 'q' to quit, '<-' to go
 Arrow keys: Up and Down to move. Right to follow a link; Left to go be
```

9 Here's another type of instruction you might find at the bottom of a screen.

Check Your E-Mail

Because connecting to the Internet the first time is somewhat complicated, your Internet service provider will usually send you instructions on how to copy the files you need and install them on your computer. These instructions are probably sitting in your e-mail box.

Your job is to use the service provider's UNIX menu to open and display the e-mail message on-screen. The *Guided Tour* shows you how to use a UNIX menu to check for incoming e-mail messages (and how to use Terminal or HyperTerminal to save the messages).

Remember, however, that your UNIX menu might have different e-mail commands and different ways of entering those commands.

Your service provider may send you instructions in a file (usually called README.TXT) instead of by e-mail. To copy this file to your computer, skip ahead to "Retrieve Files from Your Service Provider" on page 82.

Begin Guided Tour   Check Your E-Mail

```
Enter Command: Network

HELP SCREEN
(I)nfo          Get Version and Copyright Information
(T)alk          Enter Talk Menu (Talk, Chat, Query, User List)
(N)etwork       News, Email, FTP, and other network Access
(F)iles         Enter File Transfer Menu
(C)hange        Vote, Change passwd, term type, sig file and plan
(E)xit          Leave This system
(H)elp          Get Help Screen
```

1 Connect to your service provider as explained earlier. Then display the opening UNIX menu and look for the e-mail command. In this example, you must enter the **Network** command to get to the e-mail command.

```
Enter Command: Mail

Network Menu Help Screen
(F)tp           Obtain a file, via Interactive FTP
                into your personal file area
(T)elnet        Telnet to a host
(A)rchie        Locate files on the network via archie
(W)orld Web     Navigate the World Wide Web
(S)ervices      Access to misc. known good network services
(M)ail          Electronic mail access
(N)et-News      UseNet news access
(O)ffline       Offline Mail/News processing
(G)roup picker  UseNet newsgroup picking program
(1)Gopher       Use gopher to navigate the network
(I)RC           Enter IRC Chat
(P)ersonal      Manipulate files in your personal area
(E)xit          Exit Network Menu
(H)elp          Get Help Screen
```

2 The Network submenu appears, and you can see the Mail command. Select the **Mail** command and press **Enter**.

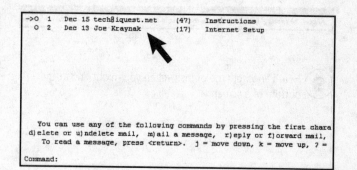

3 The Mail command displays a list of messages you've received. Hopefully, it contains an e-mail message from your service provider. Look at the bottom of the screen for instructions on how to select and display a message.

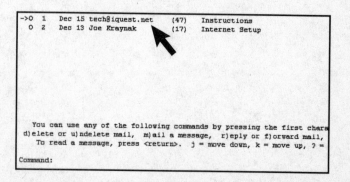

4 Follow the on-screen instructions to select and display the contents of the e-mail message from your service provider. In the system shown here, you would press **j** to move down to the next message or **k** to move to the previous message, and then press **Enter**.

Guided Tour Check Your E-Mail

```
Return-Path: < tech@iquest.net >
Date: Fri, 15 Dec 1995 09:00:17 -0500
To: kraynak@iquest.net
Subject: Instructions

Joe Kraynak

Thanks for choosing IQuest as your Internet Service Provider. Following
instructions on how to unzip, install, and set up your TCP/IP software a
use the Internet tools to access the service.

1. First, you have to download the files you need. You can use Terminal
HyperTerminal to download the files from your personal file area.

2. First, make sure you've set the transfer protocol correctly on our sy
Select Network/Personal/Options. Choose XModem if you're using Terminal
ZModem for HyperTerminal.

3. Make sure you set the transfer protocol     Terminal or HyperTerminal
match the potocol you selected in step 2.
There are 20 lines left (57%). Press <space> tor more, or "l" to return
```

5 The selected message appears on your screen. If it is long, you may have to press **Spacebar** or **Enter** to display more of the message.

6 Once the entire message appears, you can print it. First, drag over the text to select it (otherwise, you'll end up printing all the menus and other text displayed during the session). Then open the **File** menu and select **Print**.

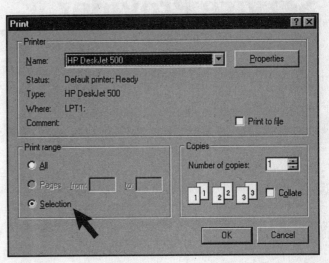

7 Click the **Selection** option button to print only the text you dragged over. Click **OK**.

```
-> 1   Dec 15 tech@iquest.net    (47)   Instructions
 O 2   Dec 13 Joe Kraynak        (17)   Internet Setup




   You can use any of the following commands by pressing the first chara
 d)elete or u)ndelete mail,  m)ail a message,  r)eply or f)orward mail,
   To read a message, press <return>.  j = move down, k = move up, ? =

Command: Quit              Move read message to "received" folder? (y/
```

8 After you print the message, enter the command to quit or exit the e-mail area.

```
Enter Command: Exit
----------------------------------------------------------
Network Menu Help Screen
(F)tp          Obtain a file, via Interactive FTP
               into your personal file area
(T)elnet       Telnet to a host
(A)rchie       Locate files on the network via archie
(W)orld Web    Navigate the World Wide Web
(S)ervices     Access to misc. known good network services
(M)ail         Electronic mail access
(N)et-News     UseNet news access
(O)ffline      Offline Mail/News processing
(G)roup picker UseNet newsgroup picking program
(1)Gopher      Use gopher to navigate the network
(I)RC          Enter IRC Chat
(P)ersonal     Manipulate files in your personal area
(E)xit         Exit Network Menu
(H)elp         Get Help Screen
```

9 You return to the menu you were at before you selected the Mail command. For now, stay connected to your Internet service provider so you can copy the files you need (as explained in "Retrieve Files from Your Service Provider," coming up next).

Retrieve Files from Your Service Provider

A good service provider supplies the files you need to connect to the Internet. These files are set up specifically to allow *your* computer and modem to connect to the service provider. The service provider enters such settings as your modem speed, the COM port your modem is plugged into, your username, and your password, so you don't have to configure the programs yourself. Most service providers also give you a Web browser, an e-mail program, and other programs for accessing the Internet.

In a few cases, the service provider mails you a disk with the essentials. In most cases, however, the service provider places the files in a special storage area on its computer. To get them, you must connect to the service provider (using Terminal or HyperTerminal), find the files, and copy them to your computer's hard disk.

You do this by setting up Terminal or HyperTerminal to receive the files and entering the command that tells the service provider's computer to send the files to you. You can then take a break while the files are transferred to your computer (this can take several minutes, depending on the speed of your modem). The *Guided Tour* walks you through the process of a typical file transfer.

> Because all service providers do not use the same system for storing files, you must ask where your files are stored. The service provider shown in the *Guided Tour* places the files in a special file area for each user.

Understand File Transfer Protocols

To ensure that the file is transferred reliably over the phone lines, you must pick a *file transfer protocol*. A protocol is a set of rules that govern the transfer of data. The sending and receiving computers must be set up to use the same protocol. If they're not, the two computers are not talking the same language, and the file cannot be transferred successfully.

In addition to making sure that both systems are using the same protocol, you should consider the features of the various protocols:

- **Xmodem** is an early protocol that is slow by today's standards. It can handle file transfers okay, but it can transfer only one file at a time. If you're using Terminal (Windows 3.1), this is the best protocol available.

- **Ymodem** is a step up from Xmodem. It is slightly faster and slightly better at detecting errors in the transfer, and it allows you to transfer more than one file at a time.

- **Zmodem** is two steps up from Xmodem. It is faster than Ymodem, allows you to transfer more than one file at a time, and recovers well when telephone line noise interrupts a transmission. If you're using HyperTerminal (with Windows 95), this is the protocol to use.

- **Kermit** is an old, slow protocol that's still in use in some educational institutions. Its claim to fame is that it is good at detecting transmission errors.

Binary or Text File Transfer?

In some cases, you might have to specify the type of file transfer you want to do: binary or text. Binary file transfers are for program files, graphics files, and any other file that's NOT a text file. Text file transfers are for text files only.

For more information about copying files from a remote computer to your computer, see "Find and Copy Files from the Internet," which starts on page 263.

Begin Guided Tour   Download Files with HyperTerminal

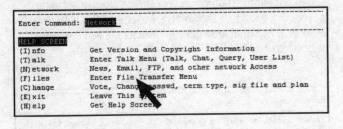

1 Connect to your service provider as explained earlier. Then display the opening UNIX menu and look for the command to access the file transfer area.

```
Enter Command: Files

HELP SCREEN
(I)nfo          Get Version and Copyright Information
(T)alk          Enter Talk Menu (Talk, Chat, Query, User List)
(N)etwork       News, Email, FTP, and other network Access
(F)iles         Enter File Transfer Menu
(C)hange        Vote, Change passwd, term type, sig file and plan
(E)xit          Leave This system
(H)elp          Get Help Screen
```

2 When you find the command you're looking for, select it. For example, in this system you would select the **Files** command and press **Enter**. This usually opens another menu that provides more specific options.

```
Enter File Transfer command: Options

File Transfer Menu Help Screen
(F)ile Area     Select a File Area
(L)ist          List the files on current Sub-board
(D)ownload      Download a file from this system
(U)pload        Upload a file to this system
(T)ext          View a text file
(O)ptions       Set personal file area options
(P)ersonal area Download from your personal file area
(E)xit          EXIT File Menu
(H)elp          Get Help Screen
```

3 Continue to enter menu commands until you reach the file transfer area and you see a command that allows you to enter file transfer options or pick a protocol. Select that command (**Options**, for example) and press **Enter.**

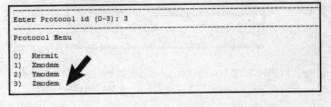

4 A list of available file transfer protocols appears. Select **Zmodem** and press **Enter**. This tells the service provider's computer which protocol to use when communicating with your computer.

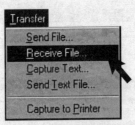

5 Next you must tell HyperTerminal how to receive files. Open the **Transfer** menu and select **Receive File**.

6 The Receive File dialog box asks you where you want the files stored and which protocol to use. Click the **Browse** button to pick a folder in which to save the files.

(continues)

Guided Tour   Download Files with HyperTerminal

(continued)

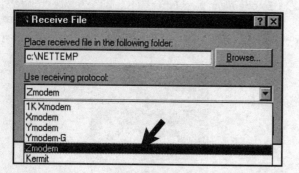

7 In the dialog box that appears, select the drive and folder in which you want to store the downloaded files. Then click **OK**.

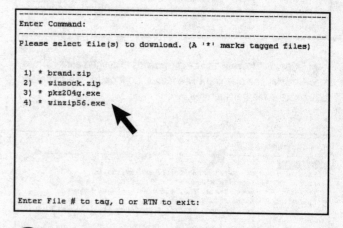

8 Back in the Receive File dialog box, you're ready to pick a protocol (which must be the same protocol you selected in step 4). Open the **Use receiving protocol** drop-down list and click **Zmodem**.

9 Click the **Close** button to close the dialog box and put the settings into effect.

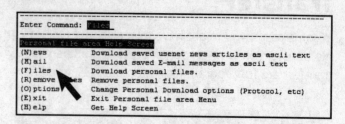

10 Use the service provider's menu to go to the area that contains the startup files your service provider set aside for you. In the example shown here, I selected **Files**, **WIN** (for Windows), **Personal area** (for my "directory"), and then **Files** (to download a file).

```
------------------------------------------------------------
Enter Command:
------------------------------------------------------------
Please select file(s) to download. (A '*' marks tagged files)

  1) * brand.zip
  2) * winsock.zip
  3) * pkz204g.exe
  4) * winzip56.exe




Enter File # to tag, 0 or RTN to exit:
```

11 A file list appears. Mark each file that you want to download by typing its selection letter or number. (Usually an asterisk appears to show that the file is selected.) When you've selected all the files you want, press **Enter**.

```
------------------------------------------------------------
Enter Command:
------------------------------------------------------------
Delete the files after downloading (Y/N):n

  1) * brand.zip
  2) * winsock.zip
  3) * pkz204g.exe
  4) * winzip56.exe
```

12 You may have to answer a couple of questions to confirm your request and specify whether you want the files deleted from the server after downloading. Answer the questions as instructed. (It's a good idea not to delete the files until you're sure they're on your computer.)

Guided Tour   Download Files with HyperTerminal

Although you should leave the startup files on the server until you're sure you have them safely on your computer, you should go back later and remove the files from the server. Most service providers charge you for the storage space you use on the server.

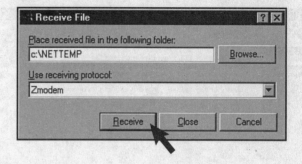

Receive File

Place received file in the following folder:

`c:\NETTEMP`   Browse...

Use receiving protocol:

Zmodem

Receive   Close   Cancel

Zmodem file receive for IQuest

Receiving:	BRAND.ZIP		
Storing as:	c:\NETTEMP\BRAND.ZIP	Files:	1 of 4
Last event:	Receiving	Retries:	0
Status:	Receiving		
File:	▓▓▓▓▓▓▓▓▓▓▓▓▓▓	16k of 20K	
Total:	▓	16k of 623K	
Elapsed:	00:00:10	Remaining: 00:06:37	Throughput: 1575 cps

Cancel   Skip file   cps/bps

13 After you answer the questions, the service provider should start sending the files, and HyperTerminal should start receiving them. If that happens, a dialog box appears, showing the progress of the transfer.

14 If the transfer does not start, you may have to tell HyperTerminal to start receiving the files. To do so, open the **Transfer** menu and select **Receive File**. In the Receive File dialog box, click the **Receive** button. HyperTerminal should start receiving the files, and then you should see the dialog box shown with step 13.

```
Enter Command: Exit
--------------------------------------------------------------------
HELP SCREEN
(I)nfo           Get Version and Copyright Information
(T)alk           Enter Talk Menu (Talk, Chat, Query, User List)
(N)etwork        News, Email, FTP, and other network Access
(F)iles          Enter File Transfer Menu
(C)hange         Vote, Change passwd, term type, sig file and plan
(E)xit           Leave This system
(H)elp           Get Help Screen
```

15 When you finish transferring files, back out of the UNIX menu system and exit. Then exit HyperTerminal.

Begin Guided Tour Download Files with Terminal

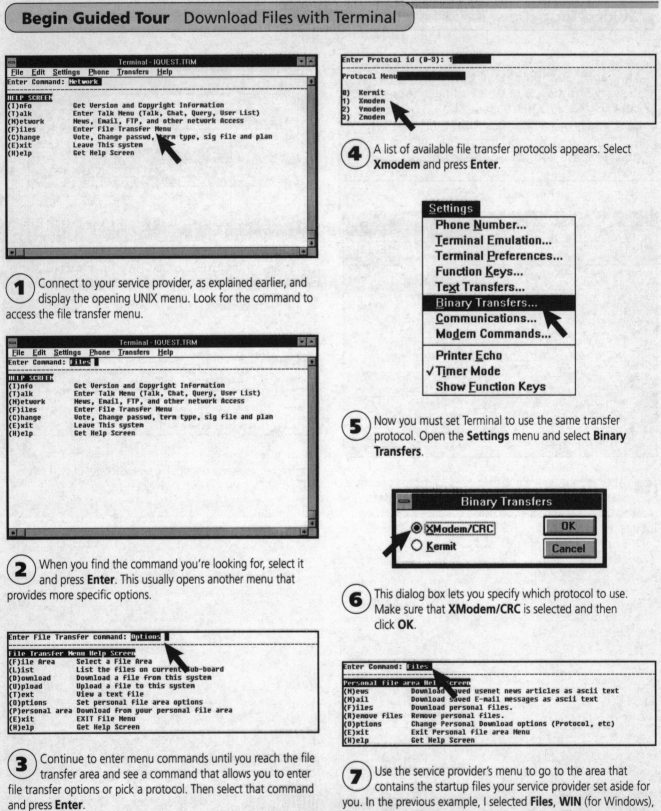

1 Connect to your service provider, as explained earlier, and display the opening UNIX menu. Look for the command to access the file transfer menu.

2 When you find the command you're looking for, select it and press **Enter**. This usually opens another menu that provides more specific options.

3 Continue to enter menu commands until you reach the file transfer area and see a command that allows you to enter file transfer options or pick a protocol. Then select that command and press **Enter**.

4 A list of available file transfer protocols appears. Select **Xmodem** and press **Enter**.

5 Now you must set Terminal to use the same transfer protocol. Open the **Settings** menu and select **Binary Transfers**.

6 This dialog box lets you specify which protocol to use. Make sure that **XModem/CRC** is selected and then click **OK**.

7 Use the service provider's menu to go to the area that contains the startup files your service provider set aside for you. In the previous example, I selected **Files**, **WIN** (for Windows), **Personal area** (for my "directory"), and then **Files** (to download a file).

Guided Tour　Download Files with Terminal

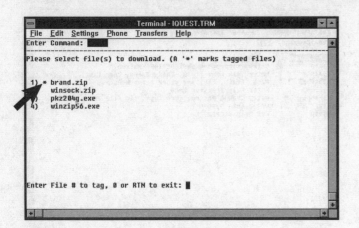

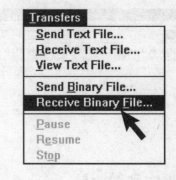

8 A file list appears. Mark the first file by typing the selection letter or number for that file. (Usually an asterisk appears to show that the file is selected.) With Xmodem, you can select and download only one file at a time. Press **Enter**.

```
Enter Command:
------------------------------------------------
Delete the files after downloading (Y/N):n

1) * brand.zip
```

9 You may have to answer a couple of questions to confirm your request and specify whether you want the files deleted from the server after downloading. Answer the questions as instructed. (It's a good idea not to delete the files until you're sure they're on your computer.)

```
Enter Command:
------------------------------------------------
Delete the files after downloading (Y/N):n
XMODEM Version 3.2 -- UNIX-CP/M Remote File Transfer Facility
File brand.zip Ready to SEND in binary mode
Estimated File Size 20K, 153 Records, 19529 Bytes
Estimated transmission time 23 seconds
Send several Control-X characters to cancel
```

10 After you've answered the questions, the server usually displays a message saying that it is ready to send the marked file.

11 You now have to tell Terminal to receive the file. Open the **Transfers** menu and select **Receive Binary File**.

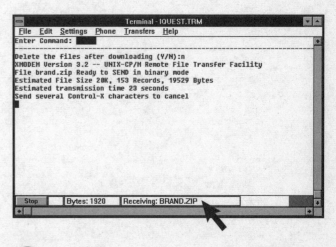

12 A dialog box appears, asking you to name the file and specify where you want it stored. Type the file's name in the **File Name** text box, select the directory where you want the file stored, and click **OK**.

13 The server starts to send the file, and Terminal starts to receive it. The bottom of the Terminal window shows the progress. Wait until the file transfer is complete.

(continues)

Guided Tour　Download Files with Terminal

(continued)

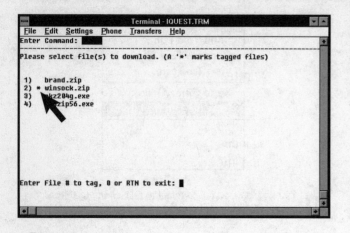

Repeat steps 7 through 13 to download any additional files that the service provider left you.

When you are done, back out of the UNIX menu system and exit. Then exit Terminal.

Copy Files from the Internet

(**Note:** If you have all the files from your service provider or if you purchased a special Internet program, you can skip this task.)

Your service provider should supply you with at least two programs: a TCP/IP (Transmission Control Protocol/Internet Protocol) program for establishing a direct Internet connection and an FTP program (which makes it easy to copy files from the Internet). With these two programs, you can easily acquire any other Internet programs you need. If your service provider does not supply the software you need, you'll have to get it yourself—from the Internet.

If you have Windows 95, you won't need the TCP/IP program. Windows 95 has built-in TCP/IP support, which you will learn how to use in "Configure Your TCP/IP Software" on page 97. However, you do still need an FTP program. If you have Windows 3.1, you'll need both a TCP/IP program and an FTP program.

The *Guided Tour* shows you how to copy the files you need from the Internet to your service provider's computer. You then use Terminal or HyperTerminal to retrieve the files from your service provider's computer.

Transfer Files Using FTP

In "Find and Copy Files from the Internet" on page 263, you will learn the details of using FTP (file transfer protocol) to copy files from the Internet directly to your computer. You will also learn how to use an FTP program or a Web browser to copy the files.

However, because you don't have a direct Internet connection yet, you cannot run a Web browser or an FTP program. Instead, you must use your service provider's FTP capabilities to copy the files.

When you use FTP from the service provider's computer (over an indirect connection), the files are copied from the Internet to your service provider's computer (not to your computer). You then have to copy the files from the service provider's computer to a folder on your hard disk.

Find the Files You Need

Various computers on the Internet have the files you need. You must know the address of the computer that has the file. Each computer on the Internet has an address called a URL (Uniform Resource Locator), which you can use to connect to that computer. A URL usually looks something like ftp.netscape.com. You'll learn all about URLs in "Go to a Specific Web Page Using a URL," on page 151.

For now, you must know the URL of the computers (FTP servers) that have the files you need. You will need two files: ws_ftp.zip (the FTP program) and winzip56.exe (a program that makes ws_ftp.zip usable). The table below shows the URLs for the servers where you can find these files, along with the folder (directory) in which the files are stored. Because you might not be able to connect to the first server you try, the table gives you the names of several servers.

For best results, try to transfer files in the early morning or after 6:00 p.m. During normal business hours, these servers are usually busy.

Essential Files to Download

File Name	Server's URL	Directory or Folder
ws_ftp.zip	earth.execpc.com	/pub/windows/winsock
	comserv.itri.org.tw	/PC/winsock
	sparky2.esd.mun.ca	/pub/winsock
	sun1.cc.ntnu.edu.tw	/pub/pc/WinSock/utility
winzip56.exe	pascal.ibp.fr	/pub6/pc/win3/util
	wuarchive.wustl.edu	/systems/ibmpc/win3/util
	ftp.sunet.se	/pub/pc/windows/winsock-indstate/ Misc_Utils/Compression
	pub.vse.cz	/pub/cica/util
	hubcap.clemson.edu	/pub/pc_shareware/windows/Archive
	cutl.city.unisa.edu.au	/pub/windows/utils
	thedon.cac.psu.edu	/pub/dos/win
	wuarchive.wustl.edu	/systems/ibmpc/win3/util

If you have an account with an online service such as Prodigy, CompuServe, or America Online, use its Web browser to copy files off the Internet. (To run a Web browser from the online service, see one of the online service sections, such as "Use America Online's Internet Connection," starting on page 37.) In the text box that shows the active page's URL, type one of the URLs from this table and press **Enter**. You can then point and click to change directories and get the files.

Begin Guided Tour   Get Files with FTP

```
IQuest - HyperTerminal                                    _ □ X
File  Edit  View  Call  Transfer  Help
[toolbar icons]

Enter Command: Network

HELP SCREEN
(I)nfo          Get Version and Copyright Information
(T)alk          Enter Talk Menu (Talk, Chat, Query, User List)
(N)etwork       News, Email, FTP, and other network Access
(F)iles         Enter File Transfer Menu
(C)hange        Vote, Change passwd, term type, sig file and plan
(E)xit          Leave This system
(H)elp          Get Help Screen




Connected 0:00:55   VT100   38400 8-N-1   SCROLL  CAPS  NUM  Capture  Print echo.
```

1 Use Terminal or HyperTerminal to log in to your service provider (as explained earlier in this section).

```
Enter Command: Ftp

Network Menu Help Screen
(F)tp           Obtain a file, via Interactive FTP
                into your personal file area
(T)elnet        Telnet to a host
(A)rchie        Locate files on the network via archie
(W)orld Web     Navigate the World Wide Web
(S)ervices      Access to misc. known good network services
(M)ail          Electronic mail access
(N)et-News      UseNet news access
(O)ffline       Offline Mail/News processing
(G)roup picker  UseNet newsgroup picking program
(1)Gopher       Use gopher to navigate the network
(I)RC           Enter IRC Chat
(P)ersonal      Manipulate files in your personal area
(E)xit          Exit Network Menu
(H)elp          Get Help Screen
```

2 Use the service provider's menu system to enter the FTP command. For this example, I had to select **Network** and then **Ftp**.

```
Enter hostname for FTP: comserv.itri.org.tw_

Press return without entering a hostname to abort ftp.


Login as 'anonymous' for anonymous ftp, otherwise a remote
username is required on the remote host.

Note: Please perform large anonymous ftp's during non-working
      hours.
```

3 A prompt appears, asking you to type the server's URL. Type the URL for the server to which you want to connect, and then press **Enter**.

```
Socket CALL
Connect CALL
Connected to comserv.itri.org.tw.
220 comserv FTP server (ITRI-CC wu-2.4(1) Wed Jun 8 03:00:45 CST 1994)
Name (comserv.itri.org.tw:kraynak): anonymous
```

4 The server prompts you for your name. Type **anonymous** and press **Enter**.

```
530-
530-http://mistral.enst.fr/netscape/
530-ftp://ftp.netscape.com
530-ftp://ftp2.netscape.com
530-ftp://ftp.pu-toyama.ac.jp/pub/net/WWW/netscape
530-ftp://ftp.eos.hokudai.ac.jp/pub/WWW/Netscape
530-ftp://ftp.nc.nihon-u.ac.jp/pub/network/WWW/client/netscape
530-ftp://ftp.leo.chubu.ac.jp/pub/WWW/netscape
530-ftp://ftp.tohoku.ac.jp/pub/network/www/Netscape
530-ftp://ftp.cs.umn.edu/packages/X11/contrib/netscape/
530-ftp://server.berkeley.edu/pub/netscape/
530-
530-
530-This list is also available via our Net site:
530-
530-http://www.netscape.com/comprod/mirror/index.html
530-
530 User anonymous access denied.
Login failed.
rftp> quit
Press [RETURN] to continue_
```

5 If the server is too busy or refuses to give you access for another reason, it displays a message saying that the login failed. Type **quit** and press **Enter**. Then repeat steps 2 and 3 but connect to another server listed in the table.

```
Socket CALL
Connect CALL
Connected to comserv.itri.org.tw.
220 comserv FTP server (ITRI-CC wu-2.4(1) Wed Jun 8 03:00:45 CST 1994)
Name (comserv.itri.org.tw:kraynak): anonymous
331 Guest login ok, send your complete e-mail address as password.
Password:
```

6 If the server gives you access, it prompts you for your password. Type your e-mail address (**jsmith@iquest.com**, for example) and press **Enter**.

```
230 Guest login ok, access restrictions apply.
rftp> cd /PC/winsock
```

7 When you are connected to the server, you see a prompt like the one shown here. Type the **cd** command, followed by a space and the directory or folder path given in the table. For example, you might type **cd /PC/winsock**. (Be sure to leave a space after cd and to type the directory or folder name exactly as it appears; capitalization matters here.)

(continues)

Guided Tour Get Files with FTP *(continued)*

```
rftp> cd /PC/winsock
250-Please read the file README
250-  it was last modified on Fri Jun 17 16:59:52 1994 - 547 days ago
250 CWD command successful.
rftp> ls_
```

8 You'll see a message such as "CWD Command Successful," which tells you that you are in the selected directory. Type **ls** and press **Enter** to see a list of files in the active directory.

```
-rw-rw-r--  1 ITRI    CC-CNS     120569 Jun 17  1994 winsock.zip
-rw-rw-r--  1 ITRI    CC-CNS      55834 Jun 17  1994 wintel1.zip
-rw-rw-r--  1 ITRI    CC-CNS     153510 Jun 17  1994 wlprs40.zip
-rw-rw-r--  1 ITRI    CC-CNS     263431 Jun 17  1994 wmos20a4.zip
-rw-rw-r--  1 ITRI    CC-CNS      82499 Jun 17  1994 wnvn082s.zip
-rw-rw-r--  1 ITRI    CC-CNS      68941 Jun 17  1994 ws_ftp.zip
-rw-rw-r--  1 ITRI    CC-CNS      57134 Jun 17  1994 ws_ping.zip
-rw-rw-r--  1 ITRI    CC-CNS     158941 Jun 17  1994 wsarchie.zip
-rw-rw-r--  1 ITRI    CC-CNS      83422 Jun 17  1994 wsatest.zip
-rw-rw-r--  1 ITRI    CC-CNS     163546 Jun 17  1994 wschesb1.zip
-rw-rw-r--  1 ITRI    CC-CNS      33494 Jun 17  1994 wsck-nfs.zip
-rw-rw-r--  1 ITRI    CC-CNS     320705 Jun 17  1994 wsg-10.exe
-rw-rw-r--  1 ITRI    CC-CNS       4758 Jun 17  1994 wshost.zip
-rw-rw-r--  1 ITRI    CC-CNS     414254 Jun 17  1994 wsirc12.zip
-rw-rw-r--  1 ITRI    CC-CNS      53332 Jun 17  1994 wslpd.zip
-rw-rw-r--  1 ITRI    CC-CNS     123482 Jun 17  1994 wsmtpd16.zip
-rw-rw-r--  1 ITRI    CC-CNS      60086 Jun 17  1994 wsock1b2.zip
-rw-rw-r--  1 ITRI    CC-CNS     142801 Jun 17  1994 wtalk11.zip
-rw-rw-r--  1 ITRI    CC-CNS     167601 Jun 17  1994 wtwsk10a.zip
226 Transfer complete.
rftp>
```

9 By the time you read this book, the name of the file you want may have changed (it may not be the same as the name in the table). Look for a name that matches or is similar to the name of the file you want. Write down the file name.

```
226 Transfer complete.
rftp> bin
```

10 To tell the FTP server that you want to perform a binary transfer, type **bin** at the prompt and press **Enter**.

```
rftp> bin
200 Type set to I.
rftp> get winsock.zip
```

11 Now you are ready to nab the file. Type **get**, followed by a space and the name of the file you want to download. For example, type **get winzip56.exe** and press **Enter**.

```
Socket CALL
200 PORT command successful.
150 Opening BINARY mode data connection for winsock.zip (120569 bytes).
```

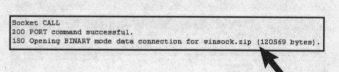

12 The FTP server starts to send the file, and your service provider's computer receives it. The file should be stored in your personal file area on the service provider's computer.

```
150 Opening BINARY mode data connection for winsock.zip (120569 bytes).
226 Transfer complete.
120569 bytes received in 13 seconds (9.2 Kbytes/s)
rftp> quit_
```

13 When the transfer is complete, a message appears telling you so. You should now leave the FTP server. At the prompt, type **quit** and press **Enter**.

```
-----------------------------------------------------------
Enter Command: Personal area
-----------------------------------------------------------
Network Menu Help Screen
(F)tp           Obtain a file, via Interactive FTP
                into your personal file area
(T)elnet        Telnet to a host
(A)rchie        Locate files on the network via archie
(W)orld Web     Navigate the World Wide Web
(S)ervices      Access to misc. known good network services
(M)ail          Electronic mail access
(N)et-News      UseNet news access
(O)ffline       Offline Mail/News processing
(G)roup picker  UseNet newsgroup picking program
(1)Gopher       Use gopher to navigate the network
(I)RC           Enter IRC Chat
(P)ersonal      Manipulate files in your personal area
(E)xit          Exit Network Menu
(H)elp          Get Help Screen
```

14 Back in your service provider's menu, you can repeat steps 2 through 12 to connect to other FTP servers and download the other files you need.

```
-----------------------------------------------------------
Enter Command:
-----------------------------------------------------------
Please select file(s) to download. (A '*' marks tagged files)


  1)    brand.zip
  2) *  winsock.zip
  3)    pkz204g.exe
  4)    winzip56.exe
```

15 When you finish downloading files to your personal file area, you must use Terminal or HyperTerminal to copy the files to your computer. See "Retrieve Files from Your Service Provider" on page 82.

Install Your Files

You now have the files you need to start. The only problem is that these files have been zipped (compressed) so that they take up less storage space on the server and travel through the phone lines faster. Actually, each file you downloaded contains several files that make up a program.

You will typically find two types of inzipped files: those whose names end in .ZIP (such as ws_ftp.zip), and those whose names end in .EXE (such as winzip56.exe). You must have a special program to decompress the files whose names end in .ZIP. However, zipped files whose names end in .EXE are self-extracting: you run the file, and it unzips itself.

The *Guided Tour* leads you through the process of unzipping the files you just downloaded. (This procedure is also useful if your service provider sent you zipped files.) First, you will unzip and install winzip56.exe, which places a program called WinZip on your computer. You can then use the WinZip program to decompress ws_ftp.zip.

Once you've unzipped ws_ftp.zip, you can learn how to use ws_ftp in "Find and Copy Files from the Internet," which starts on page 263.

Begin Guided Tour   Unzip Your Files

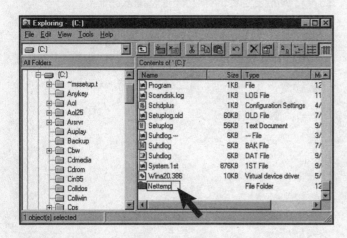

1 Create a temporary folder (call it NETTEMP) and copy winzip56.exe into it. You will use this folder only to install WinZip. Once you do that, you can delete the folder and its contents.

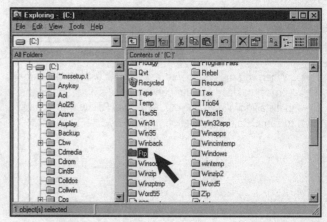

2 While you're at it, create a folder called FTP. Don't worry about moving any files into this folder yet. You'll unzip the files in ws_ftp.zip to this folder.

(continues)

Guided Tour Unzip Your Files *(continued)*

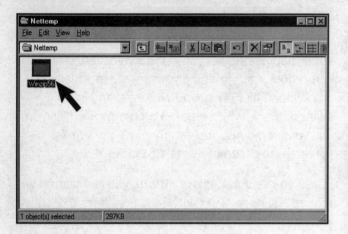

3 Open My Computer (in Windows 95) or File Manager (in Windows 3.1) and change to the NETTEMP folder. Double-click **winzip56.exe** (it may appear as just winzip56).

4 When you run winzip56.exe, it displays a series of dialog boxes that lead you through the process of unzipping the file and installing WinZip on your hard drive. Follow the instructions to complete the installation.

5 In Windows 95, the WinZip installation places WinZip on the Start menu. Click the **Start** button, point to **Programs**, point to **WinZip**, and then click the **WinZip** option.

6 In Windows 3.1, the WinZip installation creates a program group with program-item icons for WinZip. Double-click the **WinZip** icon to run WinZip.

Guided Tour Unzip Your Files

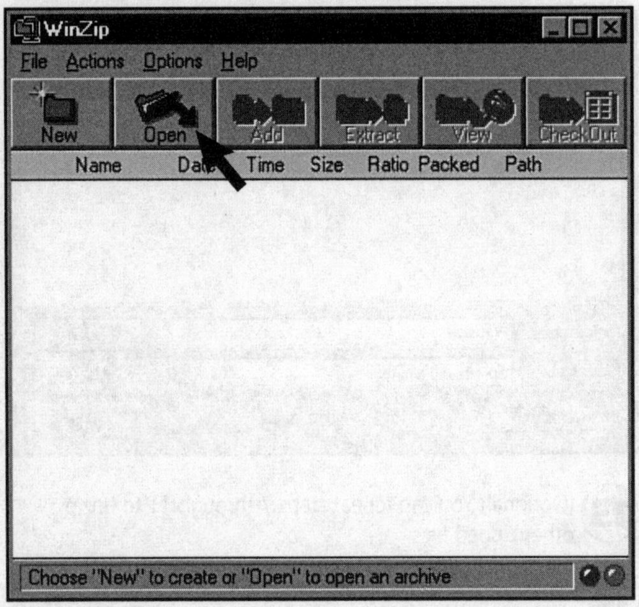

7 The WinZip window appears. You must now open an archive (one of your ZIP files). Click the **Open** button in the toolbar.

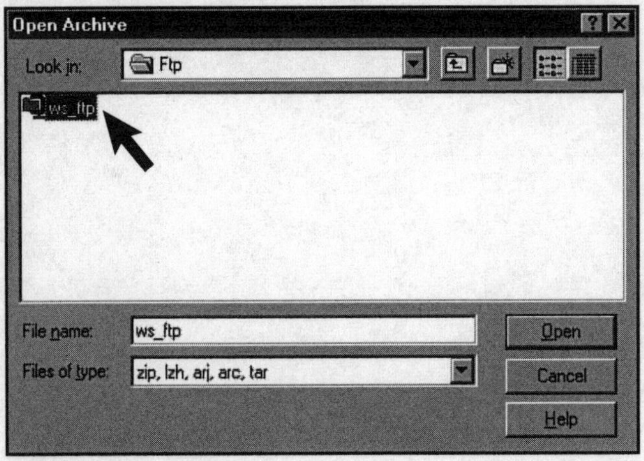

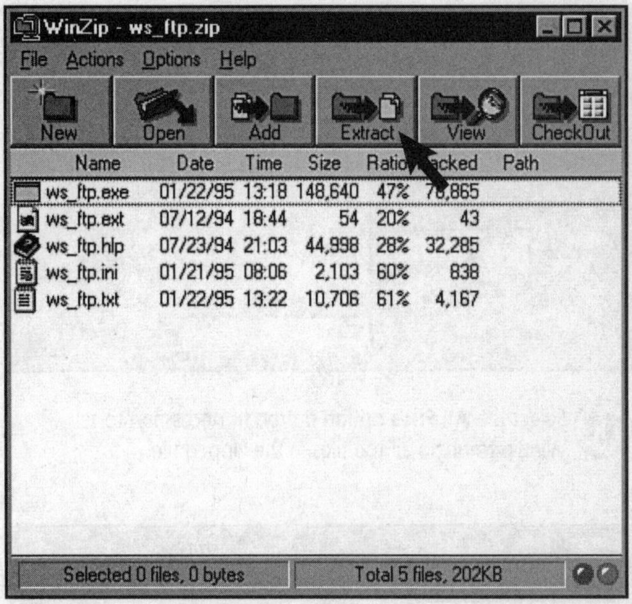

9 WinZip displays the names of all the files in the selected .ZIP file. Click the **Extract** button in the toolbar.

8 In the dialog box that appears, select **ws_ftp.zip**. Click the **Open** or **OK** button to proceed.

10 A dialog box like the one shown here appears. Select the drive and folder in which you want the unzipped files placed (the FTP folder you created earlier).

(continues)

Guided Tour　Unzip Your Files　*(continued)*

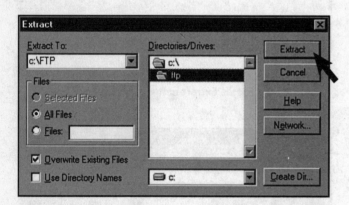

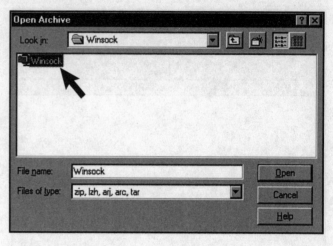

11 Select the **All Files** option button (if necessary) to tell WinZip to unzip all the files in the zipped file.

13 (Optional) You can repeat steps 7 through 11 to unzip other zipped files.

14 When you finish unzipping files, skip to "Find and Copy Files from the Internet" on page 263 to learn how to use WS_FTP.

To save disk space, you can delete from your hard disk the original files you downloaded (ws_ftp.zip and winzip56.exe).

12 Click the **Extract** button. WinZip unzips the file and stores all the extracted files in the specified folder.

HOW TO...

Configure Your TCP/IP Software

The language of the Internet is TCP/IP (Transmission Control Protocol/Internet Protocol). TCP/IP is a set of rules that control how data passes between computers on the Internet. Whether you connect to the Internet via modem or through a direct network connection, you need some kind of TCP/IP program.

If you use a direct network connection and Windows 3.1, your network administrator has taken care of installing the proper software. You can skip this section and jump to "Find and Install a Web Browser" on page 123. If you have a direct network connection to the Internet and you use Windows 95, you have to configure a program called the Direct Network Connection (that is, if your network administrator didn't already do it for you). See "Install TCP/IP Software for Windows 95" on page 98.

If you plan to connect using a modem and Windows 3.1, you need to install a TCP/IP program such as Trumpet Winsock, which is available from your service provider. If you'll connect using a modem and Windows 95, you just need to install the built-in TCP/IP program.

What You Will Find in This Section

Install TCP/IP Software for Windows 95

A protocol is a set of rules that govern the exchange of information. TCP/IP defines how information is exchanged on the Internet in particular. Therefore, you must install the TCP/IP protocol for your modem to know how to "talk" on the Internet when you connect.

If you use Windows 3.1, you'll install a TCP/IP program called Trumpet Winsock. See "Install TCP/IP Software for Windows 3.1" on page 112 for help. Windows 95, on the other hand, provides its own TCP/IP software for your use. However, it is not usually installed when Windows 95 is set up, so you will probably have to install it. The *Guided Tour* in this section shows you how to do just that.

Depending on the type of Internet connection you have, installing the TCP/IP program can be a two-step process. No matter what, you'll need to install the TCP/IP protocol. In addition, if you're using a SLIP

dial-up Internet account, you'll need to install the SLIP/CSLIP protocol. That's where you might run into a snag: To install the SLIP or CSLIP protocol, you need the CD-ROM version of Windows 95.

> Even if you've used Trumpet Winsock in the past, don't use it with Windows 95. Windows 95 prefers its own TCP/IP program; therefore, I suggest you use it instead.

In addition to installing the TCP/IP software, you must configure the Dial-Up Networking program so it can function as your Internet Connector. You need to do this whether you connect to the Internet through a modem or through a direct network connection. You learn how to configure the Windows 95 TCP/IP software in "Configure the Dial-Up Networking Program in Windows 95" (page 106).

Begin Guided Tour   Add TCP/IP Protocol

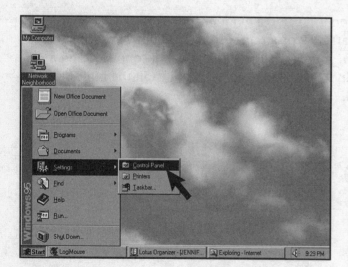

1 Click the **Start** button, select **Settings**, and click **Control Panel**.

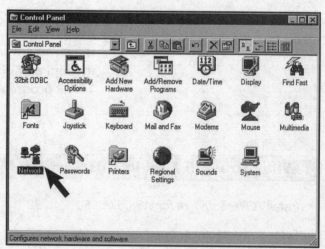

2 In the Control Panel window, double-click the **Network** icon.

Guided Tour Add TCP/IP Protocol

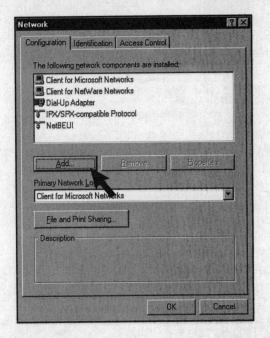

5 In the Select Network Protocol dialog box, select **Microsoft** from the **Manufacturers** list. Under **Network Protocols**, select **TCP/IP**. Click **OK**.

3 The Network dialog box appears. If you have already installed the TCP/IP protocol, skip to step 6. If not, click the **Add** button.

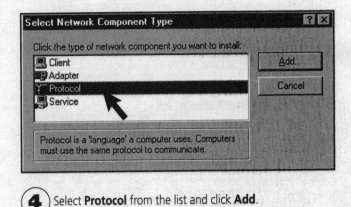

4 Select **Protocol** from the list and click **Add**.

6 If you plan to use a dial-up connection (if you will use your modem to dial into your Internet service provider), select **Dial-Up Adapter** from the network components list. To use a direct network connection (if you will connect through your company's network), select your network adapter instead. Click **Properties**.

(continues)

Guided Tour Add TCP/IP Protocol

(continued)

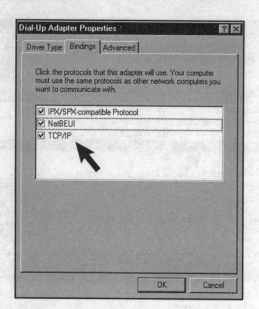

7 The Dial-Up Adapter Properties dialog box appears. Click the **Bindings** tab and select the **TCP/IP** option if it's not already checked. Click **OK**.

If you have a network card installed and you are not connecting through your network (but through a modem and a service provider instead), you should change the Properties settings of the network card so that TCP/IP is not selected on the Bindings tab (see step 7).

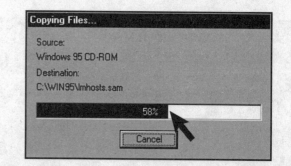

8 Click **OK** to close the Network dialog box.

9 Insert the Windows diskette or CD, and Windows 95 starts copying the appropriate files.

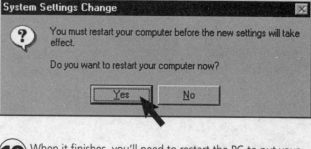

10 When it finishes, you'll need to restart the PC to put your changes into effect. Shut down your programs and click **Yes**.

Begin Guided Tour   Add SLIP or CSLIP Protocol

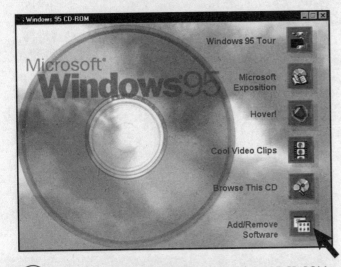

1 Insert the Windows 95 CD, and the Windows 95 CD-ROM window appears. Click **Add/Remove Software**.

To install SLIP or CSLIP protocol, you must use the Windows 95 CD-ROM. If you purchased Windows on floppy disk, you won't be able to complete this task.

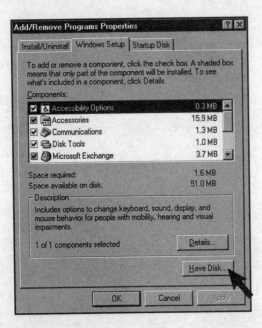

2 In the Add/Remove Programs Properties dialog box, click the **Windows Setup** tab, if necessary. Then click **Have Disk**.

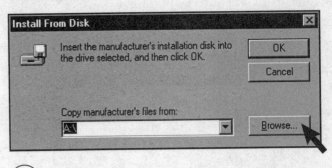

3 The Install From Disk dialog box appears. Click **Browse**.

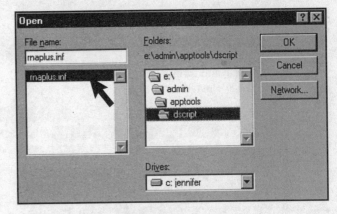

4 Change to the **Admin\Apptools\Dscript** folder, select the **rnaplus.inf** file, and click **OK**.

Install From Disk

Insert the manufacturer's installation disk into the drive selected, and then click OK.   OK
                                                                                                 Cancel

Copy manufacturer's files from:
E:\ADMIN\APPTOOLS\DSCRIPT   Browse...

5 In the Install From Disk dialog box, click **OK**.

(continues)

Guided Tour   Add SLIP or CSLIP Protocol   (continued)

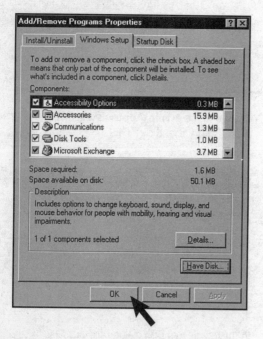

Have Disk

Click the box next to an item to add or remove a check mark. A check means you want the component on your computer; no check mark means you don't want the component.

Components:

☑ SLIP and Scripting for Dial-Up Networking   0.2 MB

Space required: 0.0 MB
Space available on disk: 50.1 MB

Description
Allows you to connect to an Internet provider, online service, or remote computer through Dial-up Networking. Supports automated script processing.

Details...

Install   Cancel

6 Select the **SLIP and Scripting for Dial-Up Networking** option and click **Install**.

Windows 95 CD-ROM

Microsoft Windows95

Windows 95 Tour
Microsoft Exposition
Hover!
Cool Video Clips
Browse This CD
Add/Remove Software

8 Close the Windows 95 CD-ROM window by clicking the **Close** button.

Add/Remove Programs Properties

Install/Uninstall | Windows Setup | Startup Disk

To add or remove a component, click the check box. A shaded box means that only part of the component will be installed. To see what's included in a component, click Details.

Components:

☑ Accessibility Options   0.3 MB
☑ Accessories   15.9 MB
☑ Communications   1.3 MB
☑ Disk Tools   1.0 MB
☑ Microsoft Exchange   3.7 MB

Space required: 1.6 MB
Space available on disk: 50.1 MB

Description
Includes options to change keyboard, sound, display, and mouse behavior for people with mobility, hearing and visual impairments.

1 of 1 components selected   Details...

Have Disk...

OK   Cancel   Apply

7 In the Add/Remove Programs Properties dialog box, click **OK**. Windows copies the appropriate files to your computer.

Enter Your Internet Account Information in Windows 95

After you install the TCP/IP protocol, you have to configure it. To do so, you enter your Internet account information, which you get from your Internet service provider. If you're connecting to the Internet through your office network, ask your network administrator to give you this information. You need to know these things:

- The IP and subnet mask (if applicable) of your connection. Depending on the type of service you get, your provider will probably assign you an address *dynamically* (each time you dial in). This allows a single provider to service a large number of users using a small number of actual

Internet connections. If you're willing to pay for it, you can have a permanent address assigned to you. An IP address consists of a series of numbers such as 198.70.144.66. Most subnet masks are 255.255.255.0, but yours may be different. Ask your service provider to be sure.

- Your host and domain name
- The DNS address and search order of the Internet server (if applicable)
- The gateway address

When you have the information you need, you're ready to configure the TCP/IP protocol.

Begin Guided Tour   Configure TCP/IP for Windows 95

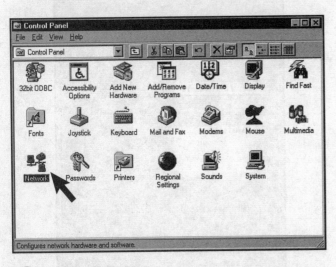

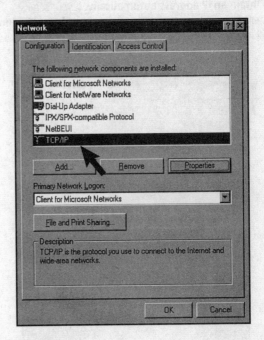

① Click the **Start** button, select **Settings**, and click **Control Panel**.

② Double-click the **Network** icon.

③ Select **TCP/IP** from the network components list and click **Properties**.

(continues)

Guided Tour Configure TCP/IP for Windows 95

(continued)

TCP/IP Properties ? X

| Bindings | Advanced | DNS Configuration |
| Gateway | WINS Configuration | IP Address |

An IP address can be automatically assigned to this computer.
If your network does not automatically assign IP addresses, ask
your network administrator for an address, and then type it in
the space below.

◉ Obtain an IP address automatically

○ Specify an IP address:

IP Address: [. . .]

Subnet Mask: [. . .]

[OK] [Cancel]

If you are connecting through your network,
you may not need to configure DNS. Check
with your system administrator.

6 Enter the **Host** and **Domain** names you were given. (This is
probably your Internet address. For example, in the Internet
address jfulton@mcp.com, the host name is jfulton, and the
domain name is mcp.com.)

7 Under **DNS Server Search Order**, enter the DNS server
address. If you're not sure what it is, try 128.95.1.4, which
is common. Click **Add** to add it. Repeat for additional DNS
servers.

8 Under **Domain Suffix Search Order**, enter the domain
name again (such as mcp.com). Click **Add** to add it. Repeat
for additional domains.

4 In the TCP/IP Properties dialog box, click the **IP Address**
tab. If your service provider assigns the address dynamically,
click **Obtain an IP address automatically**. If your service
provider gave you an actual address, click **Specify an IP address**
and fill in the **IP Address** and **Subnet Mask** boxes.

TCP/IP Properties ? X

| Gateway | WINS Configuration | IP Address |
| Bindings | Advanced | DNS Configuration |

○ Disable DNS

◉ Enable DNS

Host: jfulton   Domain: mcp.com

DNS Server Search Order

[. . .]   [Add]

| 128.95.1.4 | [Remove]

Domain Suffix Search Order

[ ]   [Add]

[ ]   [Remove]

[OK] [Cancel]

5 Click the **DNS Configuration** tab and select **Enable DNS**.

TCP/IP Properties ? X

| Bindings | Advanced | DNS Configuration |
| Gateway | WINS Configuration | IP Address |

The first gateway in the Installed Gateway list will be the default.
The address order in the list will be the order in which these
machines are used.

New gateway:

[198. 70 .144. 10]   [Add]

Installed gateways:

| 198.70.144.10 | [Remove]

[OK] [Cancel]

9 Click the **Gateway** tab.

10 Enter the gateway address and click **Add**.

Guided Tour   Configure TCP/IP for Windows 95

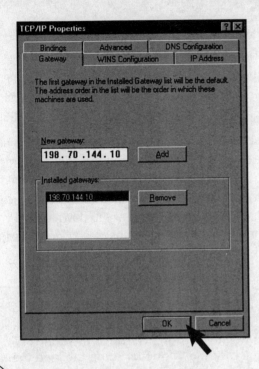

11 Click **OK** to close the TCP/IP Properties dialog box.

12 Click **OK** to close the Network dialog box. Then restart the PC to put your changes into effect.

Configure the Dial-Up Networking Program in Windows 95

Having installed the TCP/IP protocol, you're ready to configure the Windows 95 TCP/IP program that uses it: Dial-Up Networking. Before you start to configure the Dial-Up Networking program, get the following information from your service provider (if you will be using a direct Internet connection) or from your network administrator (if you will be connecting to the Internet through your office network).

- The phone number you will call to connect to your service provider (if applicable).

- Whether or not you will log in through a terminal window after you connect to your service provider. Most people don't use a terminal window. However, if for any reason, the way you log in to your Internet provider changes from day to day or week to week, and, therefore, you can't automate your login with a script, you'll want Windows 95 to display a terminal window so you can type your login manually.

- If you have a SLIP account (as opposed to PPP), you need to know whether or not your service provider uses compressed SLIP (known as CSLIP).

- Whether or not your service provider has written a *script* you can use to connect to the Internet quickly and simply. This script is usually saved to a file that you download from your service provider in the same way you downloaded your original Internet programs. See "Copy Files from the Internet" on page 89 for help.

> If necessary, install the Dial-Up Networking program before proceeding. Double-click the **Add/Remove Programs** icon in the Control Panel, click the **Windows Setup** tab, and then select **Dial-Up Networking** from the Communications options. If it's already installed, you'll find it on the Accessories menu.

Begin Guided Tour   Set Up Dial-Up Networking

1 Double-click the **Dial-Up Networking** icon in the My Computer folder, or click the **Start** button, select **Programs**, select **Accessories**, and click **Dial-Up Networking**.

> You can also access Dial-Up Networking by double-clicking the **Dial-Up Networking** icon in the My Computer folder.

2 The Welcome to Dial-Up Networking screen appears. Click **Next** or, if necessary, double-click the **Make New Connection** icon.

Guided Tour   Set Up Dial-Up Networking

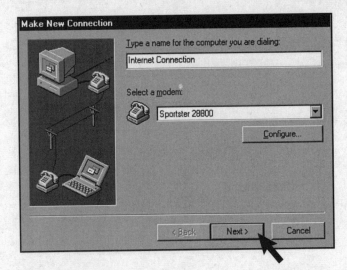

③ Enter a name, such as **Internet Connection**, for your new connection. Click **Next >**.

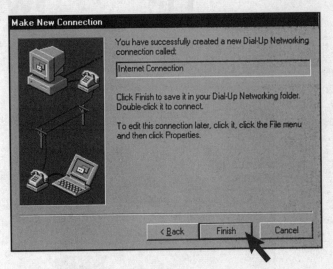

⑤ Click **Finish**, and Windows adds an icon for the new connection to the Dial-Up Networking folder.

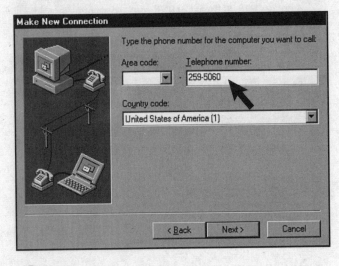

④ Enter the phone number of your service provider. If you're connecting through your network, enter any number—it will be ignored anyway. Click **Next >**.

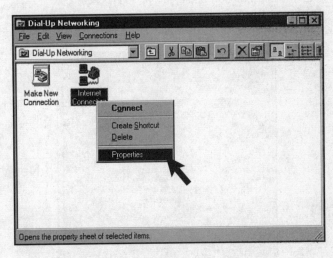

⑥ Right-click your new icon and select **Properties** from the shortcut menu that appears.

(continues)

Guided Tour Set Up Dial-Up Networking *(continued)*

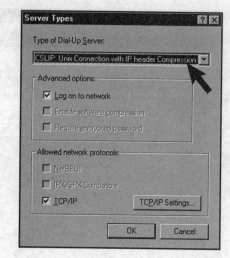

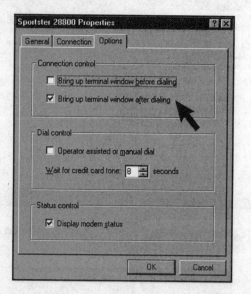

7 If your service provider told you that you will need a terminal window displayed after you connect, click **Configure**. If not, skip to step 9.

8 In the Properties dialog box, click the **Options** tab. Select **Bring up terminal window after dialing** and click **OK**.

9 In the Internet Connection dialog box, click **Server Type**. The Server Types dialog box appears.

10 In the Type of Dial-Up Server list, select the appropriate option: **PPP**, **SLIP**, or **CSLIP** (if your service provider told you to use SLIP compression). If you're connecting through your network, select **NRN: Netware Connect**. Click **OK**.

11 If your service provider gave you a dial-up script that you can use to easily configure your connection, open the **Start** menu, select **Programs**, select **Accessories**, and click **Dial-Up Scripting Tool**.

12 In the Dial-Up Scripting Tool dialog box, select your connection from the list and click **Browse**.

Guided Tour Set Up Dial-Up Networking

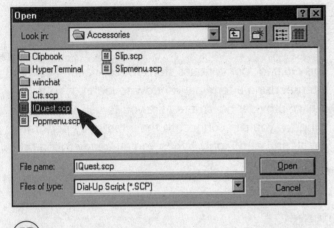

13 Select the script file from the list and click **Open**.

14 Click **Apply**, and then click **Close**.

Test Your Internet Connection in Windows 95

After you install and configure the TCP/IP protocol and you configure the Dial-Up Networking program, you need to test your new Internet connection to make sure it works. You'll need your user name and password for this. If you don't know them, contact your Internet service provider.

This *Guided Tour* contains steps for connecting to the Internet using a terminal window to log in. If your service provider doesn't require you to use a terminal window, you can connect to the Internet by performing steps 1 and 2 only. When you are ready to log off, perform step 6.

Begin Guided Tour   Log On and Off the Internet

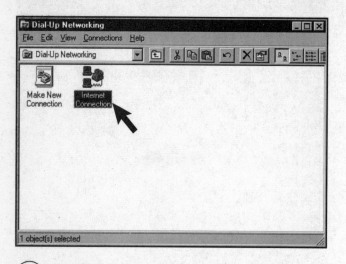

1 To connect to the Internet, double-click your new **Internet Connection** icon in the Dial-Up Networking window.

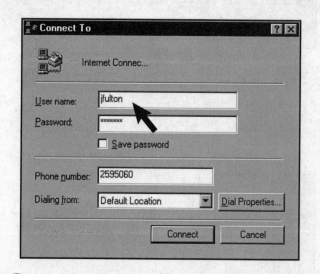

2 If you configured Dial-Up Networking to display a terminal window, do not enter your user name and password here; you'll enter them through the terminal window itself. Click **Connect**.

If you do not have to use a terminal window, enter your user name and password now and click **Connect.** Then skip to step 6.

Guided Tour Log On and Off the Internet

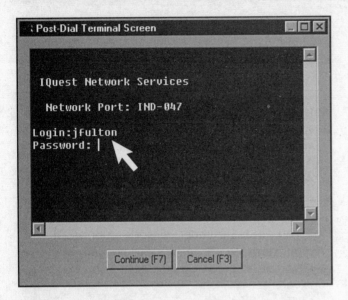

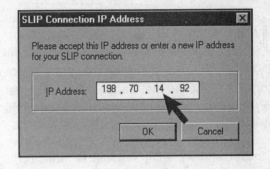

5 Enter the IP address you wrote down and click **OK**.

3 If the terminal window appears, enter your user name and password. (The password will not appear on-screen.) Then, if you are using a SLIP or CSLIP connection, continue to step 4. If not, click **Continue** and skip to step 6. (Your service provider will inform you if your login procedure differs from this.)

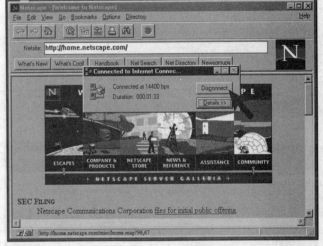

6 You should now have a working connection, and you can use any Internet programs you have, including Netscape, Mosaic, FTP, and Gopher. You can click the **Minimize** button if you want to get this window out of your way. However, when you want to log off of the Internet later on, restore this window and click **Disconnect**.

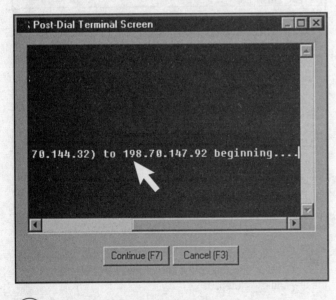

4 Use the scroll bars if necessary to see the IP address assigned to you. Write the number down and click **Continue**.

Install TCP/IP Software for Windows 3.1

Unlike Windows 95, Windows 3.1 does not include a TCP/IP program; however, you can easily obtain one. (Keep in mind that if you're going to connect to the Internet through your office network, your network administrator has done all the work for you, and you can skip this section.)

The most common TCP/IP software is Trumpet Winsock. Trumpet Winsock is a shareware program that is usually included in the software programs you download from your Internet provider when you first connect (see "Connect to Your Service Provider" on page 69 for more information). In the *Guided Tour*, I'll show you how to install and configure Trumpet Winsock. Commercial TCP/IP programs

such as Internet Chameleon are also available wherever software is sold.

> Shareware works under the assumption that you will pay for the program after a reasonable trial period, such as 30 days. After you try it out, you should register Trumpet Winsock, which is well worth the meager $25 fee.

First, you'll install Trumpet Winsock. Later, you'll configure it to log into your particular Internet service provider.

Begin Guided Tour   Install Trumpet Winsock

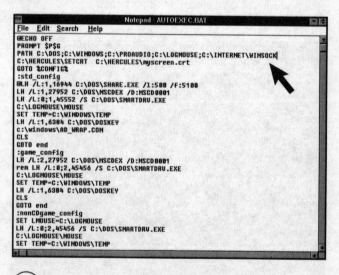

1 First, create a directory for Winsock and copy the program files to it.

2 Start Notepad and open the **AUTOEXEC.BAT** file. Add the Winsock directory to the end of the PATH statement, save the file, and exit Notepad.

Guided Tour   Install Trumpet Winsock

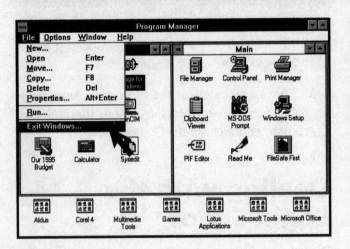

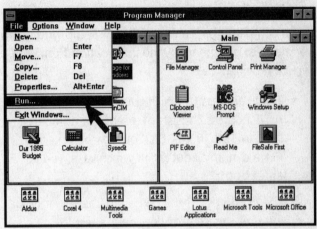

3 Open Program Manager's **File** menu and select **Exit Windows**. Then click **OK**.

4 Press **Ctrl+Alt+Delete** to restart the PC. Type **WIN** and press **Enter** to restart Windows. You're now ready to configure Trumpet Winsock.

Configure Trumpet Winsock

To complete the Trumpet Winsock setup, you'll need to get the following information from your service provider:

- The IP address to which you've been assigned. An IP address consists of a series of numbers such as 198.70.144.66. You may be asked to use a dynamic address, in which case, you'll enter **bootp**.

- The IP address of the domain name server (your Internet service provider's computer).

- The address of the time server (if any). A time server sends an updated time signal to other servers on the Internet. This is rarely used by commercial service providers, so it's very doubtful that yours will have one.

- The service provider's domain name.

- If you have a SLIP account (as opposed to PPP), you need to know whether your provider uses compressed SLIP (known as CSLIP.)

- Whether your service provider supports hardware handshaking (hardware flow control).

- The speed of your Internet connection, such as 19,200.

- Your user name and password.

- The phone number that you will call to connect to your service provider (if applicable).

In addition, during setup, you will need to set the following parameters. So while you have your service provider on the line (asking him about the previous list of stuff), ask him about these settings, too:

- MTU (Maximum Transmission Unit)

- TCP RWIN (Transmission Control Protocol Receive Window)

- TCP MSS (Transmission Control Protocol Maximum Segment Size)

- TCP RTO MAX (Transmission Control Protocol Receiver Timeout Maximum)

If your service provider can tell you specific settings for each of these parameters, use them. If not, follow my recommendations in the *Guided Tour*.

Dealing with the Login Script

During the configuration of Trumpet Winsock, you'll enter your login name and password. These variables are stored in something called a *login script*.

> A login script is a text file that contains specific commands you need to connect properly to your service provider.

Some Internet service providers include an appropriate login script with their downloadable files, making it possible for you to start on the Internet with a minimum amount of trouble. Look for a file called LOGIN.SCR. If you find one in the files you downloaded from your service provider, copy it to your Trumpet Winsock directory, and you're done.

If your Internet service doesn't provide a script, Trumpet Winsock provides a generic one into which you'll enter your login and password. If you experience problems logging into your service provider using this generic script, you can follow the steps here to edit it to fit your specific situation. You'll need to call your service provider for specifics on which elements to change. Here's a list of things you might need to change:

- Modem setup commands. By default, Trumpet Winsock turns on Data Carrier Detect (DCD) and turns off MNP data compression. Your service provider may want you to issue other commands instead—it should provide the proper codes to use.

- The type of prompt it displays. By default, Trumpet Winsock looks for a > sign.

- The login and password prompts. By default, Trumpet Winsock looks for the words "Username" and "Password" (or "username" and "password"). If your service provider uses

something else, such as "Login," you'll need to edit the login script.

- In addition, there may be other commands that your service provider might want your login script to send. You'll add these commands toward the end of the login script. (Get your service provider to supply you with exact details of the changes you'll need to make.)

Begin Guided Tour Enter Winsock Settings

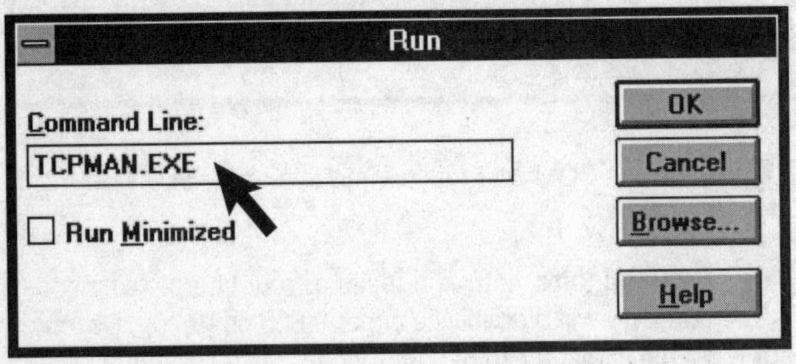

1 Open Program Manager's **File** menu and select **Run**.

2 In the Run dialog box, type **TCPMAN.EXE** and click **OK**.

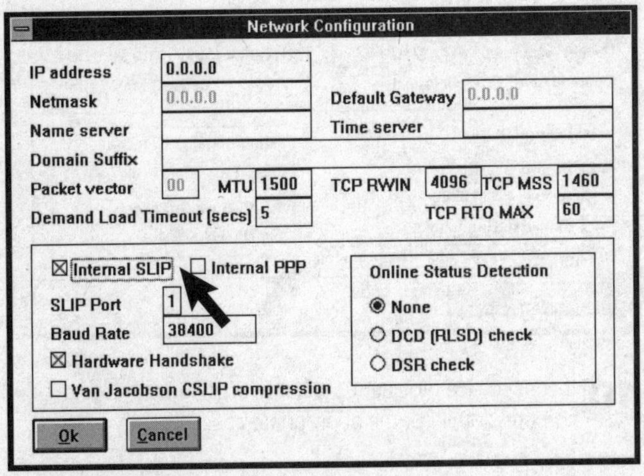

3 Click **Internal SLIP** or **Internal PPP** to indicate which type of Internet account you have.

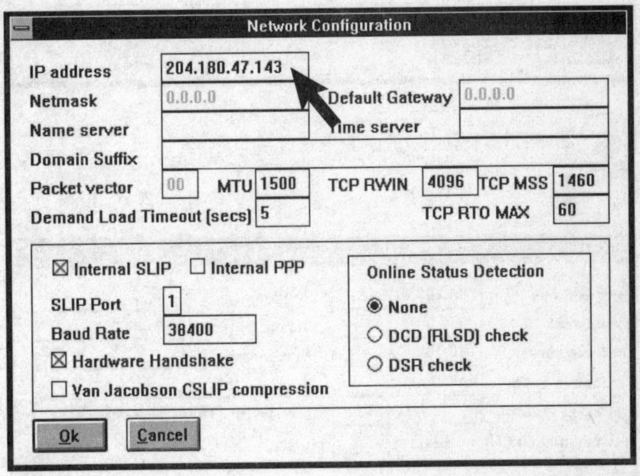

4 Enter the IP address you were given (or type **bootp** if you were told to use that instead).

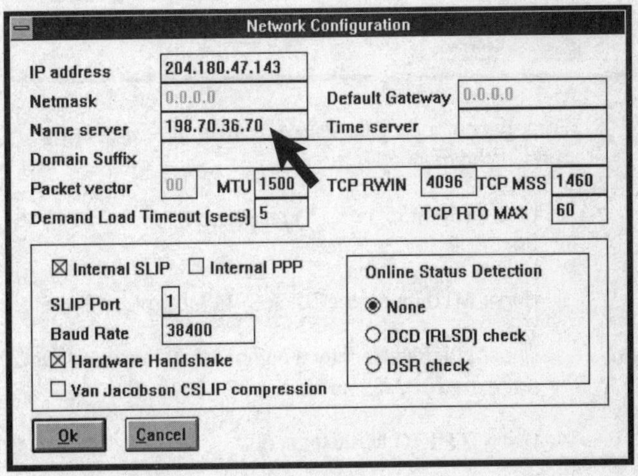

5 Enter the IP address of the domain name server, and enter the address of the time server (if there is one).

(continues)

Guided Tour   Enter Winsock Settings

(continued)

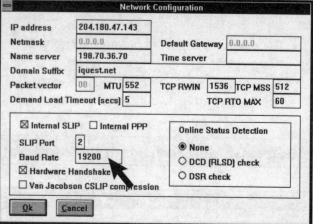

6 Enter the service provider's domain name.

8 Enter the COM port for your modem under **SLIP Port**.

9 For **Baud Rate**, enter the speed of your Internet connection. This will probably be either 9,600 or 19,200. Do not enter the actual speed of your modem, such as 14,400 or 28,800—it's not valid.

7 Enter the numbers your service provider gave you, or try these recommended settings:

Under **TCP MSS**, enter **512** if you use SLIP or **254** if you use CSLIP.

Under **MTU**, enter the TCP MSS number plus 40.

Under **TCP RWIN**, enter a number that's three to four times the TCP MSS number.

Leave **TCP RTO MAX** set at 60.

10 If your service provider uses hardware handshaking or compression, click the appropriate check box.

Guided Tour   Enter Winsock Settings

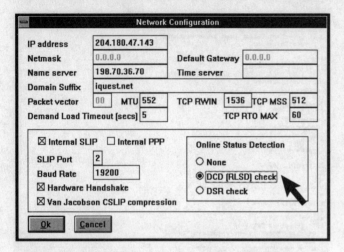

11 If your modem supports Data Carrier Detect or Data Set Ready, click the appropriate check box.

If DCD (Data Carrier Detect) or DSR (Data Set Ready) is not turned on in your modem by default, you'll need to turn it on by editing the login script. See the section, "Edit the Login Script" (next) for details.

12 Click **OK** to save your selections.

```
Trumpet Winsock
File  Edit  Special  Trace  Dialler  Help
Setup          Version 2.0 Revision B
Register       993,1994 by Peter R. Tattam
Firewall Setup rved.
PPP options    GISTERED SHAREWARE VERSION FOR EVALUATION ONLY.
Exit           river COM2 Baud rate = 19200 Hardware handshaking
My IP = 204.1__47.143 netmask = 0.0.0.0 gateway = 0.0.0.0
```

13 You'll see a message reminding you to restart Trumpet Winsock. Click **OK**. Open the **File** menu and select **Exit**. Then follow the next *Guided Tour* to edit the login script.

Begin Guided Tour   Edit the Login Script

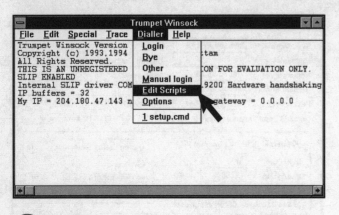

 Restart Trumpet Winsock, open the **Dialler** menu, and select **Edit Scripts**.

File Open

Filename: login.cmd

Directory: c:\internet\winsock

Files:
bye.cmd
login.cmd
setup.cmd

Directories:
[..]
[-a-]
[-b-]
[-c-]
[-d-]
[-e-]
[-i-]
[-i-]

OK
Cancel

2 Change to the **Winsock** directory, select **login.cmd**, and click **OK**.

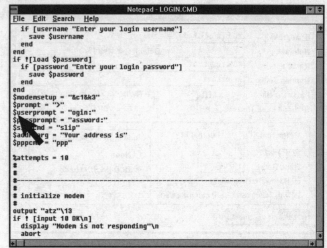

3 Scroll down to the variables area as shown in the figure. All the variables begin with a $. Change only the variables in this area; do not change the rest of the script file *unless you're specifically instructed by your service provider to do so.*

4 Only change what's needed. For example, the script is already set up to send the &c1 command to turn on Data Carrier Detect mode. If your provider has told you that you need to send additional modem commands, add them after &c1&k3. (Be sure to precede each command with an "&".) For example, to turn on Data Set Ready as mentioned earlier, add the command **&S0**.

There are many common modem commands (commonly called Hayes AT commands) that you may need to use. Check with your service provider, and if needed, see your modem's manual for a complete listing.

As another example of what to change, my provider's system prompts for Login: and not Username:, so I changed it here. Also, note that I typed "ogin" so that it will match either "Login" or "login."

Guided Tour   Edit the Login Script

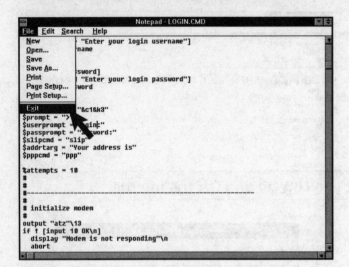

5 When you finish making your changes, open the **File** menu and select **Save**. Then open the **File** menu and select **Exit**.

Logging On and Off the Internet Under Windows 3.1

Now that you have Trumpet Winsock configured, it's time to test your Internet connection. You'll follow the procedure in the *Guided Tour* to log onto the Internet each time.

In addition, you'll learn how to log off the Internet when needed.

Begin Guided Tour Use Trumpet Winsock to Log On and Off the Internet

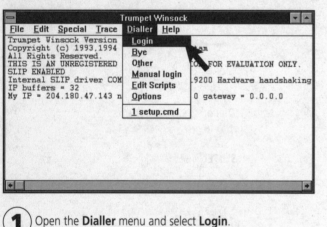

1 Open the **Dialler** menu and select **Login**.

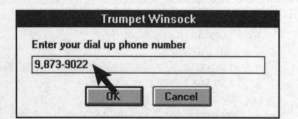

2 If this is the first time you've used Trumpet Winsock, it will prompt you for the phone number to dial. Type the number and press **Enter**.

If you need to dial a 9 or another number to get an outside line, be sure to include it, followed by a comma, in the phone number you type (as in 9,256-9090).

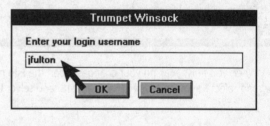

3 When you're prompted for your user name, type it and press **Enter**.

4 Enter your password and press **Enter**.

Guided Tour   Use Trumpet Winsock to Log On and Off the Internet

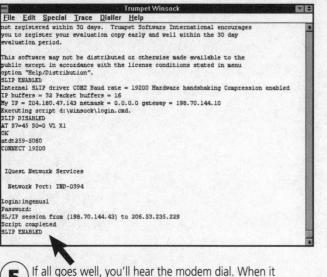

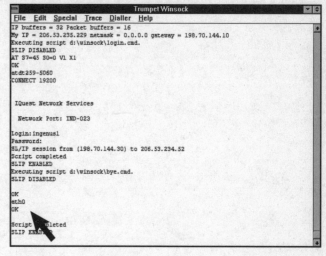

5 If all goes well, you'll hear the modem dial. When it connects, you see the message **Script completed**. Underneath that, you see **SLIP ENABLED**.

> If something goes wrong, press **Esc** to abort the script, and then skip to step 7 to log off. Look in the Quick-Finder table in Part 3 to quickly find a solution to your Winsock problem.

7 When you're ready to log off, exit any Internet programs you're using (Netscape or your FTP program, for example).

8 Open the **Dialler** menu and select **Bye**. You'll see the message **ath0** followed by **OK**, which means that your modem has hung up. You'll also see the messages **Script completed** and **SLIP ENABLED**.

> You can set Trumpet Winsock to automatically begin the login process when you start it, and to log you out when you exit Winsock. In addition, this feature closes Trumpet Winsock anytime you close all your Internet programs and don't restart any within five minutes. (If you have an Internet program open but you're not doing anything, this option will *not* close Winsock.) To set these options, open the **Dialler** menu and select **Options**. Then select **Automatic login and logout on demand** and click **OK**.

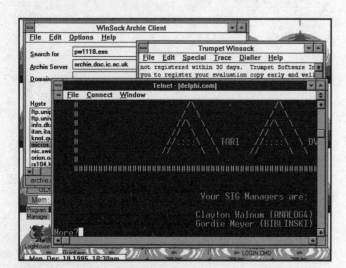

6 Once you're connected, you can run whichever Internet browser program you'd like, such as Netscape.

Find and Install a Web Browser

The World Wide Web (known as simply WWW to its friends) is a subset of the Internet itself. You may remember from earlier discussions that the Internet is basically a set of interconnected networks. Well, the Web is a set of interconnected documents located on those interconnected networks. These documents contain information on a vast array of topics; the Web attempts to connect them logically.

The documents or pages that make up the Web are connected through links. A link usually takes the form of highlighted text or a graphic. But no matter what it looks like on-screen, you simply click on a link to jump from the current WWW page to some other related page on the Web. For example, you might start on a Web page that contains information about the Environmental Protection Agency, and then click on some highlighted text or an icon to jump to a page that focuses on the industrial use of our National Parks.

In order to move around the Web, you'll need a Web browser. With it, you can view Web pages on-screen and navigate the links between them. In this section, you'll learn how to choose a Web browser, download it from the Internet (if necessary), and install it.

What You Will Find in This Section

Understand Web Browsers

The Web is like a vast book. You start on one page (called the home page because it's your starting point) but instead of turning from one page to another with your fingers, you click on some text or a fancy picture and wham! You're on a different Web page. For example, you might be looking at a page with the latest news headlines, and then, by clicking on some text that says "The Iowa Caucuses," you jump to another page with information about the "96 elections." You don't have to read the Web "book" in order, because links connect you to each of its various pages. In other words, you're free to browse the pages on the Web however you like.

When you log onto the Web with your Web browser, you start on what's called the *home page*. This is usually your service provider's main page, filled with links to what it considers the best places on the Web. (However, you *can* create your own home page and fill it with your own favorite links.)

You jump from page to page in the Web "book" by clicking on *links* (sometimes called hypertext or hypermedia links). But how does your Web browser program find each page within the vast Internet forest? It's relatively easy. Outwardly, a Web page appears to contain many links. Behind the scenes, however, the page contains a number of addresses called URLs that tell the Web browser where to find the information each link refers to.

Every Web page has its own address or *URL* (Uniform Resource Locator). A typical URL looks like this:

    http://home.netscape.com/home/
    internet-search.html

The first part of a URL address denotes the *protocol*, or language in which the information on that particular Web page is written. The second part denotes the address of the Web page.

A lot of Web pages are written in HTTP (HyperText Transfer Protocol) format. HTTP is a language that allows you to take a text document and mark it so that it contains links to other documents. When you view an HTTP document with a Web browser and you click on one of these links, you "jump" to (view) the linked document.

Web browsers support other protocols as well, such as FTP, Gopher, Telnet, and news. This is one of the things that makes Web browsers so versatile. Each protocol follows a particular format for addressing a Web page. The following table contains a list of common protocols and sample addresses.

Some Web browsers come with built-in newsreaders and mail readers; others require you to supply those programs, as well as separate Gopher, Telnet, and FTP programs. If your browser does not offer such programs, during setup you can tell your Web browser where the programs are located, and it uses them to display the corresponding data on-screen.

In addition to being able to jump from page to page on the Web by clicking links, you can jump directly to a particular page by typing its address. And if you don't know the address but you know the information you want to locate, you can use one of several Web search tools such as Lycos, WAIS, or Yahoo to look for applicable pages. See "Search for Information on the Web" on page 180 for more information. Once you find a page that's useful, you can save its address so that you can revisit it later. You can also print a page or save a page image so you can open it later using your word processor.

Web Browser-Supported Protocols

Protocol	Address Format and Sample Address
HTTP	http://*server_name*/*document_path*/*document_name* http://www.memphis.edu/egypt/main.html
FTP	ftp://*server_name*/*file_path*/*file_name* ftp://winsite.com/pub/pc/winzip.exe
Gopher	gopher://*server_name*/*document_type*/*selector* gopher://gopher.senate.gov/1
Telnet	telnet://*user_name:password*@*server_name* telnet://jfulton:secret@delphi.com
News	newsrc://*newsgroup*:*first_article-last_article* newsrc://news:/misc.writing

---

Begin Guided Tour   Tour a Typical Web Browser

1 When you start your Web browser, you automatically begin at the home page. The home page is usually the main page of your Internet provider, but you can change it to make your own home page.

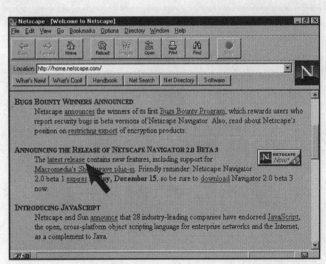

2 To jump to another Web page, click a link. Many links look like highlighted or underlined text, as shown here.

(continues)

Netscape supports framed windows, which divide a single Web page into several smaller windows. Frames make it easy to organize large amounts of information for a user to locate. This figure shows Netscape's home page with the Frames option turned on. You turn it on and off by clicking the appropriate option at the bottom of the home page.

> **Guided Tour** Tour a Typical Web Browser (continued)

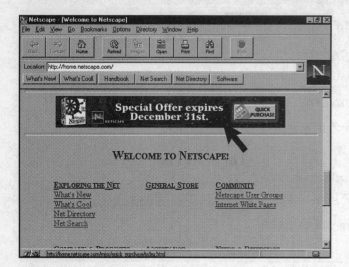

3 Some links look like a simple graphic or icon, as shown here.

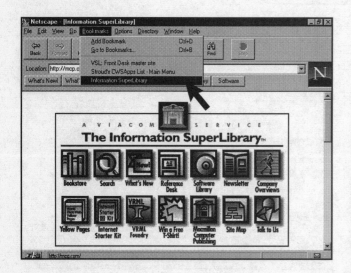

4 You can save your favorite URLs (addresses) and jump to a particular page directly.

5 By clicking a button, you can jump backward to the previous page you were on, and then you can return to your starting page by jumping forward. You can also jump to the home page at any time.

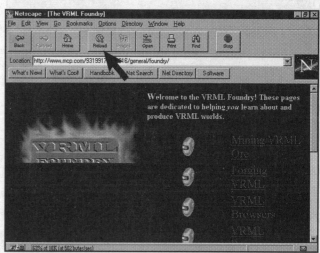

6 Sometimes your Web browser will have a problem loading the page you want to view. If that happens, you can stop the current loading process and reload the page.

> **Guided Tour** Tour a Typical Web Browser

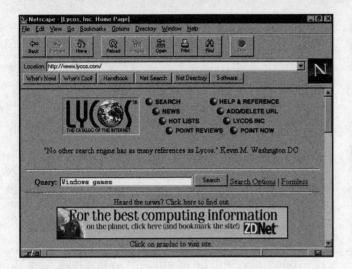

7 You'll find many search tools on the Web that can help you find a particular page. The one shown here is called Lycos.

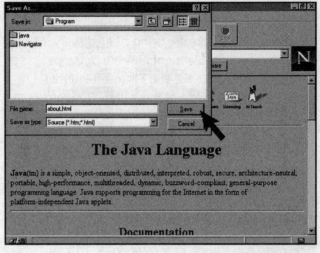

9 You can also save the image of a page you like to your hard disk.

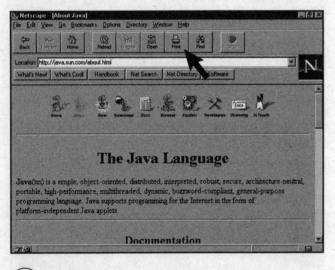

8 If you find a page you like, you can click the **Print** button to print it.

Choose a Web Browser

There are a number of Web browsers on the market, and more are being created every minute. The three most popular right now are Netscape Navigator, NCSA Mosaic, and Microsoft Internet Explorer. Check out one of these Web browsers:

- Netscape Navigator for Windows 95
- Internet Explorer for Windows 95
- NCSA Mosaic for Windows 95

If you use Windows 3.1, you might want to try one of these top-rated Web browsers:

- Netscape Navigator for Windows 3.1
- NCSA Mosaic for Windows 3.1
- I-Comm
- Quarterdeck QMosaic

In addition, Internet suites are a popular alternative. A *net-suite* is a package of programs that you can use on the Internet. The individual programs in the suite (such as the Web browser program) probably won't be as nice as programs marketed separately (such as Netscape Navigator), but getting a suite assures you of complete compatibility and ease of use. Popular suites include Internet Chameleon, Internet in a Box, Emissary, Cyberjack, Mariner, and Netshark.

> Even if you choose a suite, you may want to use Netscape Navigator as your Web browser; it's far superior to any other.

So what qualities should you look for when you're searching for the best Web browser for you? Here's a list:

- *Speed.* This is possibly the most important factor because it is time-consuming for any Web browser to display a page on-screen (especially a page filled with complex graphics); you want your browser to be as efficient as possible. The best way to judge the efficiency of a Web browser is to measure how long it takes to load graphics on-screen.
- *Video and sound support.*
- *Mail, news, and FTP support.* (The ability to send e-mail messages, browse the Usenet, and receive—download—files.)
- *Java or some other 3-D browsing support.*
- *Security features* such as the ability to block access to certain Web pages.
- *Ability to open multiple windows at the same time.*

Begin Guided Tour Look at What Your Web Browser Should Do

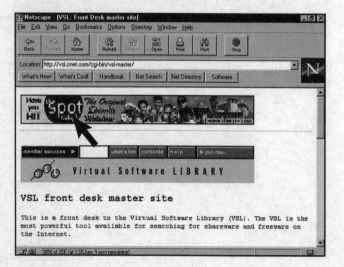

1 A good Web browser displays text on-screen as it processes graphics, so that you don't have to wait for the entire page to load before you can view it.

Guided Tour   Look at What Your Web Browser Should Do

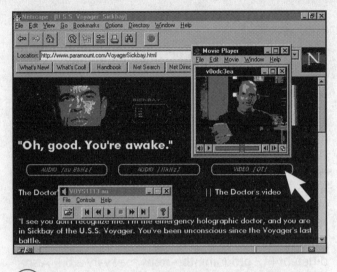

2 With a good Web browser, you can play all those video and sound clips you keep hearing about.

4 A new feature to look for is the capability to display 3-D animations—that is, pictures that look three-dimensional.

3 Your Web browser should allow you to perform common Internet functions such as downloading files with FTP.

5 Being able to open several windows at the same time allows you to get your work done quickly and more easily.

Find a Web Browser on the Internet

Some Web browsers are available for purchase at software stores. This is especially true of those that come in suite packages, coordinated with a newsreader, an FTP program, and other programs.

However, many of the more popular Web browsers are available for download from the Internet. Many of these programs are *shareware* (not freeware), which means you can "test drive" your browser before you buy it. Shareware works under the principle that you will register your program after a reasonable evaluation period. So if the Web browser you decide to use is listed as shareware, you will need to pay a small fee for its use. And even if your service provider included a Web browser with its startup files (which you downloaded using the steps in "Retrieve Files from Your Service Provider" on page 82), you'll still have to pay to register the Web browser and any other shareware programs you decide to keep.

> Some Web browsers are free to nonprofit organizations and schools. Check the documentation for details.

The most popular Web browser, Netscape Navigator, is available both through software stores and on the Internet. The fee to register the program is the same either way, so if you want to save yourself some hassle, you can simply buy Navigator instead of downloading it.

If you decide to download your Web browser from the Internet, first you have to find where its files are located and use an FTP program to download (receive) it. An FTP program was probably included with the files you downloaded from your service provider. See "Find and Install an FTP Program" on page 270 if you need more help.

> There are two Netscapes: Netscape Navigator (for ordinary people like you and me) and Netscape Gold (for people who want to create their own Web pages). You can use either one with this book; they both operate the same except for the built-in Web page editor that comes with the Gold edition.

In the *Guided Tour*, you learn how to download Netscape Navigator for Windows 95 from Netscape's FTP site using the FTP program WS-FTP. If you use a different FTP program, the steps may vary a bit. Also, if you prefer to try a different Web browser, make sure that you connect to the appropriate FTP site (as listed here).

Internet Explorer for Windows 95:
www.windows.microsoft.com/windows/download/msie20.exe

NCSA Mosaic for Windows 95:
ftp.ncsa.uiuc.edu/Web/Mosaic/Windows/Win95/mosaic20.exe

Netscape Gold for Windows 95:
ftp5.netscape.com/2.0gold/windows/g32e20.exe

Netscape Navigator for Windows 3.1:
ftp5.netscape.com/2.0/windows/n16e20.exe

Netscape Gold for Windows 3.1:
ftp5.netscape.com/2.0gold/windows/g16e20.exe

NCSA Mosaic for Windows 3.1:
ftp.NCSA.uiuc.edu/Web/Mosaic/Windows/Win31x/mosaic20.exe

I-Comm:
ftp.best.com/pub/icomm/icm109b.zip

Quarterdeck QMosaic:
ftp.qdeck.com/pub/demo/qmtry10.exe

If you use Windows 3.1, in order to run Netscape Navigator (and most of the other Windows 3.1-compatible Web browsers), you'll also need to install another program called Win32s. This *Guided Tour* also walks you through downloading the Win32s file.

After you download the Web browser of your choice, you must install it. In the next section, you'll learn how to install your Web browser.

Begin Guided Tour   Download a Web Browser

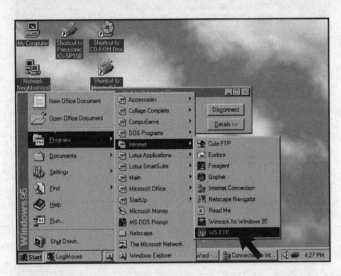

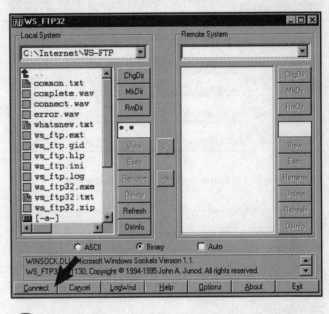

1 Connect to your Internet service provider in the usual manner and start WS-FTP.

2 Click **Connect**.

If you need help connecting via modem, see "Configure Your TCP/IP Software" on page 97. If you need help connecting through your office network, see you system administrator.

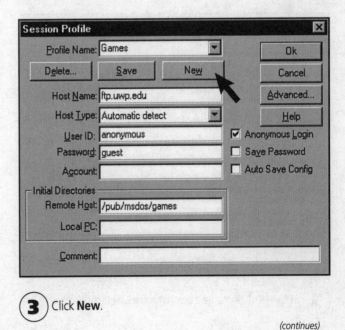

3 Click **New**.

(continues)

Guided Tour Download a Web Browser *(continued)*

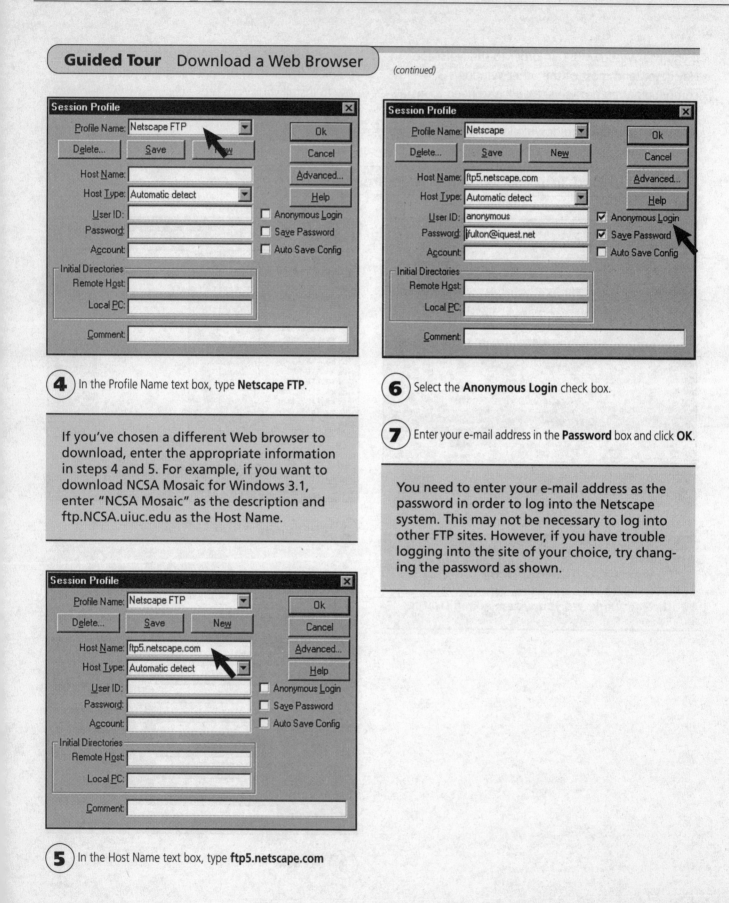

4 In the Profile Name text box, type **Netscape FTP**.

If you've chosen a different Web browser to download, enter the appropriate information in steps 4 and 5. For example, if you want to download NCSA Mosaic for Windows 3.1, enter "NCSA Mosaic" as the description and ftp.NCSA.uiuc.edu as the Host Name.

6 Select the **Anonymous Login** check box.

7 Enter your e-mail address in the **Password** box and click **OK**.

You need to enter your e-mail address as the password in order to log into the Netscape system. This may not be necessary to log into other FTP sites. However, if you have trouble logging into the site of your choice, try changing the password as shown.

5 In the Host Name text box, type **ftp5.netscape.com**

Guided Tour   Download a Web Browser

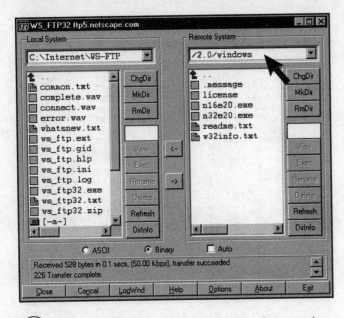

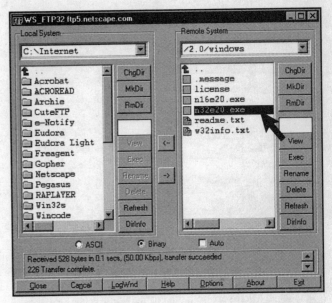

8 After you connect to the Netscape FTP site, change to the **/2.0/windows** directory.

9 On your Local System, change to a temporary directory in which you want to store the file. Then double-click the **n32e20.exe** file to download it into the temporary directory.

Begin Guided Tour   Download the Win32s File

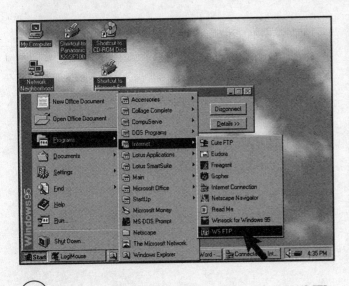

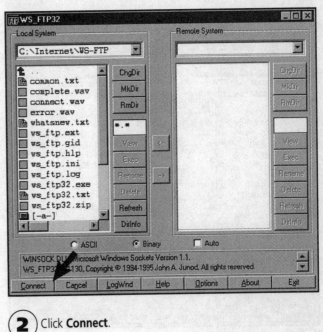

1 Connect to your Internet service provider and start WS-FTP.

2 Click **Connect**.

(continues)

Guided Tour Download the Win32s File (continued)

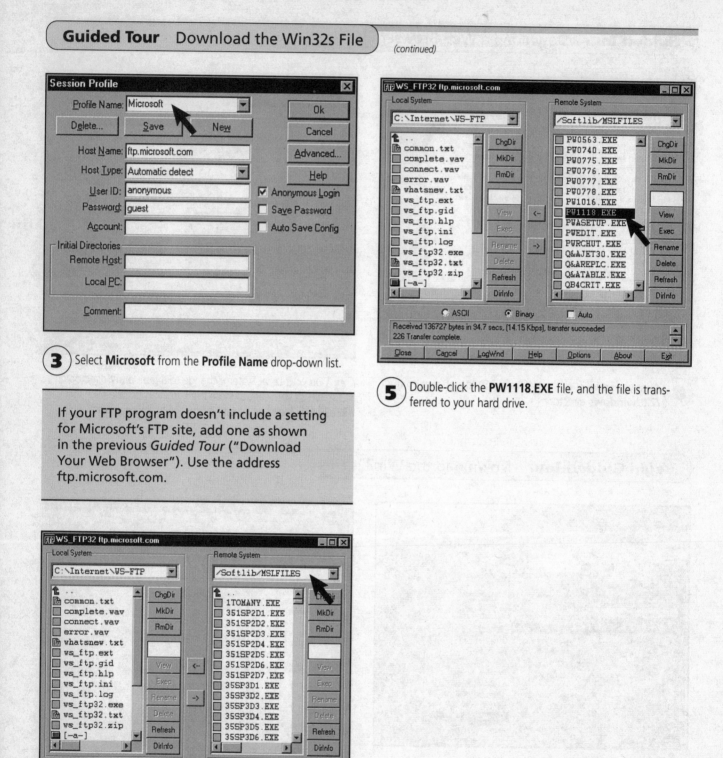

3 Select **Microsoft** from the **Profile Name** drop-down list.

If your FTP program doesn't include a setting for Microsoft's FTP site, add one as shown in the previous *Guided Tour* ("Download Your Web Browser"). Use the address ftp.microsoft.com.

5 Double-click the **PW1118.EXE** file, and the file is transferred to your hard drive.

4 After you connect to Microsoft, double-click the **Softlib** folder, and then double-click the MSLFILES folder.

Install Your Web Browser

After you download your Web browser, you'll need to install it. The file that you downloaded from the FTP site is compressed (zipped), which means that the separate files that make up the program have been condensed into one single file that's smaller and easier to download.

In order to install your Web browser, you'll need to decompress this file, which you'll learn how to do in the *Guided Tour*. After you decompress the file, it expands into its separate program files. Therefore, before you decompress the zipped file, you should move it to the folder where you want to store it permanently. One of these files allows you to finish the installation process, as you'll see in the *Guided Tour*.

> If you plan to use a Windows 3.1-compatible Web browser, you'll need to install something called Win32s first, before you actually install Netscape. It helps your Web browser run properly under Windows 3.1. I'll show you how to install this program in the *Guided Tour*. If you use Windows 95, you should not install Win32s.

After installing your Web browser, you may want to find and install a series of helper applications for it. These applications include special graphics viewers (GIF and JPEG, for example—although a lot of Web browsers handle these graphic types for you), an MPEG movie viewer, a QuickTime movie viewer, a PostScript viewer (such as GhostScript), a chat client, a RealAudio client, and a VRML viewer, for example. See "Play Sound and Video Clips with Helper Applications" on page 161 for more information.

If your Web browser does not have an FTP, Gopher, or mail server of its own, you also need to locate and install them and tell your Web browser where they're located. In the *Guided Tour*, I'll show you how to install Netscape Navigator for Windows 95. You install most other Web browsers the same way; however, if you do choose a different Web browser, you may want to read its documentation (usually found in a README.TXT or INSTALL.TXT file) before you attempt to install the program.

Begin Guided Tour   Install Netscape

1 Double-click the **n32e20.exe** file to decompress its files.

> Again, if you're using Windows 3.1, make sure that you install Win32s before installing Netscape.

(continues)

Guided Tour   Install Netscape   *(continued)*

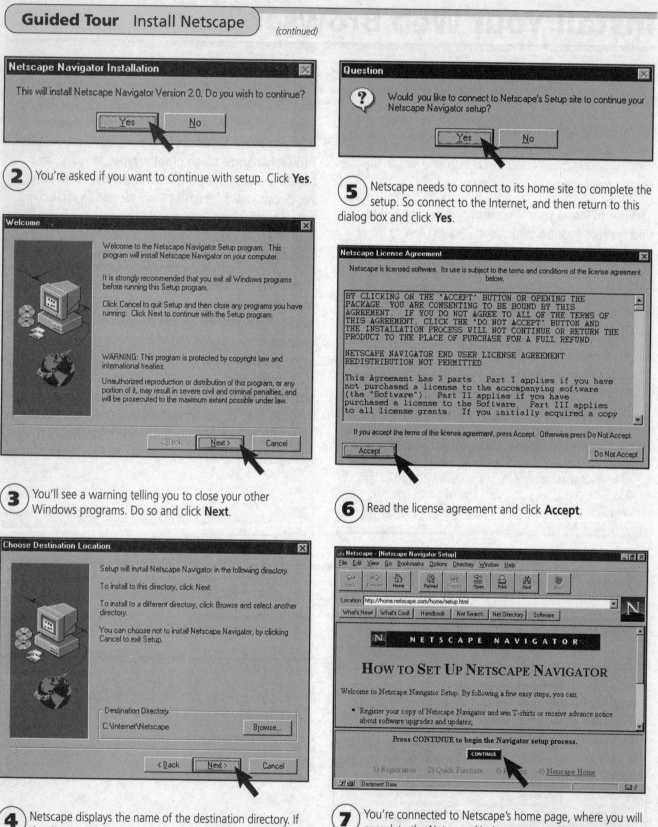

Netscape Navigator Installation

This will install Netscape Navigator Version 2.0. Do you wish to continue?

Yes   No

2 You're asked if you want to continue with setup. Click **Yes**.

Welcome

Welcome to the Netscape Navigator Setup program. This program will install Netscape Navigator on your computer.

It is strongly recommended that you exit all Windows programs before running this Setup program.

Click Cancel to quit Setup and then close any programs you have running. Click Next to continue with the Setup program.

WARNING: This program is protected by copyright law and international treaties.

Unauthorized reproduction or distribution of this program, or any portion of it, may result in severe civil and criminal penalties, and will be prosecuted to the maximum extent possible under law.

< Back   Next >   Cancel

3 You'll see a warning telling you to close your other Windows programs. Do so and click **Next**.

Choose Destination Location

Setup will install Netscape Navigator in the following directory.

To install to this directory, click Next.

To install to a different directory, click Browse and select another directory.

You can choose not to install Netscape Navigator, by clicking Cancel to exit Setup.

Destination Directory
C:\Internet\Netscape   Browse...

< Back   Next >   Cancel

4 Netscape displays the name of the destination directory. If the destination directory is okay, click **Next**. If you want to change it, click **Browse**, select the desired directory, click **OK**, and then click **Next**.

Question

Would you like to connect to Netscape's Setup site to continue your Netscape Navigator setup?

Yes   No

5 Netscape needs to connect to its home site to complete the setup. So connect to the Internet, and then return to this dialog box and click **Yes**.

Netscape License Agreement

Netscape is licensed software. Its use is subject to the terms and conditions of the license agreement below.

BY CLICKING ON THE "ACCEPT" BUTTON OR OPENING THE PACKAGE, YOU ARE CONSENTING TO BE BOUND BY THIS AGREEMENT. IF YOU DO NOT AGREE TO ALL OF THE TERMS OF THIS AGREEMENT, CLICK THE "DO NOT ACCEPT" BUTTON AND THE INSTALLATION PROCESS WILL NOT CONTINUE OR RETURN THE PRODUCT TO THE PLACE OF PURCHASE FOR A FULL REFUND.

NETSCAPE NAVIGATOR END USER LICENSE AGREEMENT REDISTRIBUTION NOT PERMITTED

This Agreement has 3 parts. Part I applies if you have not purchased a license to the accompanying software (the "Software"). Part II applies if you have purchased a license to the Software. Part III applies to all license grants. If you initially acquired a copy

If you accept the terms of this license agreement, press Accept. Otherwise press Do Not Accept.

Accept   Do Not Accept

6 Read the license agreement and click **Accept**.

Netscape - [Netscape Navigator Setup]

File Edit View Go Bookmarks Options Directory Window Help

Back Forward Home   Reload Images Open Print Find   Stop

Location: http://home.netscape.com/home/setup.html

What's New! What's Cool! Handbook Net Search Net Directory Software

N   NETSCAPE NAVIGATOR

HOW TO SET UP NETSCAPE NAVIGATOR

Welcome to Netscape Navigator Setup. By following a few easy steps, you can:

* Register your copy of Netscape Navigator and win T-shirts or receive advance notice about software upgrades and updates;

Press CONTINUE to begin the Navigator setup process.

CONTINUE

1) Registration   2) Quick Purchase   3) Patches   4) Netscape Home

Document: Done

7 You're connected to Netscape's home page, where you will complete the Netscape Navigator setup. Click **Continue**.

Guided Tour   Install Netscape

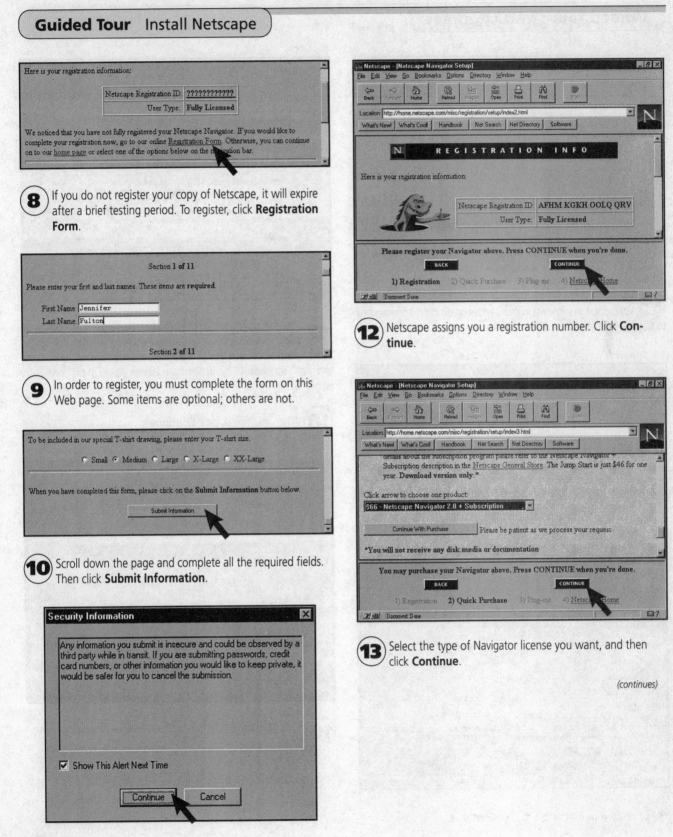

8 If you do not register your copy of Netscape, it will expire after a brief testing period. To register, click **Registration Form**.

9 In order to register, you must complete the form on this Web page. Some items are optional; others are not.

10 Scroll down the page and complete all the required fields. Then click **Submit Information**.

11 When you see this warning, click **Continue**.

12 Netscape assigns you a registration number. Click **Continue**.

13 Select the type of Navigator license you want, and then click **Continue**.

(continues)

Guided Tour Install Netscape *(continued)*

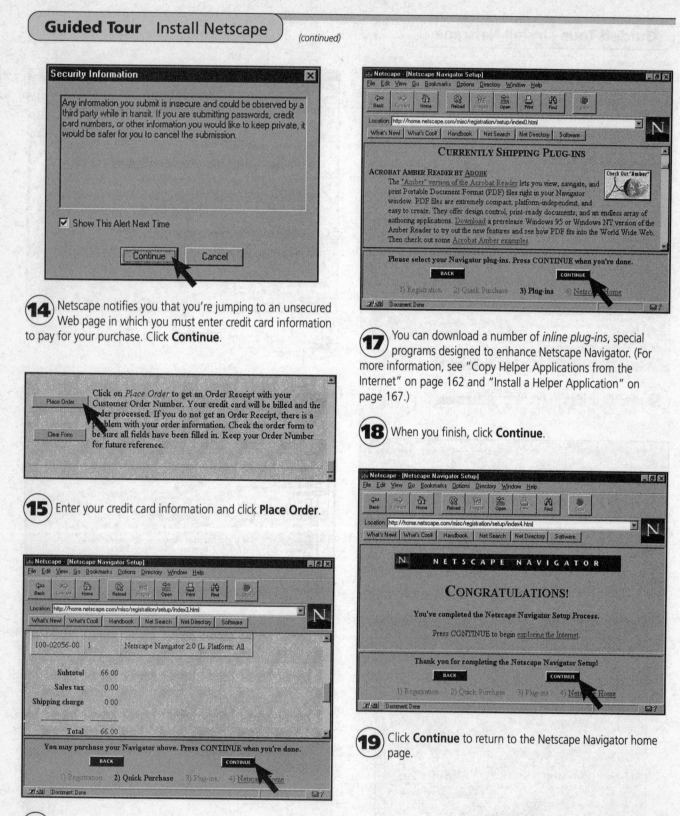

14 Netscape notifies you that you're jumping to an unsecured Web page in which you must enter credit card information to pay for your purchase. Click **Continue**.

15 Enter your credit card information and click **Place Order**.

16 Verify your purchase and click **Continue**.

17 You can download a number of *inline plug-ins*, special programs designed to enhance Netscape Navigator. (For more information, see "Copy Helper Applications from the Internet" on page 162 and "Install a Helper Application" on page 167.)

18 When you finish, click **Continue**.

19 Click **Continue** to return to the Netscape Navigator home page.

Guided Tour Install Netscape

20 When you finish browsing the Internet, click the **Close** button to close Netscape. To disconnect from the Internet, return to the Connect To dialog box and click **Disconnect**.

Begin Guided Tour Install Win32s

1 Copy the pw1118.exe file to a temporary directory.

2 Double-click the **pw1118.exe** file to decompress its files into that directory.

3 Double-click the **wb2s120.exe** file to decompress its files.

4 Double-click the **setup.exe** file.

(continues)

Install Win32s only if you're installing a Windows 3.1 Web browser that requires it. You should not install Win32s if you are installing a Windows 95 Web browser. Win32s is a component of Windows 3.1 that allows it to run certain 32-bit software (not necessarily Windows 95 software).

Guided Tour Install Win32s *(continued)*

Microsoft Win32s Setup

Welcome to the Microsoft Win32s Setup Program

This program will install the Microsoft Win32s system components. You will also have the option of installing the Win32 game Freecell to verify the correct installation of Win32s.

At the end of the installation, this program will exit Microsoft Windows and restart to load Win32s.

Make sure that any other applications are closed and that all data is saved before proceeding.

[Continue] [Exit] [Help]

5 You'll see a message telling you to close your other Windows programs. Do so and click **Continue**.

Microsoft Win32s Setup Target Directory

Setup has determined that your Microsoft Windows System Directory is:

C:\WINDOWS\SYSTEM\

Some Win32s components will be installed into this directory. The other components will be installed into the WIN32S subdirectory of this path.

Press Continue to proceed with the installation and Exit to quit.

[Continue] [Exit]

6 In the Win32s Setup Target Directory dialog box, click **Continue** to proceed with the installation.

Microsoft Win32s Setup

ℹ Win32s files successfully installed.

[OK]

7 When Win32s is completely installed (in the SYSTEM subdirectory of Windows 3.1), this dialog box appears. Click **OK**.

Freecell Setup

Microsoft Win32s has been successfully installed. You are now ready to install your Win32 application.

Freecell is a Win32 game that you may use to verify the correct installation of Win32s.

Press Continue to proceed with Freecell installation.

Press Exit to restart Microsoft Windows without installing Freecell.

[Continue] [Exit]

8 In the Freecell Setup dialog box, click **Continue** to load Freecell, a game you can use to test Win32s.

Verify Freecell Path

The setup program will copy Freecell files into the following directory.

Path: C:\WIN32APP\FREECELL\

Press Exit to restart Microsoft Windows without installing Freecell.

[Continue] [Exit] [Help]

9 Verify the Freecell path by clicking **Continue** and then **OK**.

Microsoft Win32s System Setup

The Microsoft Win32s components have been installed successfully.

Setup will now exit and restart Microsoft Windows to complete the installation.

[Continue]

10 Click **Continue** to restart Windows.

Guided Tour   Install Win32s

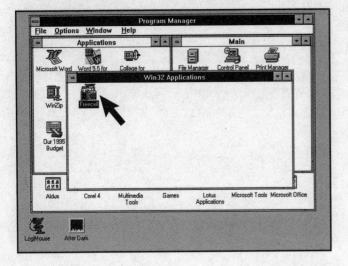

 Double-click the **Freecell** icon to start the game. If it starts, Win32s is set up correctly. Exit Freecell.

HOW TO...

Explore the World Wide Web

On the World Wide Web, you can navigate from one Internet site to another by selecting a link that appears on a Web page. A link might be a picture or some highlighted text that appears on-screen. You just click on the picture or text, and your Web browser links (jumps) you to the requested spot on the Internet. The Web protocol automatically logs you onto that requested site, down-loads a document, formats it, displays it, and logs you off—and you don't have to memorize or type any nasty UNIX commands at all. With a Web browser, surfing the Net is as simple and easy as using Windows.

As you learned in "Find and Install a Web Browser" on page 123, there are a number of Web browsers from which you can choose. Right now, the most popular Web browser is Netscape Navigator, so I'll use it in the *Guided Tours*. In this section, you'll learn how to use Netscape Navigator to explore the World Wide Web.

What You Will Find in This Section

Connect to the World Wide Web

In order to connect to the World Wide Web part of the Internet, you'll need a special program called a Web browser. In "Find and Install a Web Browser" (page 123), you learned how to download your choice of Web browsers from the Internet and how to install it. In this section, you'll use Netscape Navigator to connect to the WWW. If you're using a different Web browser, the steps in the *Guided Tour* may vary slightly; however, all Web browsers work basically the same way.

In the *Guided Tour*, you use Netscape Navigator version 2.0 for Windows 95. Netscape Navigator 2.0 for Windows 3.1 is exactly the same; however, if you have an earlier version of Netscape, what you see may look quite different. To download a current version of Netscape, see "Find a Web Browser on the Internet" (page 130).

Each Web site has its own address, called a URL (Uniform Resource Locator). The URL for the Netscape Navigator's home page looks like this:

http://home.netscape.com/home

The *home page* is your starting point. When you start Netscape Navigator, it connects you to Netscape's home page, from which you can jump to other pages on the Web. You can jump back to the home page at any time by clicking the **Home** button, as you'll see in a moment. Later, as you become more familiar with the Web, you can select a different home page from which to start if you want. See "Select a New Home Page" on page 153 for help. This new home page can be one of your favorite pages on the Web, or it can be a page designed by someone in your company or school, with links to Web pages that you'd find most useful. You can even design your own Web page as a starting point.

Each page contains links to other pages, providing a quick way for you to browse around and view pages on similar topics. You can also jump directly to a specific Web page by entering its address (URL) into the Web browser. In upcoming *Guided Tours*, you'll learn how to navigate the Web, but first you must connect to it.

Begin Guided Tour Connect to the WWW with Netscape

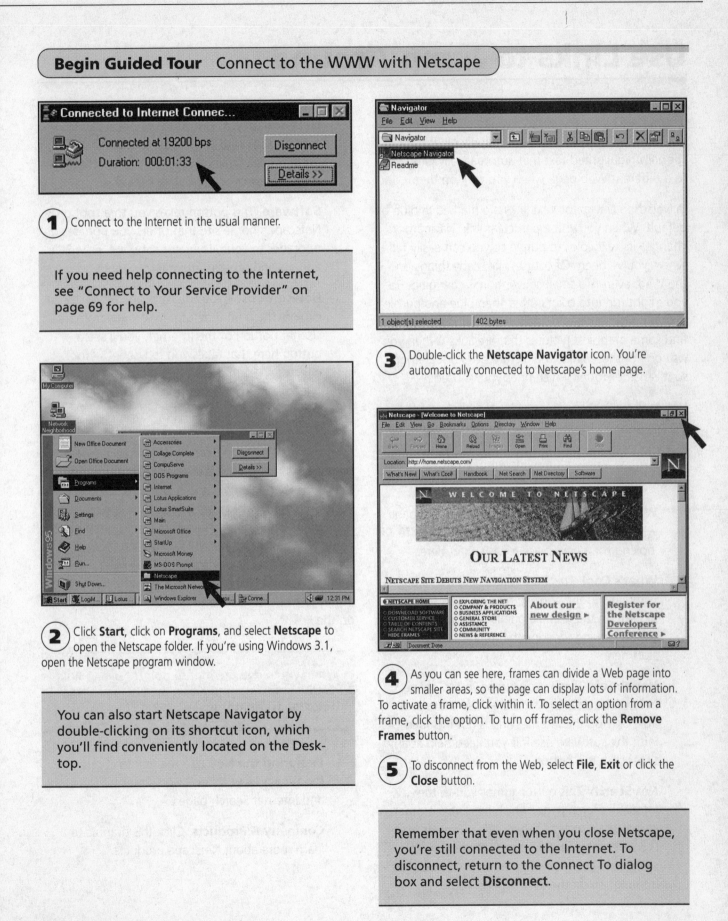

1 Connect to the Internet in the usual manner.

If you need help connecting to the Internet, see "Connect to Your Service Provider" on page 69 for help.

2 Click **Start**, click on **Programs**, and select **Netscape** to open the Netscape folder. If you're using Windows 3.1, open the Netscape program window.

You can also start Netscape Navigator by double-clicking on its shortcut icon, which you'll find conveniently located on the Desktop.

3 Double-click the **Netscape Navigator** icon. You're automatically connected to Netscape's home page.

4 As you can see here, frames can divide a Web page into smaller areas, so the page can display lots of information. To activate a frame, click within it. To select an option from a frame, click the option. To turn off frames, click the **Remove Frames** button.

5 To disconnect from the Web, select **File**, **Exit** or click the **Close** button.

Remember that even when you close Netscape, you're still connected to the Internet. To disconnect, return to the Connect To dialog box and select **Disconnect**.

Use Links to Jump Around

Links are by far the easiest way to explore the World Wide Web. Links are graphic pictures or specially highlighted text that automatically jump you to a different Web page when you click on them.

In Netscape Navigator, text links are marked in blue by default. When you visit a particular link, Navigator changes its text color to purple so you can easily tell where you've been. Of course, like many things on the Web, even this small convention is changing. So you might run into colors other than blue and purple, but you get the idea. In addition to text links, you'll find some graphical pictures that are links. When you visit one of these links, the picture does not change so it is harder to tell which ones you've used.

Netscape Navigator also provides toolbar buttons that are links to often-used places. These buttons are available to you at all times, no matter which Web site you're linked to. Here's a rundown of what each button does:

What's New This button jumps you to a page with links to the newest Web pages. If you're looking for a new place to visit, start here.

What's Cool This button jumps you to a page with links to the coolest, hippest Web pages—at least, in the humble opinion of Netscape. If you're looking for something new and different, start here.

Handbook This button jumps you to online help for Netscape Navigator—help that's available only on the Internet and is not included with the software itself. If you need help at any time, click this button.

Net Search This button jumps you to the InfoSeek search page, which has links to other search tools such as Yahoo, Web Crawler, and Lycos. You'll learn how to use these tools to search the Web for information in "Search for Information on the Web" (page 180).

Net Directory This button connects you to another tool with which you can search the Web: Excite. Again, there are links on this page to other search tools such as Yahoo.

Software This button takes you to a spot on Netscape's home site that offers you updates or upgrades to your Navigator software, as well as add-ins and other useful Internet tools.

Newsgroups If you use Netscape Navigator to explore the multitude of newsgroups from the Usenet portion of the Internet, you'll see a button here that takes you to Usenet's "root directory." For more on newsgroups, see "Read and Post Messages in Newsgroups" on page 221.

Even though Netscape Corp. redecorates its home page from time to time, it always offers the same selections for beginning your adventure through the Web. Again, unless you've set your home page to something different, you'll start at Netscape's home page, which includes the following links (located in the second frame at the bottom of the screen if frames are turned on, or at the top of the home page if they're not). To select one of these links, simply click on the link.

When you move the mouse pointer over a link, its URL (address) appears at the bottom of the Netscape Navigator screen.

Exploring the Net Use this link to connect to the What's New, What's Cool, Internet Directory, and Internet Search pages.

Company & Products Click this graphic to learn more about Netscape products.

General Store This takes you to a page with links to the many catalog services that do business through Netscape's home site. In other words, you can buy stuff here.

News & Reference This links you to a page with today's Internet-related news stories and the reference/help page for Navigator.

Assistance Click this graphic to learn where you can download helper apps such as video, graphics, and audio readers. You'll learn more about helper apps in "Play Sound and Video Clips with Helper Applications" on page 161.

Community Connect to Netscape users through this graphic link.

What to Do When a Link Fails

You need to know one important thing before you start. Sometimes when you try to connect to a Web page, it fails to load. Here's how to tell when you're in trouble. Normally, when you click on a link or enter a URL, meteors flash across the Netscape icon (the big "N" in the upper-right corner). This is good. If the meteors stop flashing, it means that Netscape Navigator has hung—which means you're getting nowhere quickly. Click the **Reload** button at the top of the Navigator window. If the meteors move again but then stop, and nothing happens for a minute or two, something's hung again. Click **Stop** to discontinue loading the Web page. Then try clicking the link again.

Begin Guided Tour Using Links

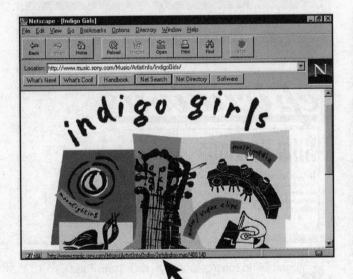

1 When you move the mouse over a link, the address of the Web page it links to appears at the bottom of the Netscape Navigator window.

2 To connect to a linked Web page, click the link.

(continues)

Guided Tour Using Links *(continued)*

3 After you visit a linked site, the text link changes color from blue to purple.

5 If a link fails, you can click **Reload** to reload the page. (You might have to do this, for example, if a page contains a lot of complex graphics; graphics often cause loading problems.)

4 Some links are graphic images instead of text. To connect to the linked Web page, just click the graphic.

6 If you fail to connect to a page, click **Stop**. This tells Netscape Navigator to stop trying to load the page. You can click the link again to retry.

Back Up and Move Forward

As you change from one page to another on the Web, you create a kind of working history of where you've been. Your Web browser saves this history for you, making it easy for you to return to any previously viewed page. The most recent of the previously viewed pages remains in Netscape's memory. So if you ever need to see one again, you can click on a button, and it pops back up in about a second.

The history that Netscape Navigator tracks is for the current session only; it is erased when you exit the program. However, if you find a Web page that you like, you can save its address permanently so that you can return to it at any time. See "Return to Your Favorite Web Pages" on page 155 for more information.

Using the history feature in Netscape Navigator is a lot like reading a book. To return to a previously viewed page, you move backward in the "book." You can move as many pages backward as you like. After moving backward, you can return to your starting point by moving forward through your previously viewed Web pages. You can also jump directly to a particular previously viewed page by selecting it from the history list.

Even if you are using a Web browser other than Netscape Navigator, your browser probably has a history feature that works very much like Netscape's. The *Guided Tour* shows you how to use this handy feature.

Begin Guided Tour Navigate with Netscape

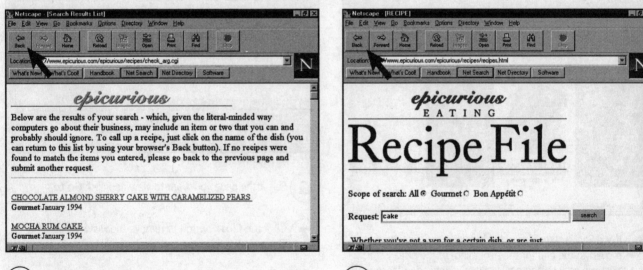

1 To return to the Web page you just viewed, click the **Back** button.

2 Move backward one more page by clicking the **Back** button again. You can repeat this as many times as you need to return to a previously viewed page.

(continues)

Guided Tour   Navigate with Netscape   *(continued)*

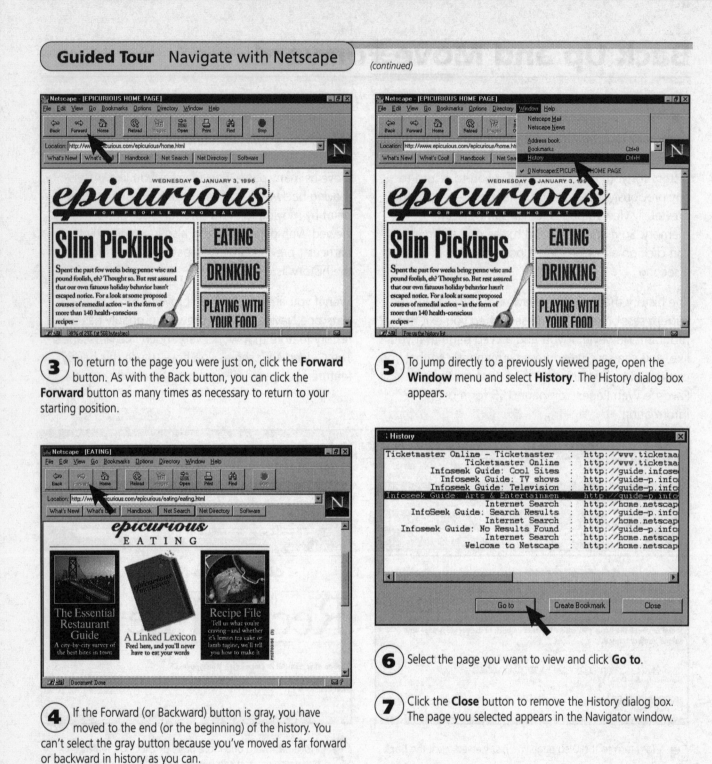

3 To return to the page you were just on, click the **Forward** button. As with the Back button, you can click the **Forward** button as many times as necessary to return to your starting position.

4 If the Forward (or Backward) button is gray, you have moved to the end (or the beginning) of the history. You can't select the gray button because you've moved as far forward or backward in history as you can.

5 To jump directly to a previously viewed page, open the **Window** menu and select **History**. The History dialog box appears.

6 Select the page you want to view and click **Go to**.

7 Click the **Close** button to remove the History dialog box. The page you selected appears in the Navigator window.

Go to a Specific Web Page Using a URL

As I've mentioned, each Web page has its own address, or URL. A typical URL looks like this:

http://pages.nyu.edu/~liaos/indigo.html

With the right address, you can jump directly to the Web page you want. If you don't know the address or even which pages you might want to view, you can search for applicable pages using a Web search tool such as Lycos. See "Search for Information on the Web" on page 180 for more information. You can also get addresses for hot Web sites from any of several Internet magazines such as *The Net*, *Websight*, and *Internet World*.

To jump directly to a Web page, you enter its address in your Web browser. A Web address identifies an official Internet resource, whose "name" is known formally as its URL. (If you hear a person talk about his site's "earl," he's referring to its URL.) Every URL has two parts: a content identifier and location.

The first part, the content identifier (or content-id for short), tells you what protocol or language was used to create the current page. For most Web pages, the basic content-id is http:// because the Web pages are written using HyperText Transfer Protocol or http. Web browsers do support other protocols such as ftp://, gopher://, telnet://, and news:// (the protocol for Usenet newsgroups). But those protocols aren't used for Web pages; they connect you to other resources you can reach through the Web. An HTTP Web page can link directly to any resource that uses one of these protocols. You can easily identify such a resource by its content-id. For instance, you can link to a site's FTP directory or to a Usenet newsgroup just as easily as you can link to another Web page—just by clicking the link. If you want to see what type of resource you're linking to before you link to it, move your pointer over the link but don't click. The URL of the link appears in your browser's status line. The content-id at the beginning of the URL tells you whether the link is a Web page (http://) or some other type of resource.

The second part of every URL identifies the location of the resource. Every resource and every Web page has its own unique location name. This name looks suspiciously like a directory path—which is exactly what it is. Every Web page is a document file that exists on someone else's computer somewhere. These directory paths follow the UNIX format, using forward slashes (/) in place of the backslashes (\) you're used to seeing in DOS and Windows. The paths also contain periods (.), which are used to categorize the resource. So, looking at the address www.microsoft.com (without going into too much detail), you see that the address refers to the Web-managing portion (www) of the computer called microsoft.com. See "Understand Web Browsers" on page 124 for examples of other types of addresses.

Once you enter an address into your Web browser, you can save it so that you can revisit it later. See "Return to Your Favorite Web Pages" on page 155 for details.

Begin Guided Tour   Enter a Web Page's Address (URL)

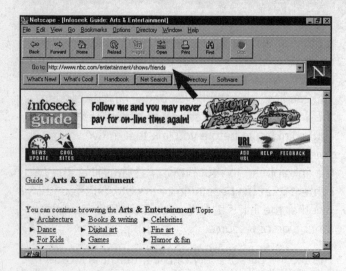

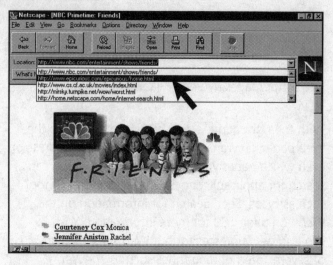

1 Type the address of the page you want to go to in the **Location** or **Go to** text box (whichever is currently visible). Make sure that you use forward slashes (/) to separate the parts of the address. Make sure you've typed the URL correctly, and then press **Enter**.

2 After you enter an address, your Web browser keeps it in a list of most recently typed addresses. To return to a previously entered address (even one from an earlier session), click the **Location** drop-down arrow and select an address from the list.

Select a New Home Page

When you install Netscape Navigator, it sets the home page (the page at which you start your Internet session) to the Netscape home page. This is a good place to start, especially if you're new to the Internet. But as you gain confidence and a certain preference for particular sites, you may want more from your home page.

Netscape and other Web browsers allow you to set the home page to any Web page. For example, if you always start your Internet session by checking out CNN for the latest headlines, you might want to set

the CNN Web page as your home page. Or suppose someone in your company or school may have designed a local Web page with links tailored to your interests, so you may want to set your home page to that. Finally, you can design your own Web page, fill it with links to your favorite places, and use that as your home page.

No matter what you choose, when you're ready to change your home page, take the following *Guided Tour* to learn how (in Netscape Navigator 2.0).

Begin Guided Tour   Change Your Home Page

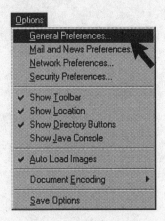

(1) Open the **Options** menu and select **General Preferences.**

(2) Click the **Appearance** tab.

(continues)

Guided Tour Change Your Home Page

(continued)

3 In the **Start With** text box, enter the URL (address) of the Web page you want to use as your home page. For example, to start at CNN's home page, type the address **http://cnn.com**.

4 Click **OK**.

Return to Your Favorite Web Pages

Web addresses (URLs) are often long and complex, which can make it difficult to enter them correctly. When you finish typing an address into your Web browser, you may not want to lose it. But there's no need to worry about it. Every Web browser provides a means of saving the addresses of the Web pages you visit.

Browsing the Web is like browsing through the pages of a large book. When you find a particular passage in a book that you want to be able to find again quickly, you insert a bookmark. You can do the same thing with your Web browser. To return to a page you've marked, you select it from the Bookmark list.

One of the most important things to know about Internet Web pages is how subject they are to change. Whereas you'll find the same Web page at a given URL address from day to day, the contents of that page may change at any time. If the address is a news-related site, such as a magazine or headline service, you can count on the contents changing. So if you like a certain Web page for what it contains more than for who's bringing it to you, keeping a bookmark for it will not be enough. You'll want to save a copy of the page to your own computer, which is usually no more difficult than saving a word processor file.

Occasionally, the URL location of a page changes. Many companies that produce Web pages rent computer storage space from a type of computer called an Internet Service Provider. And because there's a big market in Web space rental these days, some companies tend to move from one provider to another. When that happens, their URL addresses change (just as their U.S. postal addresses would if they moved their home offices). So a bookmark that you can count on one week to take you to a favorite site may not be valid the next week. When that happens, you might need to use one of the Internet's many search tools to find the new address; then you can use the browser's bookmark editor to change the old address.

In the *Guided Tour*, you'll use Netscape Navigator version 2.0 to set up and edit bookmarks. This particular version of Navigator provides a more advanced bookmark feature than most other Web browsers; it enables you to sort bookmarks, organize them in folders, and add comments.

Begin Guided Tour Set a Bookmark

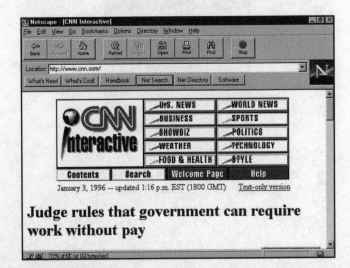

1 First jump to a page whose address you want to save.

(continues)

Guided Tour Set a Bookmark

(continued)

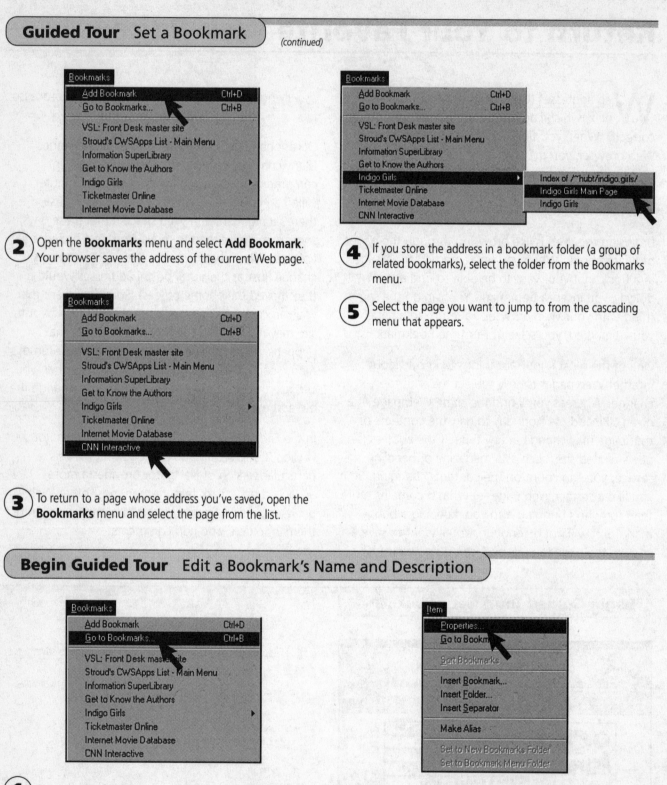

2 Open the **Bookmarks** menu and select **Add Bookmark**. Your browser saves the address of the current Web page.

3 To return to a page whose address you've saved, open the **Bookmarks** menu and select the page from the list.

4 If you store the address in a bookmark folder (a group of related bookmarks), select the folder from the Bookmarks menu.

5 Select the page you want to jump to from the cascading menu that appears.

Begin Guided Tour Edit a Bookmark's Name and Description

1 Open the **Bookmarks** menu and select **Go to Bookmarks**.

2 To change the description for a particular item, select it, open the **Item** menu, and select **Properties**.

Guided Tour　Edit a Bookmark's Name and Description

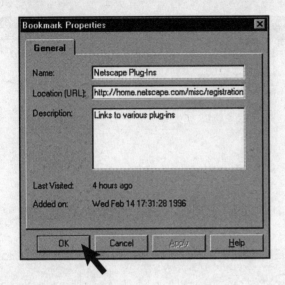

3 In the **Name** text box, change the name of the item if necessary.

4 In the **Description** area, add a description if you want. The description shows up at the bottom of the Netscape Navigator window when you select the item from the Bookmarks list. Click **OK**.

Begin Guided Tour　Organize Items into Bookmark Folders

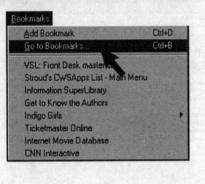

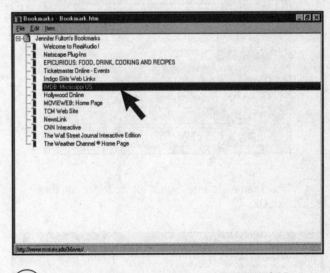

1 Open the **Bookmarks** menu and select **Go to Bookmarks**.

2 To keep similar items together, you can create a folder. In the Bookmarks list, click where you want the folder to appear.

(continues)

Guided Tour Organize Items into Bookmark Folders *(continued)*

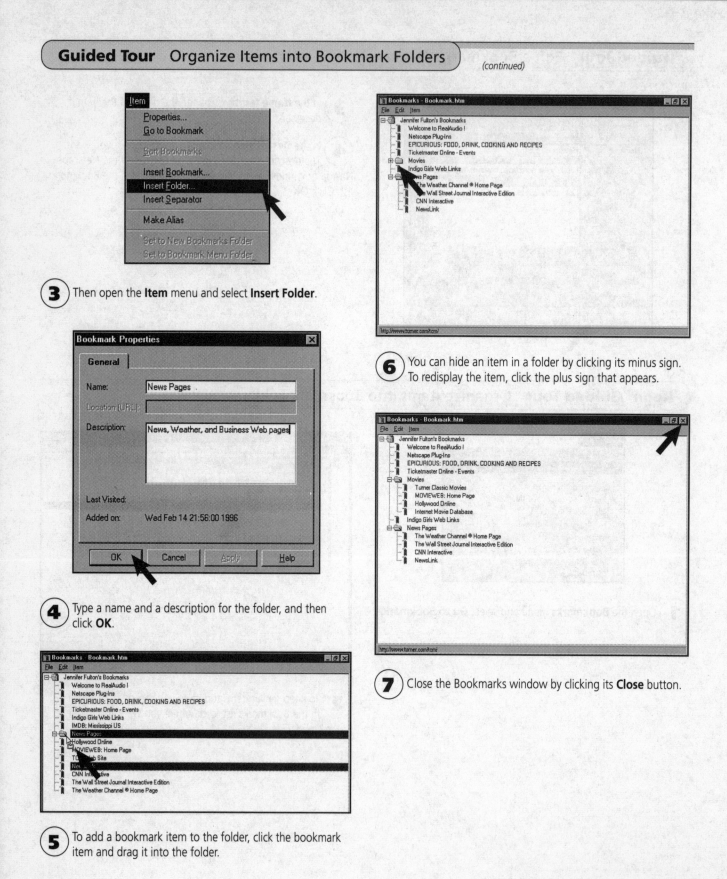

③ Then open the **Item** menu and select **Insert Folder**.

④ Type a name and a description for the folder, and then click **OK**.

⑤ To add a bookmark item to the folder, click the bookmark item and drag it into the folder.

⑥ You can hide an item in a folder by clicking its minus sign. To redisplay the item, click the plus sign that appears.

⑦ Close the Bookmarks window by clicking its **Close** button.

Fill Out Forms

At some Web pages you visit, you may be asked to fill out a form. For example, when you visit the Lycos page (a common Web search tool), you'll fill out the basic information for which you want Lycos to search the Web. Similarly, you might complete a form to order merchandise on the Web or to leave an opinion on someone's Web page. The uses for forms are as vast as the Web itself.

An on-screen form looks like a large dialog box, complete with text boxes, list boxes, check boxes, and option buttons. If you know how to work your way around a basic Windows dialog box, you'll do fine with Web forms. To complete a form, make your selections and type in data as needed. There's always some kind of button—such as Send Now, Accept, or Search—to tell the system when you've finished completing the form. Just click the appropriate button, and your information is saved for the owner of the Web page.

About Security

The Internet is basically an open system. This means that, despite what people want you to believe, the information you send over the Internet is not completely secure. However, some systems are more secure than others. In Netscape Navigator, secure Web pages use the protocol **https** instead of the usual **http**, so you can look at the address of the page you're on to see if it's secure. Another way to tell if you're on a secure page in Navigator is to look at the key icon in the status bar. A broken key represents a nonsecure channel. You need to be aware of a page's security level when you're completing forms that ask for personal information such as your social security number or credit card numbers.

> Be very careful when completing any Internet form that asks for private information such as your social security number, credit card numbers, or phone number. The Internet is not secure, so there's always a chance that someone could get the information you provide.

Also, keep in mind that even if you connect to a secure Web page, the person who retrieves that information at the other end is a suspect. Just as you should exercise caution when giving your private information over the telephone, you should make sure you know the person with whom you are doing business through the Internet before you provide him or her with your personal information. You'll learn more about Internet security in "Secure Your System and Practice Proper Etiquette" on page 307.

Begin Guided Tour   Fill Out a Form

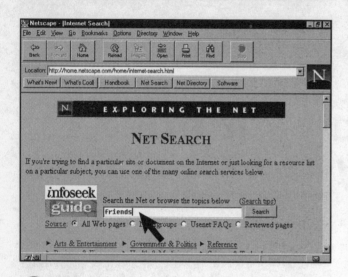

1 When you encounter a form on a Web page, treat it like you would a Windows dialog box. To enter text, click in the text box and type your information.

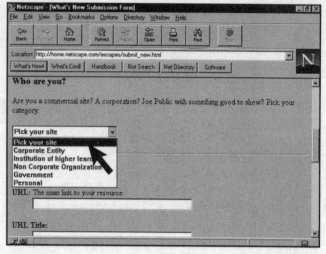

3 If the form contains list boxes, click the drop-down arrow to open the list. Then make your selection.

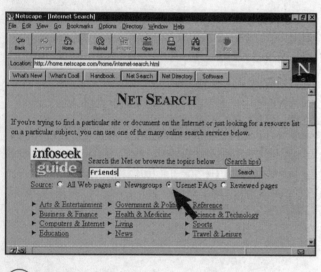

2 Many forms contain option buttons and check boxes. Simply click the option you want to select.

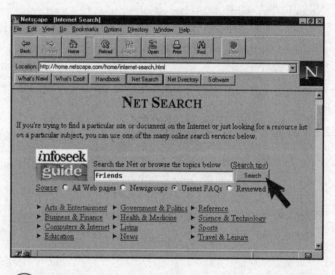

4 Click the button your system provides for letting it know you've finished making selections. In the case of the system shown here, you click **Search**.

Play Sound and Video Clips with Helper Applications

As you cruise the Internet, you'll come across text files, sounds, video clips, graphics, and other files that your Web browser (or Gopher program) may or may not be able to "play." For example, Netscape Navigator 2.0 can handle JPG and GIF graphics (files with the extension .JPG and .GIF) and AU and AIF audio files, but Navigator cannot handle MPG or AVI video clips, WAV audio files, and some other file types.

Although your Web browser (or Gopher program) may not be able to play to these types of files, it can automatically run a helper application that can play the file. Helper applications are small programs that typically run very quickly and require little memory. Whenever your Web browser (or Gopher program) encounters a file it cannot play, it copies the file to your computer and runs the helper application. The helper application automatically opens the file and plays it or displays it on the screen.

In this section, you will learn how to copy helper applications from the Internet and set them up to run automatically from your Web browser or Gopher program.

What You Will Find in This Section

Copy Helper Applications from the Internet

Various FTP (File Transfer Protocol) servers on the Internet have the helper applications (also called *viewers*) you need. You can connect to these servers with your Web browser or with an FTP program (as explained in "Find and Copy Files from the Internet" on page 263) and then download the helper application files. This *Guided Tour* shows you how to use your Web browser to get the files you need.

The procedure is fairly straightforward. In your Web browser, you enter the URL of the FTP server. Once you connect to the server, the Web browser shows a list of files and folders on the server. You can change from one folder to another by clicking links. When you find the name of the file you're looking for, you simply click (or Shift+click) its link and fill in the Save As dialog box to specify where you want the file saved.

As you proceed through the *Guided Tour*, keep in mind that FTP sites are often busy during the day. Try to download helper applications in the evening or early morning.

Which Helper Applications Do You Need?

In general, you should have at least three helper applications: one for displaying graphics, one for playing sound (audio) files, and one for running video clips. The following table shows common file types you'll find on the Internet, along with the names of popular helper applications that can handle these file types.

Find the Right Helper Application

To Play These Files...	With These File Name Extensions...	You Need This Helper Application
Graphics and Photos	JPG, JPEG, GIF, BMP	LView or PaintShop Pro
Sounds	AU, AIF	Netscape Audio Player, WHAM!, or Wplany
	WAV	Windows Sound Recorder
Video Clips	AVI	Video for Windows or Avi Pro
	MPG, MPEG	MPEGPlay or VMPEG
	MOV	QuickTime
Compressed Files	ZIP, TAR	WinZip or PKZIP
PostScript Files	EPS	GhostView

Your Web browser might already be equipped to display graphics and play sounds. For example, Netscape Navigator has a built-in viewer that can display JPG and GIF files. It also has an audio player that can play audio clips. Other Web browsers may not be able to handle any of these special files. If you are satisfied with the way your Web browser plays certain file types, you don't need to set up helper applications for those particular file types.

Find Helper Applications

You can acquire the helper applications you need from various FTP servers on the Internet. The only difficulty you face is finding the FTP server that has those helper applications. Fortunately, the Web has a few sites that can help you track down popular helper applications. Using your Web browser, try loading any of the following Web pages (as instructed in the *Guided Tour*). Then click the links to download the helper applications you want.

http://www.eden.com/music/winhelpers.html

http://www.voicenet.com/~mmax/help/win.html

http://pages.prodigy.com/Computing/help/AppleViewers.html

http://metro.turnpike.net/Rene/tools.htm

http://home.netscape.com/assist/helper_apps/windowhelper.html

If you can't connect to any of those sites, use the following table to find the helper application.

One word of caution: The file name or folder in which the file is stored may change at any time. When looking for files to download, you may have to poke around in other folders or search for a file name that's close (not necessarily identical) to the name listed in this table.

> If you know the name of a file you want, you can use an Internet tool called Archie to find the file. For details on how to use Archie, see "Find Files with Archie" on page 278.

Where to Look for Helper Applications

Helper Application	Use This URL	Look in This Folder	File Name
LView	ftp://ftp.std.com	/ftp/vendors/mmedia/lview/	lviewpro.zip
	ftp://oak.oakland.edu	/SimTel/win3/graphics/	lviewplb.zip
	http://world.std.com/~mmedia/lviewp.html	N/A (This is a Web page)	N/A
PaintShop Pro	ftp://mail.ncku.edu.tw	/pub/tools	pspro20.zip
	ftp://usc.edu	/pub/www/PC/HelperApps	pspro20.zip
	ftp://hubcap.clemson.edu	/pub/pc_shareware/windows/Graphics	pspro20.zip
WHAM!	ftp://owl.nstn.ns.ca	/pub/pc-stuff/windows/viewers	wham131.zip
	ftp://ftp.nyu.edu	/nyu-net.transition/windows	wham131.zip
	ftp://fatty.law.cornell.edu	/pub/LII/Cello	wham131.zip
Wplany	ftp://hasle.oslonett.no	/gopher/software/windows/media	wplany11.zip
	ftp://webcom.com	/pub/memcore/www/orig	wplany.exe

(continues)

Where to Look for Helper Applications   Continued

Helper Application	Use This URL	Look in This Folder	File Name
QuickTime	ftp://cecelia.media.mit.edu	/pub/eds	qtw11.zip
	ftp://ftp.hk.super.net	/.4/pub/windows/WWWUtil	qtw11.zip
	ftp://earth.execpc.com	/pub/windows/viewers	qtw11.zip
	ftp://sparky2.esd.mun.ca	/pub/winsock	qtw11.zip
MPEGPlay	ftp://ftp.hk.super.net	/.4/pub/windows/WWWUtil	mpegw32g.zip
	ftp://epas.utoronto.ca	/pub/cch/shareware/images	mpegw32g.zip
	ftp://hubcap.clemson.edu	/pub/pc_shareware/windows/Graphics	mpegw32g.zip
VMPEG Player	ftp://ftp.hk.super.net	/.6/cica/win/desktop	vmpeg12a.zip
	ftp://knot.queensu.ca	/pub/win3/winsock/www	vmpeg12a.zip
	ftp://orion.pppl.gov	/pub/pc/win3/viewers	vmpeg12a.zip
	ftp://ftp.oleane.net	/pub/.disks/.3/cica/desktop	vmpeg12a.
GhostView	ftp://ftp.eos.ncsu.edu	/pub/vlsi/sting/latex_stuff_for_bill	gsview10.zip
	ftp://huron.scd.ucar.edu	/libraries/GrADs/printing	gsview10.zip
	ftp://ftp.hk.super.net	/.6/cica/win3/util	gsview10.zip
WinZip	ftp://pascal.ibp.fr	/pub6/pc/win3/util	winzip56.exe
	ftp://wuarchive.wustl.edu	/systems/ibmpc/win3/util	winzip56.exe
	ftp://ftp.sunet.se	/pub/pc/windows/winsock-indstate/Misc_Utils/Compression	winzip56.exe
	ftp://hubcap.clemson.edu	/pub/pc_shareware/windows/Archive	winzip56.exe

---

Begin Guided Tour   Download a Helper Application

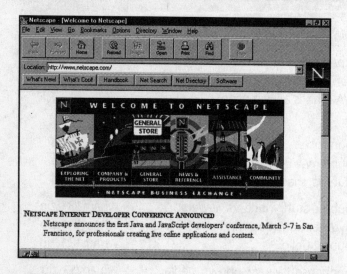

1 Connect to the Internet, and then run your Web browser as explained in "Connect to the World Wide Web," on page 144.

2 Highlight the entry in the browser's URL or Location text box. In some Web browsers, you can just click inside the text box. In other browsers, you might double-click inside the text box or drag over the entry.

3 Type the URL of an FTP server that has the helper application file you want to download (refer to the previous table). Press **Enter**.

Guided Tour Download a Helper Application

customers/	Sun May 28 00:00:00 1995	Directory
customers2/	Fri Oct 13 13:42:00 1995	Directory
customers3/	Thu Aug 03 18:11:00 1995	Directory
dist/	Thu Jun 30 00:00:00 1994	Directory
epimbe	Mon Sep 25 00:02:00 1995	Symbolic link
etc/	Fri Feb 03 00:00:00 1995	Directory
ftp	Mon Sep 25 00:02:00 1995	Symbolic link
gopher	Mon Oct 09 18:43:00 1995	Directory
lost+found	Fri Feb 11 00:00:00 1994	Directory
nonprofits	Mon Sep 25 00:02:00 1995	Symbolic link
obi/	Mon Oct 30 06:31:00 1995	Directory
periodicals	Mon Sep 25 00:02:00 1995	Symbolic link
private/	Tue Dec 20 12:38:00 1994	Directory
pub/	Wed Dec 20 11:38:00 1995	Directory
pub2/	Wed Dec 20 07:50:00 1995	Directory

4 Your Web browser connects to the FTP server and displays a list of folders. Click a link for the folder to which you want to go. Continue to click links until you reach the folder that contains the helper application.

iregistb.txt	1 Kb	Fri Sep 29 10:29:00 1995	Plain Text
iregistr.txt	1 Kb	Fri Sep 29 10:31:00 1995	Plain Text
lviewp1b.zip	305 Kb	Sat Jul 01 08:08:00 1995	Zip Compressed Dat
lviewpro.zip	312 Kb	Tue Sep 19 21:31:00 1995	Zip Compressed Dat
sregistb.txt	2 Kb	Fri Sep 29 10:29:00 1995	Plain Text
sregistr.txt	1 Kb	Fri Sep 29 10:31:00 1995	Plain Text
w32s125.exe	2233 Kb	Sun Jul 09 06:00:00 1995	Binary Executable

5 Eventually, you change to the folder that contains the helper application file you need. If you have Netscape Navigator, click the link to download the file. (In other Web browsers, you may have to hold down the **Shift** key while clicking.)

iregistr.txt	1 Kb	Fri Sep 29 10:31:00 1995	Plain Text
lviewp	Back	Sat Jul 01 08:08:00 1995	Zip Compressed Dat
lviewp	Forward	Tue Sep 19 21:31:00 1995	Zip Compressed Dat
sregis	Open that (lviewpro.zip)	Fri Sep 29 10:29:00 1995	Plain Text
sregis	Add Bookmark for this Link New Window with this Link	Fri Sep 29 10:31:00 1995	Plain Text
w32s12	Save this Link as Copy this Link Location	Sun Jul 09 06:00:00 1995	Binary Executable
	Internet Shortcut		

6 In some Web browsers, you can right-click the link and choose the **Save** option.

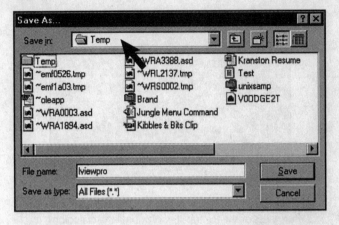

7 However you choose to download the file, a dialog box appears, asking you to pick the drive and folder in which you want the file saved. Choose the **TEMP** (temporary) folder on drive C. TEMP is a good place to store files temporarily until you install the program.

8 Click **OK** or **Save**.

(continues)

Guided Tour Download a Helper Application

(continued)

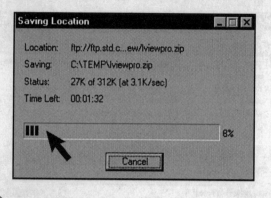

9 In most systems, a dialog box appears, showing the progress of the file transfer. Wait until the dialog box disappears, which means that the file transfer is complete.

10 Repeat steps 2 through 9 to download any other helper applications you want.

Install a Helper Application

The helper applications you just downloaded are in zipped (compressed) files. Each zipped file (any file whose name ends in .ZIP) contains all the files that make up one of the helper applications. To install a helper application, you use a file decompression program such as PKZIP or WinZip, which extracts the compressed files from the zipped file.

You may have downloaded and installed WinZip when you took the *Guided Tour* in "Install Your Files" (page 93). If you haven't installed WinZip, that's okay. The *Guided Tour* walks you through installing WinZip so you can use it to unzip the other helper applications you downloaded.

Where to Store Your Helper Applications

You should create a separate folder for each of your helper applications. For example, you might create a folder called LVIEW, another folder called MPEG, and still another folder called WHAM. You can then extract the zipped files for each helper application to its own, separate folder.

Although you can create these folders anywhere on your hard disk, they are usually placed under the WinApps folder. This is where most Windows applications place their *applets* (small programs that bigger programs share), and many Web browsers are set up to look under the WinApps folder for helper applications. If you place the helper applications under this folder, you might save yourself a little work.

Why You Have to Run a Setup Program

Most helper applications do not require that you run a setup program. You simply extract the zipped files to a folder, and you're ready to roll. WinZip is the exception. WinZip is a self-extracting zip file. When you run it (by double-clicking on it in My Computer or File Manager), WinZip extracts its files and automatically runs the setup program, which leads you through the process of installing WinZip.

Begin Guided Tour   Extract Helper Applications

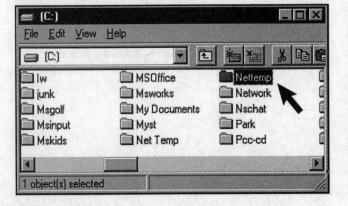

1 Create a temporary folder (call it NETTEMP) and copy winzip56.exe into it. You will use this folder only to install WinZip. After you've installed WinZip, you can delete this folder and its contents.

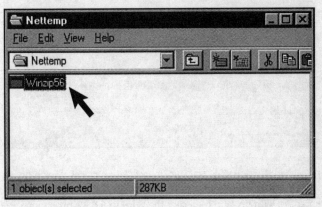

2 Open My Computer (in Windows 95) or File Manager (in Windows 3.1) and change to the **NETTEMP** folder. Double-click **winzip56.exe** (it may appear as just winzip56 in Windows 95).

(continues)

Guided Tour Extract Helper Applications

(continued)

3 When you run winzip56.exe, it displays a series of dialog boxes that lead you through the process of unzipping the file and installing WinZip on your hard drive. Follow the instructions to complete the installation.

4 Create a folder for each of your helper applications under the WinApps folder in Windows 95. You will extract the zipped helper application files to these folders.

5 In Windows 95, the WinZip installation places WinZip on the Start menu. Click the **Start** button, point to **Programs**, point to **WinZip**, and then click the **WinZip 6.0 32-bit** option.

6 In Windows 3.1, the WinZip installation creates a program group with program-item icons for running WinZip. Double-click on the **WinZip** icon to run WinZip.

7 The WinZip window appears. To open an archive (one of your ZIP files), click the **Open** button in the toolbar.

Guided Tour Extract Helper Applications

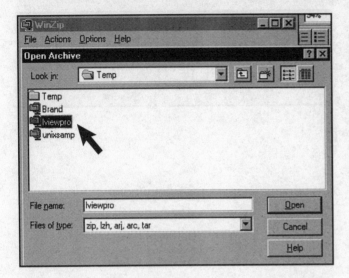

8 In the dialog box that appears, select one of your zipped helper application files. (If you followed the download instructions given earlier, they should be in the TEMP folder.) Click the **Open** or **OK** button to proceed.

9 WinZip displays the names of all the files in the selected ZIP file. Click the **Extract** button in the toolbar.

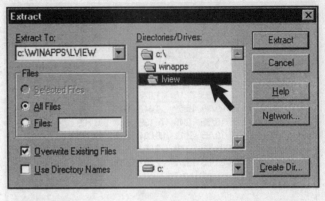

10 A dialog box like the one shown here appears. Select the drive and the folder that you created for this particular helper application. (That folder should be under the WinApps folder.)

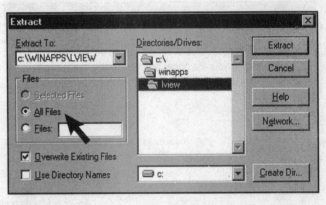

11 If necessary, select the **All Files** option to have WinZip unzip all of the files in the zipped file.

12 Click the **Extract** button. WinZip unzips the ZIP file and stores all the extracted files in the specified folder.

(continues)

Guided Tour Extract Helper Applications

(continued)

WinZip - lviewpro.zip						
File Actions Options Help						
New	Open	Add	Extract	View	CheckOut	
Name	Date	Time	Size	Ratio	Packed	Path
changes.txt	09/05/95	21:15	11,027	61%	,262	
iregistr.txt	09/05/95	15:51	1,842	57%	792	
lviewpro.exe	09/19/95	16:48	475,136	51%	233,769	
lviewpro.hlp	09/10/95	22:11	106,804	26%	78,936	
readme.txt	09/05/95	22:43	2,552	52%	1,221	
sregistr.txt	09/05/95	15:51	2,101	58%	880	

Selected 0 files, 0 bytes   Total 6 files, 586KB

After you unzip your helper applications, you can delete the original files you downloaded (the ones with the .zip extension). This will free up some disk space.

13 You can repeat steps 6 through 11 to unzip other zipped files. When you are done, proceed to the next task, in which you learn how to tell your Web browser where to look for helper applications.

Set Up Programs to Use Helper Applications

Even though the helper applications are on your hard disk, your Web browser or Gopher program doesn't know where the applications are stored or when it should use them. To remedy the situation, you must *associate* particular file types with the helper applications that can play them. For example, you might have to tell your Web browser that whenever it encounters a GIF or JPG file, it should run LView.

The steps you take to associate file types to helper applications vary according to which Web browser or Gopher program you're using. Most programs offer an Options menu, a Preferences menu, or a Configure menu that contains the command you need. That command may be called "Preferences," "Options," "Edit Viewers," or "Helper Apps." You'll have to poke around your own menu system to find its command for setting up helper applications (or viewers).

When you enter the required command, you'll see a dialog box that is basically the same no matter which Web browser or Gopher program you're using. The dialog box allows you to pick a file type (such as JPG graphic files), and then assign a helper application to that file type. Follow the *Guided Tour* to associate file types to your helper applications.

> **Begin Guided Tour**   Associate File Types with Helper Applications

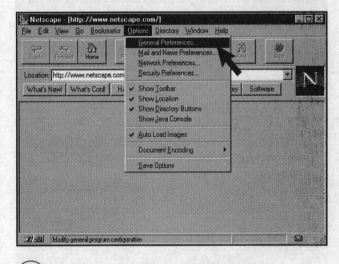

1 You don't need to be connected to the Internet to set the options for your Web browser or Gopher program. Run the Web browser or Gopher program for which you want to set up helper applications.

2 In your Web browser or Gopher program, enter the command for setting your preferences. In Netscape Navigator (shown here), you open the **Options** menu and select **General Preferences**.

(continues)

Guided Tour Associate File Types with Helper Applications *(continued)*

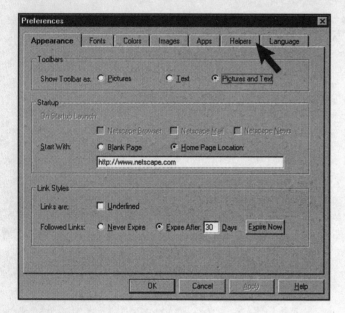

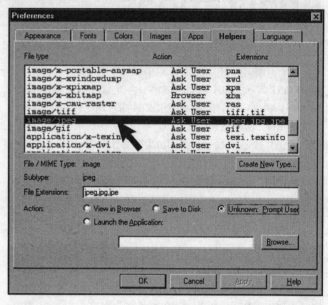

3 If the dialog box that appears has several tabs, click the **Viewers** or **Helpers** tab to bring its options to the front.

5 Click on the file type (for example, **image/jpeg**) that you want to associate with one of your helper applications.

4 The File type list shows the file types that you can associate with a helper application. The rightmost column shows the file name extensions for each file type. (You can ignore most of the file types listed.)

6 If your Web browser can open the file type you selected, you can choose **View in Browser** to use the Web browser to play the file. Or you can choose to play the file type in a helper application, as explained in the next step.

Guided Tour　Associate File Types with Helper Applications

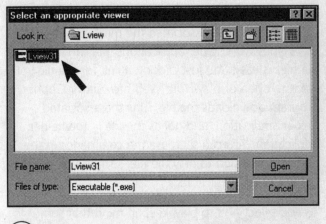

9 A dialog box appears, allowing you to select the helper application. Select the drive, folder, and name of the file that runs the helper application. Click **Open** or **OK**.

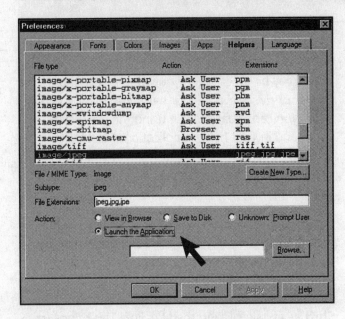

7 To use a helper application to play the file type you selected, select the **Launch the Application** option (or the comparable option in your program).

10 Repeat steps 5 through 9 to associate additional file types to your helper applications. Click **OK** when you are done to accept your changes and close the Preferences dialog box.

8 Next you must specify where the helper application is located. Click the **Browse** button.

Play Multimedia Files

After you have associated the most common file types with helper applications, playing multimedia files is easy. You just click on a link for the file you want to open or play. Your Web browser or Gopher program downloads the file, runs the associated helper application, and opens the file in the helper application. You can then use the commands in the helper application to play the file, save the file to disk, or perform other actions.

As you select files to play, keep in mind that some files may be rather large. A short movie clip, for example, might be more than one megabyte. Even if you have a fast modem, it can take well over a minute to download the file. Most Web browsers and Gopher programs display a dialog box showing the progress of the file transfer. Don't expect the file to immediately pop up on your screen.

The *Guided Tour* shows how easy it is to play graphics, video, and sound clips on the Web and from a Gopher program. For details on how to install, set up, and use a Gopher program, see "Surf the Internet Using Gopher Menus" (page 281).

Save Files to Your Disk

There may be times when you want to save a graphic, sound, or movie clip to your hard disk. After you play a file, you can usually save it using the File, Save command in your helper application. Most Web browsers also have commands that let you bypass the helper applications in case you want to save a file without playing it.

In Netscape Navigator, for example, you can right-click the link for a file, click the **Save** option on the shortcut menu that appears, and respond to the resulting dialog box. In Mosaic and some other Web browsers, you can save a file by holding down the **Shift** key while clicking the file's link. This brings up the Save dialog box, in which you select the drive and folder to which you want the file saved.

Some Web browsers, such as Netscape Navigator, let you associate a file type to the Save to Disk option (instead of to a helper application). If you select this option, anytime you select a file of the specified type, a dialog box appears, asking you if you want to save the file instead of playing it. This option is useful if you want to copy a bunch of files of a particular type to your disk.

Begin Guided Tour   Play Files from the Web

Movie poster
A larger rendition of the art at the top.
Eyelash
The closeup of Alex as he drives the car.
Alex
Alex takes control of his mutinous droogs
Alex at home.
Alex being watched by Lucy Van.
Theatre
Alex watches in agony.
Sophistos
The opera singer and friends at the Moloko bar.

Sounds (all .aiff)

Yarbles | (or here for aif version)

1 Connect to the Internet and run your Web browser. As you wander the Web, you will come across files that may require a helper application. Click a file's link to play or open the file.

Guided Tour Play Files from the Web

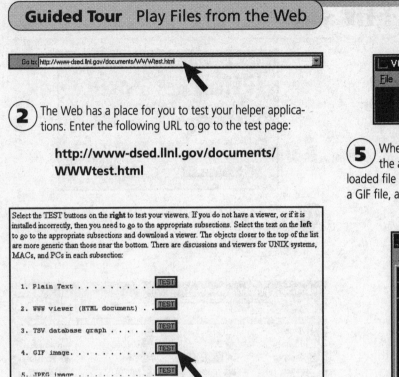

2 The Web has a place for you to test your helper applications. Enter the following URL to go to the test page:

**http://www-dsed.llnl.gov/documents/
WWWtest.html**

3 Click the test button for one of the file types you set up a helper application to play. (If you find a file type you can't play, this page also has links you can use to find and download helper applications.)

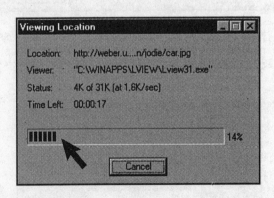

4 If you selected a file for which you've associated a helper application, your Web browser downloads the file. A dialog box like the one shown here displays the progress of the file transfer. (If the file type is not associated with a helper application, you'll see a dialog box saying so. Skip to step 8 for further instructions.)

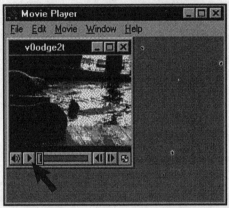

5 When the file transfer is complete, the Web browser runs the associated helper application and opens the downloaded file in the application. Here, LView displays the contents of a GIF file, a simple test pattern.

6 If your file is a sound or a video clip, you may have to click a **Play** button to start playing the downloaded file. If it's a simple graphic (such as a GIF or JPG file), the helper application displays the contents of the file immediately.

(continues)

Guided Tour Play Files from the Web

(continued)

7 Many helper applications allow you to save a file to disk. Simply open the application's **File** menu and select **Save**. Fill in the information in the dialog box that appears to specify where you want the file saved.

8 If you click on a link to play a file and you see a dialog box indicating that no helper application has been assigned to this file type, you can choose to save the file to disk (to play later).

9 Some browsers let you set up file associations on the fly. With Netscape Navigator, you can click the **Configure a Viewer** button to assign a helper application to this file type.

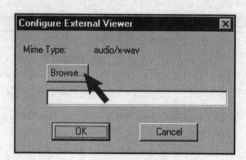

10 The Configure External Viewer dialog box displays the file type you selected. Click the **Browse** button to pick the helper application you want to use.

11 In the dialog box that appears, select the drive, folder, and name of the file that runs your helper application. Then click **Open** or **OK**.

12 After you configure a viewer for the selected file type, your browser downloads the selected file and opens it in the specified helper application.

Begin Guided Tour Play Files from Gopher

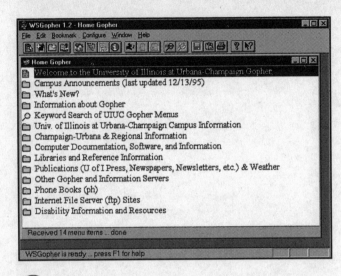

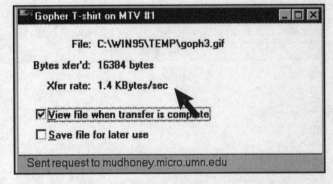

1 Although Web browsers are more graphical, you can play multimedia files from your Gopher program (assuming you've set up the appropriate file associations).

3 As Gopher downloads (fetches) the file for you, a dialog box shows you the progress of the file transfer. Wait until the file transfer is complete.

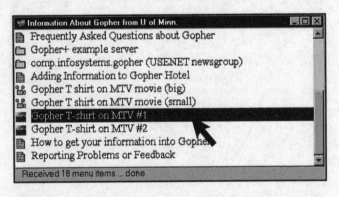

2 When you connect to a Gopher server that has multimedia files, the Gopher program usually displays a unique icon for each file type. For example, a movie camera icon appears next to each movie file. Double-click an item to play it.

4 When Gopher finishes downloading the file, it automatically runs the associated helper application and plays the file. In some sound and video helper applications, you must click a **Play** button to play the file.

HOW TO...

Search for Information on the Internet

U p to this point, you've been wandering the Web like some disoriented nomad, relying on links and recommended URLs to carry you where they may. That's fine if you're using the Internet to pass the time or for the sheer enjoyment of stumbling upon interesting sites. But if you have to use the Internet to research a topic or do some serious work, wandering is hardly the most efficient method.

Fortunately, the Internet offers several search tools that you can use to find specific information. On the Web, you can use Yahoo's home page to search various categories for information, or you can type a search term (a key term that zeros in on what you're looking for). Two other popular Web search tools, Lycos and WebCrawler, work in much the same way.

The Internet also offers search tools that you can use through Gopher. In this section, you'll learn where to find these search tools and how to use them.

What You Will Find in This Section

Search for Information on the Web

The best Internet search tools are on the World Wide Web. To search for general information, say about movies, you can go to any of several Web pages that contain lists of categories. You simply click on a category, such as Movies or Food, and the page displays a long list of links. You can then poke around and look for the general information you need.

If you need specific information in a hurry, the Web offers *forms-based* search tools. A forms-based search tool is simply a fill-in-the-blanks Web page that asks you what you're looking for. You type a specific search term, such as Casablanca or Harrison Ford, and then click a button (usually labeled Submit or Search). Within seconds, the search tool displays links that can carry you to Web pages that have the information you need.

Take the *Guided Tour* to try out some of these Web search tools. You'll find that the Web search tools often turn up additional information that you'll find on non-Web servers (such as newsgroups, FTP servers, and Gophers).

Understand How Search Tools Work

When you perform a search, you might get the impression that the search tool is rummaging through the Internet to find the information you asked for. Actually, the search itself has already been done. Each search tool uses a *search engine* that regularly explores the Internet for new information. When it finds new information, it catalogues or indexes that information, referencing each topic with a URL (an address that tells where the information is stored).

When you enter a specific search term, the search tool simply dips into the index, finds all the items that match your search term, and displays a list of links that point to the URLs where the information is

stored. By handling searches in this way, a search tool can perform a search in a matter of seconds.

Search tools that regularly wander the Web, indexing its many pages, go by such names as knowbot, robot, webcrawler, spider, and infobot. These names all focus on the nature of the search tools: they are automated and persistent. The Yahoo search tool, however, is not a robot; its directory is compiled and maintained by humans.

Narrow Your Search

If you choose to use a forms-based search tool, you should select your search terms carefully. Searching for a general term such as "food" or "books" will give you a list of links too long to be of any use. Try to pick a term that's more specific, such as "desserts" or "crime novels." You can further narrow the search by looking for "pies" or "Devil in a Blue Dress."

In addition, many search forms allow you to set additional options for narrowing your search. These search tools, for example, are set to find all topics that match any of the search terms you enter. So if you enter "Coral Snake," the search tool will find a bunch of references to "coral" and to "snake." You need to specify that you want only those items that have *both* "coral" and "snake" in the title.

You can also tell the search tool to find only those titles that *exactly match* your search terms. For example, if you perform a nonexact match for "basketball," the search tool might come up with a list of items such as "basket weaving," "basket," and "basketcase." To find titles that match "basketball," you need to specify that you want exact matches only. The *Guided Tour* shows you how to enter search options for the most popular search tools.

Stop Words and Hits

As you type search terms, keep in mind that the search tool may not look up all the terms you type. Search tools are set up to ignore certain common words, called *stop words*. These include "a," "the," and "what," and such commonly used nouns as "computer" and "internet." So, for example, if you type "What is a web robot?" the search tool is likely to search only for "robot." When you type search terms, try to include one or two unique words.

When a search tool searches its index, it determines the number of *hits* for each item. A hit means that the search tool found a word in the index entry that matched one of your search terms. When the search tool displays the resulting list of items it found, it usually places the item with the most hits first. So when you're trying to decide which link to follow, you should start at the top of the list and work down.

Other Search Tools

The *Guided Tour* covers the three most popular search tools on the Web. However, the Web offers several other search tools. Here's a list of other search tools to try, along with their URLs:

InfoSeek: http://www2.infoseek.com/

All-In-One: http://www.albany.net/allinone/

New Rider's Yellow Pages: http://www.mcp.com/nrp/wwwyp/

Wandex: http://wandex.netgen.com/cgi/wandex

World Wide Web Worm: http://wwww.cs.colorado.edu/wwww

Alta Vista: http://altavista.digital.com/

Excite: http://www.excite.com/

CUSI: http://pubweb.nexor.co.uk/public/cusi/cusi.html

Begin Guided Tour   Search from the Yahoo Home Page

1 The Yahoo home page is one of the most popular places to start wandering the Web. To go to Yahoo, type **http://www.yahoo.com** in the **Location** or **Go to** text box of your Web browser and press **Enter**.

2 Yahoo provides an extensive list of categories you can explore. Simply click a category of interest.

(continues)

Guided Tour Search from the Yahoo Home Page *(continued)*

Recreation:Sports

[text box] [Search] Options

○ Search in **Sports**   ◉ Search all of Yahoo

- **Current Sports Headlines** ✦✔
- **Indices** *(19)*

- **Adventure** *(1)*
- **Air Hockey** *(1)*
- **Archery** *(10)*
- **Auto Racing** *(184)*
- **Badminton** *(3)*
- **Baseball** *(320)*
- **Basketball** *(410)*

- **Korfball** *(3)*
- **Lacrosse** *(13)*
- **Lumbering** *(2)*
- **Magazines@**
- **Martial Arts** *(172)*
- **News@**
- **Officiating** *(3)*

③ When you click a major category, Yahoo presents you with a list of subcategories. Continue clicking links until you find the information you want or reach a dead end.

Happy Holidays! · Yahoo Survey Results · Web Launch

[Michael Jordan] [Search] Options

④ To perform a more structured search, return to Yahoo's home page and type one or two search terms in the text box at the top of the page.

Happy Holidays! · Yahoo Survey Results · Web Launch

[Michael Jordan] [Search] Options

⑤ Click the **Search** button.

Yahoo Search Results

Found 5 matches containing **michael jordan**. Displaying matches 1-5.

Entertainment:People

- Dawes, Daniel **NEW!** - A brief look at Dan Dawes. **Michael Jordan** is mentioned.
- **Jordan, Michael**

Entertainment:People:Families

- Shevik Family - Information and news on the Shevik Family. Picture of Letechia with **Michael Jordan**.

Recreation:Sports:Basketball:NBA:Players

⑥ Yahoo searches for the requested topic and displays a list of links that match your entry. Click a link to display the Web page or other Internet resource.

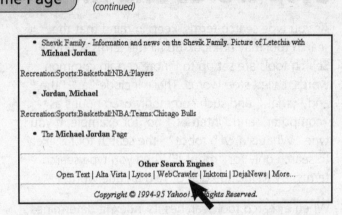

- Shevik Family - Information and news on the Shevik Family. Picture of Letechia with **Michael Jordan**.

Recreation:Sports:Basketball:NBA:Players

- **Jordan, Michael**

Recreation:Sports:Basketball:NBA:Teams:Chicago Bulls

- The **Michael Jordan** Page

Other Search Engines
Open Text | Alta Vista | Lycos | WebCrawler | Inktomi | DejaNews | More...

Copyright © 1994-95 Yahoo! All Rights Reserved.

⑦ After checking out a page, you can click the **Back** button to go back to the list of items that Yahoo found and click on another link. Also look at the end of the list of found items for links to other search tools. You can click one of these links to search for the same information using another tool.

WebCrawler Search Results

The query "Michael Jordan" found 9537 documents and returned 25:

100 Total Jordan Peugeot Home Page
089 Nothing But Net - A Tribute to Michael Jordan
059 Web Server Of The Hashemite Kingdom Of Jordan
059 *Web Server Of The Hashemite Kingdom Of Jordan*
059 *Web Server Of The Hashemite Kingdom Of Jordan*
059 *Web Server Of The Hashemite Kingdom Of Jordan*
059 *Web Server Of The Hashemite Kingdom Of Jordan*
056 Rich's Michael English Page
053 JORDAN PETROLEUM LTD. - $3 MILLION FLOW-THROUGH SHARE FINANCING
051 MICHAEL'S DARK SIDE
047 Document moved

⑧ If you click a link for another search tool, the tool automatically performs the search and displays a list of items it found in its index.

Happy Holidays! · Yahoo Survey Results · Web Launch

[Michael Jordan] [Search] Options

⑨ Although a basic Yahoo search usually finds the information you need, you can set Yahoo search options. Return to Yahoo's home page and click the **Options** link.

Guided Tour   Search from the Yahoo Home Page

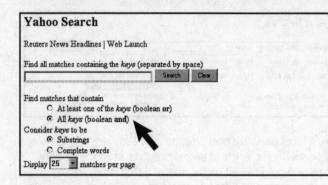

10 You can use the search options to broaden or narrow your search. Select **At least one of the keys** to broaden the search, or select **All keys** to narrow it.

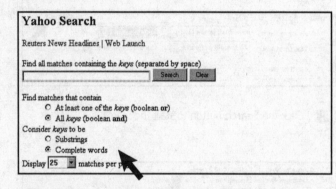

11 Yahoo normally treats your search terms as substrings, so if you type "book," Yahoo will find "book," "books," "bookstore," "bookkeeper," and so on. You can select the **Complete words** option to narrow the search.

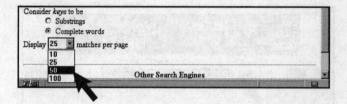

12 Yahoo typically displays up to 25 found items per page, but provides a link at the bottom of the page that allows you to change that number. If you want more items displayed per page, open the **Display ___ matches per page** drop-down list and select the desired number.

13 Type your search terms in the text box (if you haven't already), and then click the **Search** button.

Begin Guided Tour   Search with Lycos

Go to: http://www.lycos.com/

1 Lycos provides one of the most thorough Internet indexes you can find. To display the Lycos search page, type **http://www.lycos.com** in the **Location** or **Go to** text box and press **Enter**.

2 To perform a simple search for one or two terms, type the terms in the text box (as shown here) and click the **Go Get It** button. Lycos will find any items that have any of the search terms you enter.

(continues)

Guided Tour Search with Lycos *(continued)*

3 You can take more control of the search by setting the search options. To do so, click the **Enhance your search** link.

4 To narrow the search, open the **Search Options** drop-down list on the left, and click **match all terms (AND)** or one of the **match # terms** options.

5 You can further narrow the search by specifying how exact you want the match to be. Open the **Search Options** drop-down list on the right and select an option that specifies how close you want the match to be.

6 By default, Lycos displays ten of the items it finds per page and displays a link at the bottom of the page that allows you to see additional items. To display more found items per page, open the **Display Options** drop-down list on the left and select a number.

7 Lycos displays a brief description of each item it finds. To specify the length of each description, open the **Display Options** drop-down list on the right and click the desired detail option: **summary results** (short), **standard results** (longer), or **detailed results** (longest).

8 Click the **Search** button to start the search.

1) Welcome to Seurat [1.0000, 1 of 2 terms]
2) The Georges Seurat Homepage [0.8586, 1 of 2 terms]
3) The Georges Seurat Homepage [0.8463, 1 of 2 terms]
4) ARTH1003 (Erika) Introduction to Modern Art 1B [0.8261, 1 of 2 terms]
5) Seurat: Biographical Outline [0.8234, 1 of 2 terms]
6) Seurat: Biographical Outline [0.8161, 1 of 2 terms]
7) Seurat: "Esthetique" [0.8039, 1 of 2 terms]
8) WebMuseum: Seurat, Georges: The Circus [0.8006, 1 of 2 terms]
9) WebMuseum: Seurat, Georges: Young Woman Powdering Herself [0.7993, 1 of 2 terms]
10) WebMuseum: Seurat, Georges: Entree du port de Honfleur [0.7992, 1 of 2 terms]
11) WebMuseum: Seurat, Georges: The Side Show [0.7989, 1 of 2 terms]
12) WebMuseum: Seurat, Georges: The Side Show [0.7984, 1 of 2 terms]
13) WebMuseum: Seurat, Georges: The Side Show [0.7984, 1 of 2 terms]
14) WebMuseum: Seurat, Georges: Un dimanche apres-midi a l'Ile de la Grande Jatte

9 Lycos searches its index and displays a list of items that match your search instructions. You click a link for an item to access that item.

Begin Guided Tour Find Information with WebCrawler

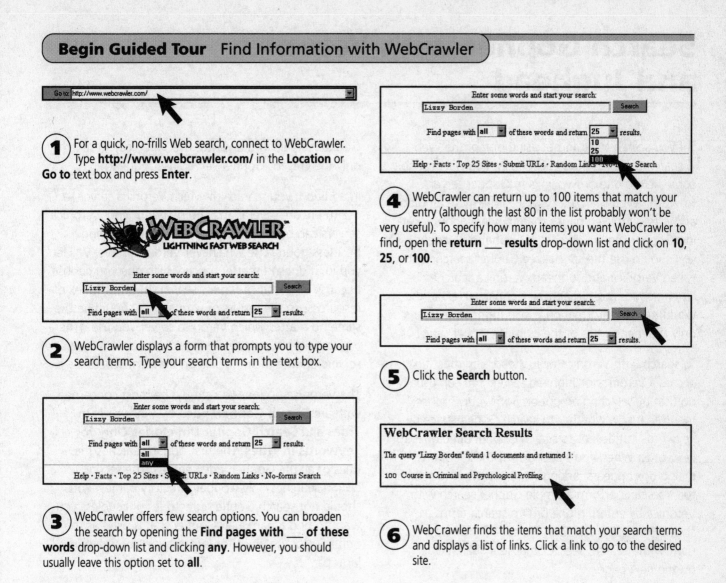

1 For a quick, no-frills Web search, connect to WebCrawler. Type **http://www.webcrawler.com/** in the **Location** or **Go to** text box and press **Enter**.

2 WebCrawler displays a form that prompts you to type your search terms. Type your search terms in the text box.

3 WebCrawler offers few search options. You can broaden the search by opening the **Find pages with ___ of these words** drop-down list and clicking **any**. However, you should usually leave this option set to **all**.

4 WebCrawler can return up to 100 items that match your entry (although the last 80 in the list probably won't be very useful). To specify how many items you want WebCrawler to find, open the **return ___ results** drop-down list and click on **10**, **25**, or **100**.

5 Click the **Search** button.

WebCrawler Search Results

The query "Lizzy Borden" found 1 documents and returned 1:

100 Course in Criminal and Psychological Profiling

6 WebCrawler finds the items that match your search terms and displays a list of links. Click a link to go to the desired site.

Search Gopher with Veronica and Jughead

If you search the Internet using one of the Web search tools described previously, you will probably come across one or two links to Gopher servers. However, Web search tools are a little more ambitious about finding Web pages than they are about locating Gopher servers. To search Gopher exclusively, you should use the specialized Gopher search tools called Veronica and Jughead. Veronica searches *Gopherspace* (presumably all Gopher servers in the world) to find information, while Jughead searches only the menu titles of the current Gopher server.

To search with Veronica or Jughead, you must first access a Veronica or Jughead server. You can usually do that by selecting an option from your Gopher menu that tells whether to search Gopherspace by keywords in titles, or to search Gopher directories for keywords. When you select one of these options, a dialog box appears, asking what you want to search for. You can perform a simple Gopher search with Veronica by entering one or two search terms as shown in the *Guided Tour*. For specifics on how to narrow the search, see "Compose a Search Query," on the next page.

> To perform a search using Jughead, you perform the same steps as in the *Guided Tour*. However, instead of selecting Veronica and searching all of Gopherspace, you select an option such as **Search this Gopher**.

Choose a Veronica or Jughead Server

The choice of whether to search with Veronica or Jughead is fairly obvious. If you want to search all the Gopher servers in the world, use Veronica. To search only the current Gopher server, use Jughead.

In addition, your choice of which Veronica server to use (there are several) may be made for you. Veronica servers can be tough to access, especially during business hours. Use whichever Veronica server will let you in. It doesn't matter much which one you choose because all Veronica servers search the same index of resources, so the results of your search should be the same no matter which Veronica server you use. (There may be a slight difference, though, because Veronica servers update their indexes on different schedules.)

The Veronica options you should be most concerned with are **Search GopherSpace by keywords in Titles** and **Search Gopher Directories Only for keywords in Titles**. The first option searches the titles of all the Gopher index entries. The second option searches only Gopher directory names. You should not search Gopher directories only unless you want to find a particular Gopher that is used as the primary storage place for information about a particular topic.

If you cannot find a Veronica or Jughead option on your Gopher menu (or if you're using your Web browser to access Gopher), try entering any of the following URLs to connect to a Veronica server:

gopher://veronica.unipi.it:2347/7

gopher://empire.nysernet.org:2347/7

gopher://veronica.psi.net:2347/7

gopher://veronica.sunet.se:2347/7

gopher://gopher.umanitoba.ca:2347/7

gopher://veronica.utdallas.edu:2348/7

Compose a Search Query

Although you can perform a simple search by typing one or two key terms, Veronica and Jughead offer additional search options you can use to control the search. These options can make a search fairly complex. The following entries are often used to control a Veronica search:

Maximum Found Items Veronica typically lists up to 200 items that match your search terms. To control the number of items listed, use the -m switch. For example, type **Bob Dylan -m50** to list only 50 items. If you omit the number after -m, Veronica lists *all* the items it finds.

Boolean Operators These are the words AND, NOT, and OR. When you perform a simple search, Veronica assumes you want to find items that have all the search terms you typed (for example, **Bob AND Dylan**). To broaden the search, you can use OR (for example, **Whitewater OR Watergate**). You can also use NOT to narrow a search, as in **Whitewater NOT Hillary**. And you can use the operators together using parentheses to group expressions, as in **movies (Coppola OR Scorsese)**.

Wildcard Entries You can use an asterisk (*) at the end of a word to broaden the search. For example, entering the search term **school experiment*** will turn up items for *experimental school*, *school experiments, and school experimentation*.

File Types To specify the types of Gopher resources you want to find, use the **-t** switch, followed by the code for the file type you want. For example, **Whitewater -t0** searches for only text files. Here's a list of common codes you can use and their corresponding file types:

0   Text file

1   Directory

5   PC binary

7   Full text index (Gopher menu)

s   Sound

I   Image (other than GIF)

g   GIF image

h   HTML (Web page)

> Use the OR operator sparingly if at all. The OR operator makes the search too broad to be of much use.

Begin Guided Tour   Search Gopherspace with Veronica

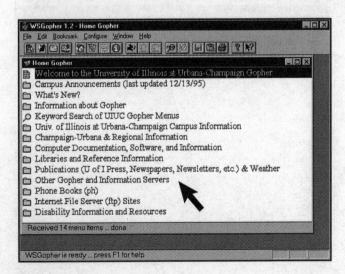

1 Connect to the Internet, and then run your Gopher program or Web browser. If you run a Gopher program, you should see an opening Gopher menu similar to the one shown here.

(continues)

Guided Tour Search Gopherspace with Veronica *(continued)*

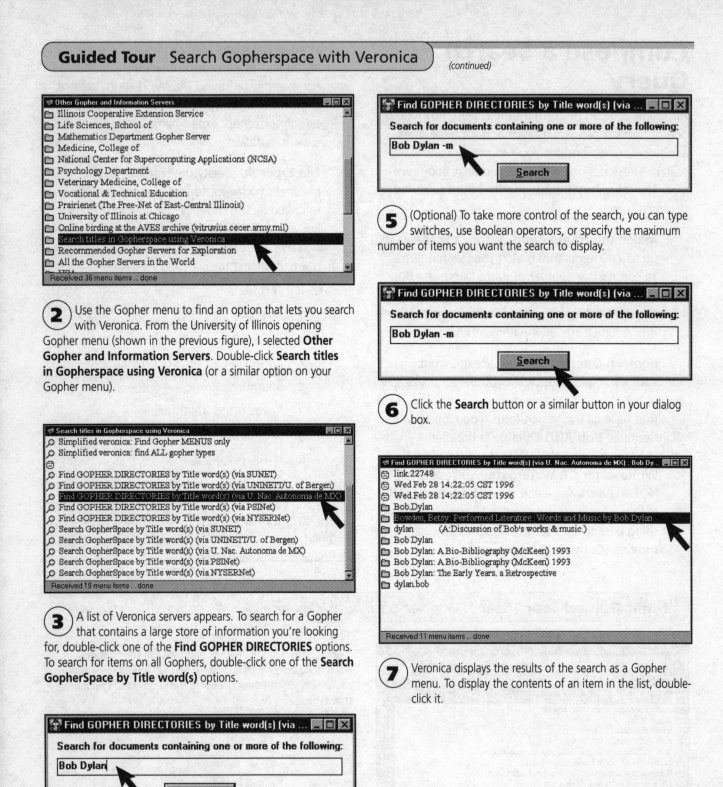

2 Use the Gopher menu to find an option that lets you search with Veronica. From the University of Illinois opening Gopher menu (shown in the previous figure), I selected **Other Gopher and Information Servers**. Double-click **Search titles in Gopherspace using Veronica** (or a similar option on your Gopher menu).

3 A list of Veronica servers appears. To search for a Gopher that contains a large store of information you're looking for, double-click one of the **Find GOPHER DIRECTORIES** options. To search for items on all Gophers, double-click one of the **Search GopherSpace by Title word(s)** options.

4 A dialog box appears, prompting you to type your search terms. Type one or two unique search terms to perform a simple search.

5 (Optional) To take more control of the search, you can type switches, use Boolean operators, or specify the maximum number of items you want the search to display.

6 Click the **Search** button or a similar button in your dialog box.

7 Veronica displays the results of the search as a Gopher menu. To display the contents of an item in the list, double-click it.

Guided Tour Search Gopherspace with Veronica

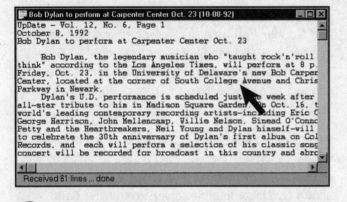

8 The contents appear on-screen. If you clicked on a sound file, movie clip, or graphic, your Gopher program may need to run a helper application to display the file (see "Play Sound and Video Clips with Helper Applications" on page 161).

Go to: gopher://dragon.dgsca.unam.mx:2347/7-t1%20%20

9 You can also access a Veronica server with your Web browser. In the **Location** or **Go to** text box, type the URL of a Veronica server and press **Enter**.

gopher://dragon.dgsca.unam.mx:2347/7-t1
Gopher Search

This is a searchable Gopher index. Use the search function of your browser to enter search terms.

This is a searchable index. Enter search keywords: `dog training`

10 A form appears, prompting you to type your search terms. Click inside the text box, type your search terms, and press **Enter** or click the **Search** button.

Gopher Menu

erCNT24389erCNT24409ink.22748ed Feb 26 14:32:40 CST 1996 Texas Tech Unive

Dog Club

Searcy, Margaret Zehmer: Wolf Dog of the Woodland Indians

Hooper, Johnson Jones: Dog and Gun: A Few Loose Chapters on Shooting, Ar

Olsen, Stanley John: Origins of the Domestic Dog: The Fossil Record

Harring, Sidney L.: Crow Dog's Case: American Indian Sovereignty, Triba

Hot Dog Folder

Dog Breeds

dog-care

11 If Veronica finds items that match your search instructions, it displays a list of links. Click a link to view the information. If the search turns up nothing, a message appears telling you so. You can use the **Back** button to return to a previous page, where you can search for something else or perform the search using another search tool.

Search WAIS with Your Web Browser

WAIS (pronounced "ways") stands *for Wide Area Information Server*. WAIS is a system that allows you to search various databases on the Internet for specific articles and other resources. For example, you might connect to a WAIS server and find a list of 500 or more databases for everything from stocks to cooking. You pick the database you want to search, and you type your subject title or other unique search text. WAIS finds the articles and resources that match your entry and lets you know how you can get to them. In most cases, you can even view the articles immediately.

What makes WAIS different from other Internet search tools is that WAIS creates an index for the contents of each article, whereas Gopher indexes only the titles of articles. With WAIS, you perform a *full-text search*, because WAIS searches the *contents* of articles.

> WAIS searches usually find all articles that have any of the search terms you enter. To specify that you want WAIS to find only those items that have all the search terms, use AND to separate your search terms. For example, type **dog AND training** instead of **dog training**.

Find Web WAIS Sites

In the days before Web browsers and Gophers, WAIS was difficult to access. You had to connect to a WAIS server and type commands at a prompt. Now, however, you can access WAIS servers through the Web

and Gopher. You then simply type your search terms in a text box and send WAIS on a search. The *Guided Tour* shows you how to use your Web browser to connect to a special Web site that performs WAIS searches.

Several companies have created special Web-to-WAIS *gateways*, which give you easy access to WAIS by way of your Web browser. A gateway is a system that allows two incompatible servers to transfer data. When you connect to one of these gateways, you're greeted with a form, complete with a text box in which you type your search terms.

You simply type one or two unique search terms and then click on a **Search** or **Submit** button just as you would if you were using a Web search tool. The WAIS server searches its databases (or only the databases you specify) to find articles that match your entry.

The *Guided Tour* shows you how to connect to and use the Einet Web-to-WAIS gateway. Einet combines a Web and WAIS technology to provide a thorough index you can search.

WAIS with Gopher

This *Guided Tour* shows the simplest way to access WAIS. However, if you prefer to use Gopher to explore the Internet, you can connect to WAIS servers and perform searches with Gopher. Try either of the following URLs to access WAIS through Gopher:

gopher-gw.micro.umn.edu

launchpad.unc.edu

Begin Guided Tour   Search WAIS Databases

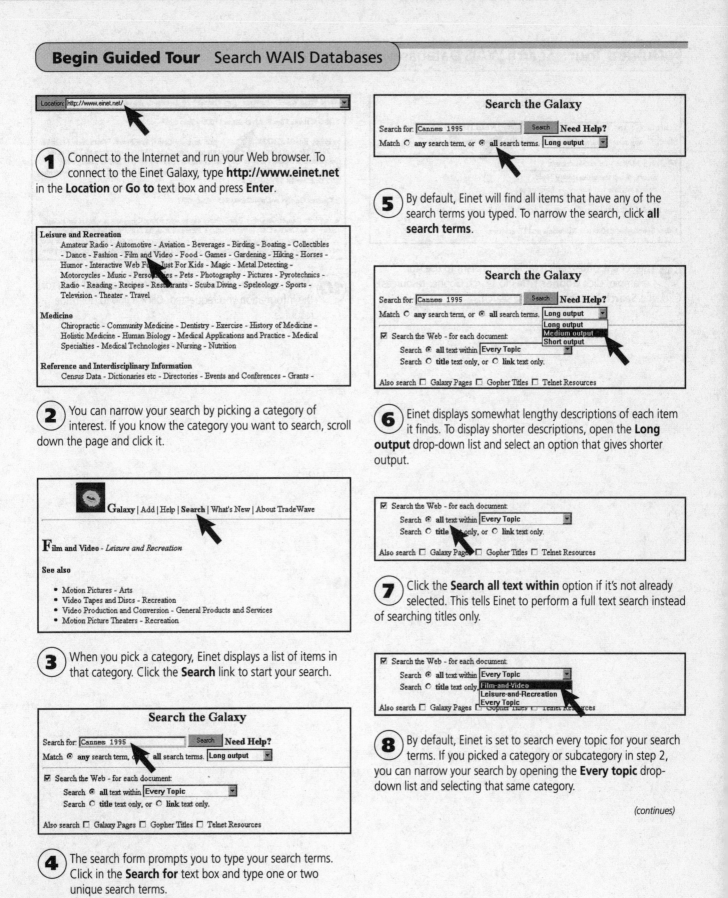

1 Connect to the Internet and run your Web browser. To connect to the Einet Galaxy, type **http://www.einet.net** in the **Location** or **Go to** text box and press **Enter**.

2 You can narrow your search by picking a category of interest. If you know the category you want to search, scroll down the page and click it.

3 When you pick a category, Einet displays a list of items in that category. Click the **Search** link to start your search.

4 The search form prompts you to type your search terms. Click in the **Search for** text box and type one or two unique search terms.

5 By default, Einet will find all items that have any of the search terms you typed. To narrow the search, click **all search terms**.

6 Einet displays somewhat lengthy descriptions of each item it finds. To display shorter descriptions, open the **Long output** drop-down list and select an option that gives shorter output.

7 Click the **Search all text within** option if it's not already selected. This tells Einet to perform a full text search instead of searching titles only.

8 By default, Einet is set to search every topic for your search terms. If you picked a category or subcategory in step 2, you can narrow your search by opening the **Every topic** drop-down list and selecting that same category.

(continues)

Guided Tour   Search WAIS Databases

(continued)

Search the Galaxy

Search for: Cannes 1995   [Search]   **Need Help?**

Match ○ **any search term,** or ● **all search terms.** [Me▾ output ▾]

☑ Search the Web - for each document:
   Search ● **all text within** [Every Topic ▾]
   Search ○ **title text only,** or ○ **link text only.**

Also search ☐ Galaxy Pages ☐ Gopher Titles ☐ Telnet Resources

Other Searchable Reference Materials and Directories

---

9 Select any other search options you want to use (for example, click **Gopher Titles** to search Gopher resources). Click the **Search** button to start the search.

World Wide Web Documents - for "Cannes." *16 documents found.*

1. **48th Cannes Film Festival**- *Score: 1000 - Size: 6967*

by Philipp Hoschka INRIA-R▮EO Sophia Antipolis Cote d'Azur France What's New ? October 2 1995 While you're here have a ▮ok at my new page: Cote d'Azur Connections All Films of the Competition at a Glance Day-to-Day Listing without Pictures. Fast Day-to-Day Listing with Pictures Official List of Movies Daily Events: What has happened ? What will happen ? Wednesday 17.5 Thursday 18.5 Friday 19.5 S...

2. **Cannes.On.Cyber Cup**- *Score: 845 - Size: 4775*

Welcome to Cannes.On.Cyber Tune in every day to our realtime Cybercast to witness the second century of the Cinema Choose your language: Please click on the flag of your language Click here for advertising and publishing information or email editor@shrine.cyber.ad.jp for more info For your viewing pleasure please use the Netscape 1.1 browser This global broadcast made possible by the

---

10 Within seconds, the Einet Galaxy displays a list of links for the information you requested. Click a link to open the resource.

HOW TO...

Send and Receive Electronic Mail

E lectronic mail (e-mail for short) is a system that enables users to send messages via modem from one computer to another. If you're connected to the Internet, you can send messages electronically to anyone else on the Internet—provided you have his or her e-mail address. An electronic mail address is similar to a U.S. postal address: it tells the Internet where to route the e-mail message.

E-mail messages sent over the Internet are restricted to text only (as in a letter, memo, or report); they cannot include graphics or special text enhancements such as bold, italics, or underline. However, you can send a file such as a spreadsheet, a graphic image, or a chart that contains such elements as text enhancements and graphics. For example, you might send a short e-mail message about recent sales figures and then send the details in a translated spreadsheet file.

When you receive an e-mail, you open it and read the message just as you would if it were a real letter. If other files have been attached to the e-mail message, you can detach them for use separately in some other program.

What You Will Find in This Section

Find and Download an E-Mail Program

In order to send and receive e-mail through the Internet, you need an e-mail program. A lot of Web browsers such as Netscape Navigator include a built-in e-mail program. However, you may not find it as full-featured as those offered separately, such as Pegasus and Eudora.

> If you already use Lotus Notes or cc:Mail, it can handle your Internet e-mail if you like. Likewise, if you use Windows 95, you can use Microsoft Exchange as your e-mail program. However, most Internet users (especially those with SLIP or PPP accounts) still prefer a separate Internet e-mail program such as Pegasus or Eudora, so that's what I will concentrate on here.

You can purchase some e-mail programs at any software store. However, you'll find a larger variety of software available for download from the Internet. Like Web browsers, the e-mail programs you'll find on the Internet are mostly shareware (not freeware), so you will need to register your program and pay a small fee after a reasonable testing period. Even if your service provider included an e-mail program with its startup files (which you downloaded using the steps in "Retrieve Files from Your Service Provider" on page 82, you'll still have to pay to register the e-mail program if you decide to keep it.

To download an e-mail program from the Internet, you have to locate its files and download (receive) them. The easiest way to locate and download files from the Internet is with your Web browser. If you haven't installed yours yet, see "Find and Install a Web Browser" on page 123 for help. Once you download your e-mail program, you'll need to install and configure it for your use.

Follow the *Guided Tour* to download an e-mail program called Eudora Light using Netscape Navigator. If you use a Web browser other than Netscape, the steps may vary slightly. To download the e-mail program, you'll jump to a Web site called Stroud's, which provides access to a lot of good Internet programs.

If you prefer a more direct method for downloading a particular e-mail program, you can connect to that program's FTP or Web site directly using one of the addresses listed here:

Eudora
http://www.qualcomm.com/quest

Pegasus
http://www.cuslm.ca/pegasus

P.O. (Post Office)
http://www.cis.ksu.edu/~novak/po.html

E-Mail Connection
ftp://ftp.connectsoft.com/pub

NETcetera II Lite
ftp://ftp.airtime.co.uk/pub

Pronto Mail
ftp://commtouch.com/pub

But the fastest way to shop around for the best e-mail program is to go to a Web site such as Stroud's, which provides links to each program along with comprehensive reviews. Another such Web site is called The Ultimate Collection of Winsock Software, or TUCOWS. Here are its Web locations:

Stroud's main site
http://www.cwsapps.com

Stroud's second main site
http://www.stroud.com

Stroud's main alternate site
http://www.enterprise.net/cwsapps

Stroud's second alternate site
http://cwsapps.wilmington.net

TUCOWS main site
http://web.idirect.com

TUCOWS main alternate site
http://tucow.niia.net

Stroud's is an excellent one-stop shopping place for all your Internet software needs. You'll probably visit it often, so you might want to create a bookmark in your Web browser to save the Stroud's Web address permanently. If you use Netscape Navigator, you create a bookmark by jumping to Stroud's, opening the **Bookmarks** menu, and selecting **Add Bookmark**.

Begin Guided Tour Download Eudora

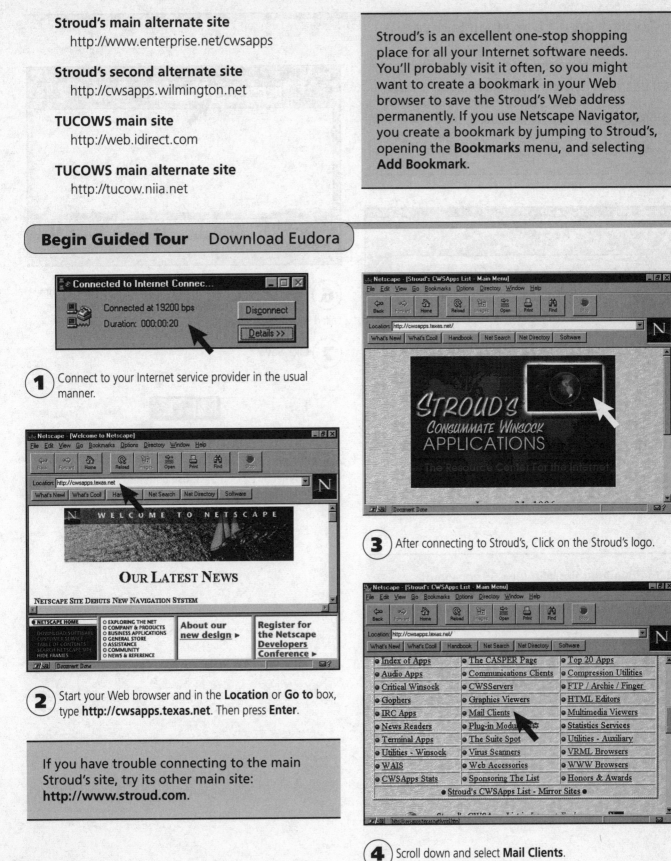

1 Connect to your Internet service provider in the usual manner.

2 Start your Web browser and in the **Location** or **Go to** box, type **http://cwsapps.texas.net**. Then press **Enter**.

If you have trouble connecting to the main Stroud's site, try its other main site: **http://www.stroud.com**.

3 After connecting to Stroud's, Click on the Stroud's logo.

4 Scroll down and select **Mail Clients**.

(continues)

Guided Tour Download Eudora *(continued)*

If you need help connecting via modem, see "Configure Your TCP/IP Software" on page [5tbd]. If you need help connecting to the Internet through your office network, see your system administrator.

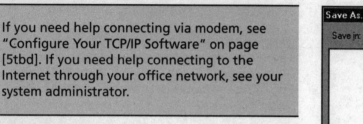

5 Scroll down the list and click the name of the e-mail program you want to download. For example, scroll down until you see Eudora Light, and then click the **Location** of Eudora Light.

To download the Windows 95 version of Eudora, click **Eudora Light 32-bit**. You'll be taken to another screen where you can click the file's location.

Also, if you want to read about an e-mail program before you download it, click the **Full Review** box in the left column.

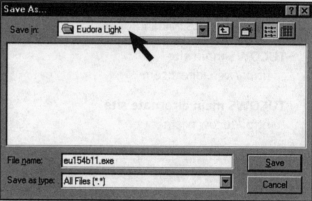

6 Select the folder into which you want to download your e-mail program. You might want to create a new folder called Eudora Light.

7 Click **Save**.

8 Once the program is downloaded, disconnect from the Internet by clicking the **Close** button so you won't waste online time while setting up Eudora.

Install Your E-Mail Program

To install Eudora (or any e-mail program), you'll need some information from your Internet service provider. For example, you'll need to know:

- The address of your Internet provider's POP (Post Office Protocol) server.

- The address of your Internet provider's SMTP (Simple Mail Transfer Protocol) server.

- Your specific e-mail address.

- Your password for getting mail (which is probably the same as your Internet logon password).

In the *Guided Tour*, you'll learn how to set up and install Eudora. If you downloaded a different e-mail program, the steps for installing it may vary. Look for a README.TXT file for help installing it.

Begin Guided Tour Install Eudora Light

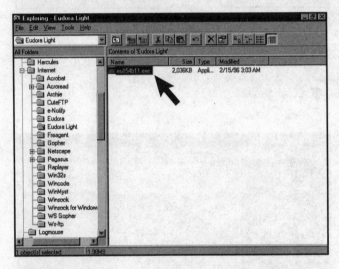

 Start Explorer or File Manager and change to the **Eudora Light** directory.

② Double-click the **eudor154b11.exe** file. The file expands into the Eudora Light directory.

 Click the **Close** button, or open the **File** menu and select **Exit** to remove the WinZip window.

Your file name may differ slightly if you downloaded a more recent version of Eudora Light.

(continues)

Guided Tour Install Eudora Light

(continued)

4 Double-click the **Setup.exe** file.

5 Click **Next**.

6 Verify the directory into which Eudora will be installed. If you want, click **Browse** and select a different directory.

7 Click **Next**.

8 Select **Eudora Light for Win 95 and NT (32 bit)** if it's not already selected, and then click **Next**.

If you use Windows 3.1, select **Eudora Light for Windows 3.x (16 bit)** instead.

Guided Tour Install Eudora Light

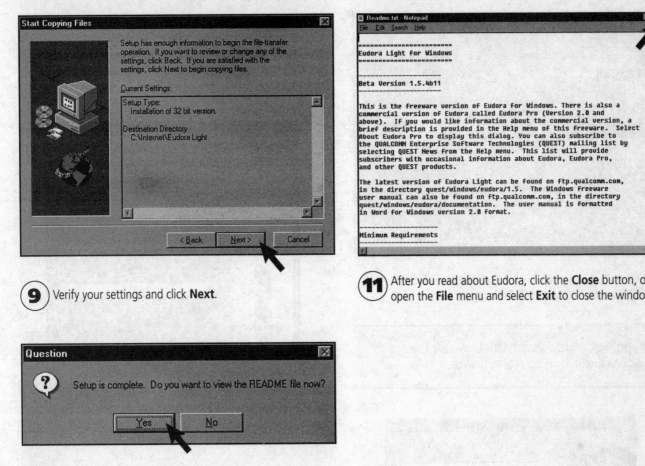

Start Copying Files

Setup has enough information to begin the file-transfer operation. If you want to review or change any of the settings, click Back. If you are satisfied with the settings, click Next to begin copying files.

Current Settings:

Setup Type:
    Installation of 32 bit version.

Destination Directory
    C:\Internet\Eudora Light

< Back   Next >   Cancel

Readme.txt - Notepad

File Edit Search Help

```
==============================
Eudora Light for Windows
==============================

Beta Version 1.5.4b11
------------------------------

This is the Freeware version of Eudora for Windows. There is also a
commercial version of Eudora called Eudora Pro (Version 2.0 and
above).  If you would like information about the commercial version, a
brief description is provided in the Help menu of this freeware.  Select
About Eudora Pro to display this dialog. You can also subscribe to
the QUALCOMM Enterprise Software Technologies (QUEST) mailing list by
selecting QUEST News from the Help menu.  This list will provide
subscribers with occasional information about Eudora, Eudora Pro,
and other QUEST products.

The latest version of Eudora Light can be found on ftp.qualcomm.com,
in the directory quest/windows/eudora/1.5.  The Windows freeware
user manual can also be found on ftp.qualcomm.com, in the directory
quest/windows/eudora/documentation.  The user manual is formatted
in Word for Windows version 2.0 format.

------------------------------
Minimum Requirements
------------------------------
```

---

9 Verify your settings and click **Next**.

11 After you read about Eudora, click the **Close** button, or open the **File** menu and select **Exit** to close the window.

Question

❓ Setup is complete. Do you want to view the README file now?

Yes   No

10 When you get the message "Setup is complete," click **Yes**.

Begin Guided Tour   Configure Eudora Light

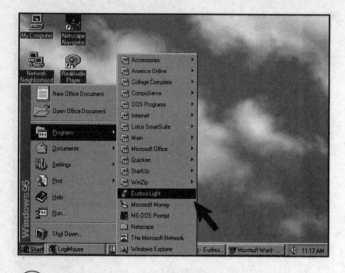

1 Start Eudora by clicking the **Start** button, selecting **Programs,** and selecting **Eudora Light**.

If you use Windows 3.1, double-click the **Eudora Light** icon to start Eudora.

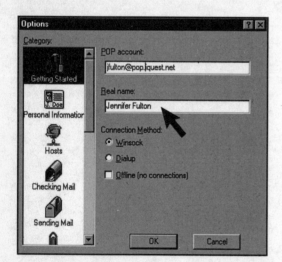

2 In the **POP account** text box, enter the e-mail address of your POP server, such as jfulton@pop.iquest.net.

3 Enter your name in the **Real name** text box.

4 Select **Winsock** if you plan to dial into the Internet directly or through a network. Select **Direct** if you're going through an online service such as CompuServe or America Online. Do not click **Offline** unless you will be sending your mail through a network to the Internet.

5 Click the **Personal Information** icon on the left side of the window.

6 Enter your **Return address**.

7 Enter a **Dialup username** if you use an online service or a network where you need to log in with a different username from the one in the POP account.

8 If your Internet provider uses a separate SMTP, Ph, or Finger handler, click the **Hosts** icon and enter the appropriate address.

Guided Tour Configure Eudora Light

The SMTP server's address may be the same as the POP server's. In that case, you can just skip to step 9.

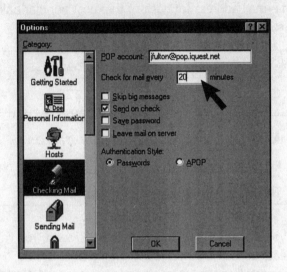

 9 If you want Eudora to check for mail periodically while you're online, click the **Checking Mail** icon.

10 Enter a time interval in the **Check for mail every __ minutes** blank.

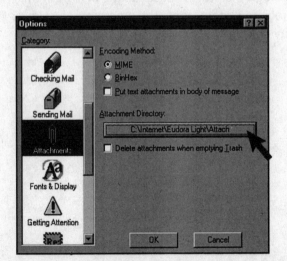

11 You should tell Eudora where to put files that you receive as attachments to e-mail messages. Click the **Attachments** icon, and then click the **Attachment Directory** button.

 12 Select the directory in which you want Eudora to store attached files. Then click **Use Directory**.

13 If you connect to the Internet via modem, click **Dialup** and enter the information required for connecting to your service provider.

14 You can make additional changes to the setup if you want. Simply click a button or icon on the left side of the screen and change the settings on the right. (For example, you can change the font used in e-mail messages.) Once you've made all your selections in Eudora, click **OK**.

Send an E-Mail Message

When you finish installing your e-mail program, you're ready to send a message. Remember that an e-mail message can only contain text. If you want to send a file as an e-mail message, see "Send Files As Messages over the Internet" on page 210.

You can send e-mail—either directly or indirectly (such as through CompuServe or America Online)—to anyone who's connected to the Internet. All you need to know is his or her e-mail address. An Internet address looks something like this:

jnoname@que.mcp.com

The first part of the address is the person's user name (the name by which she is known to her home system). Most user names consist of the person's first initial and last name run together. An at symbol (@) always comes after the user name. The part that follows the @ sign is a location, in this case, the address of Que (the company that published this book). The smaller parts of that address tell you that Que is part of Macmillan Computer Publishing— hence que.mcp—and that it is a commercial (.com) business venture. The last part of an address will always be .com (commercial), .edu (educational), .net (an Internet server), or .mil (military).

When you're on the Internet, you must be careful to use upper- and lowercase letters exactly as they are given to you. If someone tells you that his Internet e-mail address is SAMBeldon@imagineTHAT.com, you must type the address exactly that way. He will not receive his mail if you address it to sambeldon@imaginethat.com because that is a completely different address.

If you're sending e-mail to a person who connects to the Internet through an online service such as CompuServe, you'll find that entering the address is a bit trickier. The following list shows you the format of an e-mail address for each of the most popular online services.

Online Service	Sample Address
CompuServe	71354.1234 @compuserve.com
America Online	joeblow@aol.com
Prodigy	joeblow@prodigy.com
The Microsoft Network	joeblow@msn.com

If you have several e-mail messages to send, you can create each one while you're offline (that is, not connected to the Internet) and save it in your Outbox. Then when you're ready to send the messages, you can connect to the Internet and send all the messages in the Outbox at once. This *Guided Tour* walks you through the process of sending e-mail from the program Eudora Light. The process will be similar in any other e-mail program.

Begin Guided Tour   Send an E-Mail Message with Eudora Light

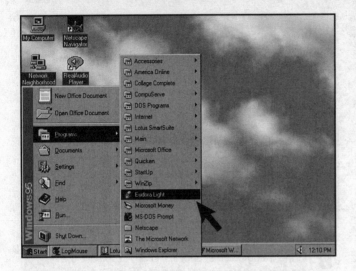

1 Click **Start**, select **Programs**, and then select **Eudora Light**. If you use Windows 3.1, double-click the **Eudora Light** icon to start Eudora.

You do not have to connect to the Internet in order to use your e-mail program. In fact, it's less expensive to create your e-mail messages offline and then connect to the Internet and send all your messages at the same time.

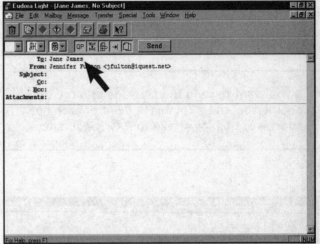

3 In the **To:** line, type the Internet address of the person to whom you want to send your e-mail message. To enter a second address, separate it from the first address with a comma.

Eudora lets you save the addresses of people who send you e-mail (see "Retrieve and Read E-Mail Messages" on page 205. To create a new e-mail message for a person whose address you have saved, skip steps 2 and 3; instead open the **Message** menu and select **New Message To**. A list of saved addresses appears. From this list, select the name of the person to whom you want to send a message.

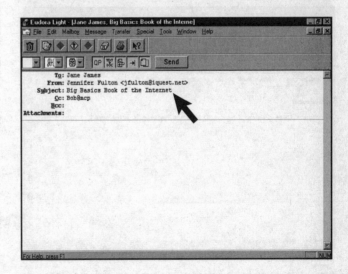

2 Open the **Message** menu and select **New Message,** or click the **New Message** button.

4 Enter a subject on the **Subject** line.

(continues)

Guided Tour Send an E-Mail Message with Eudora Light

(continued)

5 If you want to send a copy of this e-mail to other people, enter their addresses on the **Cc** (carbon copy) and or **Bcc** (blind carbon copy) lines.

> If you want to send this message to more than one person, use a comma in front of each new address as in jblow@fake.com,tsilly@duh.net.

> If you don't want to send additional messages, you can simply connect to the Internet and click **Send**.

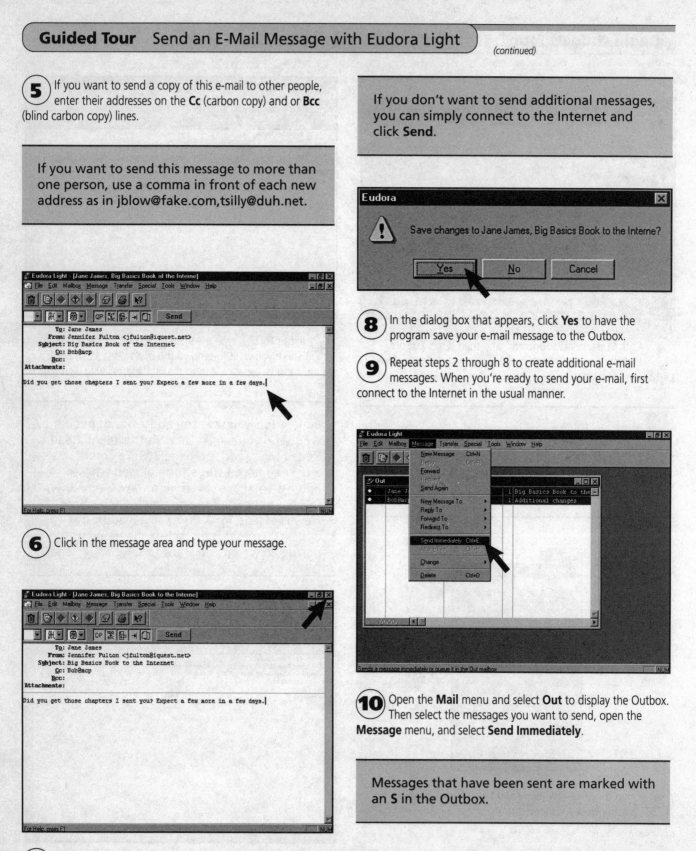

6 Click in the message area and type your message.

7 When you finish entering your message, click the **Close** button.

8 In the dialog box that appears, click **Yes** to have the program save your e-mail message to the Outbox.

9 Repeat steps 2 through 8 to create additional e-mail messages. When you're ready to send your e-mail, first connect to the Internet in the usual manner.

10 Open the **Mail** menu and select **Out** to display the Outbox. Then select the messages you want to send, open the **Message** menu, and select **Send Immediately**.

> Messages that have been sent are marked with an **S** in the Outbox.

Retrieve and Read E-Mail Messages

Besides sending messages, the other basic function of a good e-mail program is retrieving messages. Retrieving an e-mail message is like going to your mailbox and checking for mail. If there's mail in your mailbox, you take it out, open it, and read it. Your e-mail program does the same thing: it goes to your electronic mailbox, located on your Internet provider's computer, checks for mail, and brings back anything it finds.

You can configure your e-mail program to automatically check for mail every so often, or you can initiate the checking process whenever you want. Once you

retrieve your mail, you "open" it to read it. You can print an open message if you want, save the contents of the message in a file to use in another program, or reply to the message by sending a message back to the originator (see "Respond to a Message" on page 208.

In this *Guided Tour*, you'll learn how to retrieve your mail using Eudora Light, how to configure Eudora Light to check your mail automatically, and how to print your mail. If you use another e-mail program, the steps may vary.

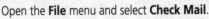

Begin Guided Tour   Retrieve Mail

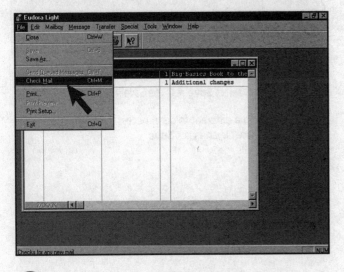

3 Type your password and click **OK**. Eudora connects to your Internet service provider's computer and searches your mailbox for new mail. If you have new messages, it copies them to your system.

1 Connect to the Internet in your usual manner and start your e-mail program, such as Eudora Light.

2 Open the **File** menu and select **Check Mail**.

4 If you have new mail, the New Mail dialog box appears, telling you so. Click **OK**, and Eudora places your new e-mail in the In box. If you don't have any e-mail, you'll get a message telling you so. Click **OK.**

(continues)

Guided Tour Retrieve Mail

(continued)

Once you get your e-mail, disconnect from the Internet so you don't have to pay connect charges while you view each message.

6 If you want to print your e-mail message, click the **Print** toolbar button or open the **File** menu and select **Print**.

5 To view the contents of a particular message, double-click the message in the In box.

7 To save the contents of the message in a file, open the **File** menu and select **Save As**. The Save As dialog box appears.

8 Change to a different folder if necessary. Then type a name for the new file and click **Save**.

Begin Guided Tour   Check Your Mail Automatically

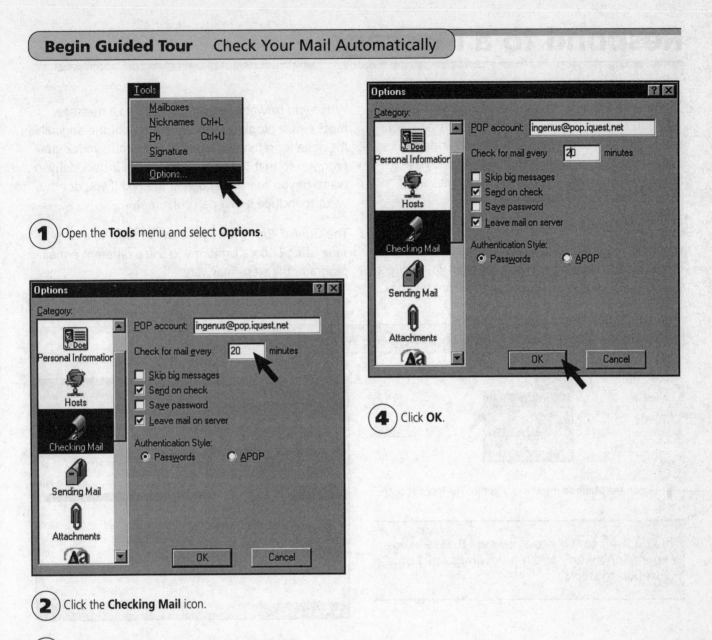

1 Open the **Tools** menu and select **Options**.

2 Click the **Checking Mail** icon.

3 Enter a time interval in the **Check for mail every __ minutes** blank.

4 Click **OK**.

Respond to a Message

You can reply to, forward, or redirect any message you receive. When you reply to a message, your e-mail program automatically fills in the address of the originator in your new message. All you have to do is type your reply and then send the message.

When you forward a message, your e-mail program sends a copy of the original message to the person you indicate. Redirecting a message is similar to forwarding a message, except that when you redirect, the program adds your address to the From text box.

When you forward, redirect, or reply to a message, most e-mail programs include the text of the original message for reference. You can customize your e-mail program so that the original text is not included if you want, or you can simply delete the text if you don't want to include it in a particular reply.

The *Guided Tour* shows you how to reply to a message using Eudora Light. If you use a different e-mail program, the steps may vary.

Begin Guided Tour   Reply to a Message with Eudora Light

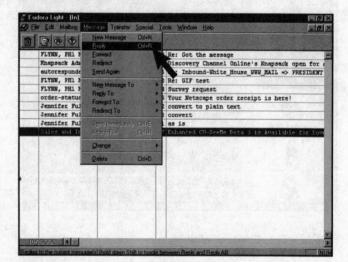

 1 Open the **Mailbox** menu and select **In**. The Inbox appears.

If you want to reply to a message that's already open, don't worry about following steps 1 or 2. Just skip to step 3.

 2 Select the message to which you want to reply.

 3 Open the **Message** menu and select **Reply**, or just click the **Reply** button. (If you want to forward or redirect the message instead, select the appropriate command.)

Guided Tour   Reply to a Message with Eudora Light

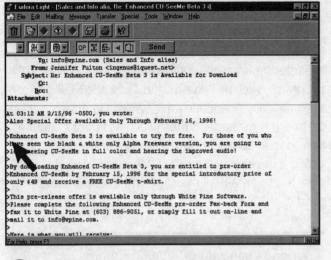

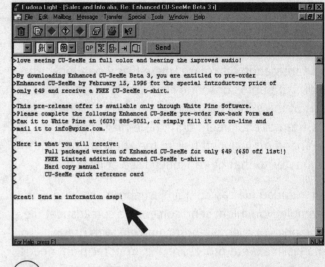

4 Your e-mail program updates the header information, filling in the To:, From:, and Subject: lines. In the message area, the text from the original message appears. Each line of the original message is marked with an arrow (>).

If you want to delete any of these original lines, just select them and press **Delete**. In addition, you can type your reply in between lines of the original message; simply place the cursor at the end of an original line and press **Enter** to create a blank line on which you can type.

5 Type your message under the copy of the original message.

6 Save and send your message as usual.

Send Files As Messages over the Internet

You can send files over the Internet as e-mail messages. Of course, these files won't look like charts or photos or sound like sounds when they're part of the e-mail message. But if the recipient set up his Internet equipment right, his e-mail application can hand off included files to the applications on his computer so that he can indeed see or hear them.

An included file can contain just about anything. For example, you might send someone a spreadsheet file, a graphic, or even a report complete with graphic images in a word processing file. Your recipient needs some way of reading the contents of the file. For example, if you send a Lotus 1-2-3 spreadsheet file as an e-mail message, your recipient must have a copy of Lotus 1-2-3 (or some other program that can read 1-2-3 files) in order to read the information in the file.

Normally, messages sent over the Internet contain text only, with none of the coding necessary to display fancy fonts, text enhancements (such as bold), or graphics. Therefore, before you can send a file over the Internet, it has to be converted into these basic text codes (7-bit characters). There are several ways to convert files for transmittal over the Internet, each of which has its pros and cons.

One process that's included in most e-mail programs is called MIME (Multipurpose Internet Mail Extension). MIME places a header in the e-mail message just before the file's data to show that what follows is not text. The MIME header also indicates the file type (such as a bitmap graphic or a word processing document). The recipient's e-mail recognizes the MIME header and sends the data after the header to the indicated program for translation. Unfortunately, if the recipient of your file uses an online service to access the Internet, his e-mail program may not make sense of MIME coding. For example, WinCIM (the e-mail program used on CompuServe) does not recognize MIME information; if you send a MIME-encoded file to a CompuServe address, the recipient cannot use it.

The most dependable process for sending files over the Internet is called *uuencoding*. Some e-mail programs, such as Pegasus and Netscape Mail, automatically uuencode a file when you attach it to an Internet message. Others, such as Eudora, require you to uuencode the file manually using a program called a uuencoder. Once the file is encoded, you can attach it to an e-mail message within Eudora and send it.

A good uuencoder is WinCode, which you can download from the Stroud's site (http://www.cwsapps.com). Follow the *Guided Tour* in the section "Find and Download an E-Mail Program" (page 194) to locate and download a uuencoder.

Another common encoding scheme is BinHex, which began as an encoding format for Macintosh computers and later spread to PCs. The theory behind BinHex and uuencoding is much the same, but the methods and results are somewhat different. Because uuencoding is the method of choice among UNIX users, and UNIX forms the backbone of much of the Internet, BinHex is a less common encoding scheme. If you're sending your file to someone who uses a PC, BinHex is not a good choice.

In the *Guided Tour*, you'll learn how to use Eudora to send files. Because Eudora does not automatically uuencode files, you'll learn how to use WinCode to uuencode your file first. You can then attach the uuencoded file to an e-mail message. You'll also learn how to attach a file to an e-mail message using an e-mail program such as Pegasus that automatically uuencodes the file for you. (To learn how to use Netscape Mail to send a file, see "Send and Receive E-Mail with Your Web Browser" on page 217.)

Begin Guided Tour Send a File with Eudora

1 Start WinCode (or whatever uuencoder you downloaded and installed).

2 Click the **File Encode** button.

3 Select the file you want to encode and click **OK**. The program uuencodes your file and places it in the WinCode directory.

4 Click **OK**.

5 Click the **Close** button to close your uuencoder program.

6 Start Eudora Light. Then open the **Message** menu and select **New Message**.

(continues)

Guided Tour Send a File with Eudora

(continued)

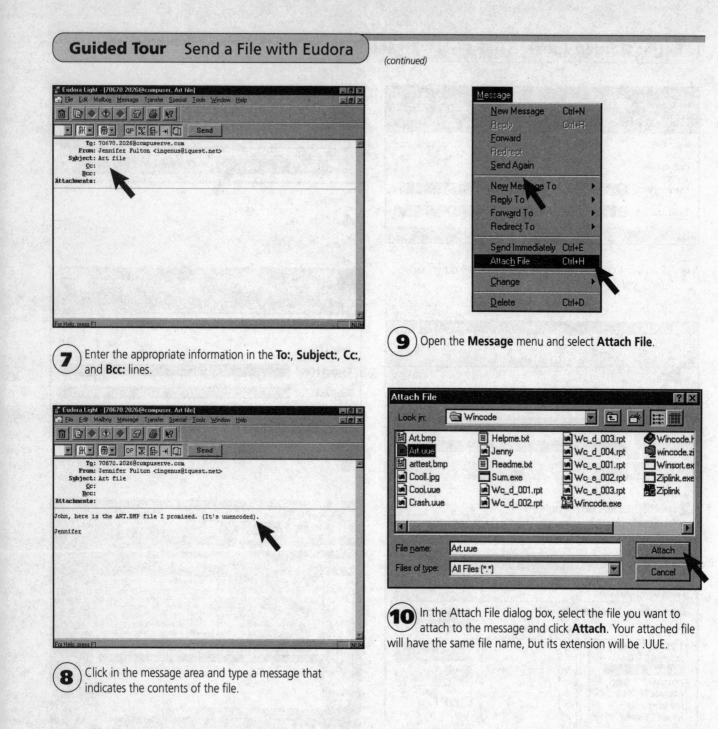

7 Enter the appropriate information in the **To:**, **Subject:**, **Cc:**, and **Bcc:** lines.

8 Click in the message area and type a message that indicates the contents of the file.

9 Open the **Message** menu and select **Attach File**.

10 In the Attach File dialog box, select the file you want to attach to the message and click **Attach**. Your attached file will have the same file name, but its extension will be .UUE.

Guided Tour   Send a File with Eudora

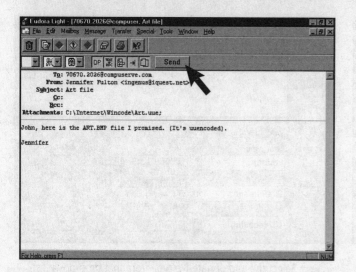

11 Click the **Send** button to send the message.

Begin Guided Tour   Send a File with Pegasus

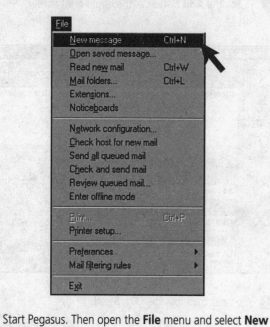

1 Start Pegasus. Then open the **File** menu and select **New message**.

2 Enter the appropriate information in the **To:**, **Subj:**, and **Cc:** text boxes.

(continues)

Guided Tour Send a File with Pegasus

(continued)

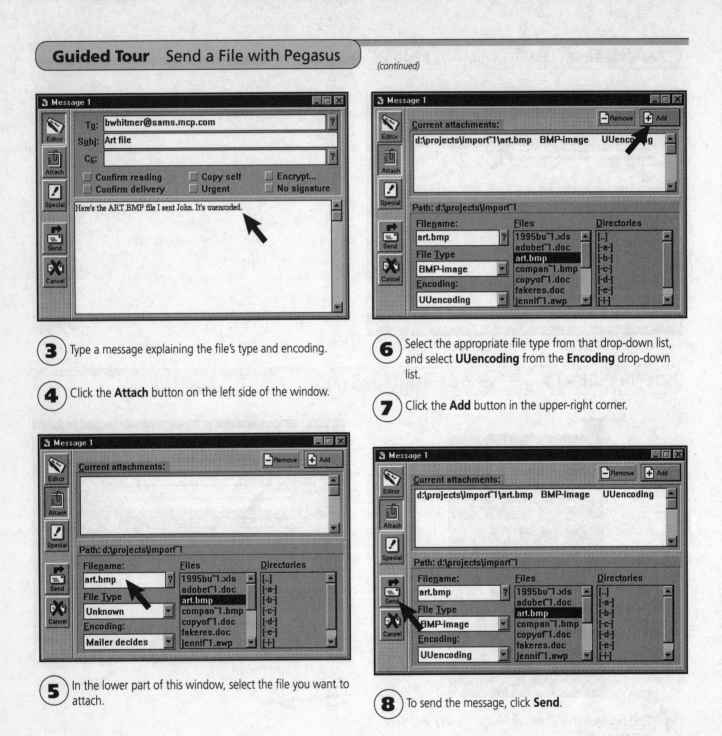

3 Type a message explaining the file's type and encoding.

4 Click the **Attach** button on the left side of the window.

5 In the lower part of this window, select the file you want to attach.

6 Select the appropriate file type from that drop-down list, and select **UUencoding** from the **Encoding** drop-down list.

7 Click the **Add** button in the upper-right corner.

8 To send the message, click **Send**.

Retrieve a File Sent As a Message over the Internet

If you receive a message with a uuencoded file, you have to use WinCode or a similar program to extract the file and decode it. Once the file is extracted, it is ready to use. Of course, you must have the program needed to open the file. For example, if someone sends you an Excel spreadsheet file, you'll need a copy of Excel (or a program that can read Excel files) in order to open and use the spreadsheet.

If someone sends you a file using MIME or BinHex encoding, you'll need to retrieve that file using an e-mail program that supports MIME or BinHex. Fortunately, all Internet e-mail programs do.

Because uuencoding is the most common method of encoding, the *Guided Tour* teaches you how to use WinCode to extract a uuencoded file from a message.

Begin Guided Tour Decode a File with WinCode

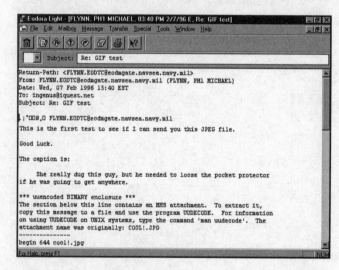

 In your e-mail program, open the message that contains the uuencoded file by double-clicking it.

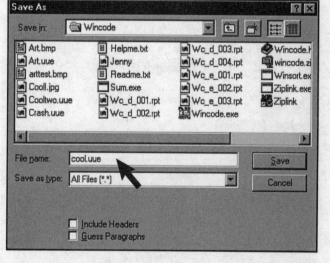

 Enter a name for the file in the **File name** text box. Make sure that you use the extension .UUE.

 Click **Save**.

(continues)

 Open the **File** menu and select **Save As**. The Save As dialog box appears.

Guided Tour Decode a File with WinCode

(continued)

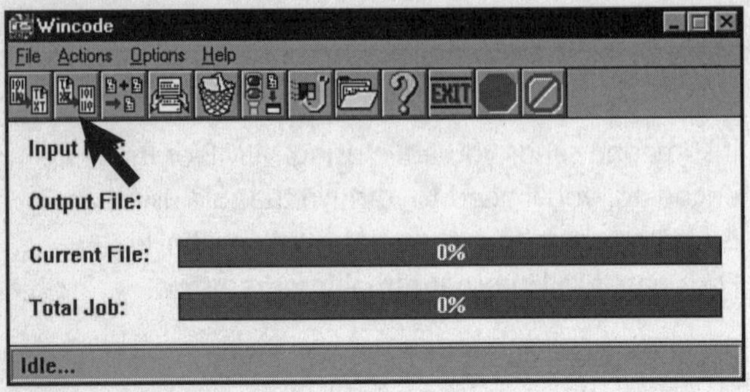

Wincode

File Actions Options Help

Input

Output File:

Current File: 0%

Total Job: 0%

Idle...

File to Decode

Filename: cool.uue

Directory: c:\internet\wincode

Files:
art.uue
cool.uue
crash.uue

Directories:
[..]
[-a-]
[-b-]
[-c-]
[-d-]
[-e-]
[-i-]
[-j-]

OK

Cancel

All Files

Clipboard >>

□ UNZIP After

Options...

5 Start your uuencoder program.

6 Click the **Decode** button.

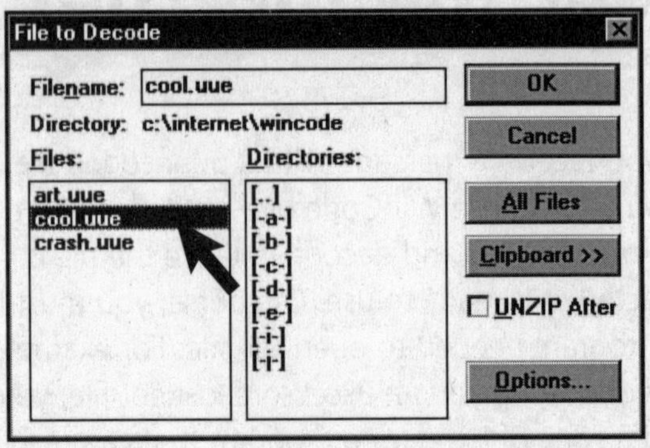

7 In the File to Decode dialog box, select the file to decode and click **OK**. The program decodes your file, changes its file name back to the original file name, and saves it to the WinCode directory. In the example, the cool.uue file was originally a jpeg file, so it is decoded and renamed cool.jpg (its original name).

Send and Receive E-Mail with Your Web Browser

With some Web browsers, such as Netscape Navigator, you don't need a separate e-mail program because they come with one built-in. The e-mail programs built into most Web browsers are not as fully functional as the ones you can get separately. But because you'll probably use your Web browser most of the time you're connected to the Internet, it might be more convenient to use its mail program to send and retrieve e-mail than to start up a separate program.

Before you can use your Web browser's e-mail program, you have to configure it. The *Guided Tour* shows you how to set up the e-mail program in Netscape Navigator. Setting up any other Web browser's program will be much the same.

> Flip back to "Install Your E-Mail Program" on page 197 if you need a refresher on the basic information you have to fill in when configuring an e-mail program.

Begin Guided Tour — Configure Netscape Navigator for E-Mail

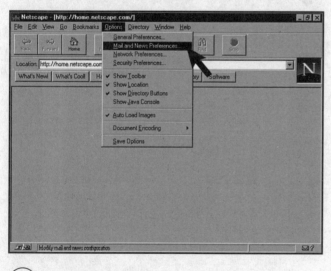

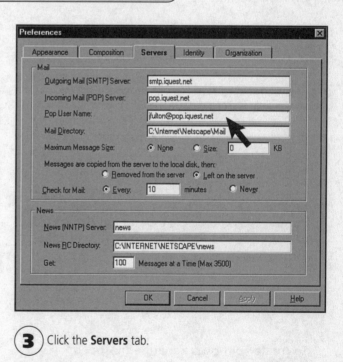

1 Start Netscape Navigator. (You do not need to be connected to the Internet.)

2 Open the **Options** menu and select **Mail and News Preferences**.

3 Click the **Servers** tab.

4 Enter the address of your incoming and outgoing mail servers.

5 In the **Pop User Name** text box, enter your address on the POP server.

(continues)

Guided Tour   Configure Netscape Navigator for E-Mail   *(continued)*

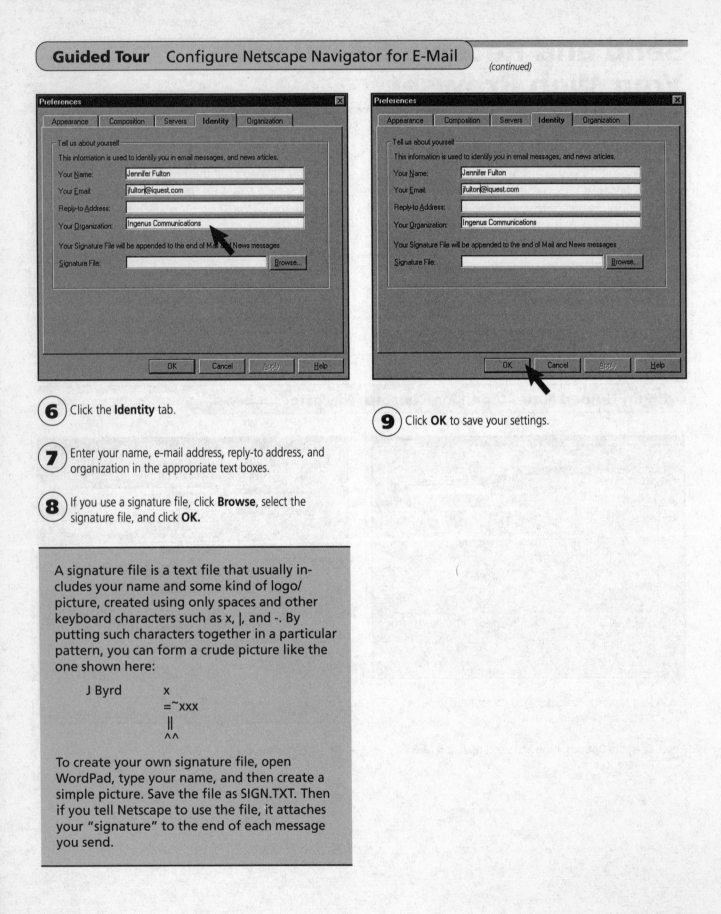

6 Click the **Identity** tab.

7 Enter your name, e-mail address, reply-to address, and organization in the appropriate text boxes.

8 If you use a signature file, click **Browse**, select the signature file, and click **OK.**

A signature file is a text file that usually includes your name and some kind of logo/picture, created using only spaces and other keyboard characters such as x, |, and -. By putting such characters together in a particular pattern, you can form a crude picture like the one shown here:

```
J Byrd        x
              =~xxx
              ||
              ^^
```

To create your own signature file, open WordPad, type your name, and then create a simple picture. Save the file as SIGN.TXT. Then if you tell Netscape to use the file, it attaches your "signature" to the end of each message you send.

9 Click **OK** to save your settings.

Begin Guided Tour Send E-Mail

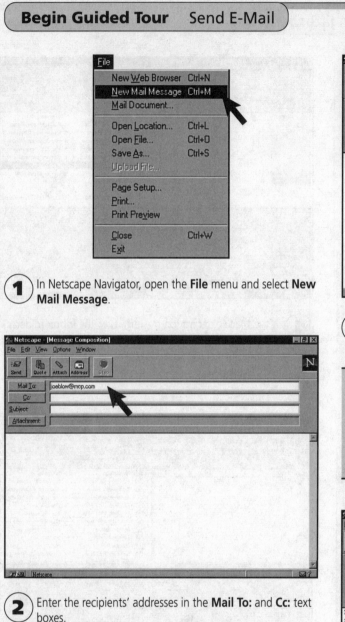

1 In Netscape Navigator, open the **File** menu and select **New Mail Message**.

2 Enter the recipients' addresses in the **Mail To:** and **Cc:** text boxes.

Netscape Navigator enables you to save addresses of the people from whom you receive mail so you can reuse them if you want. To send a message to someone whose address you've saved, click the **Address** button and select the address to which to send your message.

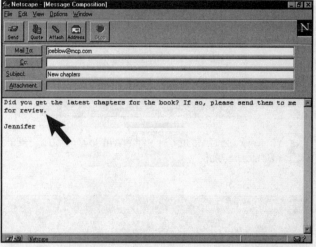

3 Enter a subject in the **Subject:** text box, and then type your message.

You can attach a file to send with your message, and Netscape Mail will uuencode it automatically. To attach a file, click the **Attachment** button, click **Attach File**, select your file, and click **Open**. Select **As Is** and click **OK**.

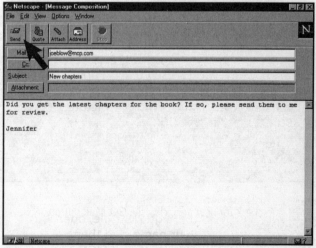

4 Click the **Send** button to send your message.

Begin Guided Tour   Receive E-Mail

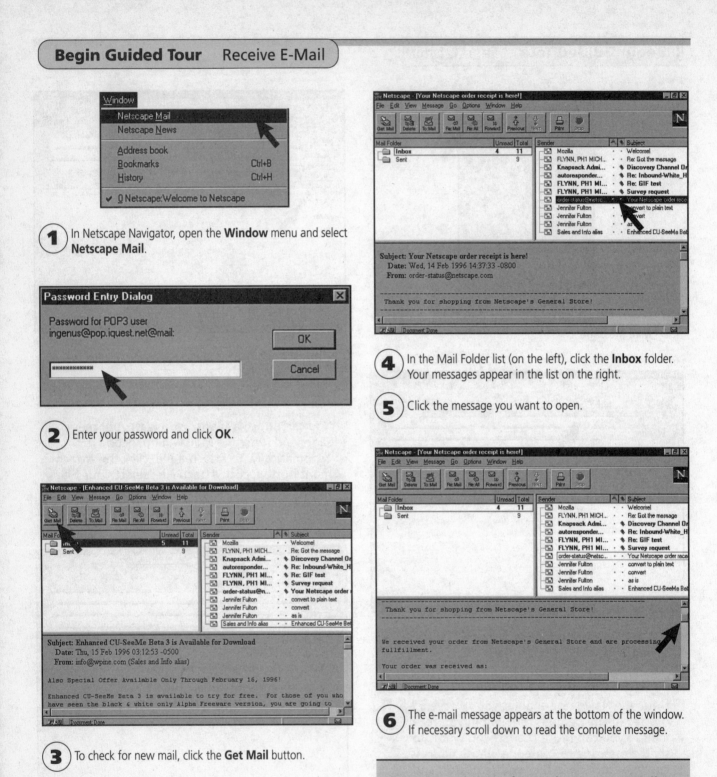

1 In Netscape Navigator, open the **Window** menu and select **Netscape Mail**.

2 Enter your password and click **OK**.

3 To check for new mail, click the **Get Mail** button.

4 In the Mail Folder list (on the left), click the **Inbox** folder. Your messages appear in the list on the right.

5 Click the message you want to open.

6 The e-mail message appears at the bottom of the window. If necessary scroll down to read the complete message.

You can reply to or forward a Netscape Mail message just as you would any other e-mail. Click the Reply, Reply All, or Forward button, and then type your message.

Read and Post Messages in Newsgroups

When you walk into a library or grocery store, you invariably see a bulletin board plastered with brochures, announcements, and want ads. When you wander around the Internet, you find newsgroups, electronic bulletin boards where users with a particular hobby or interest post questions, answers, and information that can help others.

The Internet offers thousands of newsgroups, each of which focuses on a specific interest. You can find a newsgroup for any topic imaginable—from using a PC to tattooing your body. With a special program called a newsreader, you can open any of these newsgroups and read messages that other people have posted, or you can post your own messages. For example, if you have a tax question, you can post your question in a tax newsgroup and then check every day to see if anyone has answered it (chances are, somebody will try to help).

In this section, you'll learn how to find and download a newsreader from the Internet and use it to read and post messages in newsgroups.

What You Will Find in This Section

Find and Install a Newsreader

To access newsgroups, you need a *newsreader*, a program that connects to a news server and enables you to read and post messages. You can get a freeware (no charge) or shareware (use now, pay later) version of the program you need off the Internet from an FTP server.

For details on how to download (*copy*) files from the Internet, see "Find and Copy Files from the Internet" on page 263. The following table provides a list of FTP sites where you can find the WinVN newsreader featured in this section. Remember that file names and directories can change at any time; when you get to the FTP site, look for a file name that is similar to one of the names in the table.

Follow the *Guided Tour* to download the newsreader and install it on your computer. Remember, if you ftp from your Web browser, be sure to add **ftp://** before the FTP server's URL. For example, you would enter **ftp://nisc.jvnc.net** to access the first server listed in this table.

> You can search for a newsreader using any of the search tools described in "Search for Information on the Web" (page 180). For example, go to Yahoo's home page and search for **newsreader**.

Unzip and Install the Newsreader

The newsreader file you'll download is in a compressed format. All the files that make up the newsreader program are packed into one file. You must unpack (unzip) the file you download to decompress the files and make them useable.

A special program called WinZip can decompress the file for you. You may have downloaded WinZip earlier and used it to decompress helper applications you downloaded. If you haven't downloaded WinZip yet, see "Copy Helper Applications from the Internet" on page 162. This section also shows how to use WinZip to unzip files.

Where to Find WinVN

FTP Server	Directory	File Name
nisc.jvnc.net	/pub/MSDOS/winsock	winvn926.zip
ftp.oleane.net	/pub/.disks/.3/cica/winsock	winvn926.zip
knot.queensu.ca	/pub/win3/winsock	winvn926.zip
ftp.pppl.gov	/pub/pc/win3/newswatch/winvn	winvn926.zip
ftp.std.com	/customers3/src/pc/winsock	winvn926.zip
ftp.cae.wisc.edu	/pub/todds-area	winvn.zip
scss3.cl.msu.edu	/msu	winvn.zip
ftp.iij.ad.jp	/pub/standards/winsock	winvn.zip

Specify a News Server

Before you can use a newsreader to read and post newsgroup messages, you must specify the news server you want to use. You will usually use your service provider's news server. The first time you run WinVN, it displays a dialog box, asking you for your name, e-mail address, and for the news server URL. You must enter this information to connect to the news server.

If your service provider did not give you the URL for its news server, try adding **news** to the beginning of the service provider's URL. For example, if your service provider's URL is iquest.com, try entering **news.iquest.com** as the news server's URL.

Begin Guided Tour   Download the WinVN Newsreader

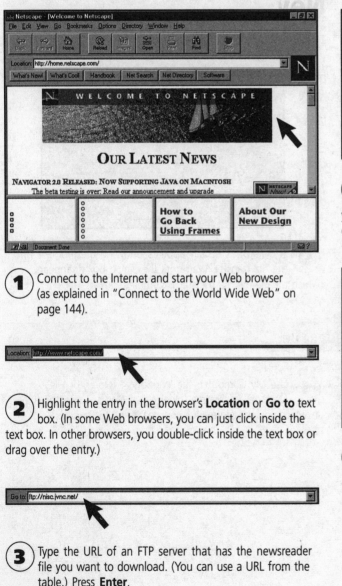

1 Connect to the Internet and start your Web browser (as explained in "Connect to the World Wide Web" on page 144).

2 Highlight the entry in the browser's **Location** or **Go to** text box. (In some Web browsers, you can just click inside the text box. In other browsers, you double-click inside the text box or drag over the entry.)

3 Type the URL of an FTP server that has the newsreader file you want to download. (You can use a URL from the table.) Press **Enter**.

.forward		Wed Aug 30 04:39:00 1995	
.notar		Wed Sep 15 00:00:00 1993	
.rhosts		Wed Aug 30 04:39:00 1995	
bin/		Wed Nov 30 00:00:00 1994	Directory
dev/		Wed Apr 06 00:00:00 1994	Directory
etc/		Tue Jun 14 00:00:00 1994	Directory
ftp		Mon Nov 13 16:59:00 1995	Symbolic link
priv/		Sat Dec 30 05:21:00 1995	Directory
pub/		Wed Jan 03 08:00:00 1996	Directory
rfc		Mon Nov 13 16:59:00 1995	Symbolic link
services		Mon Nov 13 16:59:00 1995	Symbolic link
usr/		Wed Apr 06 00:00:00 1994	Directory

4 Your Web browser connects to the FTP server and displays a list of directories. Click the link for the directory you want to go to. Continue to click links until you reach the directory that contains the winvn file.

wintelb3.zip	54 Kb	Wed Dec 14 00:00:00 1994	Zip Compressed
winter07.zip	319 Kb	Wed Dec 14 00:00:00 1994	Zip Compressed
winvn926.zip	172 Kb	Wed Dec 14 00:00:00 1994	Zip Compressed
winweb.zip	414 Kb	Wed Dec 14 00:00:00 1994	Zip Compressed
wlprs40b.zip	205 Kb	Wed Dec 14 00:00:00 1994	Zip Compressed
wmos20a7.zip	281 Kb	Wed Dec 14 00:00:00 1994	Zip Compressed
wnvndc92.zip	246 Kb	Wed Dec 14 00:00:00 1994	Zip Compressed
ws_ftp.zip	110 Kb	Wed Dec 14 00:00:00 1994	Zip Compressed
ws_ftp.zip.1	93 Kb	Tue Jan 10 00:00:00 1995	
ws_ping.zip	59 Kb	Wed Dec 14 00:00:00 1994	Zip Compressed
ws_watch.zip	26 Kb	Wed Dec 14 00:00:00 1994	Zip Compressed
wsarch06.zip	166 Kb	Wed Dec 14 00:00:00 1994	Zip Compressed
wsatest.zip	81 Kb	Wed Dec 14 00:00:00 1994	Zip Compressed
wschesb1.zip	159 Kb	Wed Dec 14 00:00:00 1994	Zip Compressed

5 Eventually, you change to the directory that contains the newsreader file you need. If you have Netscape Navigator, click the link to download the file. (In other Web browsers, you may have to hold down the **Shift** key while clicking.)

(continues)

Guided Tour Download the WinVN Newsreader

(continued)

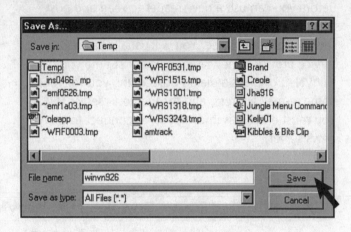

wintelb3.zip	54 Kb	Wed Dec 14 00:00:00 1994 Zip Compressed
winter07.zip	319 Kb	Wed Dec 14 00:00:00 1994 Zip Compressed
winvn926.zip	172 Kb	Wed Dec 14 00:00:00 1994 Zip Compressed

Back
Forward

Open this (winvn926.zip)
Add Bookmark for this Link
New Window with this Link
Save this Link as...
Copy this Link Location

Internet Shortcut

ws_watch.zip 26 Kb Wed Dec 14 00:00:00 1994 Zip Compressed
wsarch06.zip 166 Kb Wed Dec 14 00:00:00 1994 Zip Compressed
wsatest.zip 81 Kb Wed Dec 14 00:00:00 1994 Zip Compressed
wschesb1.zip 159 Kb Wed Dec 14 00:00:00 1994 Zip Compressed

6 In some Web browsers, you can right-click on the link and choose the **Save this Link as...** option.

8 Click the **OK** or **Save** button.

7 However you choose to download the file, a dialog box appears, asking you to pick the drive and folder in which you want the file saved. Choose the **Temp** folder on drive **C**.

9 A dialog box usually appears, showing the progress of the file transfer. Wait until the dialog box disappears, which means the file transfer is complete.

Begin Guided Tour Unzip the Newsreader File

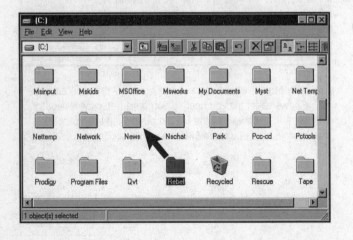

1 Use My Computer, the Windows Explorer, or File Manager to create a folder called **News**. This is the folder in which you will store your newsreader program files.

Guided Tour Unzip the Newsreader File

2 Run WinZip as explained in "Install a Helper Application" on page 167.

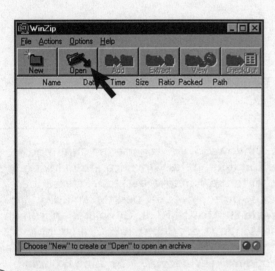

3 The WinZip window appears. To open the archive (your winvn296.zip or winvn.zip file), click the **Open** button in the toolbar.

4 In the dialog box that appears, select the zipped winvn file. (If you followed the download instructions, this file should be in the TEMP folder.) Click the **Open** or **OK** button to proceed.

5 WinZip displays the names of all the files in the selected ZIP file. Click the **Extract** button in the toolbar.

6 The Extract dialog box appears. Select the **News** folder to extract the files to it.

7 Select the **All Files** option, if necessary, so WinZip will extract all the files in the zipped file.

(continues)

Guided Tour   Unzip the Newsreader File

(continued)

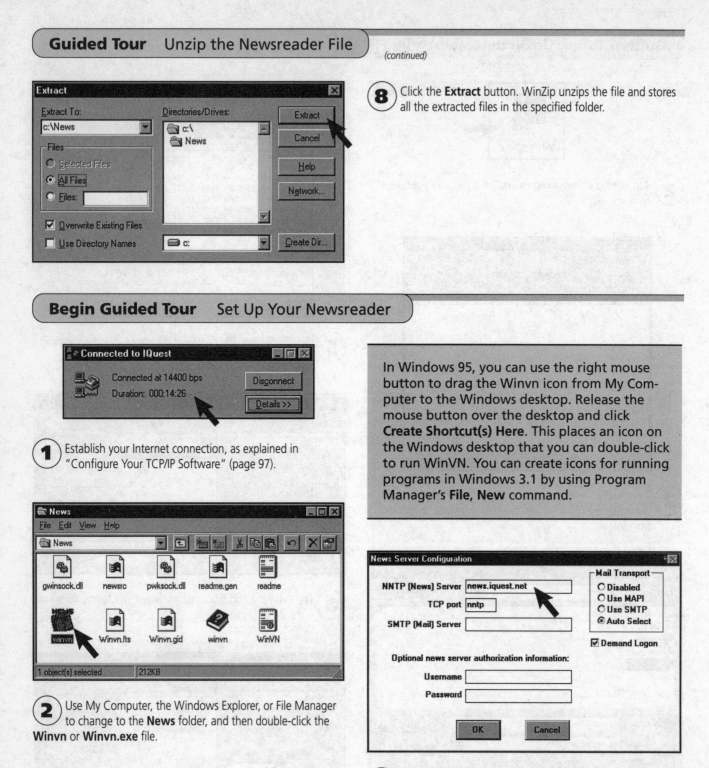

8 Click the **Extract** button. WinZip unzips the file and stores all the extracted files in the specified folder.

Begin Guided Tour   Set Up Your Newsreader

1 Establish your Internet connection, as explained in "Configure Your TCP/IP Software" (page 97).

In Windows 95, you can use the right mouse button to drag the Winvn icon from My Computer to the Windows desktop. Release the mouse button over the desktop and click **Create Shortcut(s) Here**. This places an icon on the Windows desktop that you can double-click to run WinVN. You can create icons for running programs in Windows 3.1 by using Program Manager's **File, New** command.

2 Use My Computer, the Windows Explorer, or File Manager to change to the **News** folder, and then double-click the **Winvn** or **Winvn.exe** file.

3 The first time you run WinVN, it displays the News Server Configuration dialog box, asking you to specify the URL of the news server you will connect to. Type the URL specified by your service provider in the **NNTP (News) Server** text box.

Guided Tour   Set Up Your Newsreader

4 The TCP port entry is **nntp** for most news servers. For some servers, you might have to enter a port number—usually 119. Unless your service provider specified otherwise, leave this entry alone.

6 Most news servers do not require you to enter a username or password to access the server. If your news server requires this login information, type it in the appropriate text boxes and click **OK**.

5 WinVN doubles as an e-mail program. If you want to use WinVN as your e-mail program, type your e-mail server's URL in the **SMTP (Mail) Server** text box. To learn more about e-mail, see "Send and Receive Electronic Mail" on page 193.

7 WinVN displays another dialog box that asks for information about you. Type your name in the **Your name** text box.

8 Type your e-mail address in the **Your email address** text box. See "Send an E-Mail Message" on page 202 if you need help.

(continues)

Guided Tour Set Up Your Newsreader

(continued)

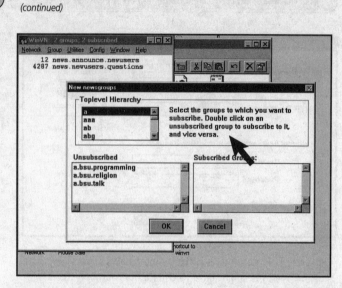

9 (Optional) If you want to supply a company name, type it in the **Organization name** text box.

10 Click **OK**.

11 WinVN connects to your news server and retrieves a list of all the newsgroups carried by the server (this may take several minutes). Eventually, a dialog box appears, asking you to specify which newsgroups you want to subscribe to. See "Subscribe to Newsgroups" on page 232.

Set Up Your Web Browser to Read Newsgroups

Some Web browsers double as newsreaders. For example, Netscape Navigator 2.0 has a built-in newsreader called Netscape News that enables you to both read and post messages. If you click a link for a newsgroup or enter its URL in the Location text box, Navigator runs the newsreader and displays a list of messages. You can then click a message's description to read it.

Although other Web browsers function as newsreaders, many don't offer all the newsreader features that Netscape Navigator does. With some Web browsers, for example, you can read the mes-

sages in a newsgroup, but you can't respond to them or post your own messages.

Before you can use your Web browser as a newsreader, you must tell the Web browser which news server to use. In most Web browsers, you do this by selecting the Options or Preferences command and then typing the URL for the newsreader. The *Guided Tour* shows you how to enter a newsgroup URL in Netscape Navigator and how to use Netscape News to read newsgroup messages. The steps may differ slightly if you use a different browser.

Begin Guided Tour   Use Your Web Browser as a Newsreader

1 Establish your Internet connection and start your Web browser. This figure shows Netscape Navigator in action.

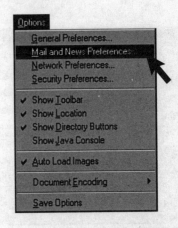

2 Enter the command that allows you to specify a news server. In Navigator, you open the **Options** menu and select **Mail and News Preferences**.

(continues)

Guided Tour Use Your Web Browser as a Newsreader

(continued)

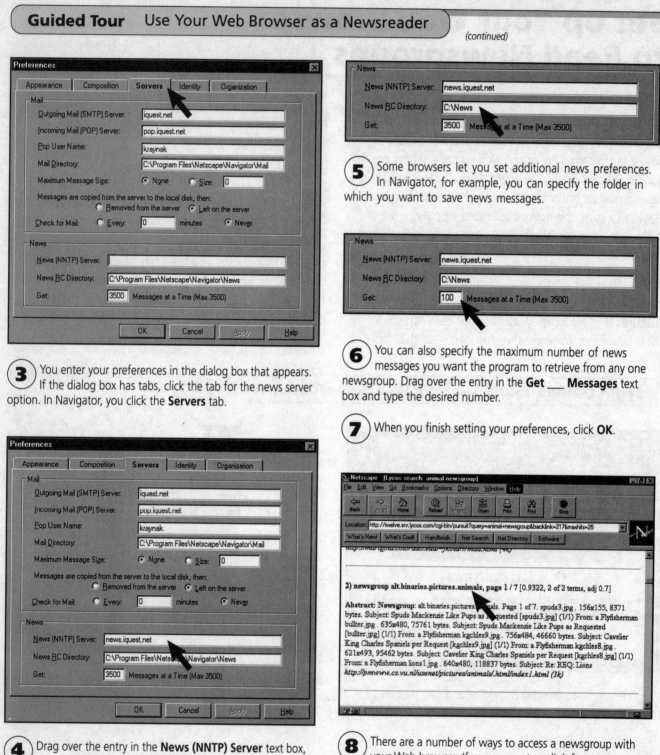

3 You enter your preferences in the dialog box that appears. If the dialog box has tabs, click the tab for the news server option. In Navigator, you click the **Servers** tab.

4 Drag over the entry in the **News (NNTP) Server** text box, and then type the URL of the news server you want to use. (NNTP stands for Network News Transfer Protocol.)

5 Some browsers let you set additional news preferences. In Navigator, for example, you can specify the folder in which you want to save news messages.

6 You can also specify the maximum number of news messages you want the program to retrieve from any one newsgroup. Drag over the entry in the **Get ___ Messages** text box and type the desired number.

7 When you finish setting your preferences, click **OK**.

8 There are a number of ways to access a newsgroup with your Web browser. If you encounter a link for a newsgroup, click the link.

Guided Tour Use Your Web Browser as a Newsreader

Go to: news:rec.skydiving

9 You can also view a list of messages in a specific newsgroup by entering the newsgroup's URL in the Location, Go to, or URL text box. As you can see here, a newsgroup URL starts with **news:**. Note that it does not contain the forward slashes you find in most URLs.

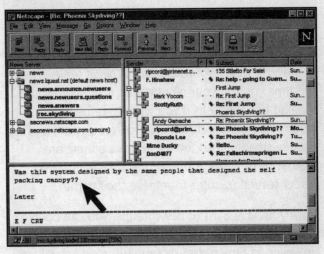

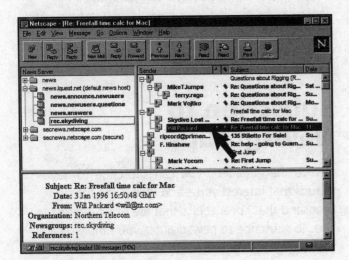

11 From here, you can read newsgroup messages, reply to them, or post your own messages, all of which are explained later in this section.

10 If you use Netscape Navigator to go to a newsgroup, Navigator runs its newsreader, Netscape News, and displays a list of messages in the selected newsgroup.

Retrieve a List of Newsgroups

Before you can become involved in a newsgroup, you need to use your newsreader to retrieve a list of available newsgroups from your news server. The first time you run your newsreader, it should display a dialog box that asks if you want to retrieve newsgroups. You simply click the OK or Yes button, and the newsreader does the rest. Because there are thousands of newsgroups, it may take your newsreader several minutes to retrieve their names.

Once you have a list of newsgroups, you can open a newsgroup and start reading and posting messages. However, as time passes, your newsgroup list will become dated. New newsgroups are created daily, and old newsgroups in which interest has faded are destroyed just as quickly. To keep your newsgroup list current, you must refresh your list as shown in the *Guided Tour*.

Understand Newsgroup Names

In order to know which newsgroups might interest you, you must know how to read a newsgroup name (or URL). Unlike most URLs, you read newsgroup URLs from left to right. For example, *alt.comedy.british* stands for "alternative comedy of the British persuasion."

The first part of the address indicates the newsgroup's overall subject area: **comp** stands for computer, **news** is for general information about newsgroups, **rec** is for recreation (hobbies, sports), **sci** stands for science, **soc** is for social topics, **talk** is for controversial debates, **misc** is for general topics such as jobs and selling, and **alt** is for topics that are somewhat off-beat.

The second part of the address indicates, more specifically, what the newsgroup offers. For example, comp.ai is about computers (comp), but specifically covers artificial intelligence (ai). If the address has a third part, it focuses even further. For example, comp.ai.philosophy discusses how artificial intelligence can be applied to philosophical questions. And, of course, rec.arts.bodyart discusses the art of tattoos and other body decorations.

Subscribe to Newsgroups

In most newsreaders, you can subscribe to newsgroups that interest you—and ignore the fifteen thousand that cover topics that are of no interest to you. To subscribe to newsgroups, you simply select the newsgroups you want from a list of all available newsgroups. The names of the newsgroups you've subscribed to then appear at the top of the newsgroup list or in a completely separate area, making them easy to access. However, you can still read and post messages in newsgroups you haven't subscribed to.

WinVN treats all newsgroups the same, whether or not you've subscribed to them, but it places subscribed newsgroups at the top of the newsgroup list. More advanced newsreaders enable you to create a separate folder for each subscribed newsgroup, and still others display only the names of those to which you've subscribed.

Begin Guided Tour   Make a List of Newsgroups

1 Establish your Internet connection and start your newsreader. If you installed WinVN earlier in this section, you can run it by double-clicking the **WinVn** icon.

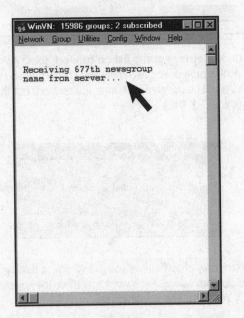

2 When you connect to your news server for the first time, WinVN retrieves the names of all the available newsgroups. A message appears, showing its progress.

3 After retrieving the names of all the newsgroups, WinVN displays a dialog box in which you subscribe to specific newsgroups. In the Toplevel Hierarchy list, click a general newsgroup category.

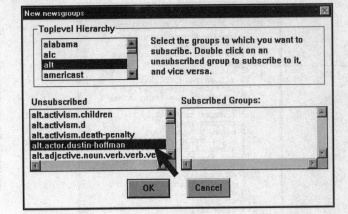

4 A list of the specific newsgroups in the selected category appears in the Unsubscribed list. Double-click the name of the newsgroup you want to subscribe to.

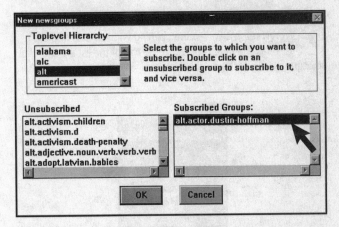

5 The name of the selected newsgroup moves to the Subscribed Groups list. You can remove a newsgroup name from the Subscribed Groups list by double-clicking on it.

6 Repeat steps 3 through 5 to subscribe to additional newsgroups. When you finish, click **OK**.

(continues)

Guided Tour   Make a List of Newsgroups

(continued)

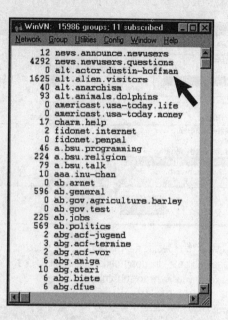

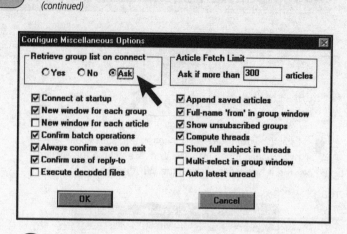

7 WinVN returns you to the opening window and displays a list of all the newsgroups. At the top of the list are the newsgroups to which you subscribed.

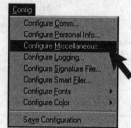

8 Newsgroups are created and deleted daily. To have WinVN refresh your newsgroup list, open the **Config** menu and click **Configure Miscellaneous**.

9 Under **Retrieve group list on connect**, select **Ask** to have WinVN prompt you each time you connect. (If you select Yes, the list will be updated each time you connect, but that takes a long time.) Click **OK**.

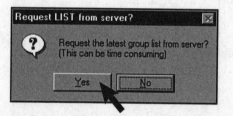

10 From now on, whenever you run WinVN, it displays a dialog box asking if you want to retrieve the newsgroup list. Click **Yes** to retrieve the latest list.

Because the list of newsgroups is long, you might have trouble finding the newsgroup you want. To help, WinVN offers a search feature. Open the **Group** menu and select **Find**. In the dialog box that appears, type a few characters of the newsgroup's name and click **OK**. WinVN displays an arrow next to the first newsgroup it finds that matches what you typed. Press **F3** to find the next newsgroup.

Read and Respond to Newsgroup Messages

Once you have subscribed to a list of newsgroups, you can start opening the newsgroups that interest you. When you open a newsgroup, your newsreader displays a list of recently posted messages. You can then select the messages you want to read (and possibly respond to).

Before you post your own messages in a newsgroup, familiarize yourself with the newsgroup. Hang out and read existing messages so you have a clear idea of the focus and tone of the newsgroup. Reading messages without posting your own messages is known as *lurking*. Newsgroups encourage lurking because it provides you with the knowledge you need to respond intelligently and to avoid repeating what has already been said.

Most messages you encounter in newsgroups are text messages. A newsgroup participant may post an opinion, a question, an answer, or simply an informative tidbit of general interest. However, you may encounter messages that have files attached. For example, in a photography newsgroup, people may trade their favorite photos. These files are usually encoded so they can be transmitted across the Internet. You will have to decode the files to view them. For information on how to decode files, see "Encode and Decode Messages" on page [11tbd].

The *Guided Tour* shows you how to read and respond to text messages in newsgroups using WinVN. The steps may differ slightly if you are using a different newsreader.

Begin Guided Tour   Read and Reply to Newsgroup Messages

1 Establish your Internet connection and run your newsreader. The figure here shows the opening WinVN window, which displays the list of available newsgroups. Double-click the name of a newsgroup.

2 The newsreader retrieves a list of recently posted messages in the newsgroup you selected (this may take several seconds). Note that each message is dated and has a description. To read a message, double-click its description.

(continues)

Guided Tour Read and Reply to Newsgroup Messages

(continued)

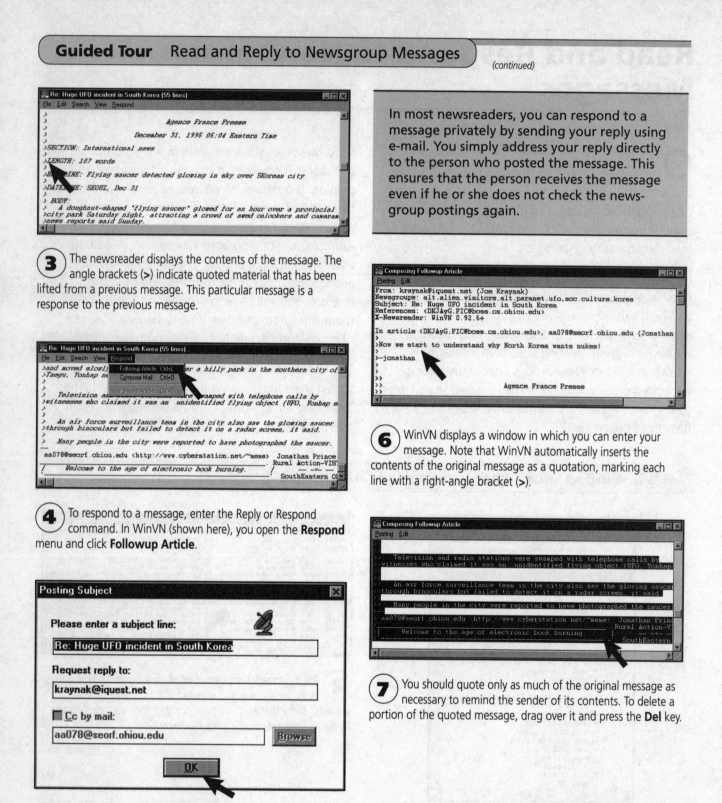

In most newsreaders, you can respond to a message privately by sending your reply using e-mail. You simply address your reply directly to the person who posted the message. This ensures that the person receives the message even if he or she does not check the newsgroup postings again.

3 The newsreader displays the contents of the message. The angle brackets (**>**) indicate quoted material that has been lifted from a previous message. This particular message is a response to the previous message.

4 To respond to a message, enter the Reply or Respond command. In WinVN (shown here), you open the **Respond** menu and click **Followup Article**.

5 The Posting Subject dialog box appears, asking for a message description. Because you are responding to a message, WinVN uses the same description as the message to which you are replying. Click **OK**.

6 WinVN displays a window in which you can enter your message. Note that WinVN automatically inserts the contents of the original message as a quotation, marking each line with a right-angle bracket (**>**).

7 You should quote only as much of the original message as necessary to remind the sender of its contents. To delete a portion of the quoted message, drag over it and press the **Del** key.

Guided Tour   Read and Reply to Newsgroup Messages

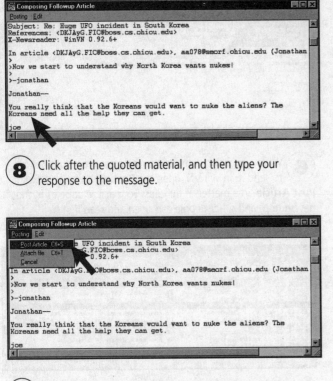

⑧ Click after the quoted material, and then type your response to the message.

⑨ Enter the command to send or post your response. In WinVN, you open the **Posting** menu and select **Post Article**.

⑩ Your newsreader sends your message to the current newsgroup. Don't expect your message to appear immediately; it can take several minutes for your reply to be posted. To see if your message has been posted, refresh the list of messages. In WinVN, open the **Articles** menu and select **Update**.

Many newsreaders enable you to sort messages by date, author, or description. They may also display *threaded* messages, which means they keep the original message and all of its responses together. This makes it easier for you to follow a newsgroup conversation. Look for a Sort menu in your newsreader to see your sorting options.

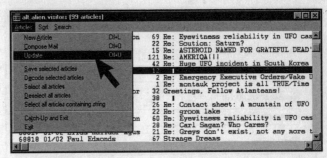

Begin Guided Tour   Post a Message in a Newsgroup

① In addition to responding to other people's postings, you can start your own conversations. To post a message in WinVN, first open the newsgroup in which you want your message to be posted.

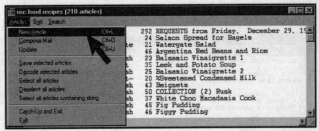

② In your newsreader, enter the command for posting a message. In WinVN, you open the **Articles** menu and select **New Article**.

(continues)

Guided Tour   Post a Message in a Newsgroup

(continued)

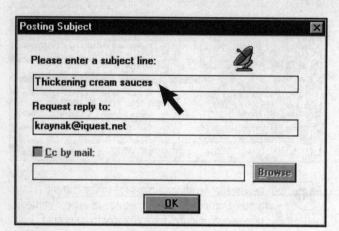

3 A dialog box appears, asking you to type a description for your message. Type a description and click **OK**.

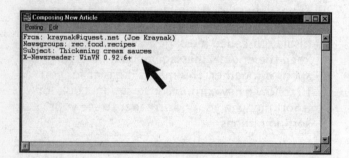

4 Your newsreader displays a window in which you can compose your message. At the top of the window, it adds a header that will be sent with the message. This header includes your e-mail address and the message description you entered.

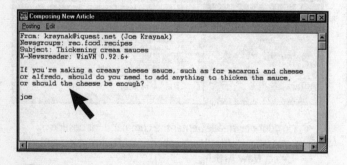

5 Click below the header area and type your message.

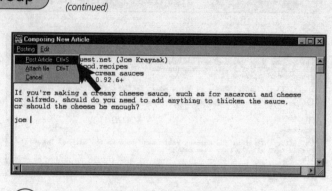

6 When you finish composing your message, you're ready to send it. In WinVN, open the **Posting** menu and click **Post Article**. In a matter of minutes, your article appears in the newsgroup, and other people can open and read it.

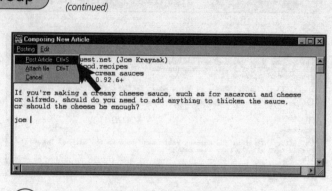

7 Check the newsgroup daily (or more frequently, if necessary) for responses to your message. When you see a response, double-click its description to read the message.

Encode and Decode Messages

Most newsgroups are essentially discussion groups where people send messages back and forth, share trade secrets, and attempt to carry on intelligent dialog. However, in some newsgroups, people swap more than just text. For instance, in a movie newsgroup, people might post photos of their favorite movie stars, or short video clips of films.

Because these types of files are binary (not just text), newsgroups have a special way of transferring them over the Internet. A special coding system called *uuencode* is commonly used to convert binary files into text. If you encounter a binary file in a newsgroup, you must get the encoded file (in its text form) and decode it to return it to its binary form.

Likewise, if you want to include a binary file with your own text message, you must encode the file before sending it. The *Guided Tour* shows you how to encode and decode files using WinVN. A more advanced newsreader may be able to encode and decode files automatically.

You have probably heard about newsgroups that focus on pornography. In these newsgroups, users commonly swap pornographic material, including nude images. If children use your system or if you find this material offensive, steer clear of any newsgroup that has "sex" in the title. In addition, see "Prevent Your Children from Accessing Specific Sites" on page 317.

Begin Guided Tour   Decode Uuencoded Files

1 If you see a message that indicates a binary file is attached, or if you see something like (0/2), (1/2), or (2/2) next to a message, you must decode the file to use it. Long files are posted in sections; (0/2), (1/2), and so on indicate the order of the sections.

2 In WinVN, you must first select all the sections of the file you want to decode. Click each message description that contains a section number for the file.

(continues)

Guided Tour   Decode Uuencoded Files

(continued)

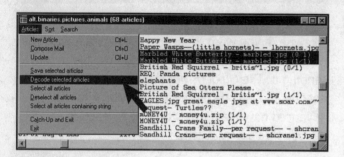

3 Having selected all the sections of an encoded file, you can decode the file. In WinVN, you open the **Articles** menu and select **Decode selected articles**.

6 Most newsreaders cannot "play" or open the binary file you just downloaded. You need to run another application (usually a helper application), and then open the file in that application. This picture shows a helper application called LView displaying a downloaded JPG file. (See "Play Sound and Video Clips with Helper Applications" on page 161 for details.)

4 A dialog box appears, asking where you want the decoded file stored. Type a path to the drive and folder in which you want the file stored. In this example, the file will be stored in the temp folder on drive C. Click **OK**.

5 Your newsreader begins to decode the file, keeping you updated on its progress. Wait until the operation is complete.

7 Netscape News is a sophisticated newsreader that comes with Netscape Navigator. In Netscape News, you simply double-click the first section of the file you want to decode.

Guided Tour   Decode Uuencoded Files

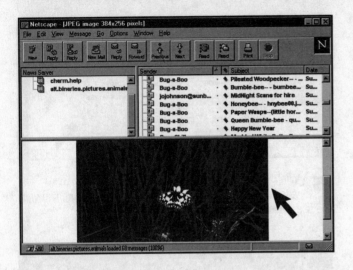

8 Netscape News automatically finds all the sections of the encoded file, decodes the file, and (if the file is one that News can handle) displays the file on-screen.

Begin Guided Tour   Encode and Post a File

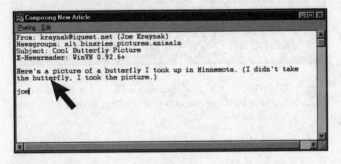

1 If you want to post a binary file—say, a picture of your-self—in a newsgroup, first you compose a message (as explained in "Read and Post Messages in Newsgroups" on page 221.

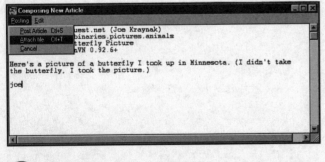

2 After composing your message, you can attach a file to it. Open the **Posting** menu and select **Attach file**.

3 A dialog box appears, prompting you to enter the name of the file you want to send. Select the drive, folder, and name of the file you want to send. Click **OK**.

(continues)

Guided Tour   Encode and Post a File

(continued)

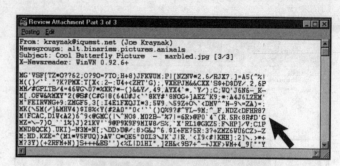

4 Once you've selected a file, you must specify the type of encoding you want to use. Open the **Encoding Type** drop-down list and select **UU** (for uuencode). Click **OK**.

5 WinVN encodes the file and inserts the encoded (text) version at the bottom of your message. This figure shows the text version of a graphic file.

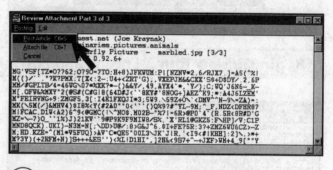

6 You can now send your message with the encoded file. Open the **Posting** menu and select **Post Article**.

HOW TO...

Chat with People on the Internet

One of the most popular pastimes on the Internet is real-time chat. Real-time chat is conversation with other users who are logged on at the same time you are. It's called real-time because the words you type instantly appear on the screens of everyone else who is participating in this activity. There's no waiting for a posted message or e-mail; the conversation happens live.

The live chat system on the Internet is called IRC, which stands for Internet Relay Chat. IRC is actually a program designed to let multiple users communicate, and it is made up of many channels. Chat channels are a lot like electronic "rooms" where people gather to talk about a common subject or just anything at all.

To use IRC, you need an IRC program, and you need to locate an Internet server that uses the IRC network. There are various ways to enter IRC, depending on your type of Internet access. If you're using an account that doesn't have a graphical interface program, you'll probably have to type IRC commands to navigate the chat channels. If you're using a SLIP or PPP account (also called a dial-in direct account), you may be using a graphical browser program such as Netscape to access the Internet, and you will be able to enter IRC commands using icons and toolbar buttons.

What You Will Find in This Section

Find and Install a Chat Program

Are you using a PPP or SLIP account to access the Internet? Unless your service provider has an IRC program you can use to connect to the IRC network, you'll probably have to find one yourself. If you're using a graphical browser program, it may or may not have a chat feature. For example, if you're using Netscape Navigator to explore the Internet, you won't be able to chat unless you use the Netscape Chat program. With Netscape Chat, an IRC chat channel appears as a separate window in which dialog scrolls by. Netscape users will have to install Netscape Chat. If your Netscape program did not come with Netscape Chat, you can find the program and download it to your computer. You'll learn how later in this section.

There are many popular programs for chatting, and all of them are available for download from the Internet. Most of them even have shareware versions. IRC programs vary in terms of how much disk space they take up on your computer and how they look and perform. As usual, some are easier to use than others. Here are a few you might look for:

- **IRCII2-6** Released in 1995, this program works a lot like the UNIX text-based programs—which means it's not very pretty to look at. It uses no-frills windows for channels, and there are no buttons or icons to use; you enter IRC commands manually just like UNIX commands. This is a good program to use if you're already used to UNIX commands, but it's not very easy to configure to your system.

- **IRC4WIN** This shareware program is fairly simple, providing toolbars and icons you use to enter IRC commands.

- **MIRC** A newer but not too flashy IRC program, MIRC lets you enter commands using a menu line option or directly in a conversation window preceded with a slash (UNIX-style).

- **WSIRC** This is the most popular IRC program for Windows users with PPP or SLIP accounts. It's available in both shareware and freeware versions, and it's updated often. WSIRC offers toolbars and icons, and it's very intuitive.

- **WinIRC** A smaller program for Windows users, WinIRC was created by the same programmer who wrote Trumpet Winsock. It's not regularly updated, and it does not contain toolbar buttons to help you enter commands.

- **Netscape Chat** Although it's a separate program, Netscape Chat is used along with Netscape Navigator to access the Internet. It's easy to use, complete with toolbar and icons. (You can learn how to install it on your computer in the *Guided Tour*.)

Many of the newer IRC programs not only let you chat but also support file exchange, let you play sound files, and trade Web pages. By far, the most popular IRC programs you'll come across are those that offer graphical interfaces and these extra features.

Locate an IRC Program

To find any of the IRC programs mentioned, you'll need to ftp to a site that stores them. Because the more popular FTP sites are often busy, you may not be able to sign onto them. However, most offer mirror sites (alternate FTP sites) that contain copies of the same files. Once you ftp to a site, look for directories with names such as irc, clients, or windows to help you find the IRC program you're looking for. Try the following sites for the latest IRC programs:

ftp.netscape.com

ftp2.netscape.com (mirror site)

ftp.winsite.com

uiarchive.cso.uiuc.edu (mirror site)

ftp.eskimo.com

cs-ftp.bu.edu

ftp.undernet.org

European sites:

> ftp.demon.co.uk
>
> ftp.funet.fi
>
> src.doc.ic.ac.uk
>
> ftp.uni-regensburg.de
>
> info.nic.surfnet.nl

For more information about using FTP to download files, turn to "Find and Copy Files from the Internet" (page 263).

For a complete list of Windows 95 or Windows 3.1 IRC programs, check out Stroud's Consummate WinSock App List Web page at http://cwsapps.texas.net/phone.html. Another good Web page source for IRC information is http://www.escape.com/~ward/ircstuff.html.

Once you find an IRC program and copy it to your computer, you can install the program and set it up to access an IRC server. (For more information about locating a chat server, read "Connect to a Chat Server" on page 249.) Since most of this book covers

accessing the Internet with Netscape, the *Guided Tour* will show you how to find and install Netscape Chat.

Find and Copy the Netscape Chat Program

If you're using Netscape to access the Internet, you should install Netscape Chat as your IRC program. You can find the program at ftp.netscape.com. You learned a little about copying files on the Internet in previous sections, but for more information, turn to "Find and Copy Files from the Internet" on page 263. In the meantime, follow the *Guided Tour* to copy and install Netscape Chat.

Using your Internet account's FTP feature, in the **Location** or **Go to** text box, type **ftp://ftp.netscape.com** or **ftp://ftp2.netscape.com**. Once you're connected, use the directory list to change to the **pub/chat** directory. Right-click either the **nc32105** file (for Windows 95) or the **nc16105** file (for Windows 3.1). Click the **Save this Link as** option to open a dialog box in which you can designate where on your computer you want the file downloaded to. A good place to store the file is in the TEMP folder or directory on your hard disk drive.

Begin Guided Tour   Install Netscape Chat

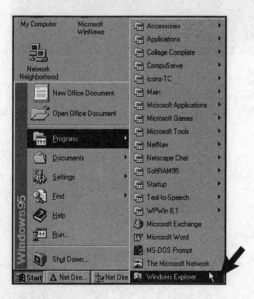

① Click the **Start** button, select **Programs**, and click **Windows Explorer**.

(continues)

Guided Tour Install Netscape Chat *(continued)*

② Open the folder into which you downloaded the Netscape Chat file, and double-click the file name **Nc32105.exe**.

③ A DOS window appears, showing the extracted program files for Netscape Chat. When the files are all extracted, close the DOS window by clicking the **Close** button.

④ To run the Netscape Chat Installation program, double-click the **setup.exe** file name or the **Setup.exe** icon in the Explorer. Follow the on-screen instructions to install Netscape Chat.

⑤ When you finish the Netscape Chat installation, the Netscape Chat icon appears on the Start menu.

Begin Guided Tour Set Up Netscape Chat

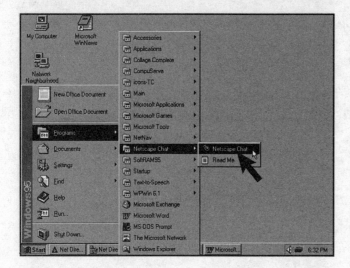

1 To set up Netscape Chat for use and make your first IRC connection, start with your Internet connection up and running. Click on the **Start** button, select **Programs**, and click **Netscape Chat**.

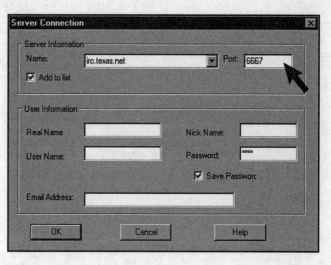

3 In the **Port** text box, type the server's port number. It's usually 6667, but if 6667 doesn't connect you, try 6668 or 6669.

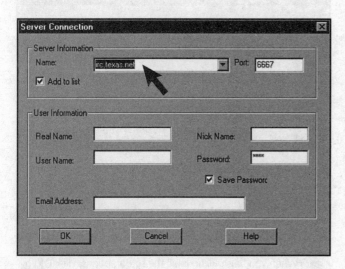

2 The Server Connection dialog box appears. In the **Name** text box (under Server Information), type the URL of the chat server you want to use, such as **irc.texas.net**.

For a complete list of IRC servers, turn to "IRC Chat Servers" on page [Pt4tbd] in the Handy Reference section of this book.

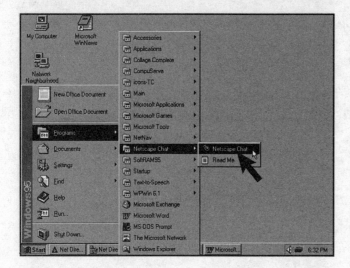

4 Check the **Add to list** option if it's not already checked. This adds the server name to the Name drop-down list so you won't have to enter the information every time.

(continues)

Guided Tour Set Up Netscape Chat (continued)

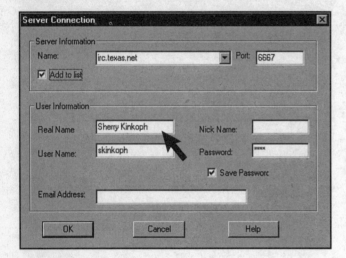

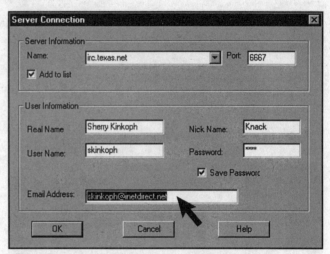

5 Under User Information, type your full name in the **Real Name** text box. In the **User Name** text box, type in your account's user name. For example, most accounts insist you use your first initial and last name for your user name, such as jsmith. (Remember, you don't have to use your real name in IRC.)

7 Type your e-mail address in the **Email Address** text box. (If you don't want anyone you meet in IRC to e-mail you, leave this text box blank.)

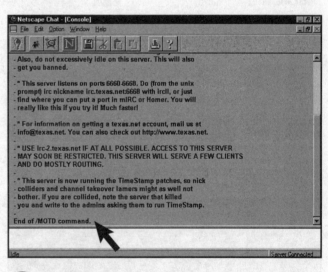

6 Click in the **Nick Name** text box and enter the nickname or handle that you want to use in the chat channels. You can use up to nine characters, but spaces aren't allowed.

8 When you finish filling in all the setup options, click **OK**. If you entered the name of a specific chat server, Netscape Chat attempts to connect you. If the connection doesn't work (it might be busy), you may have to select another chat server. If you get a list of conversation channels, select one and click **Join**.

9 If the connection is successful, information about the server will scroll by, telling you the location of the server, how many users are logged on, and any other rules or messages. Now you're ready to start chatting.

Some chat channels require you to enter a password in order to use them. If you already know the password, you can type it in the **Password** text box in the Server Connection dialog box. Then click the **Save Password** option to select it.

Connect to a Chat Server

Regardless of what type of Internet account you use, you'll have to locate an IRC server in order to chat unless your service provider offers one. Servers are bigger computers that store and manage Internet programs and data, such as IRC channels and software. The IRC network is made up of servers that are dedicated to live chat. Many Internet servers allow you to view Web pages and FTP files, but most do not want to use up their resources for mindless chat activity. For this reason, it's not always easy to find a server dedicated to IRC use.

When you log onto your chat program, you have an opportunity to choose a particular chat server to use. There are several IRC networks you can tap into to find chat servers. The various networks differ in philosophy, in terms of how the network is run, and in number of users. These are some of the more popular IRC networks.

EFNet is the largest IRC network, with over 100 connected servers. It has the most users (averaging 7,000–11,000) and the most channels, but that means it's very busy.

Undernet, formed in 1992, is one of the more famous renegade nets, offering more "attitude" and freedom than the other nets. With 200–500 users and up to 27 servers, it's considerably less congested than the EFNet.

DALnet, formed in 1994, is also less busy than the EFNet, making it a good source for IRC activity. It uses 16 servers and averages 130 users at any given moment.

IAONet, formerly known as the OverNet, has only 5 servers, but it's another choice for IRC chat.

IdealNet, formed in early 1995, has 18 servers. It's a haven for users of Linux (an operating system that grew out of UNIX), so it has lots of Linux-related channels.

Despite the fact that all of these networks support IRC, you can't chat with users on other networks. For example, if you're using EFNet, you won't stumble across any Undernet users in your EFNet chat channels.

Because each IRC network has servers, you have a choice of which one to use to start chatting. Unfortunately, not all servers will allow you to log on and use them. With some servers, you can log on only if you're near their site, and some allow only certain Internet domains to use them. Other servers have various other restrictions on who uses their site. You may have to look around for a chat server you can use. Check with your service provider or try subscribing to the **alt.irc** newsgroup (see "Read and Post Messages in Newsgroups" on page 221 for information on using Internet newsgroups).

To get you started, here are just a scant few of the many IRC servers you can try:

irc.colorado.edu (EFNet)

irc.indiana.edu (EFNet)

copper.ucs.indiana.edu (EFNet)

irc.netcom.com (EFNet)

irc.eskimo.com (EFNet)

davis.ca.us.undernet.org (UnderNet)

milwaukee.wi.us.undernet.org (UnderNet)

irc.ucdavis.edu (DALnet)

il.us.iao.net (IAONet)

il.ans.ideal.net (IdealNet)

Begin Guided Tour Change Chat Servers on Netscape Chat

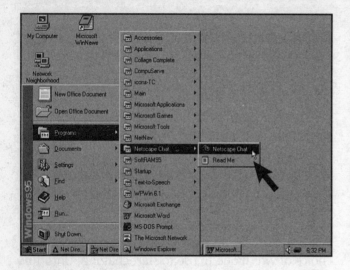

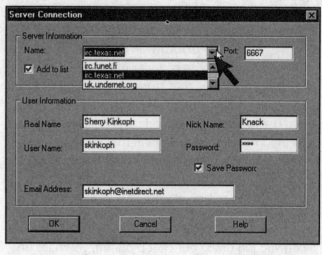

1 Open your Internet connection, and then start Netscape Chat by clicking the **Start** button, selecting **Programs**, and clicking **Netscape Chat**.

3 If you already have a list of chat servers established, click the **Name** drop-down arrow and select the server you want to use.

2 In the Server Connection dialog box, click in the **Name** text box (under Server Information) and type in the URL of the chat server you want to use, such as **irc.texas.net**.

4 (Optional) If you need to change the server's port number, type it in the **Port** text box. The port number is usually 6667; if that doesn't work, try 6668 or 6669.

Guided Tour Change Chat Servers on Netscape Chat

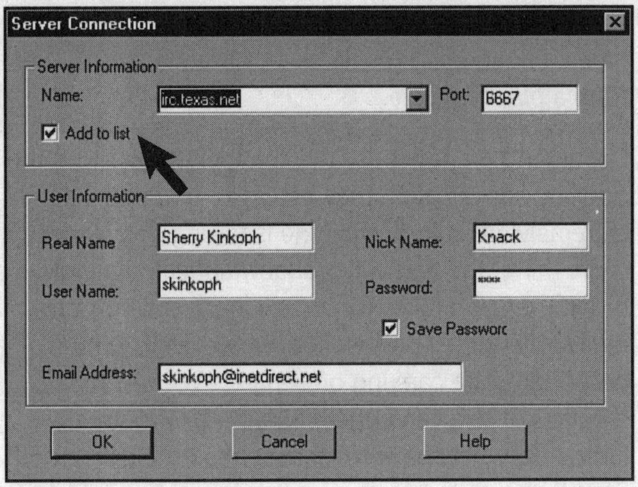

Server Connection

Server Information

Name: irc.texas.net   Port: 6667

☑ Add to list

User Information

Real Name: Sherry Kinkoph   Nick Name: Knack

User Name: skinkoph   Password: ****

☑ Save Password

Email Address: skinkoph@inetdirect.net

OK   Cancel   Help

5 (Optional) To add the server to the list of chat servers that's displayed when you click the Name drop-down arrow, click the **Add to list** option to place a check mark in the box.

6 Click **OK** to make the connection. If the connection doesn't work (the first one you select might be busy, for example), you may have to try selecting another chat server.

Converse in Channels

Having installed a chat program and connected to a chat server, you're ready to be a part of IRC. At this point, you might display a list of the various channels so you know what's available, you might create a nickname for yourself, or you might jump right into your favorite channel. You'll learn more about channels and nicknames in the following sections. If you use Netscape Chat, you can join and exit channels using icons and buttons. If you're using another type of IRC program, you must first know some IRC commands before you get started. The table below shows some common IRC commands you can use to navigate the live chat areas.

What Goes On in a Chat Channel?

IRC's chat channels are smaller areas in which people usually talk about a particular subject. When you're tuned in to an Internet chat channel, you can sit back and watch conversations scroll across your screen. When a person talks, her name appears to the left of the screen, and her text appears to the right of her name. For an observer, it's sort of like reading a script from a play or movie.

Depending on how busy the channel is, following the scrolling conversation may be easy—or it may be extremely difficult. If everyone is talking about the same thing, the text will probably appear in a logical order. Everyone takes turns "talking," and you can easily follow the conversation. However, if some participants are carrying on separate conversations, the lines of text can appear on-screen without any logical flow. You have to learn to read the dialog and associate it with the person who "spoke" it, which can be a little tricky sometimes.

When you connect to IRC, you might want to see a list of available channels, or you might just go directly to a channel you already know about. The *Guided Tour* shows you how to get to a channel both ways. If you go to a channel and you don't see any "talk," either no one is talking or they're all busy engaging in private messaging. To find out if anyone's "home," try typing **hello** and pressing **Enter**. Wait a few minutes, and if no one answers you, switch to another channel.

Common IRC Commands

Use This Command	To Do This
/join #*channelname* or /channel #*channelname*	Log on to the specified channel
/part #*channelname* or /leave #*channelname*	Exit the channel
/whois *nickname*	Find information about another person, such as his real name and Internet domain
/nick *nickname*	Change your nickname
/quit *message*	Exit the channel and display a personal message (such as "See you later," for example)
/hop #*channelname*	Exit the current channel and enter the new channel name that you designate
/help	List IRC commands and information

Some channels sponsor special conferences along with guest speakers. During such events, the channel operator sets the mode to *moderated channel*. In a moderated channel, only the designated guest speaker is allowed to converse freely; other users are given limited abilities to ask questions.

> The channels are started and run by channel operators, called *ops* or *channelops* for short. Channelops ultimately have total control over the channel, including the topic name, who's allowed in, and who gets kicked out. Channelops can easily be identified in the IRC channels; they have @ symbols in front of their names.

Nicknames

Anybody with a modem and an Internet connection can participate in live chat (where it's accessible). You'll find a variety of people from all walks of life and from all over the globe. In addition, you'll encounter all kinds of personality types. One of the best ways to express your personality is with a nickname. Before entering IRC, you need to select your own nickname (also called a handle or screen name) that will identify you to others; it can be your login name or a fun nickname.

Even if you know a user's nickname, you may never really *know* exactly who you're talking to in IRC. There's no audible voice to help you determine the person's gender or age. Just because someone's screen name is Bob doesn't necessarily mean it's a guy you're talking to. It could be a woman, a child, or even a famous celebrity. That's part of the fascination of online chat: no one really knows who you are, so you can be whoever you want to be. For example, if

you're normally a quiet, shy person, IRC offers you a chance to be as vibrant as you want to be. However, that can work to your advantage or disadvantage. Some people in the chat channels tend to be very bold in what they say, often saying things they normally wouldn't say in face-to-face conversations. Because of this, you need to approach Internet chat with a little bit of skepticism. Remember that not all of the participants are genuine and sincere; some users may have sinister motives, so be cautious.

> The Internet isn't the only place where people chat electronically. Online chat is also very popular among commercial online services, such as CompuServe and America Online, as well as the smaller BBSs (Bulletin Board Services).

Chat Rules and Guidelines

You might be ready to jump into a channel and chat as soon as you connect to IRC. However, before you do that you need to consider some loose guidelines.

IRC doesn't follow the strict rules that some areas of the Internet do. But that's not necessarily a good thing. That means it's not always easy to figure out the prevailing attitudes of the various channels and their members. So it's always best to look before leaping into the fray.

Generally, you should conduct yourself in the chat channels the same as you would in real life. Be polite and civil as necessary. Don't use crude language, sexual innuendo, or harassment unless that's what the channel is all about. Remember, you never know who might be reading what you say.

Common sense is the best way to approach live chat on the Internet. Here are a few guidelines to help you:

- Always observe the conversation first before you jump in.

- Apply the Golden Rule: Treat others as you would have them treat you.

- If you're in the middle of a conversation and must leave the room for a moment, it's a good idea to send a brb (be right back) message to let others know what happened to you.

- If someone says hello to you, it's polite to at least answer, even if you're planning to *lurk* (observe) for awhile.

- If you join a channel that requests that you speak a foreign language, don't start speaking in English. For example, if you join the #spanish channel and everyone seems to be speaking spanish, don't assume that you can just start speaking English.

> If you're concerned about your children being able to access the more risqué IRC channels, you might consider using a program such as Cyberpatrol to block out certain IRC channels. You can find the program on the Web at http://www.cyberpatrol.com. For more information, see "Secure Your System and Practice Proper Etiquette," on page 307.

If you violate chat guidelines or channel rules, you can be kicked off the channel. If you continuously violate those rules, you might be reported to your Internet service provider, in which case you could find yourself expelled from the service. Chat participants often stick together, so if someone continually annoys the rest of the group, that person may be verbally attacked by the crowd and driven from the channel. For more information about chat etiquette, see "Secure Your System and Practice Proper Etiquette," starting on page 307.

Online Emoticons and Abbreviations

It's not always easy to convey your emotion or tone while engaging in IRC conversations. For example, if someone types in "You're a looney," you can't tell from the words alone if he is serious and actually thinks you're crazy, or if he's just kidding around. To compensate for the lack of facial expressions and voice inflections, online users have created symbols, called *smileys* or *emoticons*, to express emotions.

A smiley is a face created out of keyboard symbols, such as **:)** or **: -)** (the dash for the nose is optional). To read a smiley properly, you must tilt your head to the left and look at the symbols. With a smiley, the message "You're a looney :)" takes on a light, friendly meaning. For a complete list of emoticons, turn to the Handy Reference section on page 425.

Another way to express emotions or actions on-screen is with the use of brackets of some kind, such as <grin>, [sigh], *thump*, or ::slap::. Some of the graphical-based IRC programs have action icons you can select to show physical movements. There's also an IRC command you can use, such as **/me hits head on desk**, which others on the channel read as "*ChatIdiot* **hits head on desk**" (or whatever your nickname is).

Not only will you come across strange keyboard symbols in the chat rooms, you'll also encounter a hip abbreviated form of online shorthand. Common words or phrases are abbreviated or reduced to acronyms to speed up typing time. If you're not sure what a person's acronym means, don't hesitate to ask. The following table lists a few frequently used ones.

Common Online Acronyms

Acronym	Meaning	Acronym	Meaning
brb	Be right back	cu	See you
imho	In my humble opinion	wth	What the h*** (or heck)
fyi	For your information	tia	Thanks in advance
lol	Laughing out loud	pov	Point of view
rotfl	Rolling on the floor laughing	rtm	Read the manual

Begin Guided Tour Chat on a Channel Using IRC Commands

```
NetDirect:> irc
```

1 If you're not using Netscape Chat to access IRC, these steps will show you how to use a UNIX-based IRC program. Start with your Internet connection up and running. If you have a shell account that requires you to use UNIX commands to access the Internet, type **irc** at the main menu prompt and press **Enter**. (If you're having trouble finding a chat server, turn to "Connect to a Chat Server" on page 249.)

It's not a good idea to use your full name as a nickname. Instead, use just your first name or a fun nickname such as *Smiley* or *Bobmeister*.

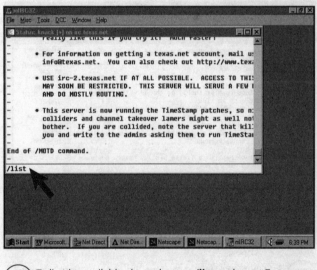

3 To list the available channels, type **/list** and press **Enter**. From the list, pick a channel you want to try.

2 Upon entering IRC, you need to enter the nickname you want to use. Type the UNIX command **/nick *nickname*** (substituting your name for *nickname*) and press **Enter**.

If you need help using the UNIX commands in IRC, type **/help** and press **Enter**.

(continues)

Guided Tour   Chat on a Channel Using IRC Commands   *(continued)*

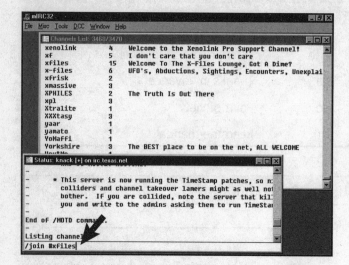

4 To join a channel, type **/join #*channelname*** or **/channel #*channelname*** and press **Enter**.

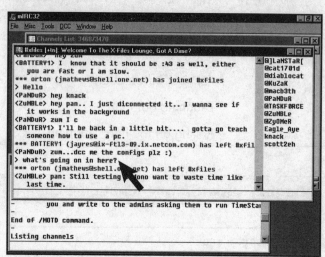

6 The text is sent to the conversation window. Continue talking by sending your responses in this way. Remember to separate IRC commands from regular conversation messages by preceding each command with a slash (/). To exit at any time, type **/leave #*channelname*** and press **Enter**.

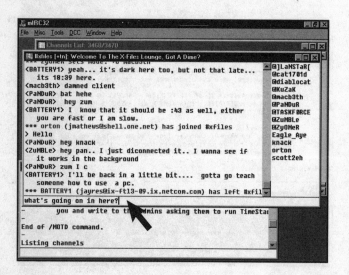

5 To join in a conversation, type the text you want to send and press **Enter**.

In some instances, there is a lag between the time you type your text /and the moment others see it. Lags are often caused by connection difficulties. One way to find out how long of a lag you're experiencing is to type **/ping *nickname*** and press **Enter** (using the name of someone else logged onto the channel). When you receive the pong reply, you know how long the lag is. (The ping command only works with IRCII, WSIRC, and IRCII2-6 for Windows.)

Begin Guided Tour   Chat with Netscape Chat

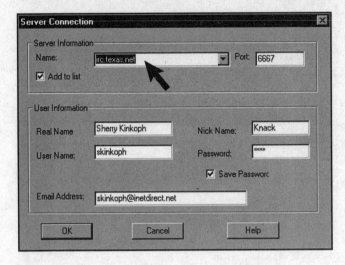

1 Start with your Internet account and Netscape Chat program up and running. Select the chat server you want to connect to in the Server Connection dialog box that appears when you first open Netscape Chat. Then click **OK** to make the connection.

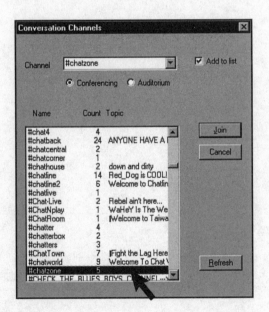

2 When you first log onto IRC, you see a lot of logon information, followed by the Group Conversation dialog box. This lists the available channels you can try. Click the channel you want to join and click **Join**.

To expand your chat channel window, click the window's **Maximize** button or drag the window's borders to a new size.

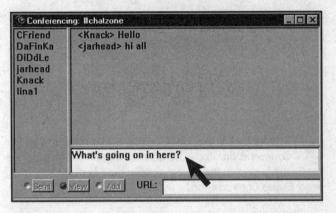

3 You're now logged on to the chat channel and can start talking. To enter your text, type it in the text box beneath the conversation window. Then press **Enter** to send it to the channel for all to read.

4 (Optional) To find out about a particular person in the room, double-click his name in the list at the left of the conversation window. The Personal Info dialog box appears, showing the person's real name and (sometimes) the e-mail address. Click the **Close** button to return to the conversation window.

(continues)

Guided Tour   Chat with Netscape Chat

(continued)

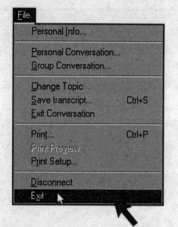

To start your own channel using Netscape Chat, open the Group Conversation dialog box. Instead of selecting a channel to join from the list, type in a unique channel name and click **OK**. It may be awhile before anyone joins you, so be prepared to wait.

5 To leave the channel, open the **File** menu and select **Exit Conversation**. To choose another channel instead, click the **Group** button on the toolbar, or open the **File** menu and select **Group Conversation**.

6 To exit Netscape Chat completely, click the **Close** button or select **File**, **Exit**.

Converse Privately

Another aspect of live chat, called *private messaging*, involves one-on-one chats that take place between two users. The conversation that takes place is separate from the chat dialog going on in the chat channel, and other users cannot see the text that's being typed.

It's not uncommon to receive a private message from another user while you're in the middle of a conversation in a channel. If you're using a text-based program, a private message appears in the middle of the channel's dialog, set apart only by the appearance of the nickname of the person who sent the message. In graphical-based programs, such as Netscape Chat, private messages appear as separate windows on the screen, with the sender's name in the title bar.

In some programs, a beep accompanies a private message, alerting you that someone is contacting you.

You can send private messages to other users on the same channel or to other people logged onto IRC. As far as what is said in a private message, well, that's private. However, you might keep in mind that not everyone welcomes a private message, so you might be rejected from time to time. Likewise, you might sometimes be annoyed by the private messages of another user. If that happens, use the IRC ignore command to stop the messages.

The following table lists the IRC commands you can use when sending and receiving private messages.

Common IRC Commands for Private Messaging

Use This Command	To Do This
/msg *nickname message*	Send a message to a user
/query *nickname*	Send all subsequent messages to the designated user (which saves you from having to type /msg every time)
/ignore *nickname* all	Ignore all incoming messages from the designated user (handy for pesty people)
/ignore *nickname* none	Turn off the ignore command
/whois *nickname*	Display information about the person

Begin Guided Tour Send a Private Message Using IRC Commands

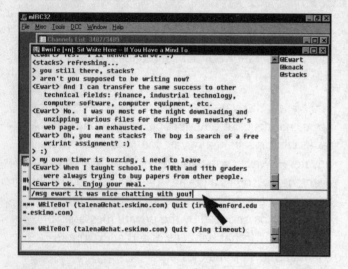
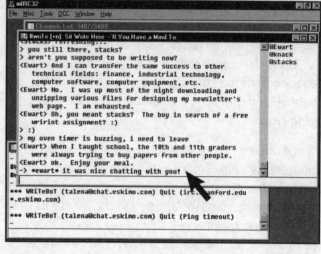

1 You first have to know the name of the person you want to contact. If you have his name, type **/msg *nickname message*** (substituting the person's name for *nickname* and the text you want to send for *message*). Then press **Enter**.

2 The message is sent and duly noted among the server notations that scroll along with the dialog.

Begin Guided Tour Send a Private Message Using Netscape Chat

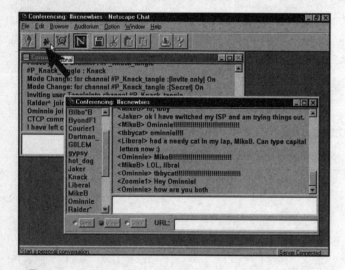
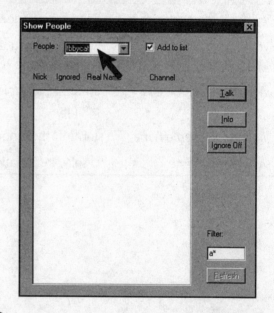

1 Open the **File** menu and select **Personal Conversation**, or click the **Personal** button in the toolbar.

2 In the **People** text box, type the name of the person with whom you want to chat privately. Then click **Talk**. This sends a private message asking if the person would like to join you in a private chat.

Guided Tour Send a Private Message Using Netscape Chat

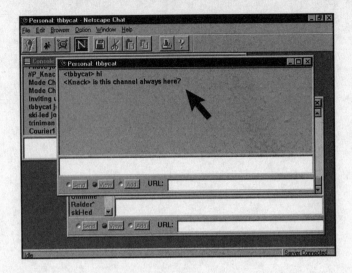

3 If the person agrees to chat with you, she clicks a **Yes** or **OK** button. A separate window appears on-screen in which you can carry on a conversation. If you're also logged onto a chat channel, you can continue to participate in the group chat while you conduct a private chat.

HOW TO...

Find and Copy Files from the Internet

One of the main reasons people want to connect to the Internet is to download (receive) some of the information that's stored there, such as the latest computer programs. The method the Internet uses for remote-to-local transfers is called FTP (File Transfer Protocol). Basically, it's a method for both computers (the FTP computer and yours) to give each other messages regarding how a file should be passed over the Internet to your computer. You can use an FTP program or a Web browser to ftp. You'll learn both methods in this section.

When you first connected to your service provider, you were probably given a copy of an FTP program so that you could download any additional Internet programs you might need. If you did not get an FTP program from your service provider, flip back to the section "Copy Files from the Internet" (page 89), which explains how you can get an FTP program from the Internet using a program included with Windows.

If for any reason you want a newer or different FTP program, you can download a more recent copy of any of several popular FTP programs from the Internet using your current FTP program or your Web browser. Once you download an FTP program, you have to install it before you can begin using it. This section explains how to do just that.

What You Will Find in This Section

Copy Files with Your Web Browser

As you've probably learned by now, your Web browser is what makes the Internet fun—mainly because it's so easy to use and understand. Just click a link, and you jump to that page. Want to go back? No problem. Want to jump directly to a particular Web page? No sweat. Want to search for stuff? Easy.

Your Web browser also makes downloading files simple. If you don't feel like learning how to use a separate FTP program, you don't have to. Your Web browser makes downloading files as simple as point-and-click: you point to a link that is connected to a file on an FTP site, and then click to begin the downloading process. Then all you have to do is select an existing folder or create a new folder into which you want the downloaded file placed.

You may want to create a single folder called Downloads for all the files you get off the Internet. That way, you can keep everything in one place until you've had a chance to use your antivirus program to verify that the files you've received are virus-free. I don't want to scare you, but downloading contaminated files from the Internet (or anywhere, for that matter) is the most common way a system becomes contaminated. So protect yourself (and your data) by double-checking the files you receive.

To download any file from the Internet, you have to find the file first. See "Search for Information on the Web" on page 179 for help finding the information you want. A lot of Web pages contain links to files. For example, Stroud's (http://www.cwsapps.com) and The Ultimate Collection of Winsock Software—TUCOWS (http:// tucows.niia.net) contain links to many popular Internet programs such as Web browsers and FTP programs. Likewise, the Virtual Software Library (http://vsl.cnet.com) contains specialized search tools for finding just about anything else. If you find a Web page with a direct link to a file, all you have to do is click the link to get it. On the other hand, if you just discover the FTP site of the file you want, you can use its address (or URL) to steer your Web browser in the right direction. Once you're connected to the FTP site, locating your file and downloading it is simple.

Here's why you need to bother with an FTP program once in a while. Your Web browser can only link to "open" systems, that is, FTP sites that allow anonymous logins. So if you need to access an FTP site that allows only restricted access, you're going to need an FTP program.

Begin Guided Tour   Search for Files on the Virtual Software Library

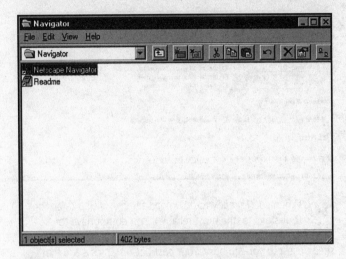

1 Connect to the Internet and start your Web browser. For example, to start Netscape Navigator in Windows 95, open the **Start** menu, point to **Programs**, and select **Netscape**. Then double-click the **Netscape Navigator** icon.

To start Netscape in Windows 3.1, open the **Netscape** program window and double-click the **Netscape Navigator** icon.

Location: http://vsl.cnet.com

2 A good source of files is the Virtual Software Library. To jump there, type **http://vsl.cnet.com** in the **Location** or **Go to** text box, and then press **Enter.**

search options

quick search

most popular

new arrivals

power search

archive search

information

3 For our example, let's look for a good antivirus program for Windows. Click **power search**.

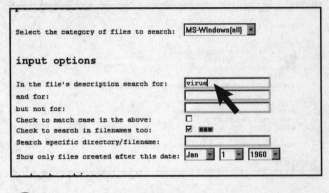

4 First, you select the category of files to search. In this case, leave it set to MS-Windows (all).

5 Type **virus** in the text box labeled **In the file's description search for**.

If you know the file name of the program you want to search for, you can enter it in the **Search specific directory/filename** text box.

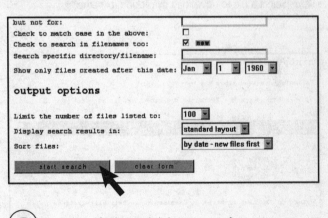

6 Scroll down further and click **start search**.

(continues)

Guided Tour Search for Files on the Virtual Software Library *(continued)*

```
    path: games/

  Virus: The Game, Version 1.1

wsc-217e.zip
      file size: 557 K (570346 bytes)
      file date: Mar 21,1995
      path: util/

  Version 2.17 of McAfee Windows Virus Scan/Disinfect

wsc-213e.zip
      file size: 526 K (538137 bytes)
      file date: Dec 01,1994
      path: misc/

  VirusScan for Windows new version 2.1.3

gatr01.zip
```

7 Scroll down to see the results of your search.

If you didn't get the results you wanted, click the **Back** button and change the information on the form, making it as specific as possible. For example, I originally searched for "anti-virus" and got nothing. When I searched for "virus," I got results.

8 Select a file to download by clicking its name.

```
hints

Estimated download times for wsc-217e.zip:

    Your access speed    Estimated download time (in minutes)

        9.6K modem   11:03

        56K ISDN     2:02

        1 Kbyte/sec   9:26
        2 Kbyte/sec   4:48
        5 Kbyte/sec   2:01
       10 Kbyte/sec   1:05

Return to the list of sites to download from. Reliablity ratings

    The reliability ratings are based on our test program's success
```

9 The page that appears has links to various FTP sites that contain your file. Scroll down to the bottom of the screen for an estimate of the amount of time it will take to download your file (useful information).

```
Switzerland

  *** wsc-217e.zip [557 K] from nic.switch.ch

USA

  *** wsc-217e.zip [557 K] from ftp.cica.indiana.edu
   ** wsc-217e.zip [    K] from ftp.marcam.com
    * wsc-217e.zip [    K] from ftp.cdrom.com

United Kingdom

  **** wsc-217e.zip [557 K] from src.doc.ic.ac.uk

hints

Estimated download times for wsc-217e.zip:

    Your access speed    Estimated download time (in minutes)
```

10 When you're ready to download the file, click a three- or four-star site (the most reliable). You do not have to use a site close to you, but that might be faster. Often, however, the sites closest to you are busy. Your best bet is to pick a site that's in a time zone where it is the middle of the night; such sites are often less busy.

Unknown File Type

You have started to download a file of type application/x-zip-compressed
Click "More Info" to learn how to extend Navigator's capabilities.

[More Info] [Pick App...] [Save File...] [Cancel]

11 If the file you're downloading is compressed (zipped), the Unknown File Type dialog box appears. Click **Save File**.

Save As...

Save in: Downloads

File name: wsc-217e.zip   [Save]
Save as type: All Files (*.*)   [Cancel]

12 Select a directory in which to save the file and click **Save**.

Guided Tour   Search for Files on the Virtual Software Library

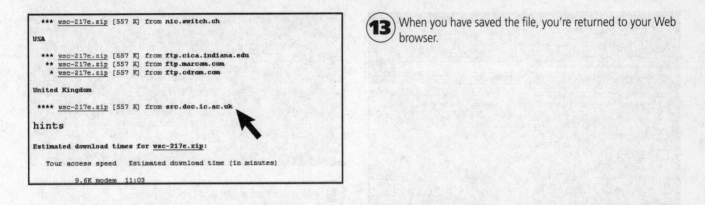

```
*** wsc-217e.zip [557 K] from nic.switch.ch

USA

  *** wsc-217e.zip [557 K] from ftp.cica.indiana.edu
   ** wsc-217e.zip [557 K] from ftp.marcam.com
    * wsc-217e.zip [557 K] from ftp.cdrom.com


United Kingdom

 **** wsc-217e.zip [557 K] from src.doc.ic.ac.uk

hints

Estimated download times for wsc-217e.zip:

  Your access speed   Estimated download time (in minutes)

        9.6K modem   11:03
```

13 When you have saved the file, you're returned to your Web browser.

Begin Guided Tour   Copy a File Directly from an FTP Site

Location: ftp://ftp.esnet.com

1 If you know the FTP site that a particular file is on, you can go directly to that site. For example, type **ftp:// ftp.esnet.com** in the **Location** or **Go to** text box and press **Enter**.

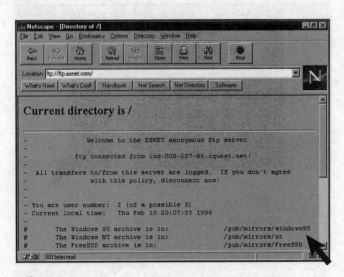

2 At the top of the page, you'll see the names of the directories in which particular files are stored. For example, Windows 95 files are in the /pub/mirrors/windows95 directory.

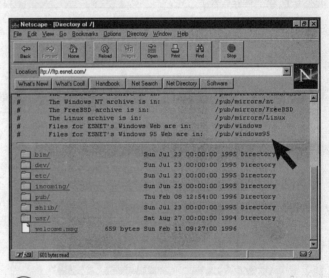

3 You're currently in the root directory of this FTP server. Scroll down to the bottom of the page to the pub directory. Click the **pub** directory, and from there you can jump to the **mirrors** directory and eventually to the **windows95** directory. (Or you can just type the address **ftp://ftp.esnet.com/pub/mirrors/ windows95** in the **Location** text box and press **Enter.**)

If you use Windows 3.1, you'll find applicable files in the **/pub/windows** directory.

(continues)

Guided Tour   Copy a File Directly from an FTP Site

(continued)

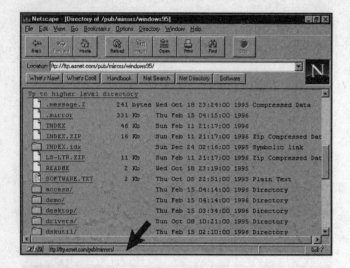

4 From here, you can dig deeper for a file.

5 To download a file, just click its name.

Begin Guided Tour   Use a Mirror Web Site

1 A lot of FTP sites provide a Web site (to use with your Web browser) that mirrors the information on the FTP site. Sometimes, you'll find links at an FTP site that you can click to jump to a Web version of that same site. Or you can go directly to the Web site by typing its address in the **Location** or **Go to** box and pressing **Enter**. For example, type **http://www.winsite.com** and press **Enter**.

2 You'll find the Web site that mirrors the popular ftp.winsite.com a lot easier to use (and faster, too). You can search for files or just browse by clicking **Browse Archive**.

Guided Tour   Use a Mirror Web Site

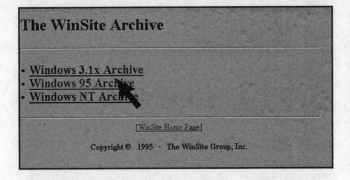

The WinSite Archive

- **Windows 3.1x Archive**
- **Windows 95 Archive**
- **Windows NT Archive**

[WinSite Home Page]

Copyright © 1995 · The WinSite Group, Inc.

Last Updated: Mon Jan 01 1996 at 11:40:48 PM EST

Filename	Size	Date	Description
bput95s.zip	643KB	11/26/95	A group of programs to make Win95 more conv
cserv.zip	27KB	12/19/95	Calculation server v.1.0 for Windows 95
dz95.zip	597KB	08/07/95	Drag and drop ZIP manager, builtin virus sc
formgx40.zip	1252KB	11/12/95	Tool for authoring interactive presentation
ifa400b4.zip	443KB	12/18/95	Long filenames in Win95
lblwz24d.zip	320KB	11/10/95	All-purpose label utility program

③ Because you're looking for Windows 95 information, click **Windows 95 Archive**.

⑤ When you find the file you want, click it to download it to your system.

If you use Windows 3.1, click **Windows 3.1x Archive** instead.

Windows Directories

Welcome to the WinSite[tm] archive.

access Microsoft Windows95 Access Files
demo Demo Windows95 Files and Crippleware
desktop Windows95 Desktop Apps, Screen, Image, and BitMap Files
drivers/other Other Win95 Drivers: SCSI, Disk, Ethernet, Scanner, etc.
drivers/printer Printer Drivers for Windows95
drivers/video Video Files, Drivers for Windows95
dskutil Windows95 Disk Utilities
excel MicroSoft Windows95 Excel Files
games Windows95 Games, Educational Software, etc.
icons Windows95 Icons and Icon Related Files
misc Miscellaneous Windows95 Files

④ You'll notice that the descriptions here are a bit more friendly. To change to a different folder, just click it.

Find and Install an FTP Program

When you originally connected to your Internet server in "Connect to Your Service Provider" (page 69), you probably downloaded an FTP program. However, after using it a few times, you may have decided that you wanted to try a different program (perhaps one that's easier to use). Or maybe you have an old FTP program, and you want to download the current version. Whatever the reason you want a new FTP program, finding one is not a problem.

After you download your FTP program, you must install it. But before you can install most programs you get from the Internet, you need to decompress them. Most files that you find will be *zipped*, which means they've been compressed with a utility called PKZIP. Compressing a file makes it smaller so that it takes less time to download. The files that make up your FTP program have been zipped into one small file. To make the files usable, you have to

decompress (unzip) them. The easiest way to deal with this unzipping nonsense is to use WinZip, which you can download from many FTP sites. For example, you'll find it at the ftp.winsite.com site in the pub/pc/win95 directory.

> You have to download and install WinZip before you attempt the *Guided Tour* because you'll need WinZip to complete the steps. Also, if you decide to keep WinZip beyond its trial period, you need to register it and pay a small fee for its use. Make sure you do.

In the *Guided Tour*, you'll learn how to download WS-FTP, one of the more common FTP programs. If you're looking for something easier to use, you might want to try downloading Cute FTP instead.

Begin Guided Tour   Download a Different FTP Program

1 Connect to the Internet as usual and start your Web browser.

2 Connect to the Stroud's site by typing **http://www.cwsapps.com** in the **Location** or **Go to** text box and pressing **Enter**.

> If you have trouble connecting to Stroud's, try their alternate site at http://www.stroud.com.

Guided Tour Download a Different FTP Program

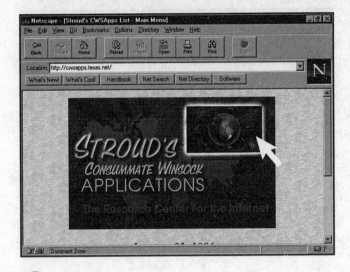

3 Click the **Stroud's** logo.

What's 竏菟	New for '95 Apps	The Newest Apps
Index of Apps	The CASPER Page	Top 20 Apps
Audio Apps	Communications Clients	Compression Utilities
Critical Winsock	CWSServers	FTP / Archie / Finger
Gophers	Graphics Viewers	HTML Editors
IRC Apps	Mail Clients	Multimedia Viewers
News Readers	Plug-in Modules 竏菟	Statistics Services
Terminal Apps	The Suite Spot	Utilities - Auxiliary
Utilities - Winsock	Virus Scanners	VRML Browsers
WAIS	Web Accessories	WWW Browsers
CWSApps Stats	Sponsoring The List	Honors & Awards

● Stroud's CWSApps List - Mirror Sites ●

4 Scroll down and select **FTP/Archie/Finger**.

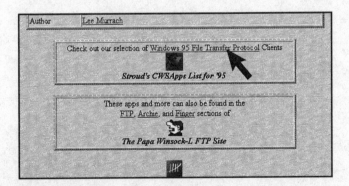

5 If you use Windows 95, scroll down to the bottom of the list and click **Windows 95 File Transfer Protocol**. If you use Windows 3.1, skip this step.

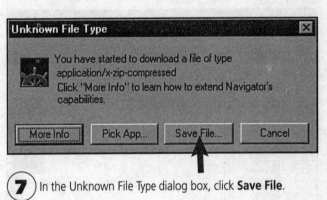

	WS-FTP 32-bit			
Full Review	Version	95.12.29	Date	12/30/95
	Rating	★★★★	Size	196 Kb
Location	ftp://ftp.csra.net/pub/win32/ws_ftp32.zip			
Description	One of the best File Transfer Protocol clients available on the 'net			
Status	Free for government, academic, or non-profit use. For any other use, contact Ipswitch			
Author	John A. Junod			
Information	About WS-FTP 32-bit			
Also Available	16-bit version. 32-bit - Alternative Location			

6 Click the FTP program of your choice. For example, click the Location of **WS-FTP 32-bit**. (If you use Windows 3.1, your program is called WS-FTP 16-bit.) Another popular program to try is Cute FTP.

> You can read more about a program before you download it by clicking the **Full Review** box at the top of the left column.

Unknown File Type

You have started to download a file of type application/x-zip-compressed

Click "More Info" to learn how to extend Navigator's capabilities.

| More Info | Pick App... | Save File... | Cancel |

7 In the Unknown File Type dialog box, click **Save File**.

(continues)

Guided Tour Download a Different FTP Program

(continued)

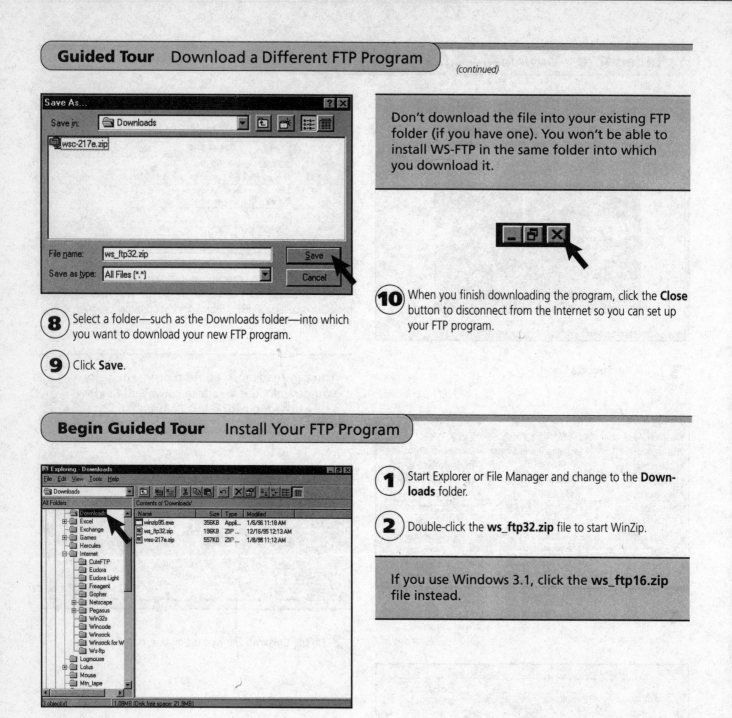

Don't download the file into your existing FTP folder (if you have one). You won't be able to install WS-FTP in the same folder into which you download it.

10 When you finish downloading the program, click the **Close** button to disconnect from the Internet so you can set up your FTP program.

8 Select a folder—such as the Downloads folder—into which you want to download your new FTP program.

9 Click **Save**.

Begin Guided Tour Install Your FTP Program

1 Start Explorer or File Manager and change to the **Downloads** folder.

2 Double-click the **ws_ftp32.zip** file to start WinZip.

If you use Windows 3.1, click the **ws_ftp16.zip** file instead.

Guided Tour Install Your FTP Program

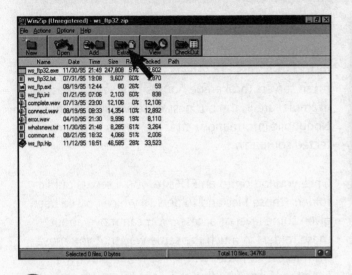

4 Select the folder in which you want the files placed and click **Extract**. WinZip decompresses the files and places them in the folder you selected. WS-FTP is now ready for use.

3 Click the **Extract** button, and the Extract dialog box appears.

Before you unzip the file, you can use WinZip to check it for viruses, provided you have an antivirus program on your system. Just click the **CheckOut** button.

Use an FTP Program to Copy Files

Although you can copy (download) files from the Internet with your Web browser, the process is a bit slower than if you used a separate FTP program. Of course, there is a trade-off. You'll probably find that locating files you want to download is easier with your Web program.

In any case, the bottom line is this: in order to connect to any computer out there and grab a copy of one of its files, you're going to need the computer's address. You might get the address in any number of ways. You might, for example, find the address in a book or a magazine that recommends the FTP site, or you might get the address through a program called Archie that helps you locate files on the Internet (see "Find Files with Archie" on page 278). This table lists some sites where you can start.

A computer that allows you access to its files is called a host computer. You are its guest. To gain entrance, you need the password. In most cases, the password is a simple one: "anonymous." In other cases, it is something like "guest." Without a doubt, you *will* need a password in order to gain access to an FTP site. If "anonymous" or "guest" doesn't work, the server probably requires that you have a special type of account with it, in which case you're given a

special password. This doesn't necessarily have anything to do with money, but it might. Some restricted-access FTP servers do charge fees. Generally, those servers (brokerage houses or research labs, for example) are in the business of selling information. Nonpublic information, after all, needs to be protected somehow.

Once you log on to an FTP site, you'll see its public folders (those files and folders to which you've been given some level of access). You can move about these folders in much the same way that you move from folder to folder within File Manager or the Explorer. When you find the right folder, you select the file you want. If you have "read" rights to that file, the FTP program copies it back to your hard disk. (Read rights designate a file you can see, but you can't touch.) Of course, you can also select which folder on your system your FTP program copies the file to.

In the *Guided Tour*, you'll learn how to copy files using WS-FTP. If you use another FTP program, the steps will vary slightly. Another popular FTP program is Cute FTP (it comes in both Windows 3.1 and Windows 95 versions); you'll discover tips on where it differs from WS-FTP in the next section.

Recommended FTP Sites

Site	URL	Site	URL
CICA Windows Archive	ftp.winsite.com	America Online	ftp.aol.com
Netscape	ftp1.netscape.com	Mirrors to Popular Sites	mirrors.aol.com
Mosaic	ftp.NCSA.uuic.edu	SimTel Archives	ftp.coast.net
Oakland Archives	oak.oakland.edu	ESNET	ftp.esnet.com
Microsoft	ftp.microsoft.com	GARBO Archives	garbo.uwusa.fi

Tips on Using Cute FTP

Cute FTP differs from WS-FTP (which is used in the *Guided Tour*) in the following ways.

To connect to an FTP site, select it from the Sites Manager and then click **Connect**. If your site is not in the list, click the folder to which you want to add the site, and then click **Add Site**. Add the required information and click **OK**. To edit an existing site (for example, to edit the CICA site information as mentioned in the *Guided Tour*, select the CICA site and click **Edit Site**. Make the necessary changes and click **OK**.

With Cute FTP, your local system is not displayed initially. To get to it, right-click in the left window panel and select **Change dir** from the shortcut menu. Enter a directory such as **C:** and click **OK**. You can

change from folder to folder on your local system the same way that you do on the remote system—by double-clicking on the folder to which you want to change.

Another way in which Cute FTP differs from WS-FTP is in the way it handles file descriptions. The moment it assimilates a remote directory, Cute FTP looks for a file called index.txt and automatically downloads it—without permission from you. As a matter of courtesy, most systems have an index.txt file for each directory, which contains a list of all the files in that directory, along with descriptions of what those files are. (You'd probably download this file yourself anyway.) Cute FTP then reconciles the information in the index.txt file with the directory listing it actually sees, and automatically writes each file's description next to its listing in the download folder. This is all automatic.

Begin Guided Tour   Copy Files with WS-FTP

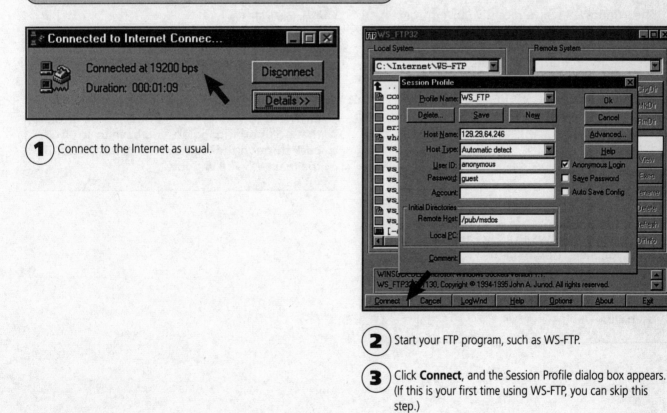

1 Connect to the Internet as usual.

2 Start your FTP program, such as WS-FTP.

3 Click **Connect**, and the Session Profile dialog box appears. (If this is your first time using WS-FTP, you can skip this step.)

(continues)

Guided Tour Copy Files with WS-FTP

(continued)

Session Profile

Profile Name: CICA WinSock Files

Delete... | Save | New

Host Name: ftp.cica.indiana.edu
Host Type: Automatic detect
User ID: anonymous
Password: guest
Account:

Anonymous Login
Save Password
Auto Save Config

Initial Directories
Remote Host: /pub/pc/win3/winsock
Local PC:

Comment:

Ok | Cancel | Advanced... | Help

Session Profile

Profile Name: Windows Archive

Delete... | Save | New

Host Name: ftp.winsite.com
Host Type: Automatic detect
User ID: anonymous
Password: jfulton@iquest.net
Account:

Anonymous Login
Save Password
Auto Save Config

Initial Directories
Remote Host: /pub/pc/win3/winsock
Local PC:

Comment:

Ok | Cancel | Advanced... | Help

4 In the **Profile Name** drop-down list, select the FTP site you want to visit. For example, select **CICA WinSock Files**.

The Windows Archive recently moved from the ftp.cica.indiana.edu site listed here. As a result, you'll have to change it in your copy of WS-FTP. To do that, type the new address (ftp.winsite.com) under **Host Name**. You might also want to change the description to **Windows Archive**. You'll also need to make the password change as described in step 4 and save the changes by following step 5.

If the site you want to visit isn't in the list, you can add it within WS-FTP. Click the **New** button, type a description in the **Profile Name** text box, and type the FTP address (such as **ftp5.netscape.com**) in the **Host Name** text box. Select the **Anonymous Login** check box, and then click **OK**.

5 You'll need to change the password to your e-mail address. For example, I changed mine to jfulton@iquest.net. Type your e-mail address and click **Save**.

6 Click **Save** to save your changes, and then click **OK** to dial into the FTP site.

If you skip step 4 and try to log onto the Windows Archive, you'll get an error message telling you that you need to change the password to your e-mail address. To see errors that occur during log on, you have to scroll back through the login list in the lower part of the main WS-FTP window.

Guided Tour Copy Files with WS-FTP

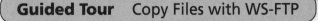

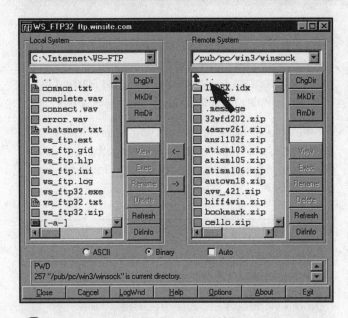

7 After you connect to the FTP site, change to the directory that contains the files you want. For example, change to the pub/pc/win95 directory by clicking the dot-dot (**..**) to move up one level. Then double-click the **win3** folder and the **util** folder.

8 On your Local System, change to the temporary folder into which you want to download the file.

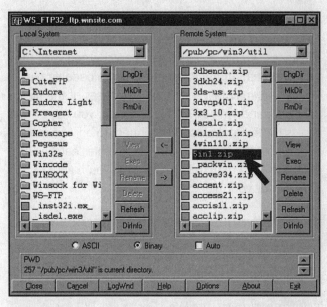

9 Double-click a file to download it into the folder you selected. For example, double-click the **5in1.zip** file.

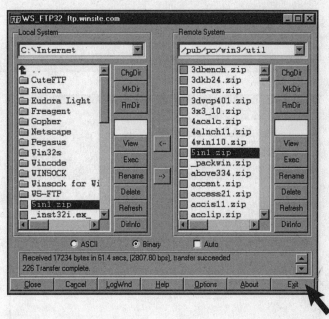

10 After the file has been copied to your system, click **Close** to disconnect from the FTP site.

11 Click **Connect** if you want to connect to another FTP site. When you finish, click **Exit** to exit WS-FTP.

Find Files with Archie

Archie is a program designed to find files on FTP sites. Archie servers have been charged with the task of searching the Internet for downloadable files. The servers maintain their own databases of the files they find, and with an Archie program, you can access these databases. You connect to an Archie site and ask for the file you want, and Archie searches its database for a match. If it finds one, you have a location for your file.

If you decide to download files from the Internet using your Web browser (and not an FTP program), you can locate files using one of the many Web search tools. See "Search for Information on the Web" on page 180 for more information.

You can't use Archie to actually download the file for you. So once you know the file's location, you fire up your FTP program to download it as you learned in "Use an FTP Program to Copy Files" (page 274).

Let me give you one tip before you begin. Some Archie sites are more up-to-date than others. If you don't find a file at one site, try looking for it on another one.

You'll need an Archie program in order to complete the *Guided Tour*. I use WS Archie for Windows 95, which I downloaded from the Stroud's site (http://www.cwsapps.com). You'll find a Windows 3.1 version there as well. See "Download a Different FTP Program" on page 270 for details on connecting to Stroud's to get such a program.

Begin Guided Tour   Find Files with WS-Archie

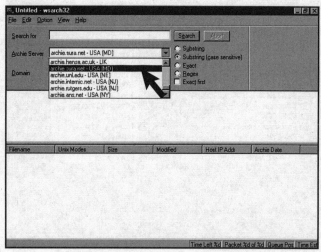

1 Connect to the Internet and start WS-Archie.

2 In the **Archie Server** drop-down list, select the Archie site you want to search.

Guided Tour   Find Files with WS-Archie

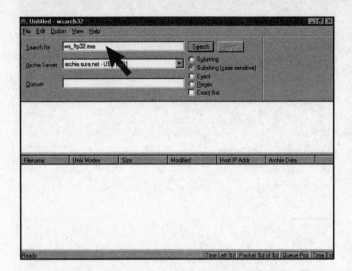

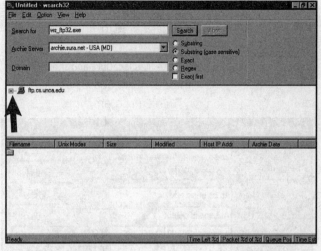

3 When you're connected to the Archie site, enter the file name you want to search for in the **Search for** text box. For example, type **ws_ftp32.exe**. If you use Windows 3.1, search for the file ws_ftp16.exe instead.

If you want to limit your search to a particular domain, enter it in the **Domain** text box. For example, if you know that your file is on a government site somewhere, enter **.gov**. Other domains include .com (for business or commercial use), .edu (for educational use), and .net (for Internet servers).

4 Click **Search**.

5 When the Archie program finds your file, it displays the file's location in the top panel. Click the **plus sign** to expand the listing.

6 To view more information about the file, click it.

(continues)

Guided Tour Find Files with WS-Archie (continued)

7 Finally, make a note of the file's location, and then click the **Close** button to exit your Archie program.

Session Profile ☒

Profile Name: U. of NC ▾	Ok
Delete... Save New	Cancel
Host Name: ftp.cs.unca.edu	Advanced...
Host Type: Automatic detect ▾	Help
User ID: anonymous	☑ Anonymous Login
Password: guest	☐ Save Password
Account:	☐ Auto Save Config

Initial Directories
Remote Host: /pub/ibmpc/winsock/apps/ws
Local PC:

Comment:

8 To download the file, use your FTP program to connect to the site. See "Use an FTP Program to Copy Files" on page 274 for help.

HOW TO...

Surf the Internet Using Gopher Menus

Gopherspace is a smaller part the Internet itself; the Gopher servers that make up Gopherspace are an interconnected index of entries that you can use to quickly find a particular file or document you might be looking for. Each Gopher server presents you with a list (menu) of categories that coincide with the job function of the server itself; for instance, a Gopher on Stanford University's science server contains Gopher links to documents about mineralogy, physics, chemistry, and the like. These documents may be located on the same server, or they may be found on any other server in the Internet—and that's part of the beauty of using Gophers.

You can generally find a file by its category or title without really knowing where it's located beforehand. In Gopherspace, you travel from one Internet location to another by selecting increasingly more specific topics from a series of menus. Eventually, you'll narrow the topic down to a particular file that meets your needs. You can reach Gopherspace through your Web browser, or you can reach it through a separate Gopher program, as you'll see later in this section. In addition, you have the choice of two search tools: Veronica and Jughead.

What You Will Find in This Section

Use Gopher Through Your Web Browser

A Gopher server maintains a large database that contains links to directories or files all over the Internet. Generally, these links are directly related to the interest or job function of the people or institution running the Gopher server. When you connect to a Gopher server, you do not see a page full of splashy, graphically typeset information like you see when you use the Web. Instead, what you see looks similar to the Explorer or File Manager. When you find what you've been looking for, your Gopher program will download it for you, and it will be a file on your own computer. This file can be of any type. Although it's generally just text, it could also be graphics, a pro-gram file, or a compressed file that contains an entire shareware application.

The information that you typically find in Gopherspace varies a lot from what you find on the Web. Most Gopher servers are connected to universi-ties, so the information in Gopherspace tends to be fairly academic. If you're doing research, chances are that you'll find more information using your Gopher program than you will browsing the WWW.

However, since you're probably pretty used to your Web browser, you might prefer to use it to travel Gopherspace. In "Find and Install a Web Browser" on page 123, you learned that a Web browser can handle many protocols. A *protocol* is the language in which the information on a particular Web page is written. The most common protocol on the WWW is HTTP, but your Web browser can handle many others as well, including FTP and Gopher.

Basically, this means that you can connect to a Gopher site simply by typing its URL address in the Location box of your Web browser. The address will look something like this:

gopher://gopher.tc.umn.edu

The first part tells your Web browser that this is a Gopher site. The second part is the actual address of the Gopher site.

Begin Guided Tour   Connect to a Gopher Site with Netscape Navigator

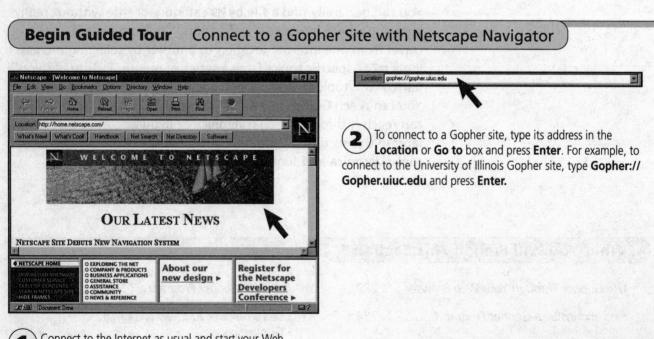

2 To connect to a Gopher site, type its address in the **Location** or **Go to** box and press **Enter**. For example, to connect to the University of Illinois Gopher site, type **Gopher:// Gopher.uiuc.edu** and press **Enter.**

1 Connect to the Internet as usual and start your Web browser.

Guided Tour Connect to a Gopher Site with Netscape Navigator

Gopher Menu

📄 Welcome to the University of Illinois at Urbana-Champaign Gopher
📁 Campus Announcements (last updated 1/17/96)
📁 What's New?
📁 Information about Gopher
🔭 Keyword Search on UIUC Gopher Menus
📁 Univ. of Illinois at Urbana-Champaign Campus Information
📁 Champaign-Urbana & Regional Information
📁 Computer Documentation, Software, and Information
📁 Libraries and Reference Information
📁 Publications (U of I Press, Newspapers, Newsletters, etc.) & Weather

3 After you connect to a Gopher site, select an item from the list by clicking it. For example, click the **What's New** folder.

Gopher Menu

📄 What's New?
📄 About "Find Items Changed" Items
📁 Find Items Changed Since 2 Days Ago
📁 Find Items Changed Since 5 Days Ago
🔭 Find Items Changed Since X Calendar Days Ago (see "About" file)

4 Items with folder icons (such as the What's New folder) are like directories on your hard disk; selecting them reveals their contents. Clicking the What's New folder in step 3 brought up this list of the What's New folder's contents.

If you want to know more about using a Gopher program, see "Use Your Gopher Program" on page 288.

```
NEW STUFF:

- 10/25/94 - Files from the Illinois Researcher Information Service
  (IRIS) are now available in three places in Gopher: under Libraries
  on the main menu; under Libraries/University of Illinois Library
  at Urbana-Champaign; and under U of I Campus Info/Academic Information
  (College, School, Department, Centers,...)/Library.  The files have
  been indexed and users may do a keyword search on the IRIS files.

- 10/25/94 - A file containing the latest scores of various athletic
  teams/clubs has been added under the Sports and Recreation Menu.
  Thanks to several alumni for this suggestion.

- 10/22/94 - A new section on "Campus Recycling and Waste Management"
  has been added under Campus Services (Health, Legal, Fellowships,
  Recycling,...)

- 10/12/94 - The menu title "Departmental Information" has been changed
```

5 Items with a page icon are documents that you can read. To open one, double-click its icon. For example, if you click the **What's New** page icon shown in the previous figure, you'll see this screen.

gopher://gopher.uiuc.edu:8002/7since
Gopher Search

This is a searchable Gopher index. Use the search function of your browser to enter search terms.

This is a searchable index. Enter search keywords: [   ]

6 Items with a binoculars icon (or a magnifying glass icon in Web browsers besides Netscape Navigator) lead you to some type of search system that generally requires typed input from you. For example, if you click the binoculars icon in step 4's figure, you'll see this screen.

See "Use Veronica or Jughead to Search Gopherspace" on page 292 for more information on using Veronica and Jughead.

Find and Install a Gopher Program

As you learned in the previous task, your Web browser can take you into Gopherspace. However, for all its convenience, you'll probably find that using a separate Gopher program is faster than using your Web browser to go Gophering. In any case, it's handy to have a good Gopher program around for times when you need it.

In the *Guided Tour*, you'll learn how to download the most popular Gopher program: WS Gopher. There is only a Windows 3.1 (16-bit) version of WS Gopher currently available; however, it will run just fine under Windows 95. To locate a copy of WS Gopher, go to the Stroud's site on the World Wide Web,

located at www.cwsapps.com and www.stroud.com. There are other sites from which you can download popular Internet programs, such as the Virtual Software Library (vsl.cnet.com), The Ultimate Collection of Winsock Software (tucows.niia.net), and the Winsite Archive (www.winsite.com).

After you download the WS Gopher program, you'll have to install it. Luckily, there's not much to do in that department. The task "Use Your Gopher Program" on page 288 explains how to use the program you will download and install in the *Guided Tour*.

Begin Guided Tour Download a Gopher Program

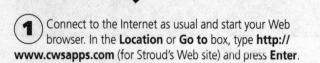

(1) Connect to the Internet as usual and start your Web browser. In the **Location** or **Go to** box, type **http://www.cwsapps.com** (for Stroud's Web site) and press **Enter**.

If you have trouble connecting to Stroud's main site, try their other main site: http://www.stroud.com or one of their alternates: http://enterprise.net/cwsapps or http://cws.wilmington.net.

● Introduction	● Windows 95 Section	● Top Ten Tips
● What's 🆕	● New for '95 Apps	● The Newest Apps
● Index of Apps	● The CASPER Page	● Top 20 Apps
● Audio Apps	● Communications Clients	● Compression Utilities
● Critical Winsock	● CWSServers	● FTP / Archie / Finger
● Gophers	● Graphics Viewers	● HTML Editors
● IRC Apps	● Mail Clients	● Multimedia Viewers
● News Readers	● Plug-in Modules 🆕	● Statistics Services
● Terminal Apps	● The Suite Spot	● Utilities - Auxiliary
● Utilities - Winsock	● Virus Scanners	● VRML Browsers
● WAIS	● Web Accessories	● WWW Browsers
● CWSApps Stats	● Sponsoring The List	● Honors & Awards

(2) Click the Stroud's logo, and then scroll down and select **Gophers**.

Guided Tour   Download a Gopher Program

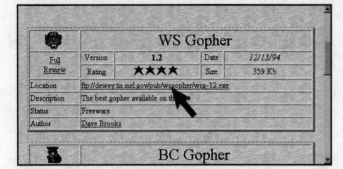

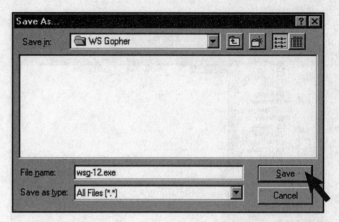

3 Click the Location of **WS Gopher**.

You can read more about a program before you download it by clicking the **Full Review** box in the left column.

4 Select a folder into which you want to download your new Gopher program. I created a WS Gopher folder.

5 Click **Save**.

6 Once the program is downloaded, close Netscape and disconnect from the Internet so you can set up your Gopher program.

Begin Guided Tour   Install Your Gopher Program

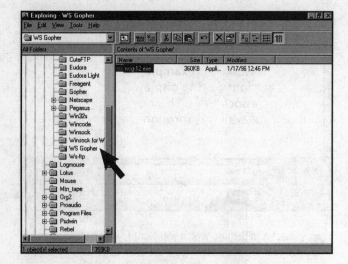

1 Start the Explorer in Windows 95 (or open the File Manager in Windows 3.1) and change to the **WS Gopher** folder (or the folder in which you downloaded the Gopher program).

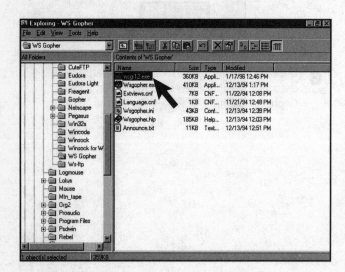

2 Double-click file **wsg-12.exe**. Its files are decompressed into the WS Gopher folder. Close the Finished-WSG-12 window.

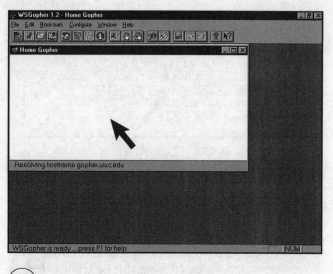

3 Double-click **Wsgopher.exe**. The program starts.

Because you're not currently connected to the Internet, you'll probably get an error message after a few minutes. If that happens, click **OK** in the box that appears.

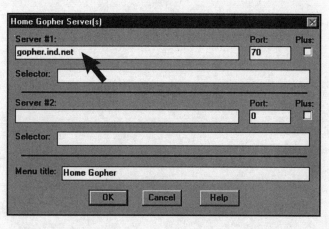

4 Open the **Configure** menu and select **Home Gopher Server**.

5 Enter the address of the nearest Gopher site in the **Server #1** text box and click **OK**. (For example, I chose the Indiana University Gopher site at gopher.ind.net. Notice that I did not use the Web-style addressing method covered earlier; I left out the "gopher://" part.)

Guided Tour Install Your Gopher Program

If you don't know the address of a nearby Gopher site (such as a university Gopher), you can continue to use the default, which is Gopher.uiuc.edu. However, you'll get faster service if you use a Gopher that's closer to your location. Next time you're on the Internet, search for one under All the Gopher Servers in the World. Just start WS Gopher, open the **Bookmark** menu, and select **Fetch**. Then click **Gopher Services** and **All the Gopher Servers in the World**. Click **OK**.

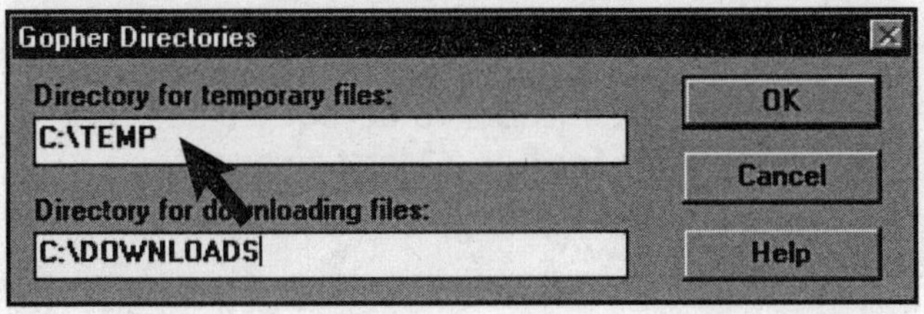

You can change some other options if you want, but it's not necessary in order to get WS Gopher to work. For example, you can select a different font for the display and add additional file associations. These additional options are available through the Configure menu.

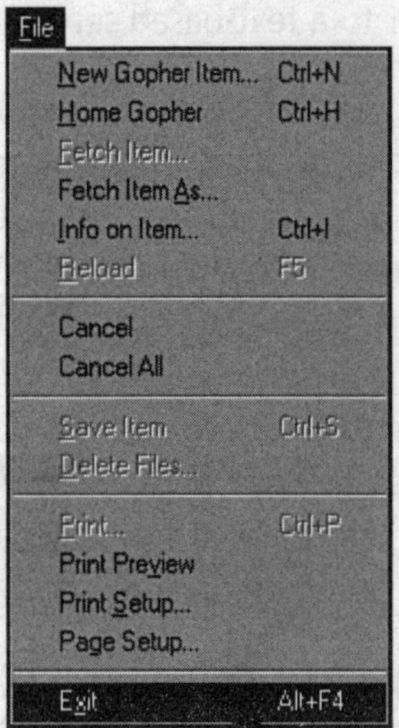

Gopher Directories

Directory for temporary files:
C:\TEMP

Directory for downloading files:
C:\DOWNLOADS

OK
Cancel
Help

6 Next, open the **Configure** menu and select **Local Directories**.

7 Enter the path of the folder in which you want Gopher to store its temporary and downloaded files, and click **OK**. I use my TEMP and DOWNLOADS folders for this purpose, but you might prefer some other folders.

File

New Gopher Item...	Ctrl+N
Home Gopher	Ctrl+H
Fetch Item...	
Fetch Item As...	
Info on Item...	Ctrl+I
Reload	F5
Cancel	
Cancel All	
Save Item	Ctrl+S
Delete Files...	
Print...	Ctrl+P
Print Preview	
Print Setup...	
Page Setup...	
Exit	Alt+F4

8 When you finish configuring WS Gopher, open the **File** menu and select **Exit**.

Use Your Gopher Program

Gopher was originated at the University of Minnesota, whose Internet engineers promptly named it after the University of Minnesota team mascot. You use Gopher to browse the Internet through a series of menus or directories. Select one option off a menu (directory), and you're usually given another menu (subdirectory) to narrow your choice. Eventually you will get to a file you can view, download, or print, or to a text-based search form.

So what will you encounter as you dig deeper and deeper into Gopher menus? Well, you might find text documents or graphics files that you can view, download, or print. You might also encounter *ask forms*, which are like dialog boxes. These forms help you search special Gopher + sites for information. Gopher + sites are enhanced versions of regular Gopher sites ("enhanced" because they provide ask forms for quick searching and usually more than one version of a file for downloading).

To jump to a specific Gopher site, you *fetch* it. Fetching involves connecting to the remote site, logging in, and finally displaying a menu of its main directory. WS Gopher contains a list of sites you can fetch in its Bookmarks menu. You can add additional bookmarks, or delete or rearrange them.

Fetching has another meaning in Gopherspace. When you locate a file that you want to keep, you can *fetch it* (display the contents of that item on-screen). You can then save the item (copy the item onto your hard disk), print it, or copy its contents to the Windows Clipboard.

> If you fetch a program file, it is displayed on-screen as text, which will look like a complete mess. Don't worry; just save the file to disk and use your uuencoder to decode it. (See "Retrieve a File Sent As a Message over the Internet" on page 215.)

The WS Gopher Toolbar

WS Gopher provides a handy toolbar that gives you quick access to common commands. The following table shows you what each button does.

WS Gopher Toolbar Buttons

Button	Function
	Displays the current Fetch Bookmark menu
	Adds current item to bookmarks list
	Adds current folder to bookmarks list
	Enables you to edit bookmarks
	Returns to your home Gopher
	Returns to the top of the current listing
	Backs up one level

Button	Function
	Displays information about the current item
	Displays (fetches) the current item
	Cancels the current transaction
	Cancels all transactions
	Searches for particular text in the current window
	Repeats the previous search
	Saves the current item to disk
	Copies the current item to the WIndows Clipboard
	Prints the current item
	Displays WS Gopher version info
	Turns on context help

Begin Guided Tour   Use WS Gopher

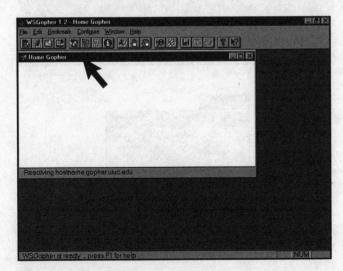

1 To start WS Gopher, change to its directory and then double-click the **Wsgopher.exe** file. You're connected to your home Gopher site. You can return to the home site at any time by clicking the **Home Gopher Site** button.

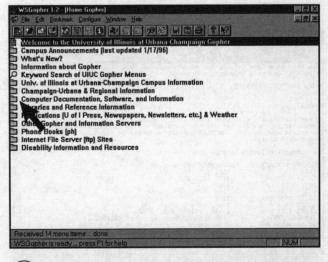

2 From here, simply double-click an item to select it. If you click a folder icon, Gopher fetches it (displays its contents). For example, double-click the **Computer Documentation, Software, and Information** folder.

(continues)

Guided Tour   Use WS Gopher   *(continued)*

If you didn't change your home site when you configured WS Gopher, your home site is the University of Illinois. For this example, I'll just use the default site—U of I.

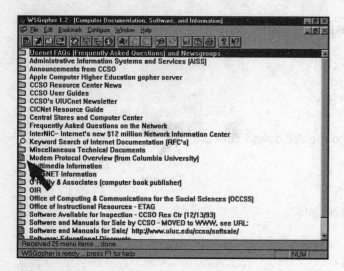

3 You can continue to dig deeper and deeper into this Gopher's directory system (called an outline) by clicking on other folders, such as **InterNIC**. To return to the Computer Documentation, Software, and Information folder, jump back one level in the outline by clicking the **Back up** button.

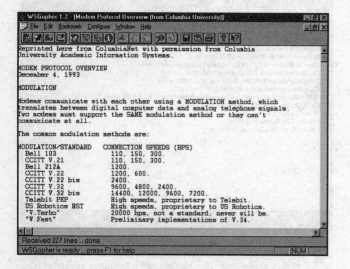

4 You can double-click a page icon or click the Fetch toolbar button to read the associated document. For example, double-click the **Modem Protocol Overview (from Columbia University)** page icon shown in the previous figure, and you'll see this screen.

Once an item's displayed, you can print it, copy it to your hard disk, or copy it to the Clipboard by clicking the appropriate toolbar button.

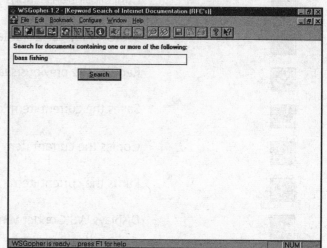

5 Items with a magnifying glass icon lead you to Veronica or Jughead search screens. So if you double-click a magnifying glass icon, you'll see something like this screen.

See "Use Veronica or Jughead to Search Gopherspace" on page 292 for information on how to search.

6 To fetch a particular Gopher site, open the **Bookmark** menu and select **Fetch**.

Guided Tour Use WS Gopher

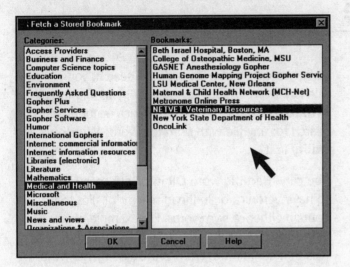

7 Select a category from the **Categories** list on the left side of the window.

8 Then select a bookmark from the **Bookmarks** list and click **OK**. WS Gopher connects you to the site you selected.

9 When you're done, click the **Close** button, or open the **File** menu and select **Exit**.

Use Veronica or Jughead to Search Gopherspace

The Gopher system has two search tools that you can use to locate items in Gopherspace: Veronica and Jughead. To use Veronica, you type in a search string, such as "bass fishing." Veronica searches Gopher sites for files that contain the words "bass fishing," and then Veronica presents the results of its search to you. If you were looking for a copy of a Windows utility, you could search for the word "IBM" to locate IBM (DOS-compatible) files. You might also search under the word "Windows." Keep in mind that whether you get good results depends on you searching for the right combination of words.

After connecting to a Veronica site, you'll find that you must choose between two different kinds of searches. For a quick search of each Gopher site, select **Directory Only**. For a more thorough (and time-consuming) search, select **Gopherspace**.

Unlike Veronica, which searches all Gophers, Jughead searches only the current Gopher site. Usually, you'll initiate a Jughead search without knowing it. For example, on a Gopher list, you might see an option such as "Search Gopher titles at the University of Minnesota." If you select this option, it'll take you to what looks like a Veronica screen. You enter the words to search for, just as you would in Veronica. However, in this case, Jughead searches only the files stored on the U of M Gopher site, and not all the Gophers in the world.

Searching Tips

When you select Veronica or Jughead from a Gopher menu, you're taken to an ask form, which is similar to a dialog box. In the ask form, you enter the information for which you want to search. Once Veronica or Jughead has successfully located an item for you, you can fetch that item for viewing by double-clicking it.

As mentioned earlier, to initiate a search, you just type in a key word or two. For example, you might type **Windows utility**. This tells Veronica or Jughead to search for any file with *both* the words **Windows** and **utility** in it.

You can insert the word **OR** into your search string to have Veronica or Jughead search for files that contain either of two words. For example, if you type **Windows OR utility**, the search tool will display all files that contain the word **Windows** or the word **utility**. This will most likely get you files you don't want, such as *Windows* games, *Windows* communications programs, and *Windows* help files, in addition to DOS *utilities* and UNIX *utilities*. So avoid using OR in your search string if possible.

Okay, there is one way to use OR to aid in a search. If you were looking for information on bass or striper fishing, you could use the following search string that includes parentheses to group the two related items: **fishing (bass OR striper)**. This would get you files related to either bass fishing or striper fishing.

You can use NOT in a search string to narrow a search if you want. For example, you can type **Windows NOT 95** to display only Windows 3.1 related files, and not Windows 95 files.

You can also use the wild-card character ***** to aid your search. For example, if you typed, **drug*** you'd get "drug," "drugs," "drugstore," and so on. Note, however, that you can't use an asterisk in the middle of a search string, as in **dr*g**. All you'll get for your cleverness is an error message.

Normally, Veronica limits its results to the first 200 items it finds that match your search string. You can also narrow a search by limiting the number of items listed, and/or by limiting the type of file Veronica searches.

To limit the number of files listing in the result, add **-m***number* to the end of your search string, like this:

> **english literature -m10**

To have Veronica list everything it finds, don't type a number, like this:

> **english literature -m**

To limit the type of file Veronica searches for, add **-t***type* to the end of your search string, like this:

> **utilities -t1**

This tells Veronica to search only for file type #1, which is directory. Here's a complete list of file types you can use with this command:

0	Text file
1	Directory
2	CSO name server (phone book)
4	Mac HQX file (BINHEX)
5	PC binary file (program file)
6	UUENCODed file
7	Gopher menus
8	Telnet session
9	Binary file
s	sound
e	event
I	Image (other than GIF file)
M	MIME e-mail message
T	TN3270 session
c	Calendar
g	GIF image
h	HTML document

Begin Guided Tour   Search Gopher Sites with Veronica and Jughead

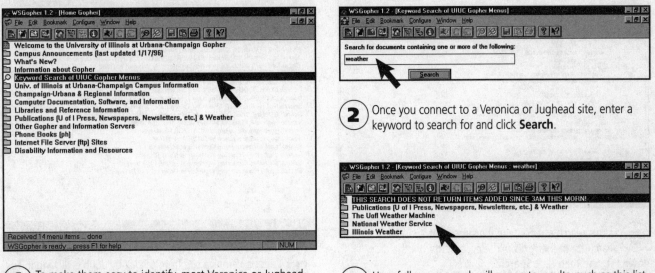

1 To make them easy to identify, most Veronica or Jughead searches are marked with a magnifying glass icon. To start your search, double-click any magnifying glass icon on a Gopher menu.

2 Once you connect to a Veronica or Jughead site, enter a keyword to search for and click **Search**.

3 Hopefully, your search will generate results, such as this list. To narrow your search further, double-click a folder such as National Weather Service.

(continues)

Guided Tour Search Gopher Sites with Veronica and Jughead *(continued)*

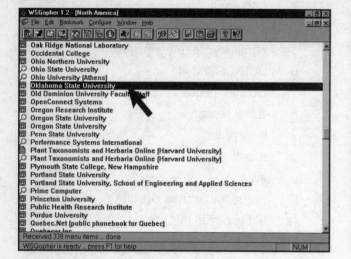

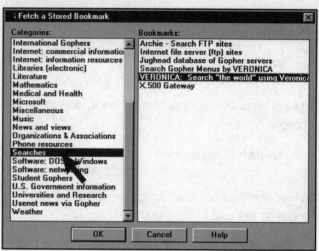

(4) Sometimes a Veronica or Jughead option won't be marked with a magnifying glass icon, but with something else such as the phone icon shown here. What type of icon is used depends on the associated Gopher menu's ultimate purpose. Double-click the phone icon.

(6) Another way you can fetch a Veronica or Jughead site is by opening the **Bookmark** menu and selecting **Fetch**.

(7) From the Fetch dialog box, select **Searches** from the **Categories** list, select either **Jughead** or **VERONICA** from the **Bookmarks** list, and click **OK**.

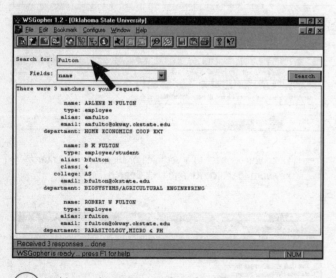

(5) In this search screen, type the information you want to search for in the text box. Select a field from the drop-down list, and then click **Search**.

(8) Select a Veronica site from the list by double-clicking it. For example, double-click **Search GOPHER DIRECTORIES by Title Word(s) [UNAM]**. Gopher servers are often busy, so you may have to try several different server sites before you get a response.

Guided Tour   Search Gopher Sites with Veronica and Jughead

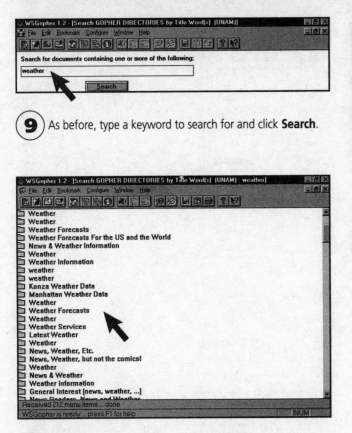

9 As before, type a keyword to search for and click **Search**.

10 When you use Veronica, you're searching all Gopher sites everywhere; therefore, your results list is longer than when you searched a single Gopher site (as you did in step 3).

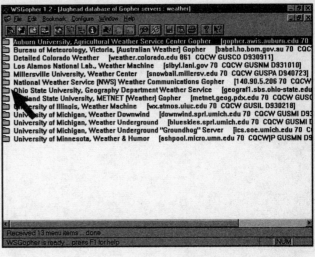

11 However, if you use Jughead instead of Veronica to search, your list is not as complete because Jughead only searches a single Gopher site. A Jughead search is typically faster than a Veronica search.

HOW TO...

Find and Play Java Applets

One of the most hyped Web topics of late is Java, a programming language that lets people create interactive, multimedia applications for the World Wide Web. Using Java, programmers can create small programs called Java applets, that can be placed on a Web page. A Java applet can be an animation (like a cartoon), a movie clip that plays automatically, or a form that gives you immediate feedback.

For example, one Java applet I recently encountered on the Web is a worksheet for calculating loan payments. When you connect to the Web page that has this applet, you are presented with a fill-in-the-blanks form. You type the amount you intend to borrow, the interest percentage, and the number of payment periods, and the applet calculates the amount of your monthly payments.

In this section, you will skip around the Web to find and play some of the more interesting Java applets and other small online programs.

What You Will Find in This Section

Play Sample Java Applets

Currently, programmers are using Java to create demos—small, interesting little applications that show the capabilities of Java. These demos include an online painting application, a tic-tac-toe game, an animated Christmas card that plays a jingle, a cross-word puzzle, a loan calculator, and other nifty playthings.

However, as programmers develop their skills with the Java programming language, they will begin to create more complex Java applets. The possibilities include interactive classes, where students can study at their own pace, take tests, and receive immediate feedback; online games you can play, just as if they were installed on your computer; and even online graphs that can show you your investment earnings.

What Makes Java Special?

On the surface, Java might seem like just another programming language. What makes Java so special is that its applets can be run on nearly any type of computer—a PC running Windows, a Macintosh, a UNIX workstation, or any other computer that can connect to the Internet. The only essential you need for running a Java applet is a Web browser that can handle Java applets.

Currently, two Web browsers can play Java applets: Netscape Navigator (version 2.0) and HotJava (a Web browser created by the company that developed Java). By the time you read this, most Web browsers should have this capability. Because Java applets can run on virtually any computer system, they are ideal for the Internet. And, because these applets can easily be placed on any Web page, they are very accessible.

> Unlike full-fledged applications that can run on their own, Java applets need a host program in which to run. The Web browser acts as the host program for Java applets.

Find Java Applets

As soon as businesses, educational institutions, and individual programmers get up to speed with the Java programming language, you'll be bumping into Java applets at every turn on the Web. And, because Java applets are embedded in Web pages, you probably won't even realize that you're using Java applets. You'll just point, click, and type, while the applet performs its magic behind the scenes.

For now, however, you'll have to search for Java applets. Because Sun Microsystems and Netscape are the major promoters of Java, you can usually find sample Java applets at their Web sites. The *Guided Tour* takes you to these sites and shows you some sample Java applets in action.

Begin Guided Tour Play Java Applets

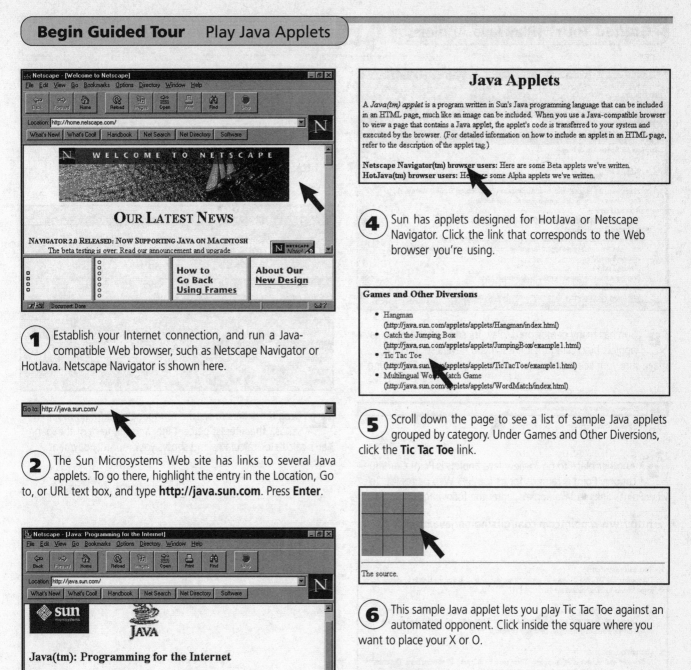

1 Establish your Internet connection, and run a Java-compatible Web browser, such as Netscape Navigator or HotJava. Netscape Navigator is shown here.

2 The Sun Microsystems Web site has links to several Java applets. To go there, highlight the entry in the Location, Go to, or URL text box, and type **http://java.sun.com**. Press **Enter**.

3 Sun's home page appears, displaying several links that give you access to more information about Java. Click the **Applets** link.

Java Applets

A *Java(tm) applet* is a program written in Sun's Java programming language that can be included in an HTML page, much like an image can be included. When you use a Java-compatible browser to view a page that contains a Java applet, the applet's code is transferred to your system and executed by the browser. (For detailed information on how to include an applet in an HTML page, refer to the description of the applet tag.)

Netscape Navigator(tm) browser users: Here are some Beta applets we've written.
HotJava(tm) browser users: Here are some Alpha applets we've written.

4 Sun has applets designed for HotJava or Netscape Navigator. Click the link that corresponds to the Web browser you're using.

Games and Other Diversions

- Hangman
  (http://java.sun.com/applets/applets/Hangman/index.html)
- Catch the Jumping Box
  (http://java.sun.com/applets/applets/JumpingBox/example1.html)
- Tic Tac Toe
  (http://java.sun.com/applets/applets/TicTacToe/example1.html)
- Multilingual Word Match Game
  (http://java.sun.com/applets/applets/WordMatch/index.html)

5 Scroll down the page to see a list of sample Java applets grouped by category. Under Games and Other Diversions, click the **Tic Tac Toe** link.

The source.

6 This sample Java applet lets you play Tic Tac Toe against an automated opponent. Click inside the square where you want to place your X or O.

7 When the game is over, click anywhere in the Tic Tac Toe grid to clear the grid and start a new game. When you're done playing, enter the command to go back to the previous page.

(continues)

Guided Tour Play Java Applets

(continued)

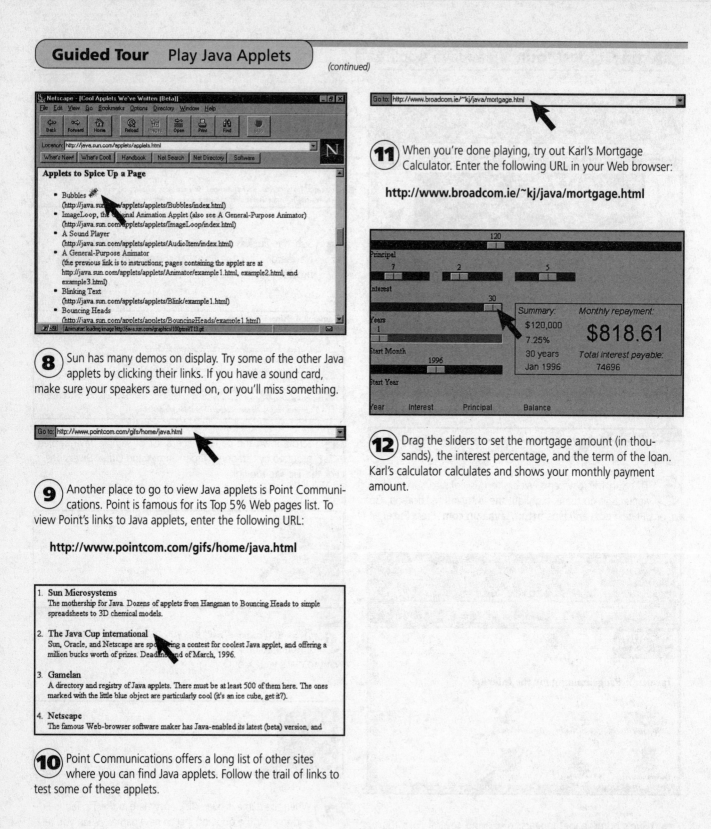

8 Sun has many demos on display. Try some of the other Java applets by clicking their links. If you have a sound card, make sure your speakers are turned on, or you'll miss something.

9 Another place to go to view Java applets is Point Communications. Point is famous for its Top 5% Web pages list. To view Point's links to Java applets, enter the following URL:

http://www.pointcom.com/gifs/home/java.html

1. **Sun Microsystems**
   The mothership for Java. Dozens of applets from Hangman to Bouncing Heads to simple spreadsheets to 3D chemical models.

2. **The Java Cup international**
   Sun, Oracle, and Netscape are sponsoring a contest for coolest Java applet, and offering a million bucks worth of prizes. Deadline end of March, 1996.

3. **Gamelan**
   A directory and registry of Java applets. There must be at least 500 of them here. The ones marked with the little blue object are particularly cool (it's an ice cube, get it?).

4. **Netscape**
   The famous Web-browser software maker has Java-enabled its latest (beta) version, and

10 Point Communications offers a long list of other sites where you can find Java applets. Follow the trail of links to test some of these applets.

11 When you're done playing, try out Karl's Mortgage Calculator. Enter the following URL in your Web browser:

http://www.broadcom.ie/~kj/java/mortgage.html

12 Drag the sliders to set the mortgage amount (in thousands), the interest percentage, and the term of the loan. Karl's calculator calculates and shows your monthly payment amount.

Understand JavaScript

As you encounter Java applets, you might come across a reference to JavaScript. Don't confuse JavaScript with Java. Java is a full-featured programming language, which is somewhat difficult for the average computer user to learn (as is any programming language). JavaScript is simply a coding system that allows Web page creators to embed Java applets in Web pages and to create simple applets.

If you don't plan to create your own Web pages, you don't have to worry about JavaScript. It works behind the scenes. However, if you decide to try your hand at creating Web pages, you might want to insert a Java applet on your page or use JavaScript to make your Web page more interactive.

The following *Guided Tour* shows you some sample JavaScript codes and demonstrates how they are used. If you're serious about writing your own Java applets, nab a copy of *The Complete Idiot's Guide to JavaScript*.

Begin Guided Tour   Look at a Sample JavaScript

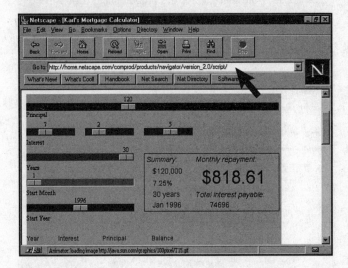

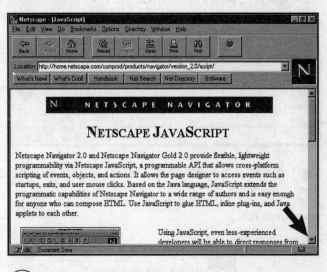

1 The best place to check out JavaScript is at Netscape's Web site. In your Web browser (Netscape Navigator is used here), enter the following URL:

http://home.netscape.com/comprod/products/navigator/ version_2.0/script/

2 Netscape's Web site explains JavaScript in greater detail. Scroll down the page to view some samples of how JavaScript can be used.

(continues)

Guided Tour Look at a Sample JavaScript *(continued)*

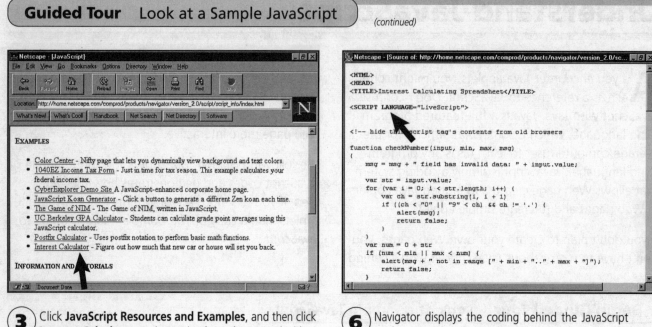

3 Click **JavaScript Resources and Examples**, and then click **Interest Calculator** to view a simple applet created with JavaScript.

# of Payments	Interest Rate	Principal	Monthly payment		
360	0.0762	120000	849.35249	Compute	Reset
				Compute	Reset
				Compute	Reset

4 This calculator determines your monthly payment amount based on the amount borrowed, the interest rate, and the length of the loan. Enter the requested data and click the **Compute** button.

6 Navigator displays the coding behind the JavaScript applet. Note that the applet's programming code is set off from the rest of the document by the `<Script>` code.

7 Following the `<Script>` code are the programming commands that perform the calculations required to determine the monthly payment amount. This is a fairly complex JavaScript applet.

5 To see how this JavaScript applet is constructed, open Navigator's **View** menu and select **Document Source**.

Guided Tour   Look at a Sample JavaScript

8 Click the **Close** button to close the Document Source window and return to Netscape Navigator.

A simple script might check the time of day and display the appropriate background or photograph.

Postfix Calculator Example
(requires Netscape Navigator 2.0b2)

Interest Calculator Example
(requires Netscape Navigator 2.0b2)

Scripting Information

Next Feature

9 The Netscape Web site offers additional information about JavaScript. If you are interested in learning more, go back to the opening Java page you saw in step 2, click **JavaScript Resources and Examples**, scroll down to the Information and Tutorials section, and click **Scripting Information**.

Netscape - [JavaScript Authoring Guide]
File Edit View Go Bookmarks Options Directory Window Help

Location: http://home.netscape.com/comprod/products/navigator/version_2.0/script/script_info/index.html

What's New!   What's Cool!   Handbook   Net Search   Net Directory   Software

Introduction

Learning JavaScript
Using JavaScript in
HTML

**The JavaScript
Language**

Values, Names, and
Literals
Expressions and
Operators
JavaScript Object
Model

The Mother of all Disclaimers
JavaScript and its documentation are currently under development. Some of the language is not yet implemented. That which is implemented is subject to change. Information provided at this time is incomplete and should not be considered a language specification. JavaScript is a work in progress whose potential we'd like to share with you, the beta users, in this developmental form.

Learning JavaScript

JavaScript is a compact, object-based scripting language for developing client and server Internet applications. Netscape

Document: Done

10 Netscape presents complete documentation to help you learn how to use JavaScript. Click a link in the left frame to display information about a specific JavaScript topic.

Play VRML Applets

Although Java has received the most press, there are other programming languages designed for the Internet. The strongest contender is VRML (which rhymes with "gerbil" and stands for *Virtual Reality Modeling Language*). Like Java, VRML is used by programmers to create small applications that can be placed on Web pages. These applications are just like Java applets in that they can display animations, video, and interactive forms on a page.

To play a VRML applet, you need a special VRML-compatible Web browser, or a helper application. One such helper application is called VR Scout. You can set up VR Scout to run from your current Web browser. You can use your Web browser to download a copy of VR Scout. (See "Find and Copy Files from the

Internet" on page 263.) Connect to the following Web page, and follow the links to download this valuable helper application:

http://www.chaco.com/vrscout/plugin.html

Once you download the file, run it and follow the on-screen instructions to install the program. The installation program asks you to specify the Web browser you're using. It then sets up VR Scout to run automatically from the Web browser whenever you click a VRML applet link.

After setting up VR Scout (or another VRML player), take the *Guided Tour* to play some sample VRML files.

Begin Guided Tour   Play Sample VRML Applets

1 Establish your Internet connection, and run your Web browser. The picture here shows Netscape Navigator, which is compatible with VR Scout.

2 Point Communications has links to several sites that have VRML demos. To view Point's links to VRML applets, enter the following URL in your Web browser's **Location** or **Go to** text box:

http://www.pointcom.com/

3 In addition to links for the Top 5% of Web pages, Point Communications offers links to Java and VRML sites. Click the **VRML** link.

Guided Tour Play Sample VRML Applets

1. **Paper Software**
   Makers of the highly-rated WebFX VRML browser, whose Java functionality allows a greater degree of interactivity.

2. **Microsoft**
   Microsoft (always a major player) has just unveiled a new VRML viewer for its Internet Explorer browser. A beta version of the viewer, known as Virtual Explorer 1.0, is available through the Microsoft Web site.

3. **Chaco's Virtual Jack-O-Lantern**
   If you suffer from "an irrational fear of knives or pumpkin guts," then generate your own custom VRML Jack-O-Lantern at this fun site.

4 A list of sites appears for both VRML players and VRML applets. Click a link for one of the VRML applets. Here, I clicked **Chaco's Virtual Jack-O-Lantern** to display a pumpkin carving applet at the VR Scout site. If you can't get there from Point Communications, try this URL:

http://userwww.chaco.com/~glenn/jack/

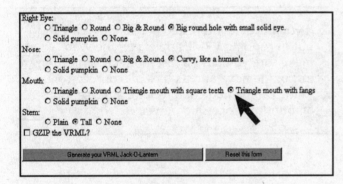

5 The pumpkin carving applet lets you complete a form for the type of pumpkin you want. Make your selections, and then click the **Generate Your VRML Jack-O-Lantern** button.

6 It takes Navigator a while to download the selected VRML applet, run VR Scout, and display your pumpkin. Click **Headlight**, at the bottom of the screen, to give your jack-o'-lantern some color.

7 Now for some cool stuff. Click the **Examine** button, and then use your mouse to drag the pumpkin head. This spins the jack-o'-lantern around, so you can see all of its sides.

8 Click the **Walk** or **Fly** button, and drag the mouse pointer slowly near the jack-o'-lantern. Watch as it walks or flies across the screen.

9 When you are done playing with your pumpkin, enter the following URL to go to the vrmLab VRML warehouse:

http://www.newcollege.edu/vrmLab/Warehouse/

(continues)

Guided Tour Play Sample VRML Applets

(continued)

Index of /vrmLab/Warehouse/

Name	Last modified	Size	Description
Parent Directory	19-Dec-95 11:42	-	
AirAndSpacecraft	10-Oct-95 11:44	-	*sub-directory*
BooksAndPens	05-Oct-95 09:53	-	*sub-directory*
Buildings	19-Dec-95 11:42	-	*sub-directory*
ComputerEquipment	05-Oct-95 08:34	-	*sub-directory*
CouchesAndChairs	03-Nov-95 15:31	-	*sub-directory*

10 The vrmLab warehouse contains lots of VRML files grouped in separate folders. Click around in the folders to find a VRML applet that interests you.

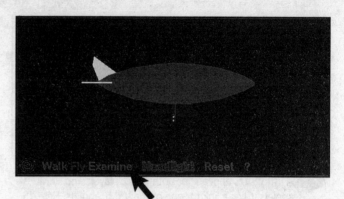

11 The VRML applet shown here is a representation of a zeppelin. Don't forget that you can use the **Walk**, **Fly**, **Examine**, **Headlight**, and **Reset** buttons to play with any VRML object you happen across.

If you become interested in making a career out of running VRML applets on the Web, make sure you have a fast modem connection, lots of memory, and a quick microprocessor. VRML can be huge and require a tremendous amount of processing power.

HOW TO...

Secure Your System and Practice Proper Etiquette

As a citizen of the Internet, you have special concerns and responsibilities. You need to protect your computer and yourself from intrusions, and you must follow the rules of the Internet to avoid insulting another user or tying up a connection during the Internet "rush hour."

In this section, you will get the information you need to become a good Internet citizen. You'll learn how to protect your system against viruses that might infect your system (and spread to other systems on the Internet). You'll find out how to send sensitive material (such as credit card numbers) safely through Internet connections. You'll learn how to act in newsgroups to prevent sparking unproductive arguments. And, if you have children, you'll learn how to screen out material that may (or at least should) offend them.

What You Will Find in This Section

Understand Internet Security

The Internet is like a big, electronic city that offers everything from massive electronic libraries and art museums to electronic pornography and online criminals. And, because the Internet is a computer playground, it has the added threat of computer viruses—bugs that can bring your computer to a grinding halt and wipe out all the programs and data you spent months accumulating.

In order to protect yourself, your family, and your computer from harm, you should give some thought to securing your system. To ensure that your system is secure, you must take the following three steps:

- Use a secure Web browser (such as Netscape Navigator), and if you enter any personal information (using an online form), make sure that you do it at a secure site. See "Send Information Securely," on page 311 for details.

- If you have children, obtain and use a program that filters out inappropriate information and prevents your kids from accessing specific sites. You can use a free program such as Cyber Patrol. For details, see "Prevent Your Children from Accessing Specific Sites," on page 317.

- Back up your system regularly, and use an antivirus program to check for viruses. Because you will be downloading and running programs from the Internet, you risk infecting your system with a virus. Although viruses are uncommon, they can do a lot of damage if not detected early. See "Avoid Viruses," on page 324, for details.

The following *Guided Tour* provides a basic overview of what you must do to secure your system. Other *Guided Tours* in this section provide details on how to use various programs to ensure that your system is secure.

Begin Guided Tour Secure Your System on the Internet

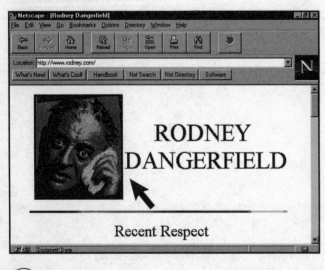

1 If all you do is wander the Internet with a Web browser, looking at Web pages, you don't have to worry too much about securing your system.

2 If you download and run programs (even small helper applications) from FTP sites, you run the risk of infecting your computer with a virus.

Guided Tour Secure Your System on the Internet

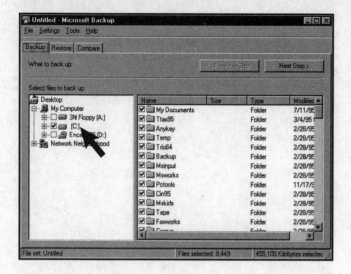

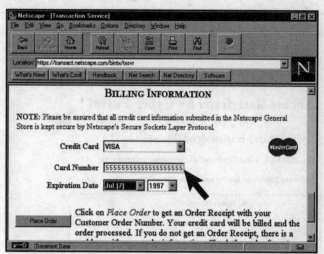

3 To prevent viruses from damaging your system, the best defense is a recent backup of your programs and data. Be sure to back up your system regularly.

5 Whenever you fill out a form on the Internet, you risk having the information you enter fall into the wrong hands. Give sensitive information (credit card numbers, phone numbers, and so on) only to reputable companies.

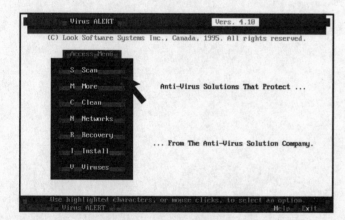

4 Although most antivirus programs cannot prevent a virus from infecting your system, they can detect a virus early and help you get rid of it so that it does as little damage as possible. Run your antivirus program regularly.

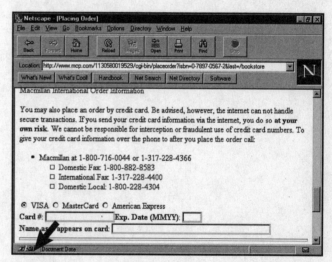

6 Some forms have special security features that prevent other users from intercepting the data you enter. When entering sensitive data, make sure you are at a secure site. Navigator displays the broken key icon shown here to indicate that a site is *not* secure.

(continues)

Guided Tour Secure Your System on the Internet

(continued)

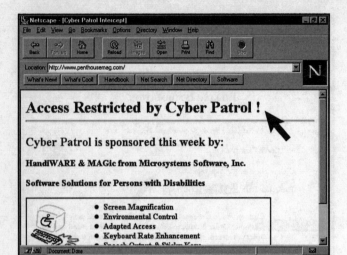

7 When you send your kids out on the Internet, you're sending them into a big city. Protect them from the criminal element by installing a special filter that screens out pornography and prevents them from accessing inappropriate material.

Send Information Securely

Whenever you use a credit card, or give someone your telephone number or address, you run some risk of having that information fall into the wrong hands. For example, if you decide to order something over the phone using a credit card, the company you are ordering from might not be legitimate. It can be a phony company that's set up just to scam credit card numbers. Or the company's phone lines might be tapped by some kid who's trying a creative way to earn money for college.

You run the same risks when you transmit sensitive information on the Internet. For that reason, you should never give someone your phone number or credit card number on the Internet unless you feel confident that the company taking your order is legitimate. Also, if you transmit the information over a connection that is not protected by some security system, you run the risk of having your credit card

number or phone number intercepted by a nefarious computer hacker.

Fortunately, with a little common sense and a Web browser that shows which sites are secure, you can feel as comfortable entering sensitive information on the Internet as you would giving this information over the phone. The *Guided Tour* shows how to use Netscape Navigator to ensure that you are entering information at a secure Web site.

If you're worried about security, and you use a Web browser other than Netscape Navigator, you should consider switching to Navigator. To take advantage of Netscape's security features, you have to use Navigator and you have to connect to a server that uses Netscape's security system.

Begin Guided Tour   Use Netscape Navigator's Security Options

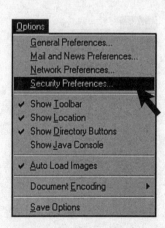

1 Before you enter any sensitive information on the Web, make sure Navigator's security features are turned on. Open the **Options** menu and select **Security Preferences**.

2 Navigator's security options tell you when you are entering and leaving a secure site, and when you are about to enter information (any information) at an unsecure site. Make sure all the options have a check mark next to them.

(continues)

Guided Tour Use Netscape Navigator's Security Options *(continued)*

Preferences

General | Site Certificates

Java
☑ Disable Java

Security Alerts
Show an Alert Before:
☑ Entering a Secure Document Space (Server)
☑ Leaving a Secure Document Space (Server)
☑ Viewing a Document With a Secure/Insecure Mix
☑ Submitting a Form Insecurely

OK | Cancel | Apply | Help

③ Because the Java feature runs applications on your computer, if you enable Java, you introduce a slight risk of infecting your computer with a virus. If you want to be extremely careful (and miss out on neat Java applets), you can disable Java support by clicking the **Disable Java** option. Click **OK**.

Security Information

You have requested a secure document. The document and any information you send back are encrypted for privacy while in transit. For more information on security choose Document Information from the View menu.

☑ Show This Alert Next Time

Continue | Cancel

④ Whenever you connect to a Web server that is protected by Netscape's security features, a dialog box appears, telling you that the site is safe. Companies have to register with Netscape to prove they are "safe" sites. Click **Continue**.

Security Information

You have requested an insecure document. The document and any information you send back could be observed by a third party while in transit. For more information on security choose Document Information from the View menu. ‖

☑ Show This Alert Next Time

Continue | Cancel

⑤ If you enter information at a site that is not secure, Navigator displays a dialog box, warning you that the information you've entered might get intercepted. If the information is not of a sensitive nature, don't worry about entering it. Click **Continue**.

> You will receive Navigator's warning messages even if you submit a form to search for a particular topic. You can ignore these warnings, because you are not entering data that anyone else might want.

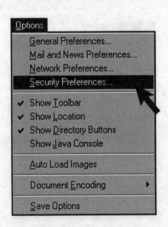

Options
General Preferences...
Mail and News Preferences...
Network Preferences...
Security Preferences...
✔ Show Toolbar
✔ Show Location
✔ Show Directory Buttons
Show Java Console
Auto Load Images
Document Encoding ▶
Save Options

⑥ If you never enter any sensitive information on the Web, you can turn off the security warnings. Open the **Options** menu and select **Security Preferences**.

Guided Tour　Use Netscape Navigator's Security Options

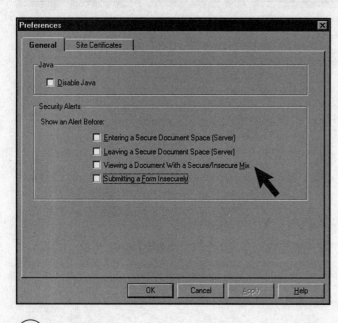

9 The key icon in the lower left corner of the Navigator window also indicates whether a site is secure. If the key is broken, the site is not secure.

Your Information

Last Name (as it appears on your credit card):	
First Name and Middle Initial (as it appears on your credit card):	
Credit Card Number:	
Card Type:　☐ American Express ☐ Mastercard ☐ VISA	
Credit Card Expiration (Month/Year):	
E-Mail Address:	
Phone Number:	
Address1:	

7 The security warnings can become annoying. To turn them off, click each warning option to remove its check mark. Click **OK**.

Location: `https://merchant.netscape.com/binms/review_cart.cgi/netstore/soft/nav/items/leaf/1008.html`

8 Even with the warnings off, you can tell when you are at a secure site. First, look in the Location or Go To text box. If the URL begins with **https** instead of **http**, the site is secure.

10 Before entering any sensitive information, ask yourself if you are confident that the company requesting this information is legitimate. If you don't feel comfortable about supplying requested information, don't enter it.

Practice Proper Internet Etiquette

Although the Internet is a massive network of computers, it is also a network of people, and whenever people assemble, you have to start worrying about etiquette—the proper way to behave in social situations. In addition to making you look bad, improper behavior may result in you losing privileges to some sites or being inundated with angry e-mail messages.

The rules of the Internet are simple. First, don't download big files (more than one megabyte) from FTP sites during business hours. Second, don't make anybody angry. It's this second rule that requires some explanation.

Downloading files during the off hours is best for everyone. It benefits the FTP site by reducing traffic during the busiest times. It benefits you, because you're more likely to be able to connect during off-hours, and the file transfer will proceed much more quickly.

There are all sorts of ways to upset people on the Internet. If you type in ALL UPPERCASE characters, for example, users think you're shouting at them, and they become suitably annoyed. If you ask questions that have already been answered earlier in a newsgroup, or if you voice an opinion in a newsgroup about which you know little or nothing, people are likely to become upset. Likewise, spouting off in chat rooms is considered bad form.

The following *Guided Tour* shows you how to behave on the Internet. With this *Guided Tour*, and a little common sense and empathy, you will be well on your way to becoming the Miss or Mr. Manners of the Internet.

Begin Guided Tour   Behave Yourself on the Internet

```
README          16 Kb    Tue Jan 03 00:00:00 1995
README.F         1 Kb    Thu Jan 12 00:00:00 1995
SGI/                     Mon Oct 31 00:00:00 1994 Directory
```

1 When you connect to an FTP site, there is usually a text file (often called README) that contains the rules of the site. Click the link to read this file.

```
The National Center for Supercomputing Applications           1/2
Anonymous FTP Server General Information

This file contains information about the general structure, as well as
information on how to obtain files and documentation from the FTP server.
NCSA software and documentation can also be obtained through the the U.S.
Mail.  Instructions are included for using this method as well.

Information about the Software Development Group and NCSA software can be
found in the /ncsapubs directory in a file called TechResCatalog.

THE UNIVERSITY OF ILLINOIS GIVES NO WARRANTY, EXPRESSED OR IMPLIED, FOR THE
SOFTWARE AND/OR DOCUMENTATION PROVIDED, INCLUDING, WITHOUT LIMITATION,
WARRANTY OF MERCHANTABILITY AND WARRANTY OF FITNESS FOR A PARTICULAR PURPOS
```

2 The README file usually contains an explanation of where files are stored and instructions on how to access files. README might also tell you the best times to download files.

Guided Tour Behave Yourself on the Internet

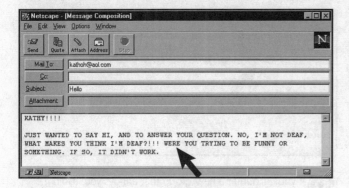

3 When composing e-mail or talking in a chat room, don't shout. Using ALL UPPERCASE characters and overusing exclamation points is the equivalent of shouting, and it is very annoying.

4 When composing e-mail or a response to a newsgroup posting, you should quote any message to which you are responding. If the e-mail program doesn't quote the message for you, type a right angle bracket (>) to the left of each quoted line, and keep quotes brief (about three lines maximum).

5 Word your e-mail messages tactfully. Humor and sarcasm can easily be misinterpreted in typewritten messages. You can often use emoticons to add a smile to a phrase that might be taken wrong, to show you are joking. See page 493 for a list of emoticons.

6 Delete any e-mail messages you've received and read from your service provider's computer. Most e-mail programs have an option that automatically copies e-mail messages to your hard disk and then deletes them from the service provider's system.

(continues)

Guided Tour Behave Yourself on the Internet

(continued)

7 Spend some time in a newsgroup reading messages before you post your own messages or respond. Many newsgroups have a FAQ (frequently asked questions) file that you should read to learn more about the group. The more you know about a newsgroup, the more intelligently you can respond to the messages it contains.

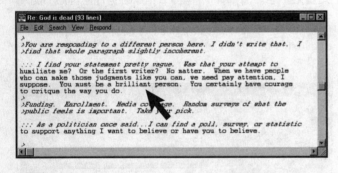

8 Avoid insulting a particular newsgroup member's opinion. This can start a *flame war* (a typically unproductive war of words).

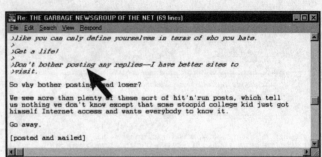

10 If you encounter a newsgroup that annoys you, avoid it. Don't enter a newsgroup simply to insult its members.

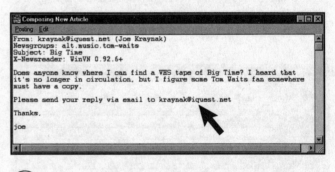

11 If you ask a specific question in a newsgroup, request that answers be sent to you via e-mail. That way, the newsgroup won't become cluttered with 20 of the same answers to the same question. You can post the best answer later, for those who might be curious.

> In addition to these proper manners, keep in mind that you must follow state and federal laws, as well. You cannot use the Internet to harass people, sell or trade child pornography, steal, or destroy a person's work or reputation.

9 Don't use newsgroups as a way to advertise (unless the newsgroup is specifically for listing services or products for sale).

Prevent Your Children from Accessing Specific Sites

Unleashing young children, unprotected, on the Internet is like sending them into a major city without an escort. Although most people and most Internet sites are fairly responsible and safe, there are a few sick individuals and several inappropriate sites on the Internet. And, because children are so curious and vulnerable, they will certainly stumble across these Internet red-light districts and possibly become victims of individuals who like to harass children.

A parent's first impulse might be to prohibit a child from accessing the Internet. However, you don't want to prevent your child from encountering the fun, educational Internet sites. Instead, a parent must find an Internet escort: a program that can prevent a child from accessing the deviant areas of the Internet.

One such program is Cyber Patrol. This free program is made available by the creators of Cyber Sentry, a program designed to prevent workers from accessing certain Internet sites during work hours. The following *Guided Tour* shows how to download, install, and use Cyber Patrol to limit a child's Internet access.

Take Control of Cyber Patrol

Cyber Patrol comes with a built-in set of safeguards. It has a list of Web sites that are off limits and a list of words that it uses to block access to any site whose name or URL suggests indecency. For example, the Playboy Web site is listed as off limits, and Cyber Patrol blocks access to any newsgroups, Web sites, chat rooms, or URLs that have "bondage" in their names.

However, you can customize Cyber Patrol to prevent access to additional sites. The *Guided Tour* shows you how to modify the list of words that Cyber Patrol uses to block access, and update the list of Web sites that are blocked.

Begin Guided Tour   Download and Install Cyber Patrol

1 The easiest way to download files is to use your Web browser. Enter the following URL to go to the Cyber Central Web page:

http://www.cyberpatrol.com

> Cyber Patrol 2.10 hits the streets!
>
> - Built-in support for the SafeSurf system. Gives you even more control over the sites your children can access.
> - The first and only Internet filter that works with all browsers, including 32-bit browsers (example: Microsoft Internet Explorer).
> - And, **Cyber Patrol Home Edition** - basic internet filtering component of Cyber Patrol, available to home users **free of charge**. For more info, read the press release.
>
> Download Cyber Patrol 2.10 for Windows NOW!
> Cyber Patrol 2.10 for Macintosh will be available next week. Download the current version for Mac now and upgrade later!

2 Cyber Patrol is a free program. To download it, click the **Cyber Patrol for Windows** link.

(continues)

Guided Tour Download and Install Cyber Patrol *(continued)*

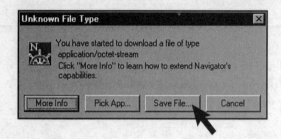

(**3**) A dialog box appears, asking if you want to save the file. Click the **Save File** button.

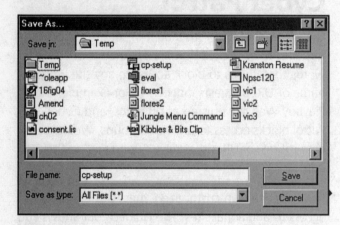

(**4**) Another dialog box appears, asking you where to store the file. Click the drive and folder where you want the file stored, and click **Save**. (The TEMP folder is a good choice.)

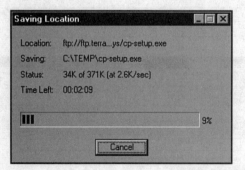

(**5**) The Saving Location dialog box shows the progress of the download. Wait until this dialog box disappears. That means the file has been transferred successfully.

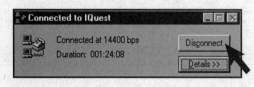

(**6**) Before installing Cyber Patrol, exit your Web browser and disconnect from the Internet.

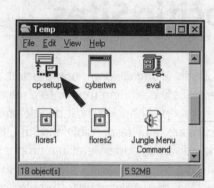

(**7**) The file you downloaded is self-extracting and automatically runs the installation program. Run My Computer, the Windows Explorer, or File Manager and change to the directory or folder where you saved the file. Then double-click the **cp-setup** icon to run the file.

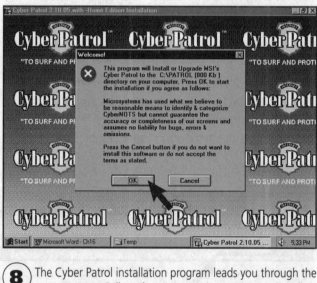

(**8**) The Cyber Patrol installation program leads you through the setup process. Follow the on-screen instructions to install Cyber Patrol.

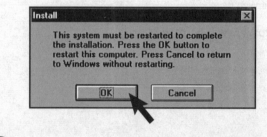

(**9**) When Cyber Patrol finishes installing itself, it restarts Windows and runs automatically in the background, keeping track of your Internet sessions. Click **OK** to restart Windows.

Guided Tour Download and Install Cyber Patrol

10 Whenever you start Windows, Cyber Patrol runs. Cyber Patrol uses a list of newsgroups, Web pages, and other Internet sites to limit access. If you try to access a prohibited site, you receive a message saying that access to the site has been denied.

If you decide to remove Cyber Patrol from your system, switch to Cyber Patrol (by clicking on it in the taskbar or by using **Alt+Tab**). Then open the **File** menu and select **Uninstall Cyber Patrol**. Do not try to remove the program manually.

Begin Guided Tour Control Internet Access with Cyber Patrol

1 To change Cyber Patrol's access limitations, you must go to the Cyber Patrol Access Checkpoint. In Windows 95, click **Cyber Patrol** in the taskbar. In Windows 3.1, use the **Alt+Tab** key combination to switch to Cyber Patrol.

2 A dialog box appears, prompting you to type a password. Type a password that you'll remember but that your kids won't guess. (You'll need to enter this password to change any options or uninstall Cyber Patrol.) Click **Validate Password**.

3 Cyber Patrol Checkpoint lets you change the Internet access limitations. To prevent someone from using the Internet during certain hours, click the **Press to Set Hours of Operation** button.

(continues)

Guided Tour   Control Internet Access with Cyber Patrol   *(continued)*

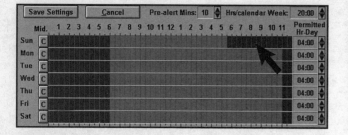

4 Red blocks mark hours during which Internet access will be blocked. Green blocks show hours where Internet access is permitted. Click a red block to turn it green, or click a green block to turn it red. You can drag over blocks to select them.

5 To allow Internet access for all hours, click the **C** button for a given day. (C stands for Clear.)

6 Click the arrows next to **Pre-alert Mins** to specify the length of time a user will be warned that he is nearing a prohibited time period.

7 You can specify the number of hours per day or per week that users can access the Internet. Click the arrows next to **Hrs/calendar Week** and **Permitted Hr-Day** to set the allowable times.

8 The **Access to specific Internet services** area lets you prevent access to specific Internet features. The **Full** option gives complete access to a feature. **None** completely locks out the feature. **Selective** blocks access to areas that are known to offer inappropriate material.

9 Cyber Patrol has a list of prohibited Internet services. To prevent access to additional services or to allow access to features on Cyber Patrol's list, click a button in the **Access to specific Internet services** area.

If the entire URL won't fit inside the text box, you can chop the end off the URL.

⌒ **Guided Tour** Control Internet Access with Cyber Patrol ⌒

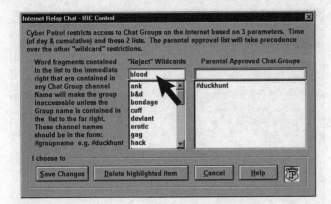

10 If you click the **IRC - Relay Chat** button, a list of keywords appears. Cyber Patrol will prevent access to newsgroups that have these words anywhere in their names. To add a word, type it in the **"Reject" Wildcards** text box and press **Enter**.

12 To approve a specific chat room that Cyber Patrol may not allow access to, type its name in the **Parental Approved Chat-Groups** text box and press **Enter**. When you are done, click **Save Changes**.

11 To remove a word from the "Reject" Wildcards list, click the word, and then click **Delete highlighted item**.

13 The **WWW, FTP & Other** button allows you to limit access to certain sites based on their URLs. Cyber Patrol already prevents access to a list of known adult sites, but if you want to lock out additional sites, click this button.

14 To prevent access to a specific site, type its URL in the **Additional Parental Service Restrictions** text box and press **Enter**.

(continues)

Guided Tour Control Internet Access with Cyber Patrol
(continued)

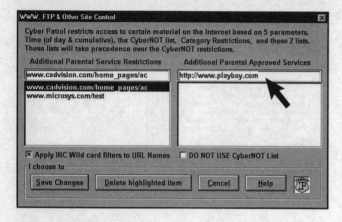

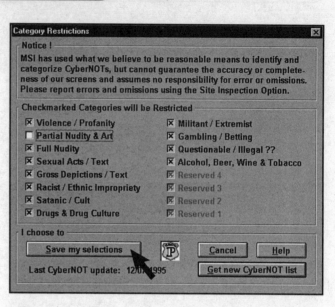

15 To override an item in Cyber Patrol's no-no list and allow access to a site, type the site's URL in the **Additional Parental Approved Services** text box and press **Enter**.

16 Now that you have the hang of this, try using the other two buttons to control access to newsgroups and to applications on your computer.

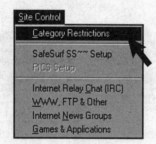

17 To prevent or allow access to certain off-beat topics, open the **Site Control** menu and select **Category Restrictions**.

18 The dialog box that appears allows you to block areas that you feel are inappropriate. Initially, all the topics are blocked (checked). To remove the X and allow access to a topic, click its name. Click **Save my selections** when you're done.

19 The makers of Cyber Patrol are constantly updating their no-no list as more sites appear on the Internet. To update the list, open the **File** menu and select **Update CyberNOT List**.

Guided Tour Control Internet Access with Cyber Patrol

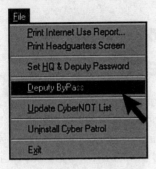

20 To bypass Cyber Patrol and open access to all Internet services, open the **File** menu and select **Deputy ByPass**.

This *Guided Tour* has shown you the basics of working with Cyber Patrol. For information about additional features, check the Help menu.

Unless you register for the full version of Cyber Patrol, it automatically reduces the number of features it offers after a certain number of days and prevents you from updating the CyberNOT list. You can register and pay for the full version by opening the **Options** menu and selecting one of the **Registration** options. The **Home Edition Registration** option lets you keep using Cyber Patrol for free but disables the configuration options, so you end up using Cyber Patrol with its default settings (which isn't bad for free).

Avoid Viruses

The only way to completely protect yourself against viruses on the Internet is to disconnect your modem and stop using the Internet. As long as you are connected to other people's computers and are downloading and using software from FTP sites, there is some risk that a virus in one of those programs will infect your computer.

However, you can minimize the risk by downloading files only from reputable sites. Most companies are careful to regularly check for viruses on their sites and in the programs they offer for downloading. If users catch a virus from one of the company's programs, the company can lose business and develop a bad reputation. As long as you download files from well-known companies or from online services, you are relatively safe.

Try to avoid programs from individuals on the Internet. If someone offers to send you a file, ask the person where he got the file, and then download the original file from that FTP site. If you don't know the individual, he might be intentionally trying to infect your system. Even if you *do* know the individual, the person's computer might be infected with a virus, and the program might carry the virus to your computer. Work only with original files.

In addition, avoid getting and running programs from newsgroups. Although some newsgroups are monitored, others allow anyone to post files, and these files might contain viruses.

The following *Guided Tour* shows you how to download a virus checking program called Virus ALERT and use it to check your system for known viruses.

> Most viruses are transmitted through program files. Before running a program on your computer, you should check it for viruses, as explained in the *Guided Tour*.

How Antivirus Programs Work

Antivirus programs protect your system by waging a three-pronged attack against viruses. First, the antivirus program scans all the files on your computer for *signatures* of known viruses. A signature is a piece of computer code that is unique to a virus. Second, the antivirus program scans for the effects of viruses, such as modified system files, unauthorized file deletions, and so on. Finally, antivirus programs help identify viruses in programs you haven't yet run, thus preventing your system from becoming infected.

To prevent your system from becoming infected, and to reduce the amount of damage in the event that your computer does become infected, you should perform the following tasks:

- Scan all the files on your computer every week or so for known viruses. By detecting and eliminating a virus early, you prevent it from causing extensive damage.

- Before running any programs you download from the Internet, scan the program files for known viruses. This prevents your computer from becoming infected in the first place.

- Update your virus list regularly. Every antivirus program has a list of known viruses. If a new virus is developed, it won't be on the list. By updating your list, you enable the antivirus program to check for the latest viruses.

- Before you place any files on the Internet or send them to an individual, check the files for viruses. This prevents spreading the virus to other computers.

Back Up Your System

Viruses typically infect program files and destroy both program and data files. They don't destroy the hardware that makes up your computer. The best way to protect your program and data files is to back them up regularly. I further recommend that you back up your data files (the files you create) separately from your program files.

This book does not cover the steps required for backing up your files. You can use Microsoft Backup (which comes with Windows 95 and DOS versions 5.0 or later) to perform the backups, or you can purchase and use a specialized backup program. Refer to your DOS or Windows documentation for details. If you have Windows 3.1, look for a program group called Microsoft Tools. It should have an icon for Microsoft Backup.

Following are a few tips for using backups to protect your system against viruses:

- Write-protect your program disks before installing a program, so your original program disks will not become infected. If the program becomes infected on your hard disk, you can then delete it and reinstall it from the floppy disks. (Don't worry about CDs.)

- Back up program files and data files (the files you create) separately. Because data files rarely become infected, if your system does catch a virus, you can delete all the programs, reinstall them, and then restore the data files from your backups.

- Some backup programs can check for viruses during the backup operation. If your backup program has this option, turn it on.

- If your system becomes infected, reinstall clean copies of your programs from the original disks, not from the backups. The backed up files might be infected. Restoring the files could reinfect your system.

> Create a separate folder (or directory) called DATA for the files you create and save. You can create subfolders under the DATA folder. You can back up all the files in this folder separately from your program files.

Begin Guided Tour   Download and Install Virus ALERT

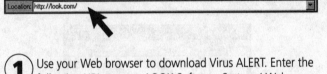

1 Use your Web browser to download Virus ALERT. Enter the following URL to go to LOOK Software Systems' Web page:

http://look.com/

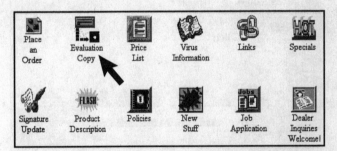

2 LOOK Software Systems greets you with its opening home page. Scroll down the page and click the **Evaluation Copy** link.

(continues)

Guided Tour Download and Install Virus ALERT

(continued)

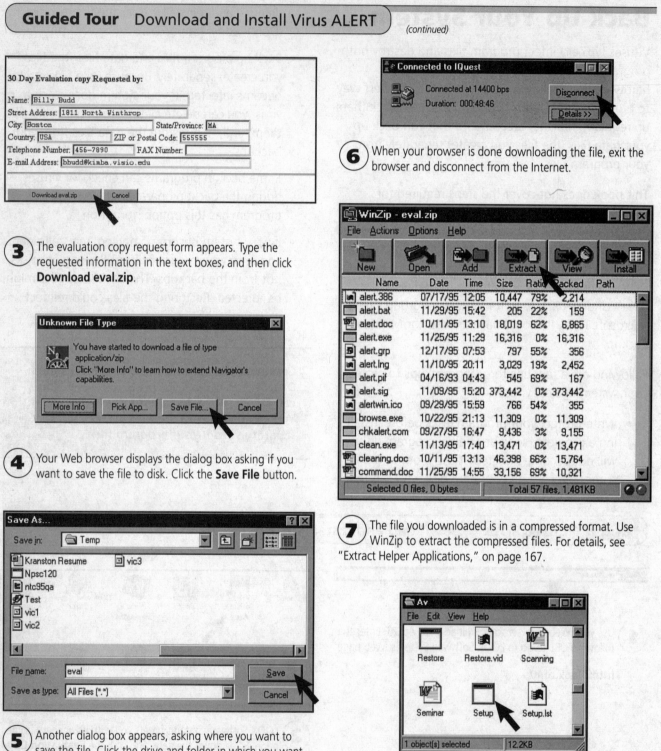

30 Day Evaluation copy Requested by:

Name: Billy Budd
Street Address: 1811 North Winthrop
City: Boston   State/Province: MA
Country: USA   ZIP or Postal Code: 555555
Telephone Number: 456-7890   FAX Number:
E-mail Address: bbudd@kimba.visio.edu

Download eval.zip   Cancel

3 The evaluation copy request form appears. Type the requested information in the text boxes, and then click **Download eval.zip**.

Unknown File Type

You have started to download a file of type application/zip
Click "More Info" to learn how to extend Navigator's capabilities.

More Info   Pick App...   Save File...   Cancel

4 Your Web browser displays the dialog box asking if you want to save the file to disk. Click the **Save File** button.

Save As...

Save in: Temp

Kranston Resume   vic3
Npsc120
ntc95qa
Test
vic1
vic2

File name: eval   Save
Save as type: All Files (*.*)   Cancel

5 Another dialog box appears, asking where you want to save the file. Click the drive and folder in which you want the file saved (C:\TEMP is a good place). Click **Save**.

Connected to IQuest

Connected at 14400 bps   Disconnect
Duration: 000:48:46   Details >>

6 When your browser is done downloading the file, exit the browser and disconnect from the Internet.

WinZip - eval.zip

File Actions Options Help

New   Open   Add   Extract   View   Install

Name	Date	Time	Size	Ratio	Packed	Path
alert.386	07/17/95	12:05	10,447	79%	2,214	
alert.bat	11/29/95	15:42	205	22%	159	
alert.doc	10/11/95	13:10	18,019	62%	6,865	
alert.exe	11/25/95	11:29	16,316	0%	16,316	
alert.grp	12/17/95	07:53	797	55%	356	
alert.lng	11/10/95	20:11	3,029	19%	2,452	
alert.pif	04/16/93	04:43	545	69%	167	
alert.sig	11/09/95	15:20	373,442	0%	373,442	
alertwin.ico	09/29/95	15:59	766	54%	355	
browse.exe	10/22/95	21:13	11,309	0%	11,309	
chkalert.com	09/27/95	16:47	9,436	3%	9,155	
clean.exe	11/13/95	17:40	13,471	0%	13,471	
cleaning.doc	10/11/95	13:13	46,398	66%	15,764	
command.doc	11/25/95	14:55	33,156	69%	10,321	

Selected 0 files, 0 bytes   Total 57 files, 1,481KB

7 The file you downloaded is in a compressed format. Use WinZip to extract the compressed files. For details, see "Extract Helper Applications," on page 167.

Av

File Edit View Help

Restore   Restore.vid   Scanning

Seminar   Setup   Setup.lst

1 object(s) selected   12.2KB

8 Run My Computer, the Windows Explorer, or File Manager, and change to the folder to which you extracted the compressed files. Double-click the **Setup** icon.

Guided Tour   Download and Install Virus ALERT

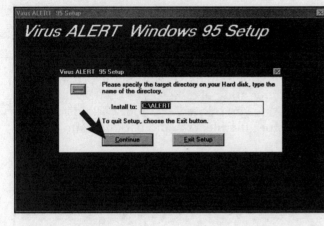

9 The setup program displays a series of dialog boxes that leads you through the process of installing Virus ALERT. Follow the on-screen instructions to proceed.

Begin Guided Tour   Scan Your Computer for Viruses

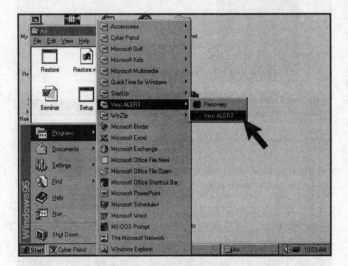

1 In Windows 95, the setup program places the Virus ALERT program on the Start menu. Open the **Start** menu, point to **Programs**, point to **Virus ALERT**, and click **Virus ALERT** on the submenu.

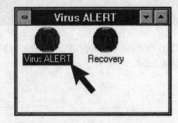

In Windows 3.1, the setup program creates a program group for Virus ALERT. Open the Virus ALERT program group window and double-click the **Virus ALERT** icon.

2 Virus ALERT runs from DOS. To display Virus ALERT full-screen, press **Alt+Enter**. Press **Enter** to display the main menu.

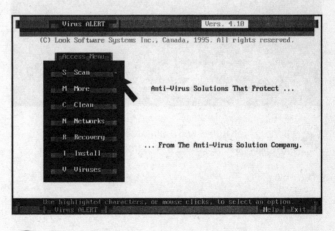

3 If this is your first time running Virus ALERT, click the **Scan** option to scan your hard disk for viruses.

(continues)

Guided Tour Scan Your Computer for Viruses *(continued)*

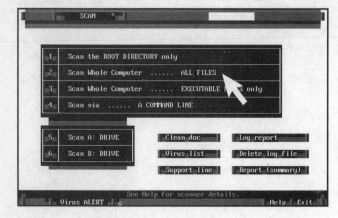

4 The Scan menu allows you to scan your entire disk or a portion of it. Select option **2 Scan Whole Computer**.

If the virus infected a file (as opposed to the boot sector of your hard disk), the cure is to delete the infected file. If the infected file is a program file, you must reinstall the program from your original diskettes or CD-ROM. If the file is one you created, use your backup copies to restore the file. (You did back up, didn't you?)

Number of infected files	0
Number of viruses in memory	0
Number of viruses in boot area	0
Number of different virus kinds found	0
Number of files scanned	9712
Number of files deleted	0
Total number of known viruses	4762

5 Virus ALERT scans your computer's memory and all the files on your computer for known viruses (this can take several minutes). If Virus ALERT does not find a virus, you'll see a report like the one shown here.

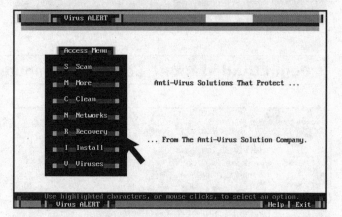

7 After you have checked your system for viruses, you should create a recovery disk to help you restore your system in the event that a virus wipes out your hard drive. Return to the main menu and select **Recovery**.

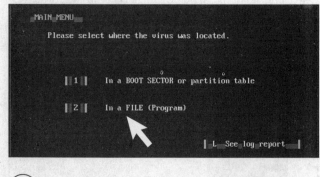

6 If Virus ALERT does find a virus, follow the on-screen instructions to remove the virus from your computer.

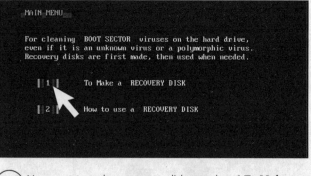

8 You want to make a recovery disk, so select **1 To Make a RECOVERY DISK**.

Guided Tour Scan Your Computer for Viruses

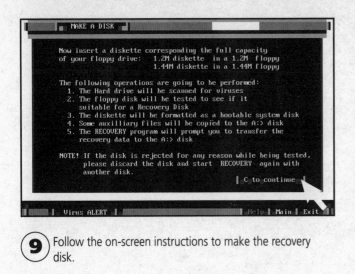

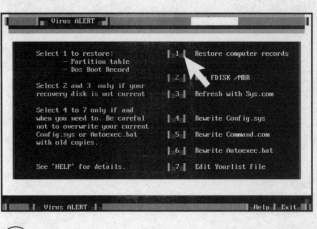

9 Follow the on-screen instructions to make the recovery disk.

11 After rebooting, you are greeted by the menu shown here. Use this menu to remove the virus and restore your system to its original condition.

10 When you finish making the recovery disk, write-protect it to protect it from viruses. If a virus ever wipes out your hard drive, you can boot your computer from the floppy disk. Simply insert the disk into one of the floppy disk drives and press **Ctrl+Alt+Del**.

PART 2

Do It Yourself

n Part 1 of this book, you learned how to establish an Internet connection and how to use a Web browser, an FTP program, and Gopher. In addition, you learned how to send and receive e-mail, read newsgroup messages, and chat. By now, you should be feeling fairly comfortable with those various Internet programs.

But just knowing how to use these programs won't make you feel at home on the Internet. As a matter of fact, you're probably thinking, "Okay, so I can get on the Internet. But what do I do once I'm there?" In this part, you'll explore the possibilities of what you can do by working through some simple step-by-step projects. Of course, these projects don't represent all that you can do on the Internet, but they will show you how to accomplish some of the more common tasks. And they might just inspire you to explore some of the other things you can do on the Internet.

What You Will Find in This Part

Take an Internet Scavenger Hunt

Now that you know your way around the Internet, you've probably developed some techniques for sniffing out the information you want. Maybe you have a favorite search tool (such as Yahoo), or maybe you've developed a knack for just guessing a site's URL. However you decide to cruise the Internet, you'll continue to find topics that pose new research challenges.

This project is designed to intentionally challenge your ability to cruise the Internet and find specific items. This project includes a list of topics, Web pages, files, and other Internet goodies for you to find. Use your favorite Internet search tool or technique to find the item, and then chalk up a point for each item you find. Don't stop until you've found all 20 items! Use the following form to keep score.

The Great Internet Scavenger Hunt

The ultimate challenge of net surfing skills for the chance to win big money $$$! Sign up now! Next contest February 1st! Check it out!

It's what all the Internet is talking about! Only once a month, the Great Internet Scavenger Hunt takes place throughout the entire Information SuperHighway. At exactly 12:01 AM CST on the first day of the month, the race begins with a simple e-mail clue to all eligible participants. Then it's up to you to surf the net, solving riddles and puzzles in order to get to the final treasure, $$$$$$$$$$$. The best part is that it is solely based on

---

In searching for these items, try to go beyond the World Wide Web. You can look for answers in newsgroups or chat rooms (where you can ask other people for the answers), you can use Archie to find files, and you can even send a Gopher to root out a server.

Score	Item Found	Score	Item Found
_____	Pikes Peak "live" photo	_____	China's home page
_____	Interactive model railroad	_____	The Jerry Garcia Memorial
_____	Cujo the parrot at the Virtual Zoo	_____	Michael Jordan's home page
_____	Number of 1995 Emmy nominations for *Seinfeld*	_____	Smileys (emoticons) list
_____	Chocolate chip cookie recipe	_____	Latest Netscape Navigator Beta
_____	Painting of Mona Lisa	_____	Newbie chat room
_____	Today's *Dilbert* cartoon	_____	Hate Barney newsgroup
_____	The Shakespeare Web	_____	Meteor Shower calendar
_____	Encyclopedia Britannica's *Britannica Online*	_____	Cool Site of the Day
_____	The Caffeine archive	_____	Online Scavenger Hunt (for Money)

Begin Do It Yourself Find Lost Treasures

1 Some Web sites broadcast "live" pictures of such scenes as the Space Needle in Seattle and San Francisco Bay. Find the picture of Pikes Peak. (Hint: you can only view Pikes Peak during the day.)

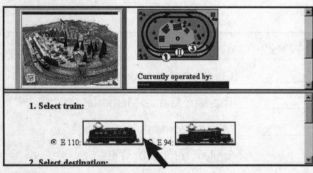

2 In addition to "live" video, some sites have *telerobots*, which are devices that you can control from your computer. Find the model railroad at the University of Ulm.

3 Okay, one more camera site. Visit the Virtual Zoo and say hello to Cujo the parrot for me.

4 Let's combine a bit of trivia with a search for a Web page. In 1995, how many Emmy nominations did the TV show *Seinfeld* receive?

Shellie's chocolate chip cookie recipe

2 c. whole wheat pastry flour
1/4 c. oat bran
1 heaping tsp. baking soda
sprinkle salt

1 stick butter, 1 stick low-fat margarine, very soft
   (Warning: the cookies tend to run together if you use all butter)
2 jumbo egg whites (or three whites from smaller eggs)
1 1/4 tsp. almond extract
1/2 c each brown sugar and granulated sugar

3-4 c (1.5 to 2 bags) chocolate chips (I prefer Nestle)

5 Find a recipe for chocolate chip cookies.

Do It Yourself   Find Lost Treasures

6 Where's Mona Lisa? She's on the Internet somewhere. Track her down, and chalk up another point.

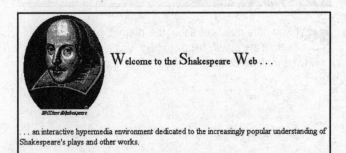

7 If you've never seen *Dilbert*, you're in for a treat. This cartoon character has been keeping Internet surfers in stitches for years. Take a break from your wanderings to have a laugh.

Welcome to the Shakespeare Web...

... an interactive hypermedia environment dedicated to the increasingly popular understanding of Shakespeare's plays and other works.

8 Shakespeare is making a comeback, this time in Hollywood. Find the Shakespeare Web and learn more about this famous playwright.

BRITANNICA

An Information Service from the Editors of *Encyclopædia Britannica*

**Welcome to *Britannica Online*,
the first encyclopedia on the Internet!**

From the editors of the *Encyclopædia Britannica*, *Britannica Online* combines the authority and breadth of the highly respected print version of *Britannica* with the vast resources of the Internet to put reliable and comprehensive information at your fingertips. Sign up for a free trial or an annual

9 If you don't want to clutter your house with a set of encyclopedias, consider using an encyclopedia on the Internet. Find *Britannica Online* from the editors of *Encyclopedia Britannica*.

The Caffeine Injection

Please sign our Guest Book.
You may also Search This Server.

alt.drugs.caffeine FAQ
Frequently Asked Questions on Caffeine from UseNet.
Boyer's Coffee
Coffee company.
Coffee Reference Desk
Detailed coffee information.
Coffee Talk Magazine
Online Magazine.

10 If this scavenger hunt is making you sleepy, maybe you need a lift. Visit the Caffeine archive...if you can find it.

China Home Page

This page is provided by the Institute of High Energy Physics, Beijing (IHEP). It includes only public scientific, technical, and business information about China.

General Information

- General Information on China
- Introduction to Computer Networks in China

11 Anyone can find the White House, but can you find China's home page?

(continues)

Do It Yourself Find Lost Treasures   (continued)

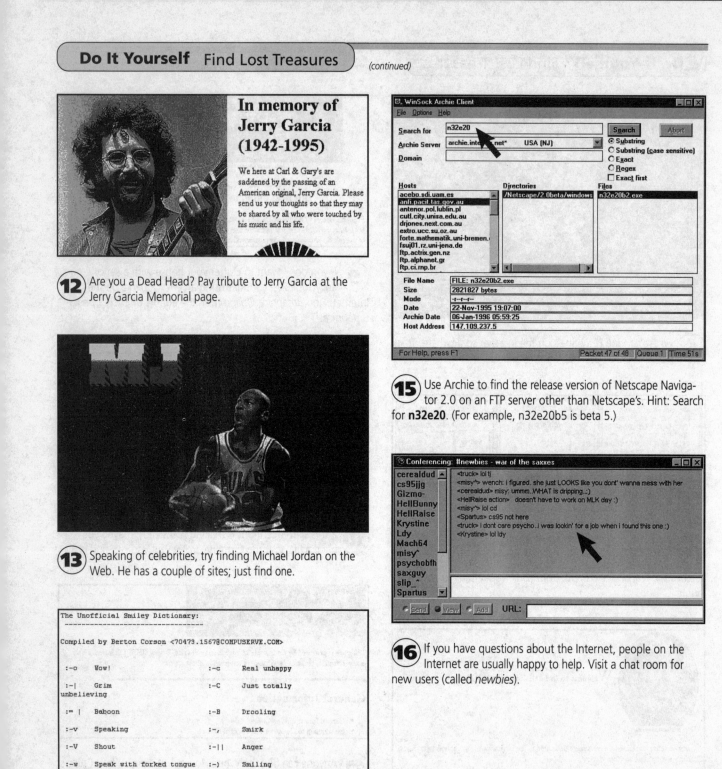

12 Are you a Dead Head? Pay tribute to Jerry Garcia at the Jerry Garcia Memorial page.

13 Speaking of celebrities, try finding Michael Jordan on the Web. He has a couple of sites; just find one.

14 Let's jump off the Web for a while. Use Gopher to find a list of smileys (emoticons) on the Internet. This list will come in handy when you visit chat rooms or write e-mail.

15 Use Archie to find the release version of Netscape Navigator 2.0 on an FTP server other than Netscape's. Hint: Search for **n32e20**. (For example, n32e20b5 is beta 5.)

16 If you have questions about the Internet, people on the Internet are usually happy to help. Visit a chat room for new users (called *newbies*).

Do It Yourself   Find Lost Treasures

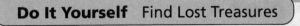

```
┌─ alt.barney.dinosaur.die.die.die [130 articles] ──────── ▼ □ ✕ ─┐
│ Articles  Sort  Search                                          │
│ >26786 01/08 Mr. Vinodchandra S    2 black.cat              ▲   │
│  26810 01/10 oO -The HooDeD oNE   16 ▌                          │
│  26835 01/10 Arthur Sankey         6 ▌                          │
│  26787 01/08 Mr. Vinodchandra S    2 black.cat                  │
│  26788 01/08 Dawn Marie Friesen  132 Re: aarrggghh!             │
│  26789 01/08 Pinhead the Cenobi   38 Re: Whats bad about barney.│
│  26791 01/08 Dawn Marie Friesen   13 Another way to get rid of Barney│
│  26792 01/08 Dawn Marie Friesen   42 Re: Whats bad about barney.│
│  26793 01/09 Vandit Kalia         16 Re: DIANA ROSS__TAKE ME HIGHER│
│  26801 01/09 Wotan                20 ▌                          │
│  26794 01/07 ASCII Express Allh    7 Re: Whats bad about barney.│
│  26795 01/08 Svartalf             26 Re: aarrggghh!             │
│  26785 01/09 Norman J. Landis     19 ▌                          │
│  26796 01/08 Mike Sawyer          30 Parents of Barney Watchers Annonymous│
│  26790 01/09 David Hibbs          60 ▌                          │
│  26807 01/08 vupdegr@ibm.net       1 ▌                          │
│  26832 01/09 ASCII Express Allh   10 ▌                          │
│  26867 01/09 Michael D. Mast      58 ▌                          │
│  26797 01/07 FaXel                19 NEWS FLASH!!!! Barney Killed in Freak│
│  26838 01/10 Lictalon             16 ▌                          │
│  26798 01/09 Wotan                10 Re: DIANA ROSS__TAKE ME HIGHER ▼│
│ ◄ ▌                                                          ► ▼│
└─────────────────────────────────────────────────────────────────┘
```

17 Use your newsgroup reader to find out why so many people dislike Barney the purple dinosaur.

Meteor Showers: A Descriptive Catalog

During 1988, my book *Meteor Showers: A Descriptive Catalog* was published. The book has been out of print for several years, but I still get requests for it. I have included a condensed version of this catalog below, divided by month.

- January
- February
- March
- April
- May
- June
- July
- August
- September

18 Okay, back to the Web. When will the next meteor shower occur in your area? There's an online calendar that gives you the answer.

19 Now for a surprise. Find the Cool Site of the Day.

The Great Internet Scavenger Hunt

The ultimate challenge of net surfing skills for the chance to win big money $$$! Sign up now! Next contest February 1st! Check it out!

It's what all the Internet is talking about! Only once a month, the Great Internet Scavenger Hunt takes place throughout the entire Information SuperHighway. At exactly 12:01 AM CST on the first day of the month, the race begins with a simple e-mail clue to all eligible participants. Then it's up to you to surf the net, solving riddles and puzzles in order to get to the final treasure, $$$$$$$$$$. The best part is that it is solely based on

20 If you enjoy the challenge of a good scavenger hunt, find an online version of a scavenger hunt. If you're good at this, you can win money and prizes.

Find Free Stuff on the Net

You've probably already snatched a few free programs off the Internet—maybe a couple of helper applications, a Web browser, a Gopher program, and some other choice tidbits. The Internet is packed with software, files, games, and other loot that's free for the taking. The only catch is that you have to know where to look.

This project takes you on a tour of the Internet in search of freebies. You'll learn where to go to get everything from computer games to shampoo samples, from online coupons to financial calculators. You'll even learn how to use some of the Internet's search tools to help you find more free stuff!

> When looking for deals and freebies, be careful. If a deal seems too good to be true, it probably is. Avoid giving out your credit card number or any other information that someone could use to rip you off.

Free Stuff for Crafters!

Prime Publishing, Inc. maintains an extensive database of FREE and postage only offers from many categories and industries. Our editors regularly review thousands of offers from hundreds of publications and manufacturers. The best offers are then individually contacted by our company for verification and review. The very best offers are then added to our state-of-the-art computer database and used to compile our bi-monthly newsletter and our now famous directory "Free Stuff For People Who Enjoy Crafting, Sewing And More". Each directory published by the company is designed to give consumers hundreds of dollars worth of "Free Stuff" - just by writing. Participating manufacturers do not pay to be listed in the directory.

This project shows you a few places where you can get freebies, but don't stop there. Use other Internet search tools to search for specific items (such as vacations, cars, or shareware) that you might be able to use for free or to find out about drawings and contests you can enter and win (if you're into that sort of thing). Try searching with Lycos, Yahoo, WebCrawler, and the other tools described in "Search for Information on the Internet" (page 179).

Begin Do It Yourself   Find Free Stuff

Freebies

Check here for a complete listing of software you can download and other freebies from mall advertisers.

Are you Ready For? A complete set of software which you can use to test your readiness to take specific college level courses such as algebra and calculus. This is great stuff if you are getting back into education, have a child who is about to take a new course, or just want to test your knowledge. Special thanks to David Lovelock and the Math Department at the University of Arizona.

1 For free educational software, check out the EduMall at **http://edumall.com/edumall/freebies.html**.

---

1 (800)235-9794   kit with information on medication and lifestyle changes to help you live heartburn-free.

1 (800)544-5680   Call to join the Chef BoyArDee Kid's Club and get recipes!

1 (800)445-9088   Free sample of Simply Whispers earrings. (I hadn't seen this one for a while!) Earrings are especially for those with sensitive ears. They offer a lot of styles and really are great for sensitive ears!

1 (800)667-7377   Free video explaining the best way to save for a child's university/college fees. Canadian Scholarship Trust Plan will pay out three times the amount saved for a child. For parents or grandparents! Can also e-mail a request to: peter_miller@mindlink.bc.ca

or check out the full details available at http://mindlink.bc.ca/Peter_Miller/CST.html

2 Thanks to Julie Pederson for her *Next to Nothing!* online magazine of freebies (or nearly freebies). Visit this site at **http://www.winternet.com/~julie/ntn.html**.

Do It Yourself Find Free Stuff

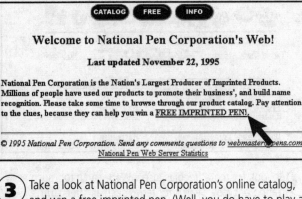

CATALOG   FREE   INFO

Welcome to National Pen Corporation's Web!

Last updated November 22, 1995

National Pen Corporation is the Nation's Largest Producer of Imprinted Products. Millions of people have used our products to promote their business', and build name recognition. Please take some time to browse through our product catalog. Pay attention to the clues, because they can help you win a FREE IMPRINTED PEN.

© 1995 National Pen Corporation. Send any comments questions to webmaster@pens.com
National Pen Web Server Statistics

3 Take a look at National Pen Corporation's online catalog, and win a free imprinted pen. (Well, you do have to play a game for it.)

Free Stuff for Crafters!

Prime Publishing, Inc. maintains an extensive database of FREE and postage only offers from many categories and industries. Our editors regularly review thousands of offers from hundreds of publications and manufacturers. The best offers are then individually contacted by our company for verification and review. The very best offers are then added to our state-of-the-art computer database and used to compile our bi-monthly newsletter and our now famous directory "Free Stuff For People Who Enjoy Crafting, Sewing And More". Each directory published by the company is designed to g consumers hundreds of dollars worth of "Free Stuff" - just by writing. Participating manufact do not pay to be listed in the directory.

4 If you're into sewing or crafts, visit Prime Publishing for a list of companies that give away crafty stuff. Here's the URL you'll need:

http://www.craftnet.org/prime/freestuff.html

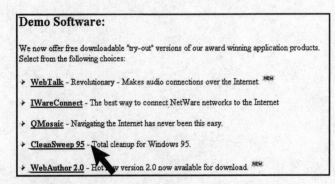

Demo Software:

We now offer free downloadable "try-out" versions of our award winning application products. Select from the following choices:

➤ **WebTalk** - Revolutionary - Makes audio connections over the Internet. NEW

➤ **IWareConnect** - The best way to connect NetWare networks to the Internet

➤ **QMosaic** - Navigating the Internet has never been this easy.

➤ **CleanSweep 95** - Total cleanup for Windows 95.

➤ **WebAuthor 2.0** - Hot new version 2.0 now available for download. NEW

5 Quarterdeck Software offers several demo programs of its software products, including CleanSweep (an uninstaller program for Windows), QMosaic (a Web browser), and WebAuthor (an HTML editor). Download the demos from **http://www.qdeck.com/qdeck/demosoft/**.

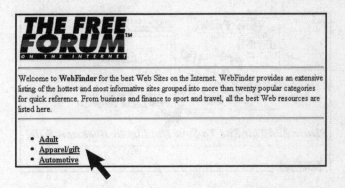

THE FREE FORUM™
ON THE INTERNET

Welcome to WebFinder for the best Web Sites on the Internet. WebFinder provides an extensive listing of the hottest and most informative sites grouped into more than twenty popular categories for quick reference. From business and finance to sport and travel, all the best Web resources are listed here.

- **Adult**
- **Apparel/gift**
- **Automotive**

6 For a list of free stuff grouped by category, visit the Free Forum at **http://www.ven.com/webfind.html**.

If you need PKUNZIP, you can get the latest version here.

Big Finance This is a great program for calculating almost everything. It will assist you from measurement conversions to helping you to determine future values of investments.
College Cost Estimator Figure out how much you will need to save now to pay for future college costs.
Mortgage Estimator Find out how much of a house you can afford.
National Debt Clock you thought you were deep in debt look at how our government is going fur er and further in debt every second. Very nice presentation.

7 For some free (and useful) financial programs, such as a mortgage calculator, visit the Debt Counselors home page at **http://debt-experts.com/item-8.html**.

MUSIC BOULEVARD
WWW.MUSICBLVD.COM

Pop & Rock   Country   Classical   Jazz   All MUSIC

On Sale   What's New   Newsstand   Backstage Pass   Customer Service   Help
Order   Contest   Music Wire   Site Seeing   Registration   Exit

8 Are you into music? Visit Music Boulevard, where you can download audio clips of your favorite groups. To go there, use the URL **http://www.musicblvd.com**.

(continues)

Do It Yourself Find Free Stuff

(continued)

Please Add This Site To Your Hot List Or Bookmark File!

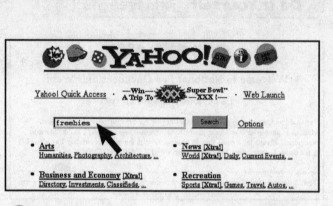

9 If you're a coupon hound, you can find coupons online at **http://www.actionpack.com/**. You can even place your name on a mailing list to receive coupons in the mail.

11 To look for more freebies, use a Web search tool such as Yahoo or Lycos. Search for terms such as "free stuff," "freebies," "free offers," "contests," "demos," and "shareware."

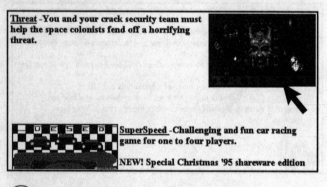

Threat -You and your crack security team must help the space colonists fend off a horrifying threat.

SuperSpeed -Challenging and fun car racing game for one to four players.

NEW! Special Christmas '95 shareware edition

10 Do you want to try out some free computer games? Connect to the Game Factory at **http://www.gamefactory.com/**. The Game Factory offers the first episode of each of its games for free.

Play Games on the Internet

Although many people like to pretend that they use the Internet mainly for business and educational purposes, if you were to sneak up on them, you very well might find them downloading GIFs, chatting, or playing one of the thousands of interactive games the Internet offers.

The biggest reasons many people *don't* play games is that they don't know where to find them or that they don't feel comfortable with the rules. In this project, you'll visit several Web sites and a couple of chat rooms where you can try your hand at some games. Play a little, until you don't feel so awkward.

Java Games

In Chapter 15, you learned about Java applets: small applications that you can play on the Internet. You may have even played the tic-tac-toe game. Java has been used to create other games on the Web, including Tetris, Reversi, Othello, The Game of Life, Mine Sweeper, and video poker.

This project shows you where to find the more popular Java games. To find more Java games, use a search tool such as Yahoo (http://www.yahoo.com) or WebCrawler (http://www.webcrawler.com) and search for "java game."

Trivia Games and Tests

Trivia games and quizzes have always been a staple of the gaming world. Whether answering questions to win prizes or just to have fun, people get hooked on testing their knowledge and their ability to remember important or unimportant information.

You can find several quiz and test sites on the Internet. You can play name-that-flag, fill out a purity questionnaire, answer questions about bats, or even determine whether you qualify as a bona fide nerd!

This project shows you a few of the more unique quiz sites.

Interactive Role-Playing Games

By far, the most popular games on the Internet are MUDs. A MUD (short for Multi User Dimension) is an interactive role-playing game that involves many users from all over the world. Originally based on *Dungeons and Dragons*, MUDs have branched out into hundreds of other role-playing games on the Internet.

To play a MUD, you have to *telnet* to a MUD site. That means you connect to another computer where the MUD is played, and then—by typing commands on your keyboard—you enter the commands to play the game. The easiest way to telnet is to set up your Web browser to run your Telnet program whenever you click a Telnet link.

Windows 95 has a Telnet program, cleverly called TELNET.EXE, which is stored in the Windows folder. If you're using Netscape Navigator, you can set it up to run TELNET.EXE. To do so, open the **Options** menu, select **General Preferences**, and click the **Apps** tab.

Click the **Browse** button next to the Telnet Application text box and, in the dialog box that appears, select **TELNET.EXE** from the Windows folder.

Once TELNET.EXE is set up to run from Navigator, all you have to do is click a link for a MUD, and you can log in and start playing. This project shows you how to find a list of MUDs and what to expect when you enter the world of MUDs.

A MOO (Multi-user dimension Object Oriented) is another type of Interactive Internet role-playing game that is based on MUDs. The "object oriented" part refers to the fact that MOOs use more advanced programming tools. You'll also encounter other types of games called MUSes, MUSHes, and LPMUDs.

Chat Room Games

Although most people in chat rooms are usually playing some sort of social game, special chat rooms allow you to play games. Sometimes you play these games in a normal chat room that is specifically designed for games or contests (such as punning or trivia). Other chat games use unique chat rooms in which an automated host greets you, judges your answers, keeps score, and even insults you and the other contestants. These automated hosts are known as *bots* and are programmed to recognize certain words, answers, and questions. (For example, the *Jeopardy* bot acts sort of like Alex Trebek, greeting the contestants and listening to the contestants' responses.) This project shows you where to find some of the more interesting chat room games.

Begin Do It Yourself Play Internet Games

1 Tetris, the game where you piece together falling blocks, has found new life on the Internet. To start playing Tetris, enter the following URL in your Web browser:

http://www.mit.edu:8001/people/nathanw/java/Tetris.html

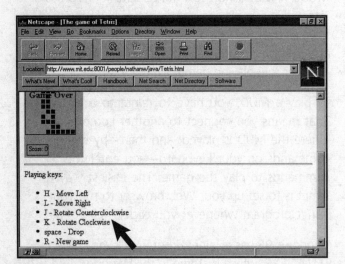

2 To play Tetris, you rotate the blocks and move them so that they interlock and form solid rows. Instructions at the bottom of the Tetris page explain the keyboard controls.

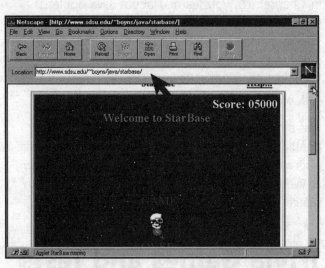

3 If you prefer arcade style games, try StarBase at **http://www.sdsu.edu/~boyns/java/starbase/**.

Do It Yourself Play Internet Games

4 In this game, objects fly at you, and you must blast them before they reach you. You press the **J** key to rotate your gun clockwise, press **K** to rotate counterclockwise, and press **Spacebar** to fire.

Some Java applets can be run in any Java-compatible browser, such as Netscape Navigator or HotJava. Other Java applets require a specific browser: they may run fine in HotJava but not run at all in Netscape. If you connect to a page that contains a Java applet you cannot run, you simply won't see the applet.

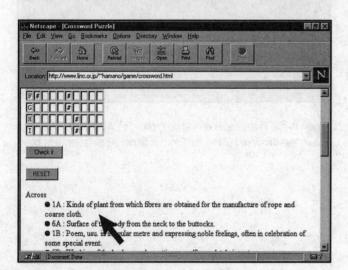

5 If you like crossword puzzles, visit the Crossword Puzzle site at **http://www.linc.or.jp/~hamano/game/crossword.html**. Scroll down the page to see the clues.

6 To enter your answer in the crossword grid, click in each text box and type the appropriate letter. You can press the **Tab** key to quickly move from one text box to the next.

7 If you like trivia and want to pit your brain against the brains of other Web walkers, visit the World Wide Trivia site at **http://www.mindspring.com/~kmims/wwt1.html**.

(continues)

Do It Yourself Play Internet Games *(continued)*

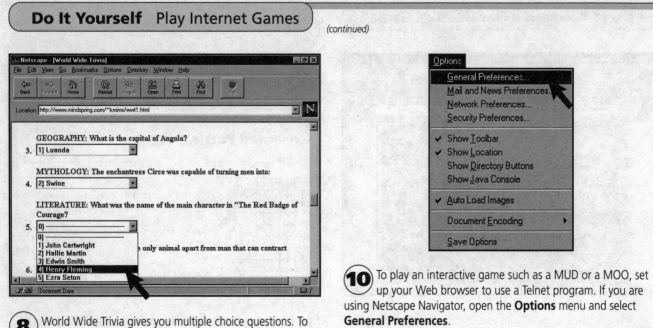

8 World Wide Trivia gives you multiple choice questions. To answer a question, open the drop-down list below the question, and click the desired answer. Check back regularly to see if you have won.

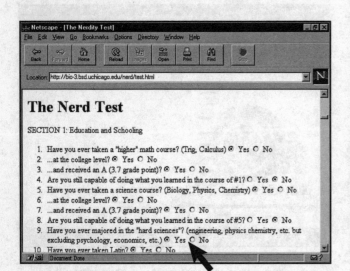

9 Think you might be considered a nerd? Take the exhaustive (500 question) nerd test to find out. It's at **http://bio-3. bsd.uchicago.edu/nerd/test.html**. Simply click **Yes** or **No** next to each question.

10 To play an interactive game such as a MUD or a MOO, set up your Web browser to use a Telnet program. If you are using Netscape Navigator, open the **Options** menu and select **General Preferences**.

11 In the Preferences dialog box, click the **Apps** tab. Then click the **Browse** button next to the Telnet Application text box.

Do It Yourself Play Internet Games

12 In the dialog box that appears, select the **TELNET.EXE** file from the folder where you installed Windows 95. Click the **Open** button, and then click **OK** in the General Preferences dialog box.

14 At the Mud Connector, click **The Mud Connector Big List** link to view an extensive list of MUDs.

13 One of the best places to start learning about and playing MUDs is the Mud Connector at **http://www.absi.com/mud/**. Here you'll find a list of more than 300 MUDs, complete with a description of each.

15 Mud Connector displays a table that shows each MUD's name, its Telnet site, and its Web page (if it has one). If the MUD has a Web page, click the link for the Web page.

(continues)

Do It Yourself   Play Internet Games

(continued)

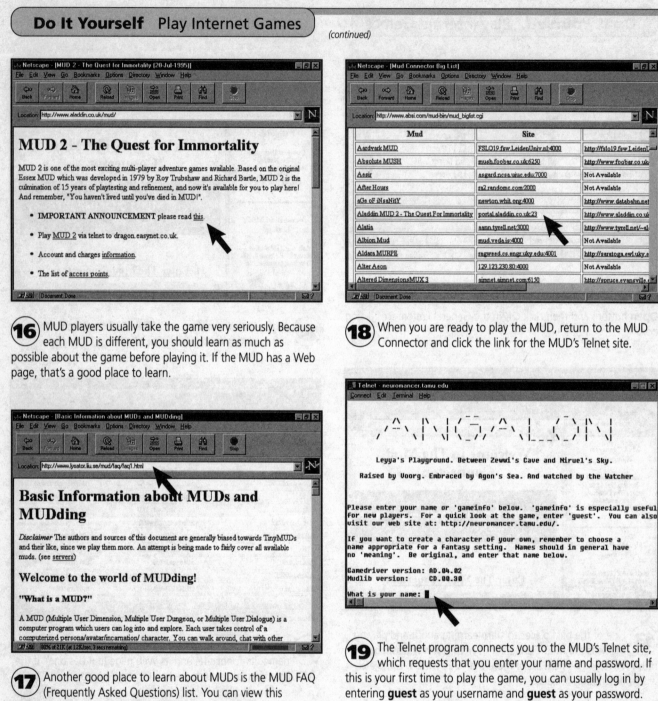

16 MUD players usually take the game very seriously. Because each MUD is different, you should learn as much as possible about the game before playing it. If the MUD has a Web page, that's a good place to learn.

17 Another good place to learn about MUDs is the MUD FAQ (Frequently Asked Questions) list. You can view this important information at **http://www.lysator.liu.se/mud/faq/faq1.html**.

18 When you are ready to play the MUD, return to the MUD Connector and click the link for the MUD's Telnet site.

19 The Telnet program connects you to the MUD's Telnet site, which requests that you enter your name and password. If this is your first time to play the game, you can usually log in by entering **guest** as your username and **guest** as your password.

Do It Yourself   Play Internet Games

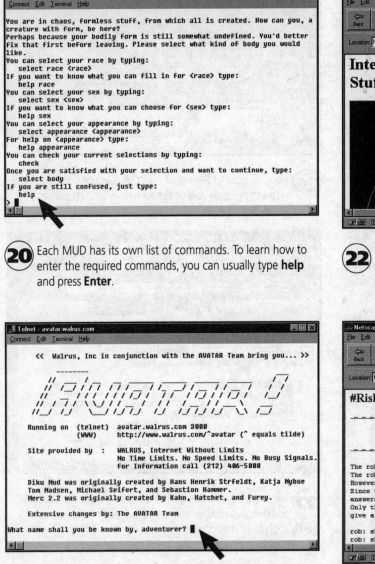

20 Each MUD has its own list of commands. To learn how to enter the required commands, you can usually type **help** and press **Enter**.

21 In some MUDs, you can create your own character and start playing. In other MUDs, you must e-mail your request to the MUD. This person will e-mail you back, sending your character name and password, and maybe a list of rules and commands.

22 If you are interested in playing chat games, check out this page at **http://phobos.cs.ucdavis.edu:8001/~mock/irc.html**.

23 This page contains information about several IRC games, including instructions on how to enter commands. Make sure you have read and understand the commands before you try to play.

(continues)

Do It Yourself   Play Internet Games

(continued)

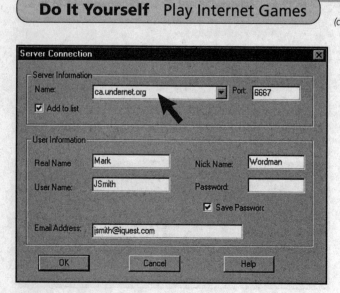

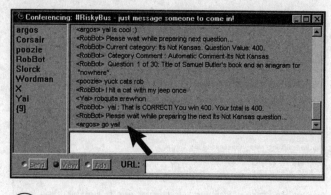

26 Here, RobBot or ReneeBot asks the questions. When responding, type **rob** or **renee** before your response.

24 To enter an IRC game, run your IRC program (Netscape Chat, for example) and connect to the specified IRC server. To play *Risky Business* (which is sort of like *Jeopardy*), try one of the following IRC servers: **irc-2.mit.edu**, **ca.undernet.org**, or **irc.qnet.com**.

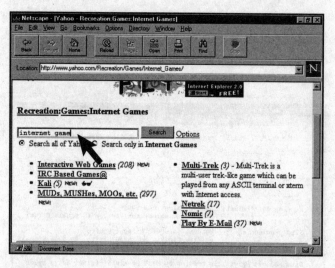

27 There are many other games on the Internet. To discover additional games on your own, use any of the Internet search tools to find information.

25 After you connect to an IRC server, you must enter the **#RiskyBus** channel. (See "Converse in Channels" on page 252 for information on how to join a channel.)

Find a Job on the Internet

In this age of downsizing and layoffs, it's important that you are aware of the changing job market and that you know where to look to find a job in your field. And here in the '90s, the Sunday want ads just won't land you the best job. More and more companies are turning to the Internet to find qualified individuals—workers who know how to use a computer and make the latest technologies work for them.

The Internet is the best tool you have for finding a job in today's market. With your Web browser and some creative thinking, you can read the want ads before they reach your local paper. You can e-mail a prospective employer almost immediately and make a direct connection instead of sending your résumé, which is likely to be added to a mountain of other résumés in the human resources department. In addition, you can show off your technological savvy by posting your résumé on the Internet, where headhunters and businesses shop for people who know their way around computers.

This project shows you some of the places on the Internet where you can start job hunting and where you can find tips that may give you an edge over other applicants. In addition, the project shows you where to post your résumé so you can save some of the running around.

Post Your Résumé in the Proper Format

Many of the sites you will encounter in your job search, as well as many companies, will request that you submit a résumé. In most cases, you will have to submit the résumé in a specific format.

In some places, you might have to create a Web page, which you can do with Notepad or WordPad as

explained in the following section, "A Sample Web Résumé." Other sites might require you to submit your résumé as a text file. Again, you can use Notepad to create the résumé, or you can use WordPad or your favorite word processor and save the résumé as a text file.

Because the requirements vary from site to site, you should be sure to read the specifications on format or length before you submit your résumé. If you don't, the company or résumé site may reject your résumé immediately.

A Sample Web Résumé

The listing below contains the text for a sample Web résumé that you can use as a basis for your own résumé. If you don't recognize some of the HTML codes in the sample résumé, refer to the table of HTML codes on page 500.

For example, the code `<A HREF = "#A2">Writing/ Editing Experience</A>` creates a link to `<A NAME="A2">`, which is directly above the section of the résumé entitled "Writing Experience." These links enable a prospective employer to jump around your document quickly and easily. The sample résumé includes similar codes that enable the reader to quickly go from the bottom of the page to the top of the page, or vice versa. At the top of the résumé is the `<A Name = "#Top">` code, and at the bottom is `<A HREF = "#Top">Top of page</A>`.

To keep this example as brief as possible, I've left out the salary history and references sections. However, you may want to include those items in your résumé. Check out "Submit Your Résumé" on page 356 to see how this résumé looks in a Web browser.

```
<title>Keaton Résumé</title>
<A Name = "#Top">
<center><h1>Jessie Keaton</h1>
<b>5525 West Market Street</b><br>
<b>Chicago, Illinois  60629</b><br>
<b>Home/Work Phone: (312) 875-0821</b><br>
<A HREF="mailto:jkeaton@iquest.com">jkeaton@iquest.com</A></center><p>
<hr>

I know you're busy, so I designed this page to make it easy to grab the information you need and then hit
the road. Just click on the link for the desired information:

<ul>
<li><A HREF = "#A1">Introduction</A>
<li><A HREF = "#A2">Writing/Editing Experience</A>
<li><A HREF = "#A3">Teaching Experience</A>
<li><A HREF = "#A4">Education</A>
</ul>

<hr>

<A NAME="A1">
<h3>Introduction</h3>

I am currently seeking a position as a writer and/or editor of technical documentation. As my résumé
shows, I have been writing, editing, and illustrating computer books for the last six years. Before that,
I wrote technical training manuals for the state of Illinois.<p>

I am trained in both task analysis and information mapping. Both of these writing tools help break down
technical information to make it easy to understand and to aid the reader in finding information and
skipping information. I also have plenty of experience transforming complex ideas into simple
graphics.<p>

I am willing to relocate to anywhere with mountains or oceans, but I am also willing to stay where I am
and telecommute (which I am currently doing).<p>

Please feel free to scan this page for my qualifications. If you wish to set up an interview, please use
the information at the top of this page to contact me.<p>

Sincerely,<p>

Jessie Keaton<p>
```

```
<hr>

<A NAME="A2">
<h3>Writing/Editing Experience</h3>

<b>1989-Present Staff Writer: Macmillan Computer Publishing</b><p>

Authored and co-authored several general computer books and software application books, including:<p>

<ul>
<li>Windows 3.1 Cheat Sheet
<li>Windows 95 Cheat Sheet
<li>Complete Idiot's Guide to Mosaic
<li>WordPerfect 5.1 Bible
<li>The First Book of Personal Computing
<li>Complete Idiot's Guide to PCs
<li>First Book of MS-DOS 6
</ul>

<b>1989-1991 Production Editor: Macmillan Computer Publishing</b><p>

<ul>
<li>Edited IBM and Macintosh software books and Nintendo game books.
<li>Coordinated production of books from manuscript stage until books were sent to printer, ensuring art
and text merged properly.
<li>Checked galleys and page proofs to ensure print and graphics were of high quality and conformed to
series design specifications.
<li>In addition to my regular duties, I helped the rest of the staff with their computer problems, and
helped develop procedures to ensure manuscripts proceeded smoothly through production.
</ul>

<b>1986-1989 Technical Writer: Training Specialists, Inc.</b><p>

Interviewed expert machine operators on the job, and developed task analysis training manuals for
Indiana's Training for Profit (TfP) program.

Wrote more than 20 manuals explaining how to operate various machines, including the following:<p>

<ul>
<li>CNC Milling Machine
<li>Autoclave
<li>Vacuum Chamber
<li>Blow-Molding Press
<li>Pin-Lift Molding Machine
</ul>

Worked closely with plant personnel to ensure accuracy of information and to target manuals to clients'
existing training program and needs.<p>

<hr>
```

```
<A NAME="A3">
<h3>Teaching Experience</h3>

1985-1986<br>
Associate Faculty: IUPUI<br>
Taught freshman English.<br>
Developed lesson plans, lectured, directed small-group activities, and evaluated student essays.<p>


<hr>


<A NAME="A4">
<h3>Education</h3>

1984<br>
Master of Arts in English: Purdue University.<br>
GPA: 5.8/6.0. Received highest grade possible on Master's comprehensive exam.<p>

1982<br>
Bachelor of Arts in Philosophy: Purdue University.<br>
GPA: 5.23/6.0.<p>


Click here to go back to the top of this page <A HREF = "#Top">Top of Page</A>.
```

Once you've created your résumé, you can post it in any of the many Web résumé banks, as explained in the following steps. You might also be able to post it on your service provider's computer. Contact your service provider for details on how to post the Web pages you create.

> Try this: Post your résumé on your service provider's computer. Then, anytime you're asked to send a résumé, ask your prospective employer if he has a Web browser. If the person has a browser, just send the URL of your online résumé. Talk about impressive!

E-Mail Your Résumé

Posting your résumé in an online résumé bank is a somewhat passive way to search for jobs; you basically have to wait till someone stumbles across your résumé. You'll have better luck e-mailing your résumé and cover letter directly to the people who might hire you. (Although some employers do not accept e-mail applications, and you might have to resort to standard mail delivery or faxes in such cases.)

When transforming your cover letter and résumé into an e-mail message, include the cover letter and résumé in the same text file and be sure to mention (in your cover letter) where you heard about the position. Also, do not type more than 70 characters per line, and press **Enter** at the end of each line. (Some e-mail readers cannot display more than 70 characters across the screen.) Because a text editing program does not have all the fancy formatting tools you'll find in a full-featured word processing program, you'll have to rely on spaces and the Enter key to make your résumé easy to read and attractive.

> When posting your résumé, keep a log of when and where you posted it. If you move or change phone numbers, or if you gain additional job experience or training, be sure to update your résumé.

Begin Do It Yourself   Read Job Postings and Other Helpful Information

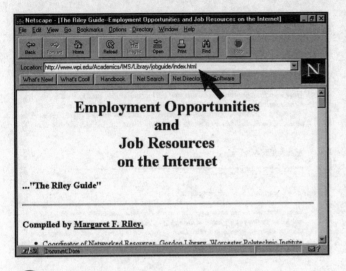

1 Listed in Point Communication's top 5% Web sites, Margaret F. Riley's Internet Job Search site is a great place to learn how to use the Internet to find a job. You can visit Ms. Riley's page at **http://www.wpi.edu/Academics/IMS/Library/ jobguide/index.html**.

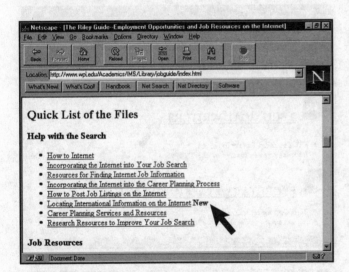

2 Scroll down the page for a list of links for files that provide general information for how to search for employment on the Internet.

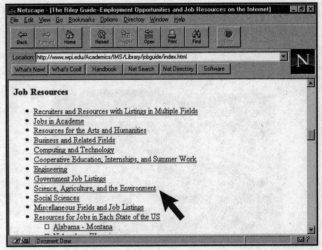

3 Scroll further down the page for files that can help you locate a potential employer. Job listings are categorized to help you locate employers in your field.

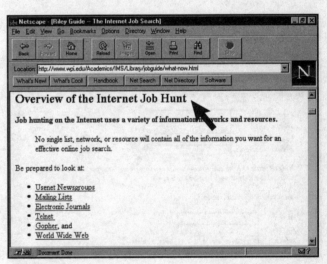

4 Before you even think about sending a résumé, read as much at this site as you can. These files contain many helpful instructions and hints on how to prepare and submit your résumé.

> When you visit a Web page that has useful job search information, create a bookmark for the page so you can return to it quickly later. You'll be skipping around on the Web more than usual during your job search.

(continues)

Do It Yourself   Read Job Postings and Other Helpful Information

5 Another great place to start your job search is at E-Span. Enter the following URL to visit its site: **http://www. espan.com/**.

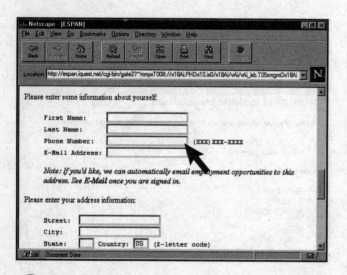

6 You can become a member of E-Span for free. Use E-Span's online form to enter information and qualifications. E-Span enters you into its pool and can automatically e-mail you job openings in your field.

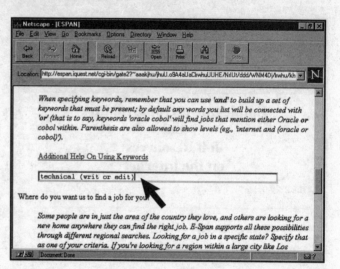

7 The online job database lets you search for job openings by state, city, job title, or anything else you want to search for. (I typed **writ** so the search would turn up "technical writer" and "technical writing.")

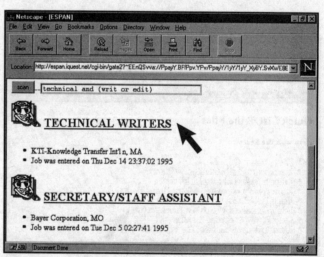

8 E-Span finds a list of employment opportunities that match your search instructions. You can click a link to view additional information about the opening.

Do It Yourself Read Job Postings and Other Helpful Information

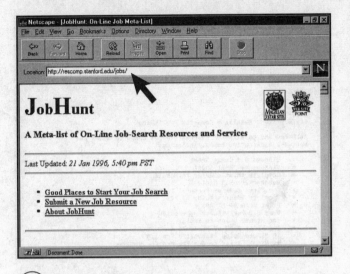

9 Stanford's Job Hunt page is another great place to start your job search. You can visit this page at **http://rescomp.stanford.edu/jobs.html**.

10 Scroll down the Job Hunt page for links to employers, general job search information, places where you can post your résumé, and much, much more. This site contains hundreds of links.

The job sites mentioned here are free. Many services charge the prospective employer for placing ads and finding candidates. Therefore, before you post your résumé or sign up for any of these services, you should check for hidden costs to you. And *don't* enter your credit card number.

Begin Do It Yourself   Submit Your Résumé

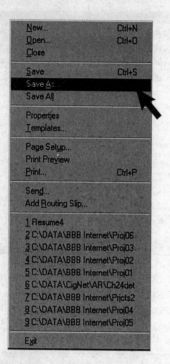

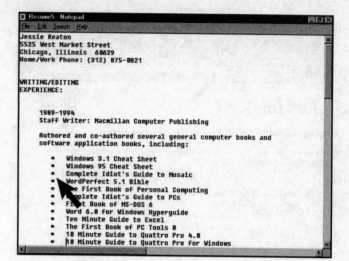

3 Text editors don't offer all the fancy formatting tools you find in a word processor. However, you can use spaces, asterisks, and other crude tools to make your résumé look professional.

1 Before you start posting your résumé or sending it off to prospective employers, create your résumé as a text file. You might be able to save your current résumé as a text file using your word processor's **File**, **Save As** command.

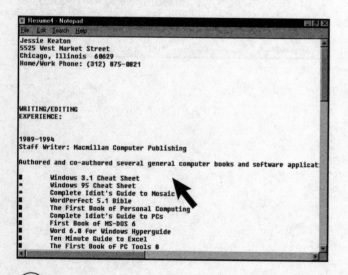

2 You can also create a text version of your résumé by typing (or pasting) it in Windows Notepad or WordPad (which has a spell checker). Be sure to include your cover letter and résumé in the same file.

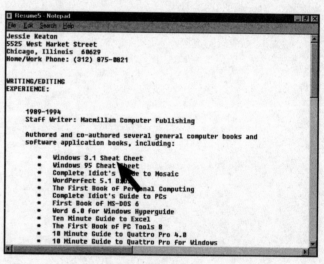

4 Before you send the résumé, proofread it carefully for spelling, grammar, and typographical errors.

Do It Yourself Submit Your Résumé

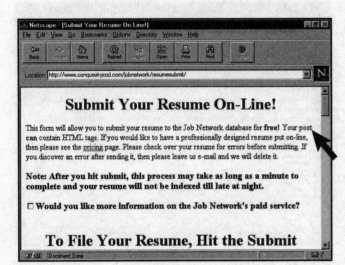

5 If you are e-mailing the résumé to a specific person or company, include a brief e-mail message describing the attached file.

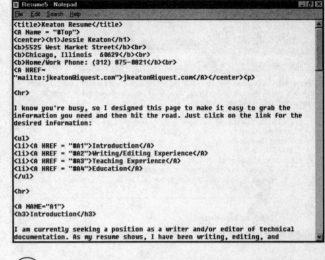

7 Use Notepad or an HTML editor to create your HTML résumé. This coded document creates a Web résumé like the one shown next.

6 If you plan to post your résumé at a Web site, the site may require that you post it as a Web document.

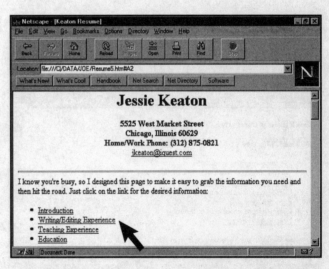

8 If you convert your résumé to a Web page, keep the opening screen brief. Include links to more lengthy material such as your résumé, references, salary history, and work samples (if applicable).

(continues)

Do It Yourself   Submit Your Résumé

(continued)

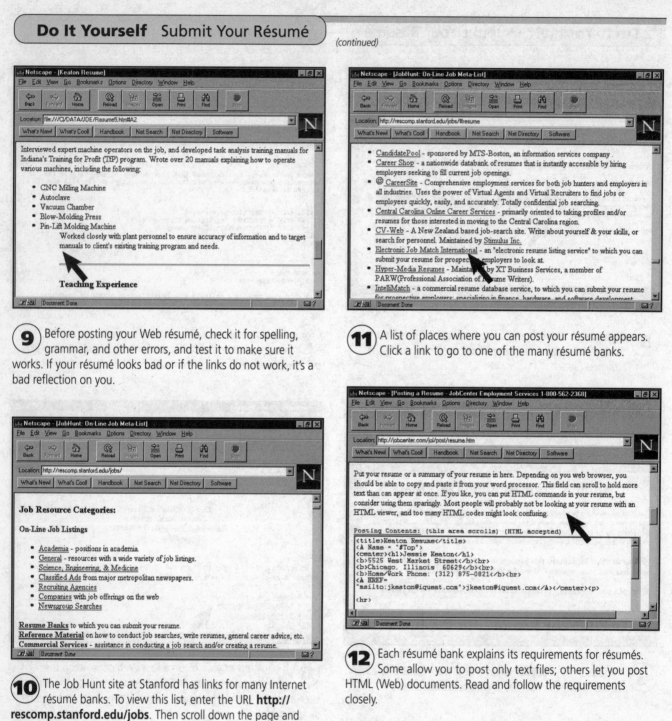

9 Before posting your Web résumé, check it for spelling, grammar, and other errors, and test it to make sure it works. If your résumé looks bad or if the links do not work, it's a bad reflection on you.

10 The Job Hunt site at Stanford has links for many Internet résumé banks. To view this list, enter the URL **http:// rescomp.stanford.edu/jobs**. Then scroll down the page and click **Resume Banks**.

11 A list of places where you can post your résumé appears. Click a link to go to one of the many résumé banks.

12 Each résumé bank explains its requirements for résumés. Some allow you to post only text files; others let you post HTML (Web) documents. Read and follow the requirements closely.

Do It Yourself   Submit Your Résumé

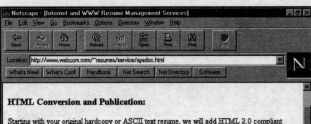

13 Many résumé banks offer links to commercial résumé services. If you do not feel comfortable creating your own HTML résumé, these services can help (for a fee).

Find the Most Recent Versions of Internet Apps

One thing about the Internet: it's always changing. You can cruise the Web every single day and still find new and interesting Web sites. They seem to pop up overnight. And along with those new sites come new ideas for putting information on the Web. Sometimes in order for you to view (and hear) the information that puts those ideas to use, you might need to get a new program or an updated version of one you already use. The best place to find the most current versions of Internet apps is on the Internet itself.

When looking for software, you can either dial into a known FTP site directly, or you can search for what you need on the Web. Your Web browser, as you may recall, can act like an FTP program when necessary, which makes it fully capable of downloading files for you. On the Web, you'll find many Web pages that connect you directly to files located on FTP sites. Some general Web sites allow you to search for just about any kind of software, and others cater specifically to people looking for Internet apps. The best of the latter type of Web site is Stroud's, from which you've downloaded a number of apps throughout the course of this book. Of course, you may run into times when Stroud's is busy and you have to try alternative sites.

Download an Internet App from Stroud's

The Stroud's site contains a list of Windows-compatible Internet applications, including FTP and e-mail clients, Web browsers, and more. Forrest H. Stroud maintains the list and provides a rating system intended to help you make the best selection. In addition, he lists the version number, size, and cost of each application. (Remember to register and pay the required fee for each shareware app you decide to keep.)

By the way, the CWS in the name CWS Stroud's stands for *consummate winsock apps.* That pretty much describes Stroud's: a complete list of winsock-related applications. About the only Internet apps you won't find at Stroud's are game-related apps such as MUDs and MOOs. Games are omitted from the CWS Stroud's list to keep it manageable.

Because the list is kept to a manageable size, Stroud's is updated daily. This ensures that you're downloading the most current version of your program available.

Tour Other Sites from Which You Can Download Internet Apps

Often, the best Web sites are also the busiest. You'll have the best success with Stroud's if you try to download your files during off-hours, which are typically between 12:00 a.m. and 5:00 a.m. local time. Use one of these two addresses:

Stroud's main site
http://www.cwsapps.com

Stroud's second main site
http://www.stroud.com

There may be times, however, when you're in a hurry to update your Internet apps or you need a particular program pronto, and Stroud's is busy. Whether that's the case, or whether you simply don't relish the thought of having to stay up all night just to beat the traffic, you can try one of Stroud's two main alternate sites (called *mirror sites* because they repeat or mirror

the same information found on the main Stroud's site). Note, though, that not all of these alternate sites are as up-to-date as the main Stroud's site.

Main alternate site
http://www.enterprise.net/cwsapps

Second alternate site
http://cwsapps.wilmington.net

If you want to find the Stroud's site closest to you, check out the Alternate Sites page where you'll find a list of all the Stroud's sites (including many located overseas) that you can try. In addition, try out other Web sites (other than Stroud's) as described in this project.

Begin Do It Yourself   Download an Internet App from Stroud's

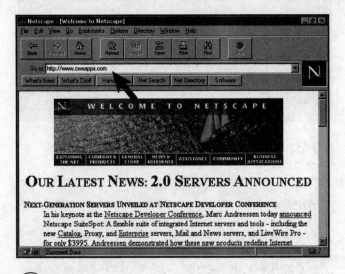

1 Connect to the Internet and start your Web browser.

2 To connect to Stroud's, type the URL: **http://cwsapps.texas.net** and press **Enter**.

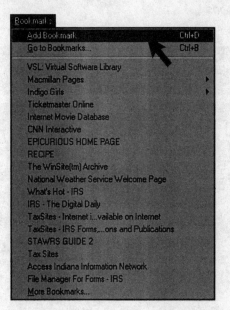

3 Once you connect to Stroud's, you'll want to save its location by adding a bookmark. In Netscape, open the **Bookmarks** menu and select **Add Bookmark**.

(continues)

Do It Yourself   Download an Internet App from Stroud's

(continued)

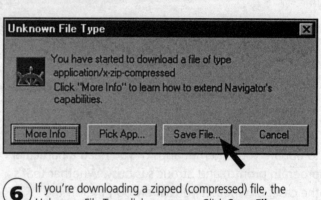

4 Scroll down the page and select the appropriate category for the Internet app you're looking for. If you just want to check out what's new and interesting, you might want to click **Top 20 Apps**.

5 Continue scrolling until you find something you like; then click its file name. Try e-Mail Notify for Windows 95.

6 If you're downloading a zipped (compressed) file, the Unknown File Type dialog appears. Click **Save File**.

7 Select a folder for your new app and click **Save**.

After you download your program, you need to install it. How you do that will vary between applications, but usually you have to extract the program files (using WinZip) from the one file you downloaded. Program files that end in .EXE are self-extracting; just double-click the .EXE file, and it extracts its own files.

When you finish decompressing the files, click the **INSTALL.EXE** or **SETUP.EXE** file to install the program. If you can't find one, there may not be any real installation procedure. In that case, double-click the program's .EXE file to start the program.

Begin Do It Yourself Tour Other Sites to Download Internet Apps

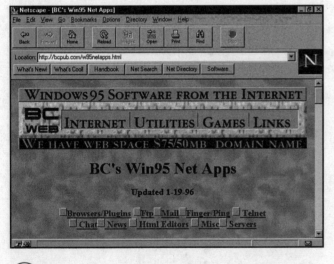

1 You can find a list of alternate Stroud's sites on the Alternate Sites page.

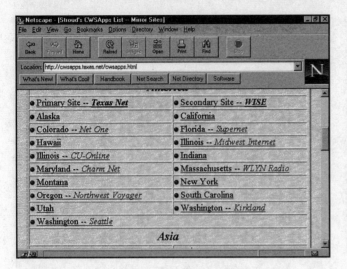

2 There's another nice collection of Internet apps on the BC's Win95 Net Apps page, located at **http://bcpub.com/w95netapps.html.**

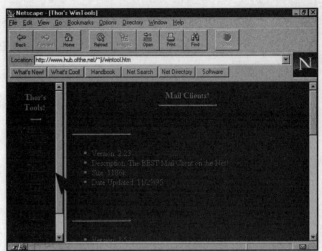

3 Thor's WinTools page, located at **http://www.hub.ofthe.net/~jl/wintool.htm**, provides a complete list of Internet apps.

4 The files at Stroud's are actually located at an FTP site called Papa Winsock. However, you can get to them on the Web using the URL **http://www.winsite.com**.

You can ftp to the Papa Winsock site if you prefer, using the address **ftp://ftp.winsite.com**. But be warned: navigating an FTP site is not an easy business.

(continues)

Do It Yourself   Tour Other Sites to Download Internet Apps   *(continued)*

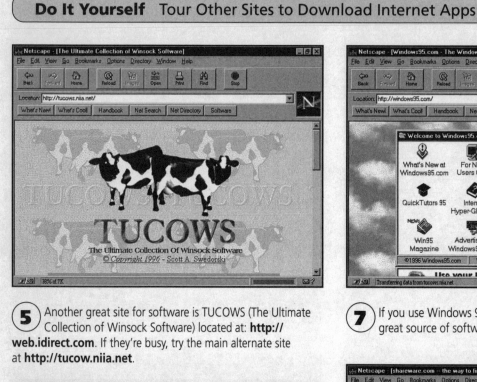

5 Another great site for software is TUCOWS (The Ultimate Collection of Winsock Software) located at: **http://web.idirect.com**. If they're busy, try the main alternate site at **http://tucow.niia.net**.

7 If you use Windows 95, you must visit **Windows95.com**, a great source of software and help.

6 The Virtual Software Library, located at **http://vsl.cnet.com**, is a great place to find software other than Internet software.

8 The site at **shareware.com** is a good source of shareware and freeware programs.

Get the Latest News Headlines

The worst thing about the news on the Internet is that there's almost too much of it. All the major news networks and many local news stations are online. Likewise, major newspapers (such as the *New York Times* and the *Wall Street Journal*), as well as local and international newspapers, are online.

In addition, many specific types of news services are on the Net, including headline news, sports news, industry and business news, financial news, and weather. And if that's not enough, there's entertainment news with direct links to pages featuring many of your favorite TV shows.

As you'll see here, there definitely is not a lack of news on the Net. And the problem is not one of how to find the news, but one of how to find the news that interests you.

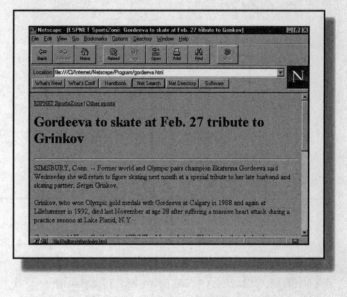

Connect to a News Source

When you're ready to get the latest news off the Net, first ask yourself, "What kind of news am I looking for, and where do I usually get it?" If the answer is that you like to get your news from the *New York Times*, start by searching for its Web page. Chances are, your favorite news source is on the Internet.

The following table lists some of the more popular national and world news sources on the Internet, along with their addresses.

Popular Internet News Sources

News Source	Address
ABC Internet Hourly News*	http://www.realaudio.com/contentp/abc.html
AP Wire Service	http://www.trib.com/NEWS/APwire.html
CBS News	http://uttm.com
ClariNet	http://www.clarinet.com
CNN Interactive	http://cnn.com
National Public Radio*	http://www.prognet.com/contentp/npr.html
NBC News	http://www.nbc.com/news/index.html
The *Nando Times*	http://www2.nando.net/nt/nando.cgi
PR Newswire	http://www.prnewswire.com

(continues)

(continued)

News Source	Address
Reuters NewMedia	http://www.yahoo.com/headlines/current/news/summary.html
TimesFax	http://www.nytimesfax.com
USA Today	http://www.usatoday.com
US Online World and News	http://www.usnews.com
Virtual Daily News	http://www.infi.net/~opfer/daily.htm
World News Today	http://www.fwi.com/wnt/wnt.html
USA Watch News	http://usawatch.com

*requires RealAudio

In order to take advantage of some news sources, you must have installed a RealAudio player for your Web browser. See "Play a Radio Broadcast with RealAudio" on page 379 for help.

For those of you who prefer local news stations and newspapers, many of them are also on the Internet. Be sure to look for your favorites. The table below lists some popular online newspapers on the local level.

Popular Local-Level Online Sources

Newspaper	Geographical Location	Online Address
Boston Globe	Boston	http://www.globe.com
Detroit News	Detroit	http://detnews.com
Electronic Telegraph	United Kingdom	http://www.telegraph.co.uk
The Gate	San Francisco	http://www.sfgate.com
Houston Chronicle Interactive	Houston	http://www.chron.com
Mercury Center	San Jose	http://www.sjmercury.com
New York Times	New York City	http://www.nytimes.com
Philadelphia Inquirer	Philadelphia	http://www.phillynews.com
TribNet	Tacoma	http://www.tribnet.com/mainnews.htp
St. Petersburg Press	Russia	http://www.spb.su/sppress

If you want to find a particular story, or if you want to look at the same story in more than one newspaper, try one of these Web pages, which provide links to multiple news sources:

Daily News

http://www.cs.vu.nl/~gerben/news.html

Extra!Extra!

http://www.fyionline.com/infoMCI/
update/NEWS-MCI.html

Infoseek's News Update

http://guide.infoseek.com/NS/
ticker?DCticker.html

Pathfinder

http://pathfinder.com

NewsLink

http://www.newslink.org

NewsPage

http://www.newspage.com

NPC Hot News Sources

http://town.hall.org/places/npc/
newsource.html

> If time is of the essence, you can subscribe to many popular news services, and they will "deliver" the news you want to know about to your computer every morning. For example, ESPN, CBS, NewsPage, *TimesFax*, the *Wall Street Journal*, and *Investor's Daily* all offer this kind of service (just to name a few). As you visit various news sites, watch for subscription offers. Each site offers complete details on pricing and how to subscribe.

If you're looking for more specific news, check out the sites in the following table, which are popular financial, industrial, and political news sources. For a lighter look at the news, try the entertainment-, weather-, and sports-related news pages listed in the table on the next page.

Serious Topic News Sources

Source	Address
Business Update	http://www.fyionline.com/infoMCI/update/BUSINESS-MCI.html
BYTE	http://www.byte.com
CNBC	http://www.cnbc.com
ClNet Central	http://www.cnet.com
C-SPAN	http://www.c-span.org
Executive Lounge	http://www.rwsa.com/executive/lounge.html
Global Internet News Agency	http://www.gina.com
HotWired	http://www.wired.com
Internet Business and Industry News	http://www.lib.lsu.edu/bus/biznews.html
Mecklermedia's iWorld	http://www.iworld.com
Wall Street Journal	http://update.wsj.com
ZDNet	http://www.zdnet.com

Lighter Topic News Sources

Source	Address
ABC	http://www.abctelevision.com
CBS	http://www.cbs.com
Discovery Channel	http://www.discovery.com
ER	http://www.nbc.com/entertainment/shows/er/index.html
ESPNet SportsZone	http://ESPNET.SportsZone.com
Fox Online	http://www.foxnetwork.com/home.html
Friends	http://www.nbc.com/entertainment/shows/friends/index.html
Comedy Central	http://www.comcentral.com
INTELLICAST	http://www.intellicast.com
NBC	http://www.nbc.com
PBS	http://www.pbs.org
People Magazine	http://pathfinder.com/@@NFza14K7ZglAQKid/people
SciFi Channel	http://www.scifi.com/dominion.html
Showtime Online	http://showtimeonline.com
Sports Network	http://www.sportsnetwork.com
Sportsline USA	http://www.sportsline.com
Travel Channel	http://www.travelchannel.com
Weather Channel	http://www.weather.com
WeatherNet	http://cirrus.sprl.umich.edu/wxnet
WebWeather	http://www.princeton.edu/Webweather/ww.html
U.S. Weather Map	http://www.mit.edu:8001/usa.html

In the "Browse for a Good News Source" steps, you'll learn how to use Netscape Navigator to find many of the news sources I've mentioned. You'll connect to a Web page called NewsLink, which provides links to many news sources. I think you'll find it a good jumping off place for your tour of Web news.

Save or Print News

From the many news sources the Internet offers, you'll soon find your favorites. And when you locate news that you're really interested in, you might want

to keep a copy of it. For example, if you're doing research for an article or a report, you might want to print out a copy of several news articles so you can refer to them later.

Even if you're not writing a report, you might want to save a copy of the news you're interested in. Why go to all that trouble? Well, connecting to the Internet costs money, and it adds up fast if you spend a lot of time reading endless news reports. You can save yourself some bucks by simply printing or saving the news articles in which you're interested. The steps under "Save or Print the News" show you how.

Begin Do It Yourself   Browse for a Good News Source

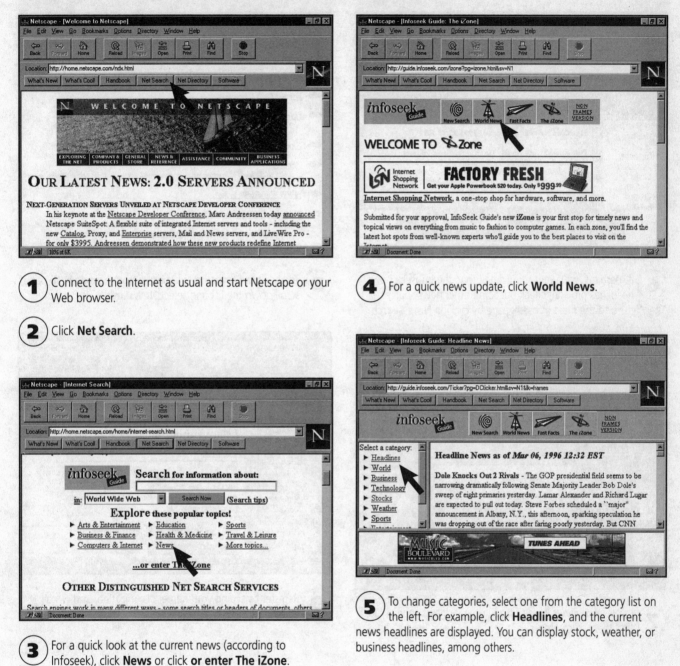

1 Connect to the Internet as usual and start Netscape or your Web browser.

2 Click **Net Search**.

3 For a quick look at the current news (according to Infoseek), click **News** or click **or enter The iZone**.

4 For a quick news update, click **World News**.

5 To change categories, select one from the category list on the left. For example, click **Headlines**, and the current news headlines are displayed. You can display stock, weather, or business headlines, among others.

(continues)

Do It Yourself   Browse for a Good News Source *(continued)*

6 If, perhaps, you want more detail than the Infoseek news headlines provide, check out some other news sources. Then return to the main Infoseek page by clicking **New Search**.

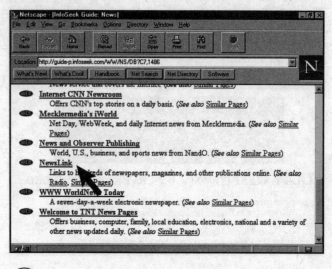

8 To check out several news sources from a single Web page, scroll down the list and select **NewsLink**.

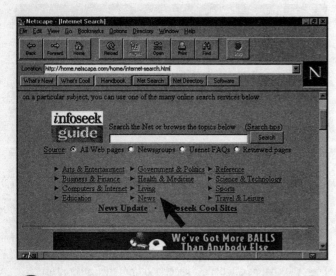

7 Infoseek provides links to many popular news sources. To find them, click **News**.

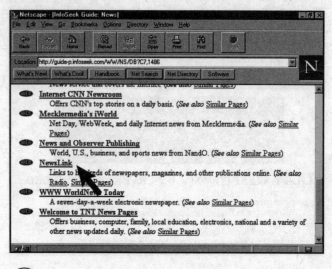

9 Register by typing your name, organization, and e-mail address.

Do It Yourself Browse for a Good News Source

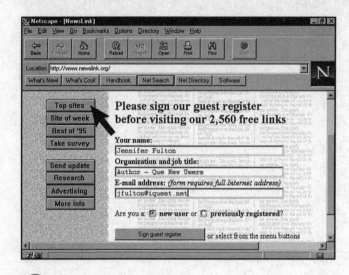

10 Click **Top Sites**.

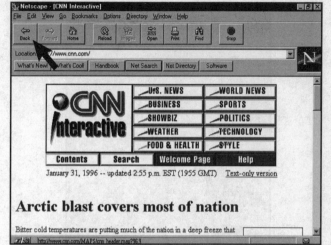

12 CNN is a good source for breaking news, business news updates, and so on. To see what other links NewsLink has, click **Back**.

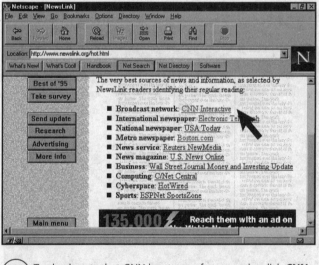

11 To check out what CNN has to say, for example, click **CNN Interactive**.

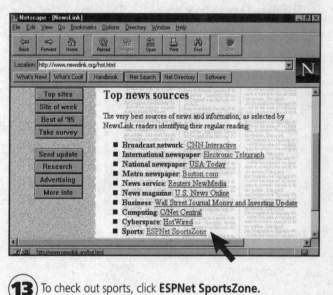

13 To check out sports, click **ESPNet SportsZone**.

(continues)

Do It Yourself Browse for a Good News Source

(continued)

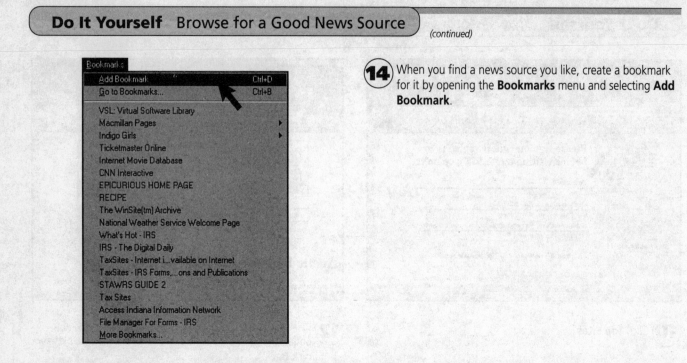

14 When you find a news source you like, create a bookmark for it by opening the **Bookmarks** menu and selecting **Add Bookmark**.

Begin Do It Yourself Save or Print the News

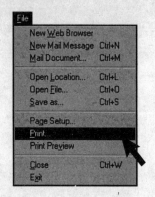

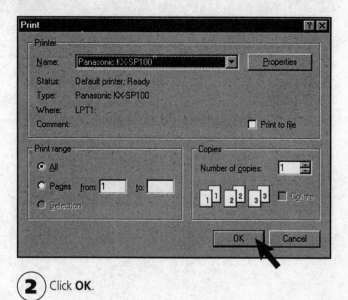

 If you find a story that you want to keep, you can print it by clicking the **Print** button or by opening the **File** menu and clicking **Print**.

2 Click **OK**.

Do It Yourself Save or Print the News

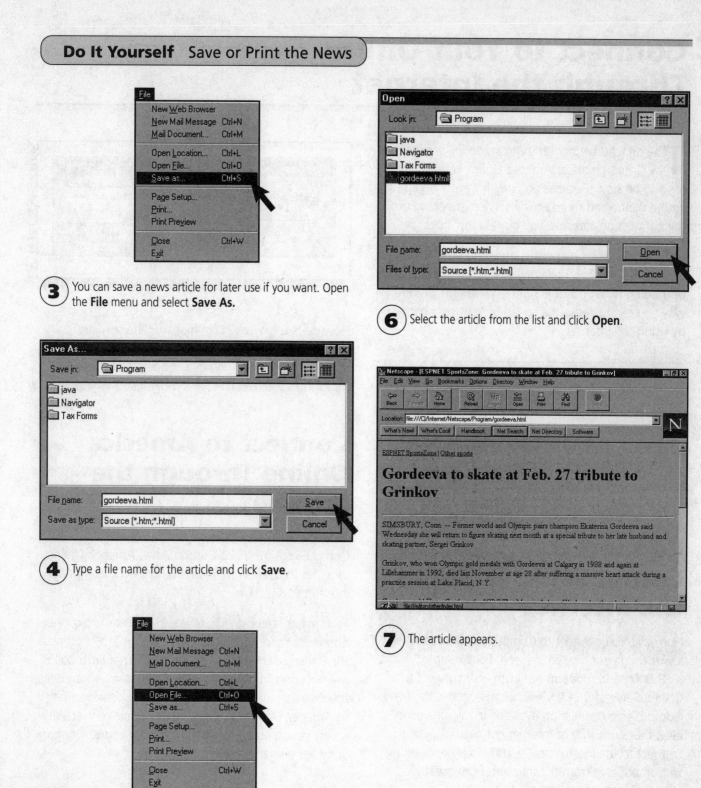

3 You can save a news article for later use if you want. Open the **File** menu and select **Save As.**

4 Type a file name for the article and click **Save**.

5 To view the article at a later date, start your Web browser, open the **File** menu, and select **Open File**.

6 Select the article from the list and click **Open**.

7 The article appears.

Connect to Your Online Service Through the Internet

The only problem with using an online service such as CompuServe or America Online is that they tend to be slow. Because you pay for every minute you're connected to an online service, speeding up the connection can save you quite a few bucks.

One way to speed up your connection time is to get a faster modem. If you already have a fast modem or if upgrading is not possible right now, there's another way you can increase the speed of your connection: by using the Internet.

> Although I've included the steps for Compu-Serve and America Online only, you can use this technique with other online services (including Prodigy) as well. The Microsoft Network does not currently offer this service, but it may sometime soon.

Connect to CompuServe Through the Internet

Normally, you connect to CompuServe at a setting lower than your modem's speed. For example, I have a 28,800 baud modem, but I can only connect to CompuServe at 9,600 baud because that is the fastest CompuServe connection available in my area. However, that's not true of Internet connections. I can connect to the Internet at 19,200. So by connecting to CompuServe from the Internet, I can greatly increase my connection speed.

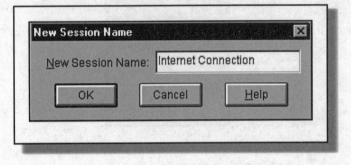

How does this work? Like many online services, CompuServe offers access to the Internet. Well, using a kind of back door, you can connect to CompuServe through its Internet link. This project shows you how.

Connect to America Online Through the Internet

America Online is a popular online service similar to CompuServe. And like CompuServe, America Online provides its users with a way to connect through an Internet connection.

In its setup screens, AOL refers to the Internet connection by its more technical name: TCP/IP. TCP/IP (short for Transmission Control Protocol/Internet Protocol) is a set of rules that define how information is sent over the Internet. Regardless, the process for connecting to America Online through your Internet connection is very similar to the process of connecting to Compu-Serve, as discussed earlier.

Begin Do It Yourself Connect to CompuServe

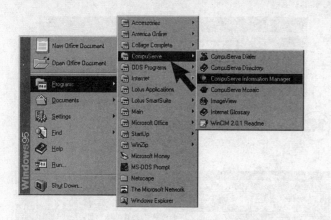

1 First, start CompuServe. Then click the **Start** button, select **Programs**, select **CompuServe**, and click **CompuServe Information Manager**. If you use Windows 3.1, double-click the **CompuServe Information Manager** icon in the Main program window.

2 Open the **Special** menu and select **Session Settings**.

3 Click **New**, and the New Session Name dialog box appears.

4 Type a name such as **Internet Connection** for your new session, and then click **OK**. You're returned to the Setup Session Settings dialog box.

5 In the **Network** drop-down list, select **Internet**.

(continues)

Do It Yourself   Connect to CompuServe

(continued)

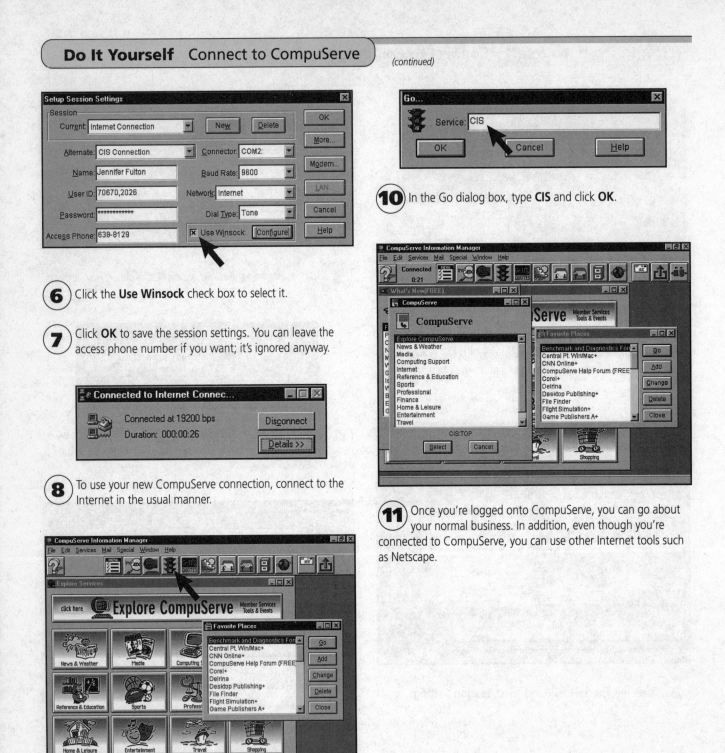

6 Click the **Use Winsock** check box to select it.

7 Click **OK** to save the session settings. You can leave the access phone number if you want; it's ignored anyway.

8 To use your new CompuServe connection, connect to the Internet in the usual manner.

9 Switch to the CompuServe Information Manager. To connect, you can select a destination from the **Favorite Places** box and click **Go**, or you can click a button in the **Explore Services** box. To connect to CompuServe's main screen, click the **Go** button.

10 In the Go dialog box, type **CIS** and click **OK**.

11 Once you're logged onto CompuServe, you can go about your normal business. In addition, even though you're connected to CompuServe, you can use other Internet tools such as Netscape.

Begin Do It Yourself   Connect to America Online

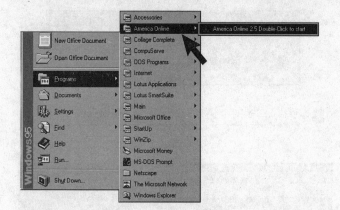

1 Click the **Start** button, select **Programs**, select **America Online**, and click **America Online 2.5.** If you use Windows 3.1, double-click the **America Online** icon in the Main program group window.

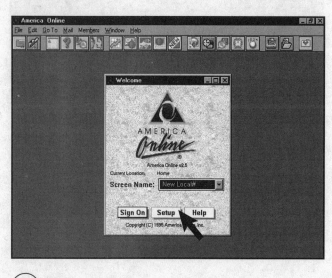

2 From the opening screen, click **Setup**.

3 Click **Create Location**.

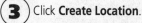

4 In the **Location** text box, type **Internet Connection**.

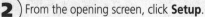

5 In the **Network** drop-down list, select **TCP/IP**. Repeat for the alternate connection (the boxes on the right side of the window).

(continues)

Do It Yourself Connect to America Online

(continued)

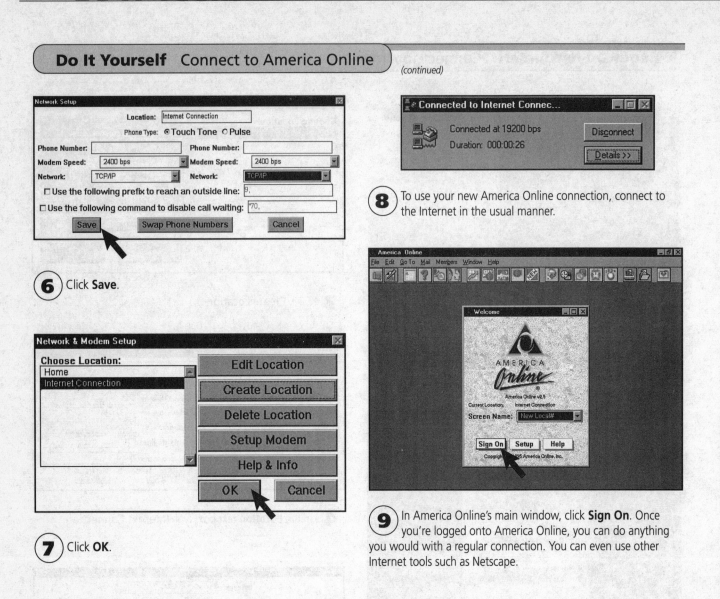

6 Click **Save**.

7 Click **OK**.

8 To use your new America Online connection, connect to the Internet in the usual manner.

9 In America Online's main window, click **Sign On**. Once you're logged onto America Online, you can do anything you would with a regular connection. You can even use other Internet tools such as Netscape.

Play a Radio Broadcast with RealAudio

RealAudio is a standard by which near-to-live radio transmissions are sent over the Internet. It's called near-to-live transmission because there's a small delay between the time the sound signal is sent and the time you actually hear it. There are other standards, but RealAudio is by far the most popular.

Normally, when you download a sound file—such as an .AU or .VOX file—from the Internet, your Web browser has to receive the entire sound file and save it to disk. Then the browser launches a sound player application, which reads the sound file in its entirety and then plays it.

RealAudio cuts a lot of time out of the audio transmission process. When you download a RealAudio sound, your RealAudio player application begins decompressing it as soon as it receives the first few thousand bytes. Then it starts playing the decompressed portion while the rest of the sound is still being transmitted. You can save a RealAudio transmission as a file if you want, but you don't have to if you only want to hear it once.

To hear a RealAudio broadcast, you'll need a RealAudio player. In this project, you'll learn how to install and configure a RealAudio player, as well as how to use it.

> To use RealAudio, your PC must have at least a 486 CPU (if you use Windows 95) or a Pentium (if you use Windows 3.1).

When you download the RealAudio player, you must complete a form with your name, address, and computer information. The RealAudio developers use that information to fine-tune each product to its actual user—you. During the installation process, RealAudio automatically ties itself in with your Web browser. This enables your Web browser to activate the RealAudio player whenever it encounters a RealAudio page on the Web.

> The steps in "Download RealAudio" (on page 380) walk you through downloading the player. After you download and install RealAudio, you'll receive a password via e-mail. Until you get it, you cannot use RealAudio; you need the password to visit a RealAudio site.

Visit a RealAudio Web Site

Several Web sites already use RealAudio, and more are moving toward it. When you connect to a Web site with a RealAudio link, your Web browser automatically launches RealAudio to play it.

In this project, you'll visit the National Public Radio Web site, which uses RealAudio. Another site that uses it that you might want to visit is the ABC Internet Hourly News site. The ABC News site is located at **www.realaudio.com/contentp/abc.html**. You'll find links to other RealAudio sites on the RealAudio home page.

Begin Do It Yourself Download RealAudio

1 Connect to the Internet and start your Web browser.

2 In the **Location** or **Go to** text box, type **http://www.cwsapps.com** and press **Enter**.

If you have trouble connecting to this main Stroud's site, try its other main site at http//www.stroud.com or one of the main alternate sites (http://www.wilmington.net or http://www.enterprise.net/cwsapps).

3 Click the **Stroud's** logo.

4 Scroll down and select **Audio Apps**.

5 In the list of audio apps, find RealAudio for Windows 3.x. If you use Windows 95, click **Windows 95 version**.

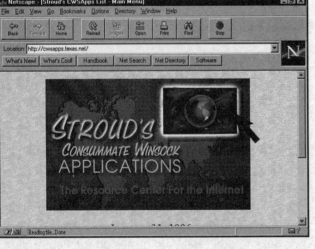

Do It Yourself Download RealAudio

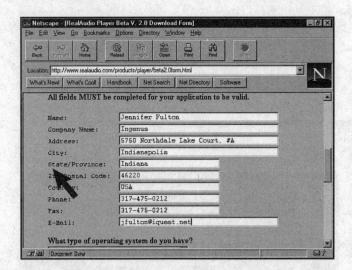

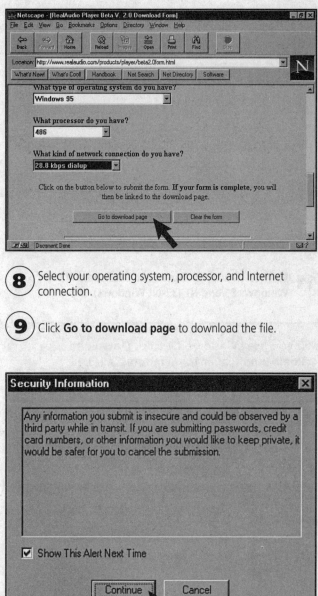

6 Click the file name of the RealAudio program (it appears in the **Location** line).

7 Complete the form for downloading RealAudio by typing your name, organization, address, and so on.

8 Select your operating system, processor, and Internet connection.

9 Click **Go to download page** to download the file.

10 The Security Information dialog box appears. Click **Continue**.

(continues)

Do It Yourself   Download RealAudio

(continued)

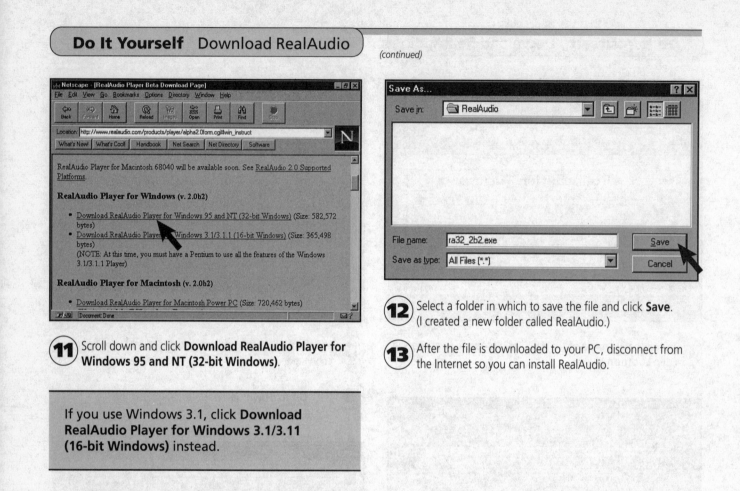

11 Scroll down and click **Download RealAudio Player for Windows 95 and NT (32-bit Windows)**.

12 Select a folder in which to save the file and click **Save**. (I created a new folder called RealAudio.)

13 After the file is downloaded to your PC, disconnect from the Internet so you can install RealAudio.

If you use Windows 3.1, click **Download RealAudio Player for Windows 3.1/3.11 (16-bit Windows)** instead.

Begin Do It Yourself   Install RealAudio

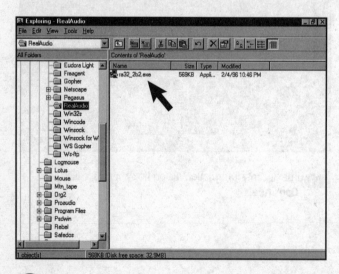

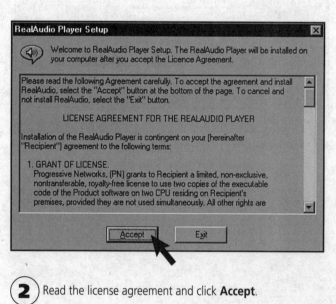

1 Start Explorer or File Manager, change to the **RealAudio** directory, and double-click the **ra32_2b2.EXE** file.

2 Read the license agreement and click **Accept**.

Do It Yourself Install RealAudio

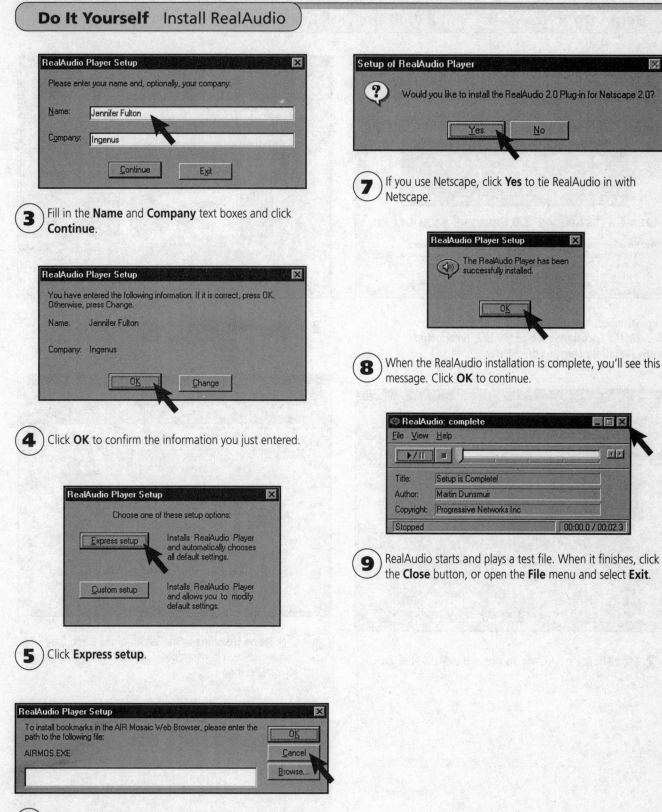

3 Fill in the **Name** and **Company** text boxes and click **Continue**.

4 Click **OK** to confirm the information you just entered.

5 Click **Express setup**.

6 If you use AIR Mosaic, enter its path in the text box. If you do not use AIR Mosaic, click **Cancel**.

7 If you use Netscape, click **Yes** to tie RealAudio in with Netscape.

8 When the RealAudio installation is complete, you'll see this message. Click **OK** to continue.

9 RealAudio starts and plays a test file. When it finishes, click the **Close** button, or open the **File** menu and select **Exit**.

Begin Do It Yourself   Visit a Web Site with RealAudio

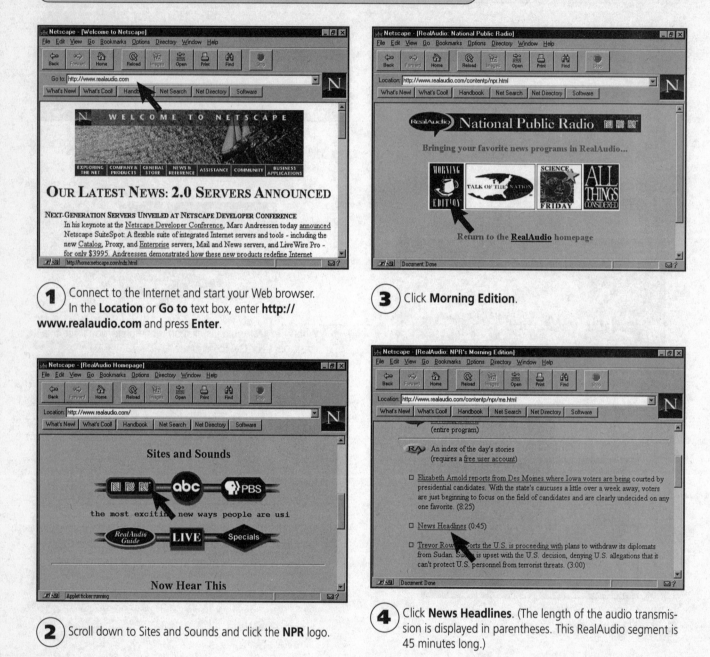

① Connect to the Internet and start your Web browser. In the **Location** or **Go to** text box, enter **http://www.realaudio.com** and press **Enter**.

② Scroll down to Sites and Sounds and click the **NPR** logo.

③ Click **Morning Edition**.

④ Click **News Headlines**. (The length of the audio transmission is displayed in parentheses. This RealAudio segment is 45 minutes long.)

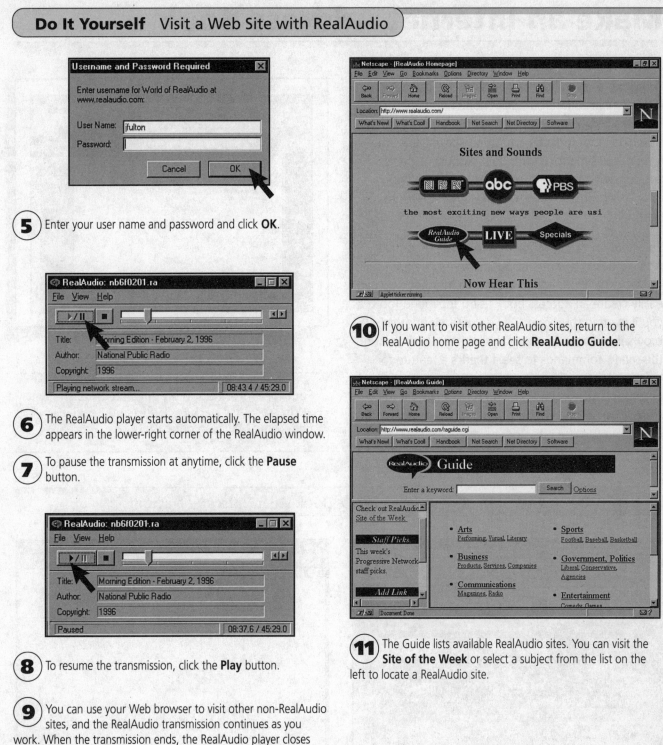

Do It Yourself Visit a Web Site with RealAudio

5 Enter your user name and password and click **OK**.

6 The RealAudio player starts automatically. The elapsed time appears in the lower-right corner of the RealAudio window.

7 To pause the transmission at anytime, click the **Pause** button.

8 To resume the transmission, click the **Play** button.

9 You can use your Web browser to visit other non-RealAudio sites, and the RealAudio transmission continues as you work. When the transmission ends, the RealAudio player closes automatically.

10 If you want to visit other RealAudio sites, return to the RealAudio home page and click **RealAudio Guide**.

11 The Guide lists available RealAudio sites. You can visit the **Site of the Week** or select a subject from the list on the left to locate a RealAudio site.

Make an Internet Address Book

Internet e-mail addresses are about as easy to remember as international phone numbers. They can be a combination of long usernames, disjointed numbers, and domain names that snake across the screen—all separated with dots. Nobody expects you to remember these addresses, but if you don't enter them precisely, your mail will never reach its destination.

The solution to this problem is to create an e-mail address book. If you're using a browser program such as Netscape Navigator to access the Internet, you can easily create an address book using the menu tools, as you'll learn in this project. If you're using another browser program to access the Internet, look through the menu commands to see if there's a feature for creating an e-mail address book. Some Internet e-mail programs (such as Eudora) also have a feature for creating an address book. Once you create an address book, you can use it to address all your e-mail messages.

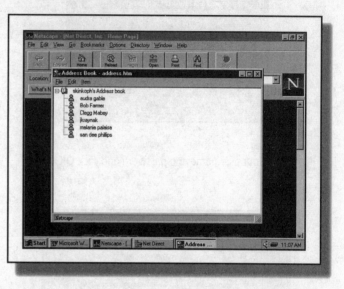

For more information on Internet e-mail addresses, turn back to "Send and Receive Electronic Mail" on page 193.

Begin Do It Yourself Create an Address Book with Netscape Navigator

1 Open the **Window** menu in Netscape Navigator or in Netscape Mail and click **Address book**. The Address Book window appears.

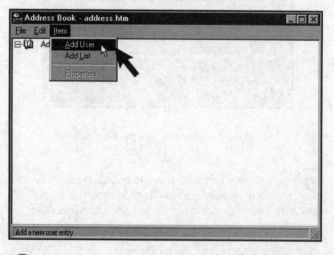

2 To add an e-mail address to your book, open the **Item** menu and click **Add User**. The Address Book dialog box appears.

Do It Yourself Create an Address Book with Netscape Navigator

You may find that you need to change an address in your address book (if a person moves or picks a new e-mail address, for example). Open the Address Book window, right-click the person's name, and click **Properties**. This opens the same dialog box you used to add the person to your address book. Simply change any of the information that is no longer correct and click **OK**.

4 Click in the **Name** text box and type the person's full name (you can include uppercase characters). This is the name that will appear in your address book.

3 (Optional) In the **Nick Name** text box, type the person's nickname as a combination of lowercase characters and numbers. (You cannot use uppercase characters.)

5 Click in the **E-Mail Address** text box and type the person's Internet e-mail address.

(continues)

Do It Yourself Create an Address Book with Netscape Navigator

(continued)

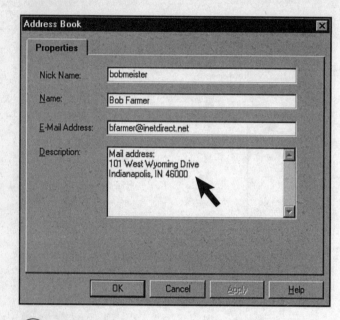

6 (Optional) You can type additional information—such as the person's phone number and mailing address—in the **Description** text box. (If you open your address book in Navigator as a Web page, the description information will appear.) To start a new line in this text box, press **Ctrl+Enter**.

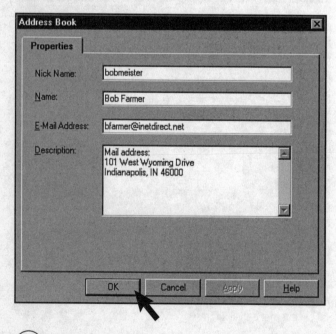

7 When you finish filling in this information, click **OK**. The address is added to the list in the Address Book window.

8 Repeat these steps as necessary to add names to your address book.

To delete a person from your address book, click the person's name and press the **Delete** key (or open the **Edit** menu and select **Delete**).

9 To use the address book and send e-mail from Netscape Navigator, open the **File** menu and select **New Mail Message**.

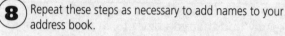

10 In the Message Composition box that appears, click in the **Mail To** text box. Then click the **Address** toolbar to display your address book.

Do It Yourself Create an Address Book with Netscape Navigator

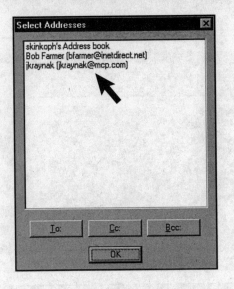

11 In the Select Addresses dialog box, click the address to which you want to send this message, click the **To** button, and then click **OK**. The selected address appears in the **Mail To** text box of your e-mail message. Now you can compose and send your e-mail message.

Take a Live Video Tour

Not only can you view text information and graphics when surfing the Internet, you can also view video clips and live video feeds. Video on the Internet has been around for a long time, but it's not always convenient to use because the video files often take a long time to download. And after you spend the time it takes to download the video file, you have to play it back from your hard drive.

Despite the downloading time constraints, Internet videos are still popular among Web surfers. Many of the hottest Web sites offer video clips you can download and view on your own computer, such as movie scenes or trailers, television scenes, music videos, and promotional videos. However, in order to view the clips, you have to have a program installed on your computer or included in your Internet browser program that allows you to see the video.

If you're using Windows 95, try the program Video for Windows that's included with it; it's a driver program you can use to view downloaded videos (you may have to install the driver yourself). If you don't like that program or if you're using Windows 3.1, you'll also find other viewer programs on the Net, such as Quicktime or Mpegplay, that you can download and use to view Internet videos.

For more information about using video viewer programs (or helper applications), turn to "Play Sound and Video Clips with Helper Applications" on page 161.

A newer aspect of Internet videos is real-time or live video (also called live video feed). Live video feed is part of the cutting edge video technology that allows Internet users to view live video shots from around the world. With live video, someone sets up a TV or video camera (sometimes called a Web-Cam) to view a particular scene (a beach or a street corner, for

example) and then feeds the digital images onto the Internet. When an Internet user opens a Web page containing live video feed, he sees a video picture that's only moments old. Most live videos are updated every couple of minutes, so it's not *exactly* live... it's more like a video snapshot.

What makes live video feed different from downloadable video clips is that the image is made into a normal data type that you can see right away on the WWW page without having to download the image onto your computer's hard drive. Most of the images appear as JPEG or GIF images, popular graphics formats.

Xing Technology Corp. and VDOnet Corp. are two companies exploring the broadcast of real-time video over the Internet. You'll find the Xing Technology home page at http://www.xingtech.com/ and the VDOnet page at http://www.vdolive.com. Both pages have instructions for downloading their respective video players and links for viewing videos on the Internet.

In this project, you'll take a live video tour on the Web using Netscape Navigator, and you can take a look at "live" video snapshots from around the world.

Because the sites you are about to visit are live video feeds, the images you see will differ from the figures shown in the project, depending on the time of day you visit a Web-Cam view. It might be night or day (don't forget to account for changing time zones). Remember, too, that the cameras update the image at different time increments. So what you see on a particular site, such as people walking by or different weather conditions, may not be what you expect.

Begin Do It Yourself   Take a Live Video Tour

1 Connect to the Internet and start your Web browser (such as Netscape). In the **Location** or **Go to** text box, enter **http://www.pointcom.com** and press **Enter**.

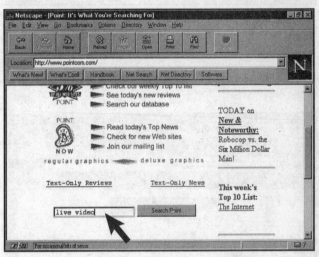

2 At the Point Communications page, you can look up the topic of live video and find out which Web sites are out there. Scroll down the page until you locate the search text box. Type **live video** in the text box, and then press **Enter** or click **Search**.

(continues)

Do It Yourself Take a Live Video Tour

(continued)

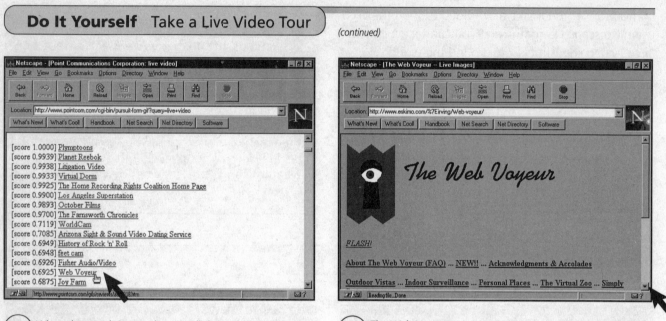

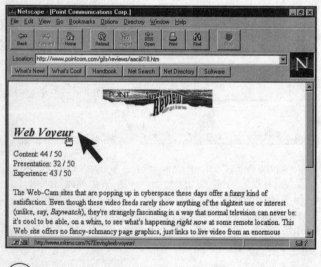

3 When the search is complete, scroll down the page to view a list of sites that match the search criteria. Some of the links will lead you to video clips; others may lead you to live video feeds. For this example, click the **Web Voyeur** link.

4 This opens a description of the Web Voyeur page, which offers you connections to all kinds of live video feeds. Click the **Web Voyeur** link.

5 The Web Voyeur page appears on your screen. You'll find a vast collection of Web-Cam sites. Scroll down the page until you see a list of links.

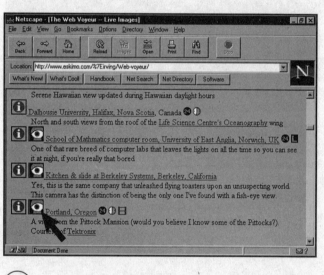

6 To tour a site in Portland, Oregon (for example), click the eye icon next to it.

Not all servers you contact among the Web Voyeur links may be operable at the time you attempt to connect. If you select one that's not working, try another link.

Do It Yourself   Take a Live Video Tour

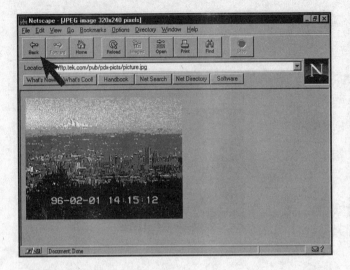

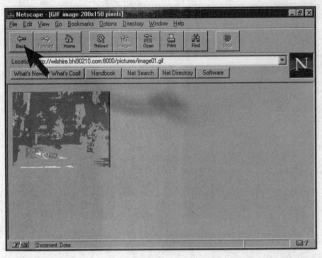

7 After the image is downloaded onto the Web page, you should see a view of Portland, Oregon similar to the one in this figure. Depending on what time of day you access the site, you may see the city with a different amount of daylight or with light reflecting on the mountain in the background.

8 To return to the Web Voyeur page, click the **Back** button on the Netscape button bar.

> Depending on the size of the image, it may take a few seconds or a few minutes to download to the Web page. Be patient.

10 You'll see a snapshot of the bus stop. Again, depending on the time of day you visit the site, you may see several people waiting for the bus, the bus itself, or no one at all. Click the **Back** button to return to the Web Voyeur page.

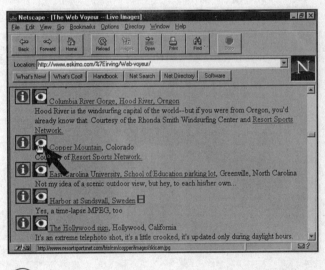

11 Next stop is the Copper Mountain ski resort in Colorado. Scroll down the list of links and click the eye icon for **Copper Mountain**, Colorado.

(continues)

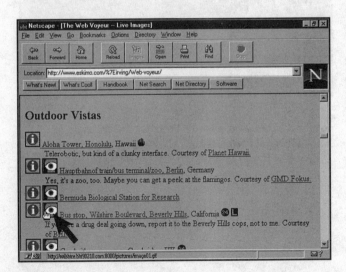

9 Back at the Web Voyeur home page, scroll down and click the eye icon for the **Bus stop, Wilshire Boulevard, Beverly Hills**, California link (listed under the category Outdoor Vistas).

Do It Yourself   Take a Live Video Tour

(continued)

12 This time you see a shot taken at the base of one of this famous resort's ski slopes. You might even catch a skier going by. Click the **Back** button to return to the Web Voyeur page.

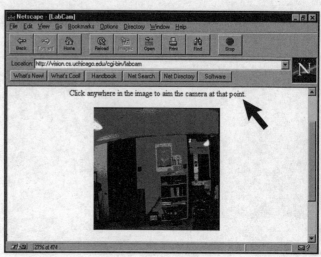

14 This camera takes you inside one of the university's labs. You can even change your view with this LabCam (just follow the instructions at the Web site). To return to Web Voyeur page, click the **Back** button.

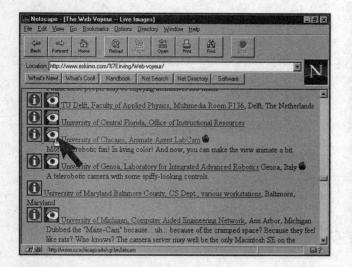

13 Outdoor scenes aren't the only live video snapshots you'll come across. You'll also find live video feeds from indoors. Under the category Indoor Surveillance, click the eye icon for the **University of Chicago, Animate Agent LabCam** link.

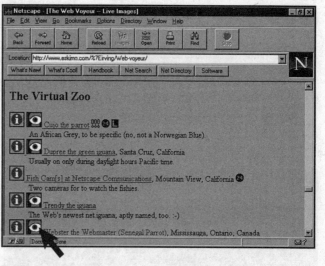

15 Click the eye icon for the **Webster the Webmaster (Senegal Parrot)** link.

Do It Yourself   Take a Live Video Tour

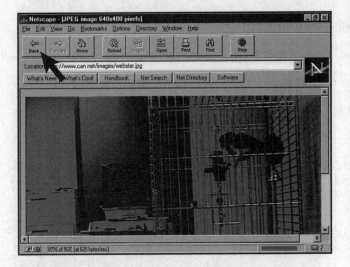

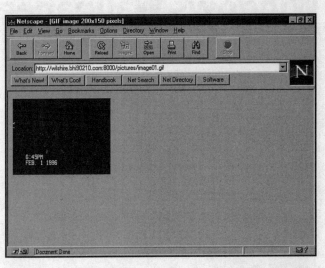

16 The scene that appears shows the interior of an office in Ontario, Canada, where there's a parrot in a cage (the parrot's name is Webster). Check this site at different times of the day, and you'll find that the parrot moves around quite a lot (although in this figure, he's sleeping). Click the **Back** button.

18 You should see some changes in the scene since your last visit in step 9. When I went back, it was dark in Beverly Hills, and you could hardly see the bus stop. But it's still there, and it's live!

19 To return to the Web Voyeur site, click the **Back** button. Then take some time to check in on other spots around the world.

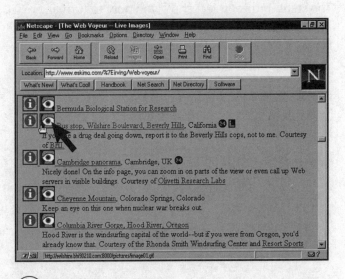

17 So you can see that the live video shots really do change, scroll up and click the eye icon for the **Bus stop, Wilshire Boulevard, Beverly Hills** link again.

Turn a Graphics File into Windows Wallpaper

One of the first things new computer users often do is experiment with the various backgrounds and wallpaper patterns available, changing the appearance of the Windows desktop. This project shows you how to take a picture you find on the Internet (such as a famous work of art) and turn it into Windows wallpaper for your desktop.

To redo your desktop at any time, open the **Control Panel** and double-click the **Display** icon. (Or for an even faster way, right-click anywhere on the desktop and select **Properties** from the menu that appears.) In the Display Properties dialog box, select the **Background** tab to see the options available for your desktop's appearance.

If you have the program LView on your computer, you can easily download an Internet picture file and turn the image into desktop wallpaper. If you don't have LView installed, you can download the program from the Web site at http://pilot.msu.edu/user/heinric6/tools.htm.

To find a picture you want to use as wallpaper, surf the Web looking for interesting GIF or JPG files (both of which are graphics files). When you find one you like, download it into LView and save it as a BMP file. A BMP file can be used for wallpaper. In the Display Properties dialog box, you can select any BMP file you want to use.

The steps in this project show you how to turn an image into wallpaper using Netscape Navigator, LView, and Windows 95.

File names that have the extension .GIF and .JPG are graphics files. Remember that a file's extension indicates the type of data the file contains. There are many types of files on the Internet, and many types of graphics files in particular. Anytime you see an extension of .GIF, .JPG, or .BMP, you can be sure the file is a graphics files.

Begin Do It Yourself Download a Graphics File and Turn It into Windows Wallpaper

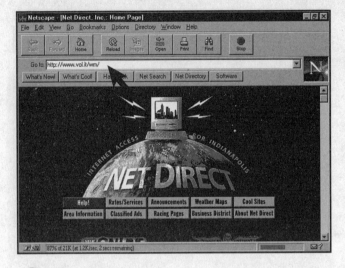

1 Start Netscape Navigator and find a graphics file you want to work with. One of the best places to look for such a file is the Web Museum. It has all the great works of art, and they make great Windows wallpaper. In the **Location** or **Go to** text box, type **http://www.vol.it/wm/** and press **Enter**.

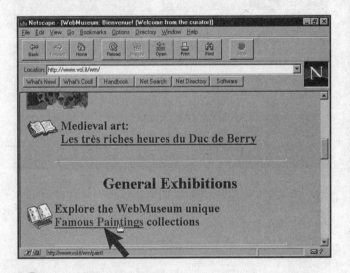

2 When the page appears, you're ready to start tracking down a graphic. (You may have to select another server to access the Web Museum; if so, follow the directions, and you'll end up at the Web Museum welcome page.) Scroll down and click the **Famous Paintings** link.

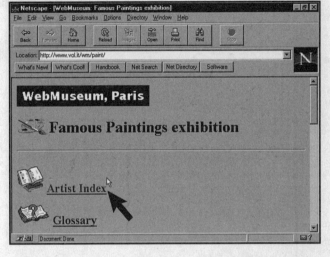

3 Click the **Artist Index** link to view a list of famous artists.

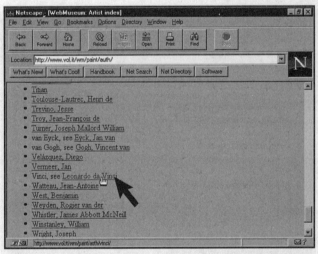

4 Click the name of the artist you want to use. For this project, download a JPG file of Leonardo da Vinci's Mona Lisa (also called La Joconde). Click the **Leonardo da Vinci** link.

(continues)

Do It Yourself   Download a Graphics File and Turn It into Windows Wallpaper   *(continued)*

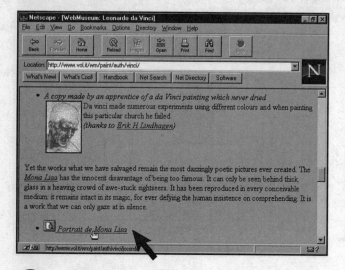

5 This Web page contains background information about the famous painter and shows some of his works. Click the **Portrait de Mona Lisa** link.

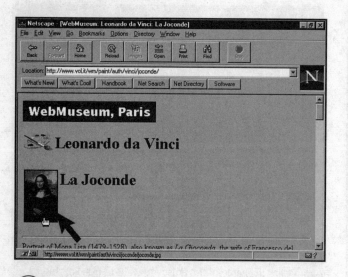

6 Finally, you see a small-scale version of the Mona Lisa. To really get a good look at it, click the image of the painting.

7 The Mona Lisa expands to full-size on your screen. To save the file, open the **File** menu and select **Save As**.

8 In the Save As dialog box, open the Lview folder and click the **Save** button to save the file JOCONDE.JPG. (If you want to store the file under another name, type the name in the **File name** text box before you click Save.)

Do It Yourself Download a Graphics File and Turn It into Windows Wallpaper

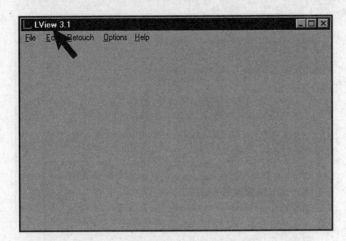

9 Exit Netscape (or minimize the Netscape window). Then double-click the **LView** program file to open the LView program.

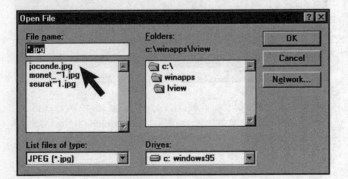

10 In the LView window, open the **File** menu and select **Open**.

11 The Open File dialog box appears. Select the Mona Lisa file (JOCONDE.JPG) and click **OK**. LView displays the graphics file.

12 In order to use the file for wallpaper, you must make it a BMP file. Open the **File** menu and select **Save as**.

13 The Save File as dialog box appears. Type a name for the file in the **File name** text box. (You might want to rename the file MONALISA.)

14 Open the **Save file as type** drop-down list and select **Windows (*.bmp, *.dib)**. Click **OK** to save the file as a BMP file and exit the box. Then close the LView program window.

(continues)

Do It Yourself Download a Graphics File and Turn It into Windows Wallpaper *(continued)*

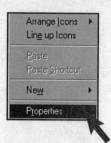

 15 Right-click anywhere on the desktop and select **Properties** from the menu that appears.

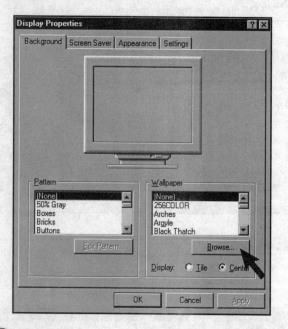

16 In the Display Properties dialog box, click the **Background** tab if necessary. Then click the **Browse** button.

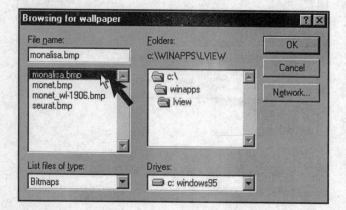

17 Select the **LView** folder and the monalisa.bmp file. With the correct file name in the File name text box, click **OK**.

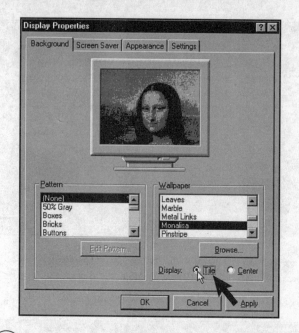

18 The name of the selected BMP file appears in the Wallpaper drop-down list. If the image is off-center in the sample monitor at the top, click the **Tile** option. To apply the image to your desktop without exiting the Display Properties box, click **Apply**. To apply it and close the dialog box, click **OK**.

19 The image of the Mona Lisa appears on your Windows 95 desktop. You can easily change it by reopening the Display Properties dialog box and selecting another wallpaper design.

Find Free Legal Advice

As you've learned throughout this book, the Internet is full of information. In some cases, you can find information online that you might have to pay for elsewhere.

This is especially true of legal advice. You'll be thankful to know that you can hunt down valuable legal advice online—without paying an enormous sum of money for it. There are dozens of WWW sites you can contact and databases you can tap into to learn about legal matters and laws. There are some exceptional Web pages out there that provide you with links to other legal sources, allow you to talk to lawyers (either by live chat or e-mail questions), search through law libraries, and locate professional law services.

In this project, you'll tour the various Web pages that offer free legal advice and access to other law-related areas. The project shows you how to access this information using Netscape, but you can use any browser program to find these sites.

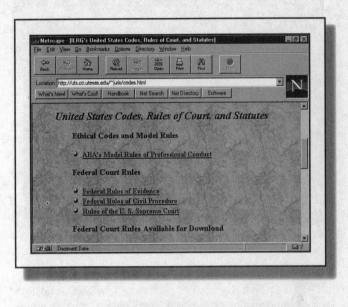

Don't forget that you can use Web search tools such as Yahoo Search (http://yahoo.com/search.html) to look up information about law and legal data on the Internet. Turn to "Search for Information on the Web" on page 180 for more information.

Begin Do It Yourself   Look for Legal Advice

1 One of the best sites to start your search for legal advice is the Legal dot Net page. In Netscape Navigator, enter the URL **http://legal.net/** and press **Enter**.

(continues)

Do It Yourself Look for Legal Advice

(continued)

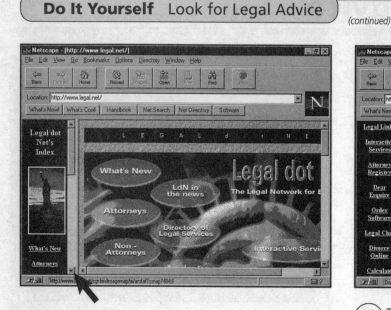

2 Legal dot Net offers several different options. To open the Legal Chat area and find out if there's any live chat going on, scroll down through the Index list (on the left) and click the **Legal Chat** link.

4 The Legal Chat room appears on your screen. Use the main window's scroll bar to move through the conversation messages.

3 The Legal Chat area opens to the right of the index. Use the main screen's scroll bar to scroll down to the Legal Chat link. Then click that link.

At the Legal dot Net site, the index always remains visible on the left side of the window.

5 Type questions or comments you want to add to the live chat in the large text box shown here. If you want to assign yourself a handle (nickname) or change your e-mail address, do so in the appropriate boxes at the bottom of the window. To send your message, click the **Refresh/Chat** button.

Do It Yourself   Look for Legal Advice

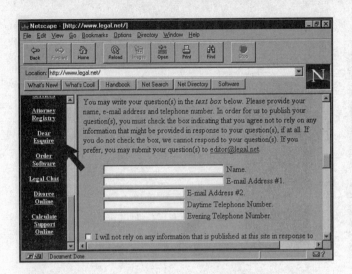

6 To post a question to a lawyer, select the **Dear Esquire** option from the index on the left. Scroll down the resulting page and fill out the form it contains. Follow all the directions before sending your message. Your questions will be answered by a legal professional.

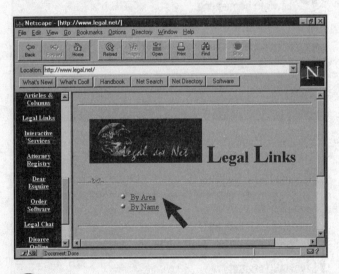

7 To access other law-related pages, click the **Legal Links** option in the index. This opens the Legal Links page. Click the **By Area** link to continue.

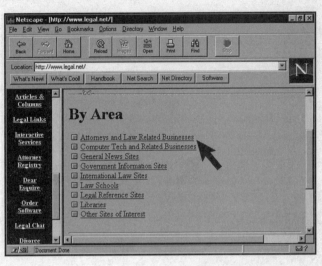

8 Click any link on this page, and another list of related links appears.

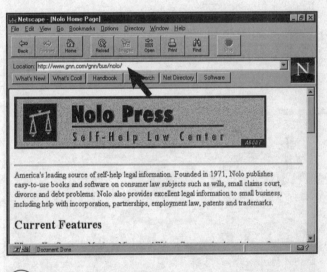

9 Now let's go to the Nolo Press Web site, a self-help source of legal information. In the **Location** or **Go to** text box, type **http://www.gnn.com/gnn/bus/nolo/** and press **Enter**.

If you have trouble connecting to any of the servers named in this project, try accessing them through http://www.pointcom.com. On the Point Communications home page, type **legal advice** in the search text box and press **Enter**. The screen that appears lists various Web sites, including the sites listed in this project.

(continues)

Do It Yourself Look for Legal Advice *(continued)*

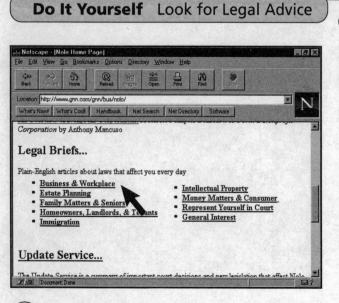

10 Scroll down to the Legal Briefs list, which contains links to legal articles pertaining to various topics. Click any category to explore related documents. The Nolo Press page also has a link to some good lawyer jokes.

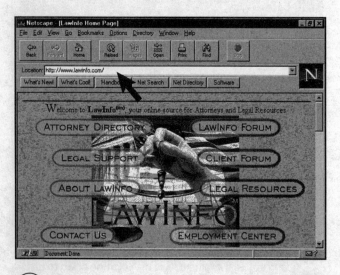

11 Moving on, enter the URL **http://www.lawinfo.com/** and press **Enter** to go to the LawInfo home page. It includes a directory of attorneys, forums, and links to legal resources on the Internet, as well as an employment center for those who are looking for jobs in the legal field.

12 Click the **Client Forum** link to open the LawInfo Self-Help page, where you'll find answers to legal questions, student research, and more. Check out the many links here; the FAQs link is a good one to start with.

13 When you finish, click the **Back** button to return to the LawInfo home page.

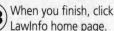

14 On the home page, click the **Legal Resources** link (or select the **Legal Resources** category and click **Index to Legal Resources on the Internet**). The page that appears (shown here) describes various resources on the Internet. From here, you can access law journals, specific topics, and law school libraries.

Do It Yourself   Look for Legal Advice

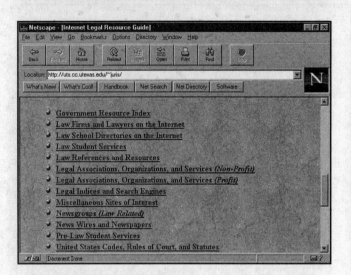

15 Next, go to the Internet Legal Resource Guide at **http:// uts.cc.utexas.edu/~juris/**. You'll find yourself at the University of Texas School of Law with access to a mega-index of law-related sites. Scroll down the page and start clicking links to search out the information you want.

16 No search of legal advice on the Internet would be complete without a stop at the Lawyer Jokes home page at **http://deputy.law.utexas.edu/jokes1.htm**. Here you'll find a little levity concerning the legal profession in general. (Humor often makes good legal advice, too.)

Find Live Help Online

Most people have been in a situation at least once where they were working with a computer and something suddenly went wrong. And some people find themselves in that predicament time and time again. Where do you turn and what do you do when that happens? Unless you're working side by side with a computer guru, you don't have a lot of options.

Granted, most of today's software programs come with online help systems to assist with specific tasks, but often the help information in those stored databases cannot solve your problem. While you can also consult a computer manual in hopes of identifying and solving your problem, manuals are typically difficult to wade through and cannot always address your problem.

Now that you have an Internet connection, there's another alternative you can try—you can ask other Internet users. Simply log onto an IRC server and find a chat channel related to computers. Once you've found a channel, pop in and ask for help. Whether or not a channel focuses on computers, it probably has people willing to answer computer questions. All you have to do is ask. And if no one on that channel can help you, try another chat channel.

For more information about using Internet Relay Chat, turn to "Chat with People on the Internet" on page 243.

Internet Relay Chat (IRC) is a perfect place to look for live help when you're experiencing difficulties with your computer (assuming the difficulties don't keep you from using your computer to contact your Internet service provider or find your way online). Talking to a real person about your problem is much easier than consulting a database or manual. With a person, you can fully explain your problem, and he can respond to you—and sympathize. You won't get that type of a response from an online help system or a technical manual.

In this project, you'll learn how to find your way onto a computer-related chat channel and ask questions of other Internet users. To do this, you must have an IRC program installed (for example, if you're using Netscape Navigator, you'll need Netscape Chat to use IRC) and you have to log on to an IRC server (an Internet server dedicated to online chat). For a list of IRC servers, turn to the "Handy Reference" section on page 487. For help installing an IRC program, refer to "Find and Install a Chat Program" on page 244.

Begin Do It Yourself Find Live Help Using Netscape Chat

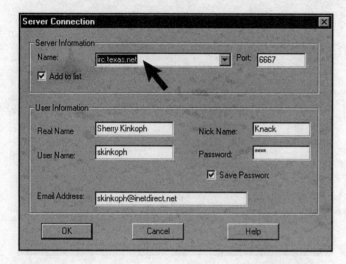

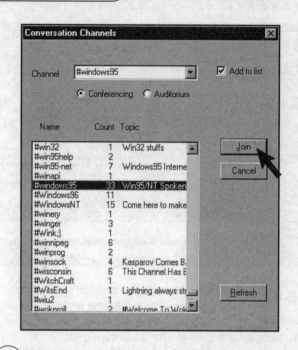

1 Start with your Internet account and Netscape Chat running. Select the chat server you want to connect to in the Server Connection dialog box that appears when you first open Netscape Chat. Click **OK** to make the connection.

3 Click the channel you want to join, and then click **Join**.

To expand your chat channel window, click the window's **Maximize** button or drag the window's borders to a new size.

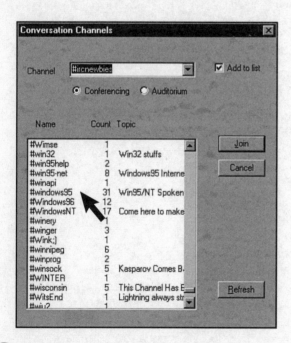

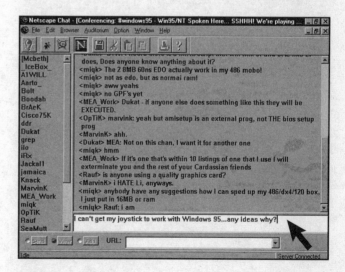

2 The Group Conversation dialog box lists the available channels. Look for a channel that seems to focus on a computer topic, such as Windows or Windows 95.

4 Once you're logged onto the chat channel, you can start talking. Type your question in the text box beneath the conversation window and press **Enter** to send it to the channel.

(continues)

Do It Yourself   Find Live Help Using Netscape Chat

(continued)

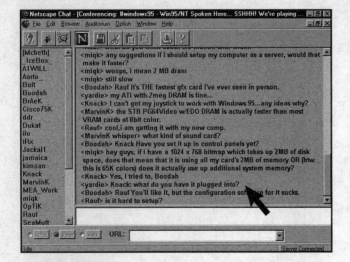

5 You may get a response to your question in no time at all—if the other people on the channel prove to be helpful. If you don't find any answers here, try another channel. To choose another channel, click the **Group** button on the toolbar, or open the **File** menu and select **Group Conversation**.

6 When you're ready to leave the channel, open the **File** menu and select **Exit Conversation**. To exit Netscape Chat completely, select **File**, **Exit** or click the window's **Close** button.

Find the Latest Financial Report

Dozens of Web sites focus on financial information and news. But you don't have to be a Wall Street wizard to enjoy money matters on the Web. You can track the latest stock reports, find out late-breaking business news—before it's in print or on network TV—and dabble in all things financial.

The cable news network CNN has its own Web site, called CNNfn (CNN financial network), that's dedicated to financial news. You'll also find the *Wall Street Journal* online. And you can even tap into the Interactive NYSE Quote Server and view stock quotes that reflect the stock market's activities as recently as 15 minutes ago.

Obviously, business users and those who are interested in financial reports will find plenty of sites to visit on the Internet. However, when you start visiting these Web sites, note that many of them require you to register before using their features. This simply means that you sign in and use a password each time you access the site. In most cases, these sites are free with registration, but others may want to charge you for use. Just be aware of this as you explore the many finance-focused avenues on the WWW.

This project takes you to some of the more popular Web sites that focus on financial matters. At any time, feel free to explore features or links that may be of specific interest to you.

One of the best places to look up more Web sites that focus on financial matters is the Point Communications site (http://www.pointcom.com). Enter **financial reports** as the search text, and you'll see a long list of Web sites related to finances and investing.

Begin Do It Yourself Tour Financial Web Sites Using Netscape

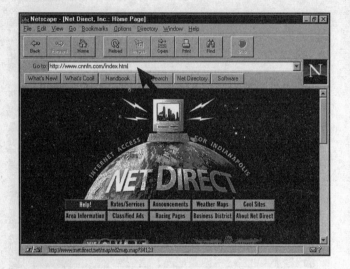

1 Connect to the Internet and start Netscape (or any other Web browser). In the **Location** or **Go to** text box, type **http://www.cnnfn.com/index.html** and press **Enter**.

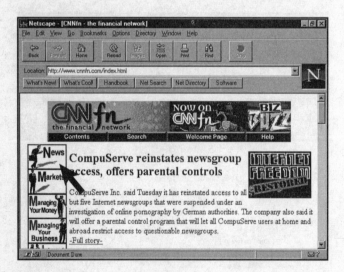

2 This is CNN's financial network site, where you'll find the latest financial news and information. The icons on the left side of the page lead you to various types of financial information. To view the latest financial news, click the **News** icon.

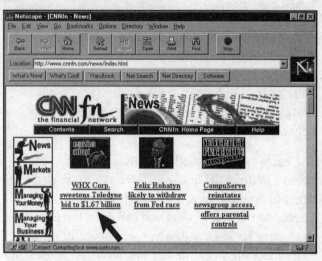

3 Explore late-breaking news reports by clicking the headlines of any stories that interest you.

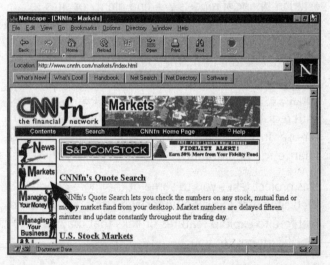

4 To explore the latest market reports, click the **Markets** icon on the left side of the Web page. This opens the Markets Main Page, from which you can explore specific financial markets.

Do It Yourself   Tour Financial Web Sites Using Netscape

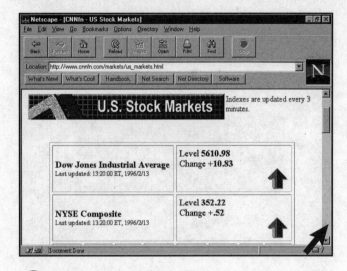

5 To take a look at U.S. stock markets, click the **U.S. Stock Markets** link.

6 On the U.S. Stock Markets page (shown here), scroll down and look at the latest figures.

7 To look up a specific stock, return to the Markets Main Page by clicking Netscape's **Back** button or by clicking the **Markets Main Page** button.

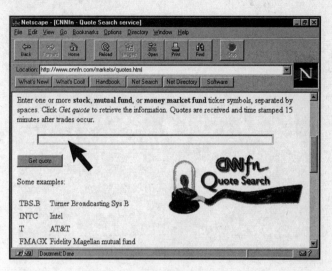

8 Click the **CNNfn's Quote Search** link to open the Quote Search page (shown here). Scroll down to the text box for entering specific stocks, type in the ticker symbol or symbols you want to look up, and click the **Get quote** button.

> If you're unsure about ticker symbols (what they are or which ones to use), scroll further down the page for tips on looking up symbols.

9 The information you asked for appears on-screen. You can return to the previous page and enter more symbols by clicking Netscape's **Back** button or the **Markets Main Page** button.

(continues)

Do It Yourself   Tour Financial Web Sites Using Netscape

(continued)

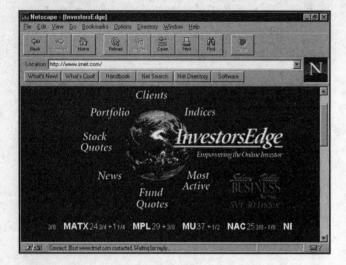

10 One of the coolest financial stops on the Web is the InvestorsEdge site. As you might expect, it provides the latest investment information; but if you stick around the home page for a moment or two, you'll see that the stock ticker scrolls horizontally across your screen with the latest figures. To access InvestorsEdge, type **http://www.irnet.com/** and press **Enter**.

Another place you can tap into the NYSE stock ticker display is on the Interactive NYSE Quote Server page (http://www.secapl.com/cgi-bin/qs).

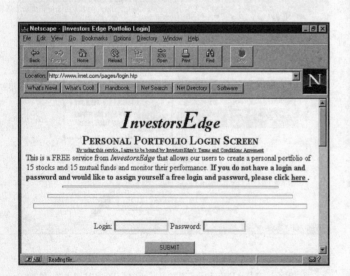

11 InvestorsEdge has a neat interactive feature that lets you build a pretend portfolio of six different stocks and then track them to see how they do. Click the **Portfolio** option and follow the on-screen instructions to create a virtual portfolio. You will have to assign yourself a user name and password.

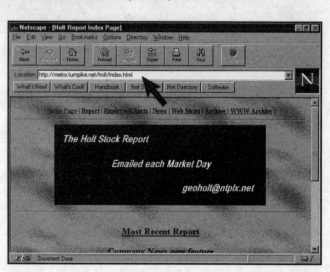

12 Another good place to check financial reports is the Holt Report Index site, which gives you access to market activity reports, financial news, archives of old reports, and links to other financial Web sites. The Holt Report Index is located at **http://metro.turnpike.net/holt/index.html**.

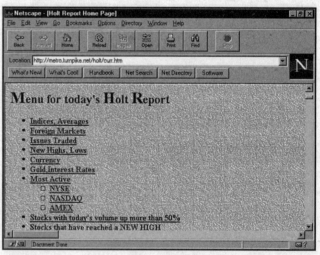

13 To check out recent reports, click the **Most Recent Report** link. Then scroll down the page to find a menu of financial features like the one shown here. Explore whichever topics interest you.

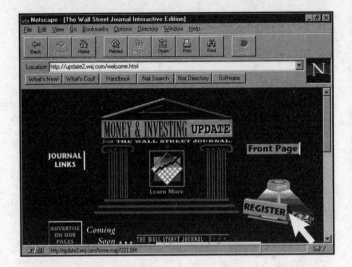

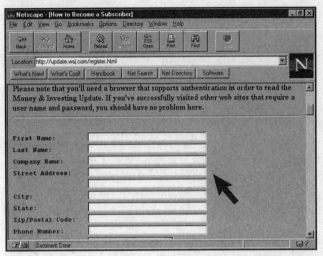

Do It Yourself   Tour Financial Web Sites Using Netscape

14 No financial tour would be complete without a visit to the *Wall Street Journal* site (http://update.wsj.com/). This figure shows the Wall Street Money & Investing Update site. To see all that the site offers, you first have to register. Click the **Register** icon.

16 Scroll down the next page to the registration form. Fill out the form one line at a time, and then click the **I Accept** button at the bottom of the page.

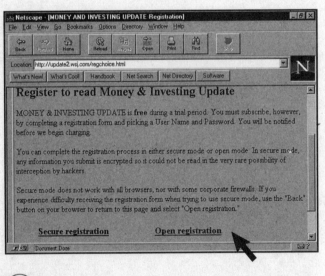

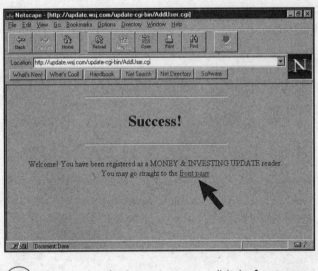

15 Read the instructions, and then click the **Open registration** link.

17 When you see the Success! message, click the **front page** link.

(continues)

Do It Yourself Tour Financial Web Sites Using Netscape *(continued)*

18 Enter the user name and password that you assigned to yourself when you filled out the registration form. Click **OK**. (You'll need to remember this information the next time you visit the site, too.)

19 Now you're free to explore the Wall Street Journal's Money & Investing site. The buttons at the top of the Web page let you use the site's features. Explore the features that interest you.

20 To exit Netscape at any time, click the **Close** button or select **File**, **Exit**.

Let Your Kids Color on a Web Coloring Book

The World Wide Web isn't just for adults; there are plenty of educational and entertaining Web sites that cater to children of all ages. Kids are just as interested in the Internet as adults and aren't as likely to be intimidated by the technology. In fact, many of today's kids know more about computers than their parents.

While you certainly don't want your children to explore the Internet without parental guidance and rules, you can help them find lots of fun things to do online. To track down kid-related sites, turn to Internet magazines that list Web sites, or use a search tool such as the Yahoo Search site (http://yahoo.com/search.html). You'll quickly find numerous Web sites with kid appeal, such as *Sports Illustrated for Kids* Online (http://www.pathfinder.com/SIFK/) and The Big Busy House (http://www.harpercollins.com/kids/).

> For help using Internet search tools, turn to "Search for Information on the Web" on page 180.

A really neat place for younger kids to visit is the Carlos' Coloring Book site. It's incredibly simple to use and offers six pictures to color. Older kids and adults are bound to like it, too. It's an interactive Web page on which the user electronically colors pictures using techniques much like those of a paint program. When you finish coloring, you can save the picture as a GIF file and use your Web browser to download it onto your own computer.

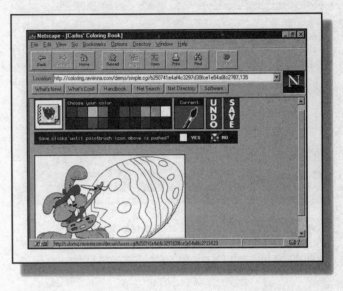

This project takes you to Carlos' Coloring Book so you can color a picture on your computer. Don't forget to let your kids have a try!

> To find links to other great kid sites on the Web, visit the Interesting Places for Kids site at http://www.crc.ricoh.com/people/steve/kids.html. I suggest you check out the Looney Tunes Home Page (http://www.usyd.edu.au/~swishart/looney.html) or the Crayola Kids page (http://www.crayola.com/crayola/crayolakids/home.html) for even more fun.

Begin Do It Yourself   Color a Picture on a Web Page

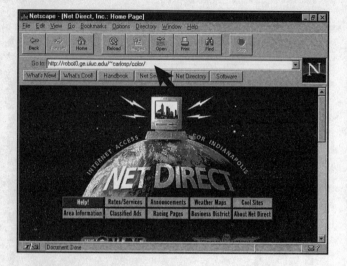

1 Connect to the Internet and start Netscape. In the **Location** or **Go to** text box, type **http://robot0.ge.uiuc.edu/~carlosp/color/** and press **Enter**.

2 The Carlos' Coloring Book Home page appears. Scroll down the page until you reach a list of pictures.

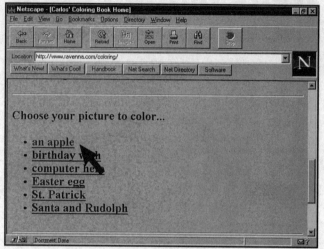

3 In the picture list, click the one you want to color.

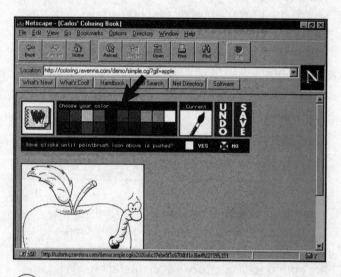

4 A color palette appears at the top of the page. Click the color you want to use, and it is displayed in the Current box (with the paintbrush icon).

Do It Yourself   Color a Picture on a Web Page

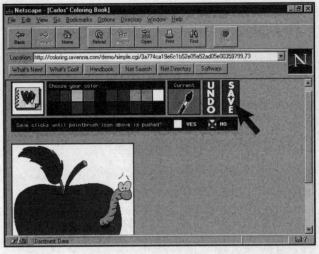

5 Move your mouse pointer to the area of the picture that you want to fill in with the selected color. You may have to scroll down the page to see the entire illustration. Click the area of the picture that you want to fill in, and it becomes the color you selected.

6 To change colors, select another color from the color palette. Repeat steps 4 and 5 as necessary until you finish coloring the entire picture.

8 To save the picture as a GIF file in a temporary directory on the server, click the **Save** button. Then follow the instructions to download the file using your Web browser.

For more information about downloading files from the Internet, turn to "Find and Copy Files from the Internet" on page 263.

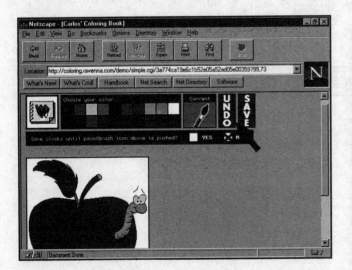

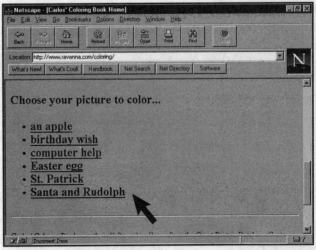

7 If you make a mistake at any time or change your mind about the color you filled in, click the **Undo** button.

9 To color another picture, return to the Carlos' Coloring Book Home page by pressing the **Back** button. Choose another picture from the list.

Look Up the Latest Weather Report

Want to find out what the weather's going to be like in your area of the country? Oh, sure, you can turn on the TV news or radio and find out—but it's just as easy to check the weather using your Internet connection. You can check dozens of Web sites for your local forecast, or you can pick up information about weather around the world.

Why check the weather with your computer? If you work in an office with no windows, you'll find it convenient: a quick visit to a weather Web site lets you know what's going on outside without ever leaving your office. Planning a business trip for the next few days? Take a peek at the extended forecast for that area so you know what to pack. Is it snowing at your favorite ski resort? That information is just a keystroke or two away. Online weather reports are constantly updated and easy to locate, as you'll learn in this project.

Not only do you have access to the latest forecasts around the world, but you can also tap into such weather information as satellite pictures, weather

history, rainfall tables, and even weather videos. Weather Web sites can be a great source of data for weather watchers everywhere and of all ages.

This project shows you several Weather-related Web sites. Feel free to deviate from the steps to follow links that may be of interest to you. There's a lot to explore when it comes to weather data.

Begin Do It Yourself Take a Tour of Weather-Related Web Sites

1 Connect to the Internet and start Netscape Navigator. Go to the *USA Today* weather page by typing the URL **http://web.usatoday.com/** and pressing **Enter**.

Do It Yourself Take a Tour of Weather-Related Web Sites

2 Click the **Weather** button.

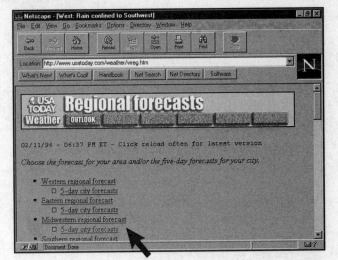

4 Select the region you're in. If you want a five-day forecast for your area, click the **5-day city forecasts** link under the region you want to look up.

3 On the *USA Today* Weather page, click the **Forecasts** button to look up your local forecast.

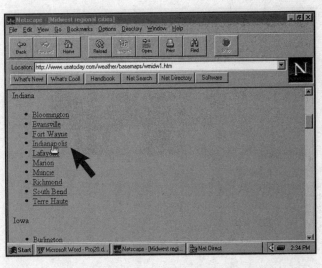

5 From the list that appears, select the city closest to where you live.

(continues)

Do It Yourself   Take a Tour of Weather-Related Web Sites

(continued)

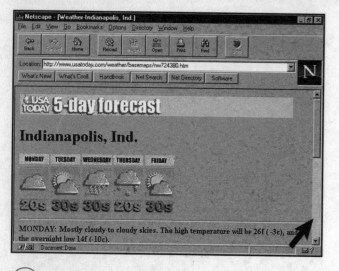

6 You'll see a five-day forecast something like this one. Scroll through the page to find out the details of each day's weather.

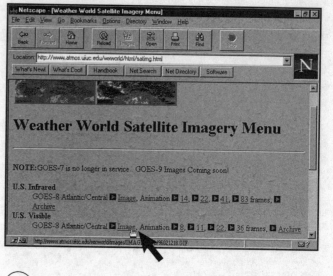
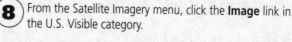

8 From the Satellite Imagery menu, click the **Image** link in the U.S. Visible category.

7 Let's jump to another Web site and look at a satellite photo. Type **http://www.atmos.uiuc.edu/wxworld/ html/detailed.html** and press **Enter** to go to the University of Illinois Weather World site. Click the **Satellite Imagery** link.

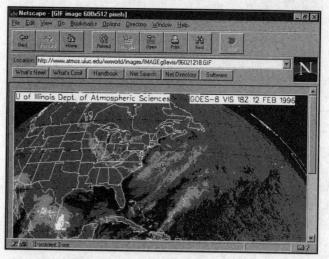

9 A satellite photo appears on-screen. From the Satellite Imagery menu, you can view an Infrared map of the U.S. If you're a weather map aficionado, this should brighten your day.

Do It Yourself   Take a Tour of Weather-Related Web Sites

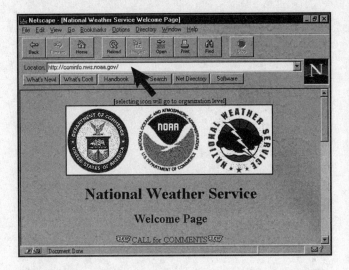

10 Make a stop at the National Weather Service site by typing **http://cominfo.nws.noaa.gov/** in the **Location** or **Go to** text box and pressing **Enter**.

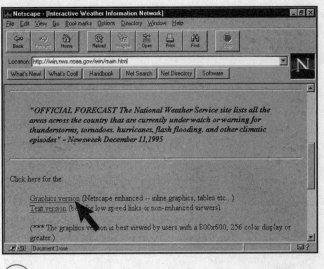

12 On the next page, scroll down and click the **Graphics version** link.

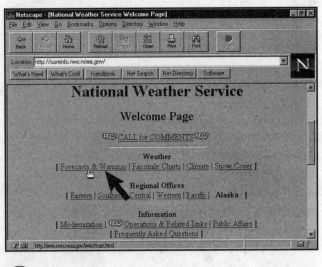

11 Scroll down the page and click the **Forecasts & Warnings** link.

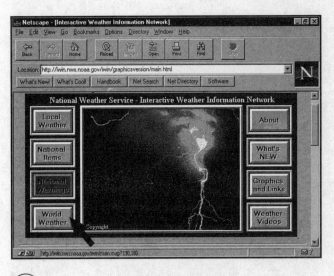

13 The National Weather Service's Interactive Weather Information Network page appears. From here, you can explore various options for viewing more weather information, and you can even download weather videos. To check the world weather report, click the **World Weather** button.

(continues)

Do It Yourself Take a Tour of Weather-Related Web Sites *(continued)*

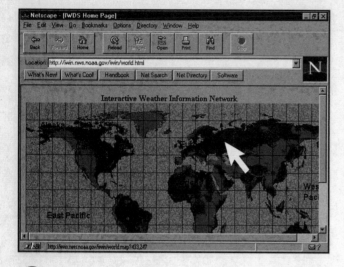

14 On the world map that appears, click the country or region for which you want to see a weather report. For example, to view a report of European cities, click over Europe.

15 You'll see a list of European cities and their weather reports. Continue to explore the weather information in your area and around the world at your leisure.

16 To quit Netscape Navigator at any time, click the **Close** button or select **File**, **Exit.**

PART 3

Quick Fixes

This is the part of the book that no one really wants to read because if you have to turn to this part, you must be having a problem. But don't despair! This part contains 101 of the most common Internet-related problems, as well as their solutions. You won't have to fumble through the whole book saying to yourself, "I know I've seen the solution in here somewhere." The solutions are all right here for easy reference.

To use this section, look for your problem in the Quick-Finder table. The problems are grouped into such categories as connection problems, e-mail problems, problems with the Web, and problems with FTP. When you find your problem in the Quick-Finder table, turn to the listed page number to find the solution.

What You Will Find in This Part

101 QUICK FIXES

Questions and Answers

Quick-Finder Table

Connection Frustrations

(continues)

World Wide Web Worries

(continues)

World Wide Web Worries *Continued*

Networking Niggles

Usenet News Jams

(continues)

Problem	Page
How much space does my account take up?	477
I don't know if I've surpassed my account quota	477
I put a program into the background	477
My account has a space quota	477
My e-mail tagline isn't showing up	478
Password was changed, but doesn't seem to work	476
Plan file not appearing when fingered	478
Preventing other users from paging me	479
Quit is not working	477
Setting permissions on the plan file	478
Strange messages are popping up on-screen	479
Strange symbols appear when I use the arrow keys	476
Text is misaligned on my screen	476
The file I downloaded to my account is corrupted	479
Using FTP to download files to UNIX	479
Words on the screen are all jumbled	476

FTP Hangups

Problem	Page
Access denied to my own account when using FTP	481
Anonymous FTP not working	480
Can't salvage a broken transfer	481
Cannot connect to my UNIX account with FTP	481
Certain files download more slowly than others	482
Don't know how to use "anonymous FTP"	480
Download aborts and garbage appears on screen	482
Download of a file quits without even starting	482
Estimated time of transfer is wrong	480
File is corrupted after Zmodem download	484
FTP download was aborted midway	480
Garbage characters appear on-screen during downloading	482
Garbled End of Line (EOL) characters	483
Interrupted download using Zmodem	481
My account refuses to download one particular file	482
No link breaks in the text file after downloading	483
Recovering a broken download with Zmodem	481

(continues)

Connection Frustrations

My modem is not receiving a dial tone.

The dial tone signals that the modem is properly attached to the actual phone line. On occasion, you may not hear a dial tone through the modem speaker, or you may receive an error message such as "No dial tone" from your communications software. There are two common causes for this problem: a bad connection or the wrong configuration.

Checking to see if the phone line is improperly or incompletely connected to the modem is easy. Check the back of the modem, and be sure that the phone line from the wall is plugged into the modem jack labeled "line" or "in." If you want a telephone or answering machine unit on the same line, it should be connected to the modem's jack labeled "phone" or "out."

Checking the configuration is slightly more difficult. To make sure you've configured your software to use the correct COM port, in Windows 95, open **My Computer,** select **Control Panel,** and click **Modems**. You should see the name of your modem. Click the **Properties** button. The dialog box shown in the following figure appears. If there is no way to select a COM port and one is already listed, Windows 95 installed your modem as a Plug and Play device and determined the correct COM port on its own. If, on the other hand, you have the option to select a COM port, you may have the wrong one selected. The thick gray cable that connects your modem to your PC plugs into your PC's serial port. Your PC's manufacturer assigned each serial port a COM number between 1 and 4. Most PCs use COM 2 for the serial port; some use 3. If you aren't sure which is correct, try each one, or contact the manufacturer.

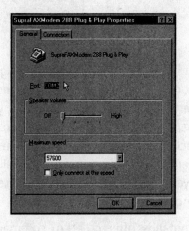

Although internal modems are not connected by cable to an external serial port, they are preconfigured to use a particular COM port, such as COM1 or COM2. Windows 95 should be able to automatically detect which COM port the internal modem is on. If it doesn't seem to be right, check the documentation or try each possibility.

If neither of those things seems to fix the problem, make sure the phone line from the wall is functioning properly. Plug a regular phone directly into the wall and check for a dial tone. Maybe you didn't pay your bill! (It happens—as I well know.)

I can't hear the modem dialing.

Most modems have a built-in speaker through which you can hear the dial and connect tones (that series of screeching sounds that would scare away even the most territorial of cats). Whether you listen to the modem's tones is usually a matter of personal preference; however, with some modems, those tones can let you know what is going on. For example, if you have an internal modem that has no other display, you may have to listen for the dial tones to make sure it is actually working.

In Windows 95, you can configure the modem speaker through the Modem Properties settings. Open **My Computer,** select **Control Panel,** and click **Modems**. You should then see the name of your modem. Click the **Properties** button. In the dialog box is a volume slider that controls the modem speaker (see the following figure). Drag the slider to any position you want, from off to low to medium to full blast.

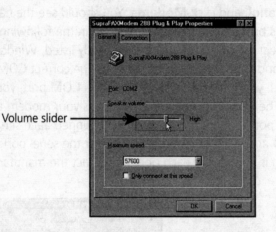

Volume slider

If you're not using Windows 95, configuring the modem speaker is a bit trickier. Most common modems share a command set, and you can send the modem commands to configure certain characteristics. To do this, you must use software that allows you to send commands directly to the modem. *Terminal programs* are the most common software packages that allow for this. If you use a terminal program such as ProComm Plus, Qmodem Pro, ComIT, or even Terminal (which is included with Windows 3.1) to connect to your Internet account, you can send commands directly to the modem before dialing your provider.

Modem commands, often called AT commands, begin with the letters AT. This tells the modem that it should pay attention to the next command. So to disable the modem's internal speaker, for example, you would type the command **AT M0** directly into the terminal program and press **Enter**. The next figure shows an example of using an AT command in HyperTerminal (the terminal program included with Windows 95).

In response to your command, the modem returns **OK** to let you know that it understood the command. Other speaker-related AT commands include the following:

AT M1   Enable internal speaker

AT L1   Set speaker volume to low

AT L2   Set speaker volume to medium

AT L3   Set speaker volume to high

The line is busy. Can I auto-redial?

Some phone numbers are constantly busy, especially if you attempt to connect at peak hours (such as prime time on weeknights). Most communications software has a feature you can use to redial automatically until a connection is made—which gives you the freedom to make popcorn or eat Ben & Jerry's instead of sitting in front of the modem for 20 minutes trying to make a connection.

Each communications package is different, so it is impossible to describe exactly how each redial feature works; however, it is usually a very basic feature. If you use Windows 95's built-in Dial-Up Networking to connect to the Internet, you may find that you need to configure it to support redialing. To do that, follow these steps.

1. In Windows 95, open **My Computer** and select **Dial-Up Networking**.

2. From the Dial-Up Networking window, select **Connections** and select the **Settings** command.

3. In the configuration window that appears, check the **Redial** option (if it's not already selected). Then enter settings for how many times you want the modem to redial before giving up, and for how much time the modem should wait between attempts.

4. When you finish, click **OK** to save your settings for auto redialing.

For users of Trumpet Winsock with Windows 3.1, the redialing capability is built into the default login script that comes with the software. You'll encounter Trumpet login scripting in a bit more detail later in this section.

The line simply rings and rings.

If the line is ringing—that is, if you hear the traditional dialing sound coming from your modem's speaker—you know that the line is functioning. Actually, when the line just rings and rings, the problem is not on your end, but on the end you are trying to connect to.

A somewhat common problem for Internet Service Providers (ISP) is called *ringthrough*. Your ISP (the people you dial to access the Internet) has a series of modems. Although you dial only one phone number, you're supposed to be connected to the first available modem in the series. Sometimes a modem goes bad, and you're connected to one of these dud modems that doesn't answer the line. It simply rings and rings and rings. That is a ringthrough, and you should certainly notify your provider if this sort of thing is happening. Sometimes they don't realize that a modem is bad; it's tough for them to know because they don't dial into their own modems. Other than that, the only thing you can do is hang up and dial again—and hope that you won't be connected to a dud modem.

The modem is connecting at the wrong speed.

Modem speeds often cause major confusion. All communications software enables you to select a baud rate for your modem connection. The general recommendation is that people with 14.4kbps modems should select a baud rate of 57,600kbps, and people with 28.8kbps modems should select a baud rate of 115,200kbps. But why?

The 14.4 and 28.8 numbers indicate the speed at which your modem can communicate with the other modem (assuming they both support the same speed). The 57.6 and 115.2 numbers indicate the speeds at which your modem and your own computer communicate. When you see communications software reporting the speed of a connection, it's important that you know which number it is telling you.

Users of Windows 95's Dial-Up Networking should note that once you're connected, a little window pops up saying **Connected at *some speed***. This is the modem-to-modem speed. If you have a 28.8kbps modem and are connecting to another 28.8kbps modem, you should see a number close to 28,800. People often are confused by this if they know they configured their modem (via the Modem Properties dialog box) to connect at, say, 57,600 or 115,200 baud. Remember that Dial-Up Networking is not reporting that setting.

Now, you do want to pay attention if a reported connection speed is lower than the speed of your modem. For example, if you have a 14.4kbps modem but receive connection speeds of only, say, 9,600 or 12,000, that is something to take note of. What might be the cause of that trouble? It's most likely a result of difficulties between the two modems attempting to connect. The trouble may lie in modem configuration settings on your end or on the other end.

On your end, the easiest solution is to try resetting the modem to factory defaults—just in case you somehow messed with certain connect speed settings. You usually do this using the **AT &F0** or **AT &F1** modem command in a terminal program; however, you should check your modem manual to be sure. If the problem is a modem on the other end, there's little you can do except notify the person who maintains that system. Then you might try dialing in again to see if you get another modem.

Lastly, two modems can connect only at the maximum speed of the slower modem. So a 14.4kbps modem can only connect at 14.4 if the other modem supports at least 14.4. Similarly, a 28.8kbps modem can only achieve that speed with another 28.8kbps modem. When a 28.8kbps modem connects with a 14.4kbps modem, however, the fastest possible connection speed is 14.4kbps. So it's good to know the speed of the modem you are calling (your provider will be able to tell you). If you connect to a modem slower than your own, you'll wind up with a connection at the slower speed.

I never connect at 28.8 even though I paid handsomely for a 28.8 modem.

Because so many variables can prevent a proper 28.8kbps connection, it's surprising that they occur at all. Analog phone lines (the kind that connect your house and the local phone company) are the remains of older technology: they were not designed for high-speed digital communications. Communication at the speed of 28,800kbps truly pushes these lines further than they can often handle. To achieve these speeds, the lines need to be of perfect quality and have no noise or interference along the way.

Many factors can cause interference. Poor-quality in-home wiring, the distance of a call, and the quality of phone lines in a general region all affect the amount of interference. In addition, the quality of the modems plays a part. A cheaper 28.8 modem is not likely to achieve 28.8kbps connections under imperfect conditions; a more expensive one may be better able to maximize your connection speed on lines with minor imperfections.

Real-world results seem to indicate that many people can achieve 28.8kbps connections on local calls between themselves and a provider who is only a few miles away. Many who can't reach 28.8 can usually reach 26.4, which is fairly close in terms of speed. However, if you are attempting to make long-distance connections, your chances of such speeds drop considerably.

I get garbage characters coming over the line.

Some people, when they are connected to their Internet account via modem, will see some garbage characters on the screen. By garbage characters, I simply mean nonsensical groups of symbols and characters, such as D##$@!~~+ . Garbage characters basically signal errors in data transmission coming over the line. These errors are often caused by noisy phone lines.

Most modern high-speed modems have built in error correction and should be able to detect such errors in transmission *before* you see the results. Upon finding an error, these modems request retransmission of the data from the other end. Of course, this error correction only works to a point: if the lines are of absolutely atrocious quality, the modem will not be able to succeed in correcting errors and will probably just disconnect. However, that's a rare exception. Most people's lines are of decent but not perfect quality, in which case, some errors will occur.

Except for some of the cheapest 14.4 and 28.8 models, most modems include built-in error correction features that can handle regular, random errors. Therefore, a properly functioning error-correcting modem should not yield garbage characters. If—as a last resort—you need to disable error-correction, try resetting the modem to its factory settings. You can usually do this with the **AT &F0** or **AT &F1** command, but check the manual for certain. Some modems use DIP switches to determine factory settings.

Slow modems, especially those as slow as 2,400 baud, may not have any built in error correction. Some do, but many do not. The ones that do not are definitely prone to spewing out garbage characters.

Letters are missing from the words when I use my account.

The problem of missing letters is called *dropping characters*, and it's as simple as it sounds: some of the data is lost on the way. Most often, this happens when you have the connection speed between your modem and the PC set higher than your PC can handle. While it is generally recommended, for example, that you configure your software to 57,600 baud for a 14.4 modem, slower CPUs may not be able to keep up.

The solution is to try lowering the speed of the computer's baud rate. If you have a 14.4kbps modem, try lowering your baud rate to 38,400. You can lower the baud rate as much as necessary until it quits dropping characters—as long as the baud rate doesn't drop lower than the speed of the modem. Although lowering the baud rate limits the maximum speed at which you can transfer data, it's better than losing characters.

To change the computer's baud rate in Windows 95, open **My Computer,** select **Control Panel,** and click **Modems**. You should then see the name of your modem. Click the **Properties** button. At the bottom of the window pictured here, notice the setting labeled Maximum Speed.

Baud rates ──→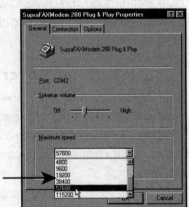

You can select the baud rate at which you want the modem to *attempt* a connection. I don't advise that you check the box marked **Only connect at this speed.** If you do enable it and the modem cannot connect at the selected baud rate, it will abort the connection attempt entirely.

Although Windows 3.1 offers a similar configuration in its Control Panel, virtually all communications software written for 3.1 ignores this setting. Instead, they provide their own configurations. So Windows 3.1 users will set the desired baud rate when setting the options of the communications software itself (such as their terminal programs).

Download speed is slower than I expected.

The first way to approach this question is to consider what you're expecting. Although modems advertisements put a lot of emphasis on a speed (such as 28.8kbps), it's not immediately obvious just how this number boils down into actual data transfer speeds.

Ultimately, data transfer speed depends on two main factors: the method of transfer (what protocols are used), and the data being transferred (how compressible is it). Making a few assumptions about these two factors, one can provide relatively accurate guidelines for what to expect.

Many large downloads consist of precompressed files (such as .ZIP files, .JPG files, and .GIF files). Thus, these files will not benefit much from the modem's built-in compression routines. For these sorts of files (and they are the most commonly transferred types), you can expect the following rough estimates.

Protocol	Modem Speed	Reasonable Expectation
Zmodem	14.4kbps	1600–1650 cps
Zmodem	28.8kbps	1.2–1.4 K/sec
FTP/WWW	14.4kbps	3200–3300 cps
FTP/WWW	28.8kbps	2.8–3.2 K/sec

Note that in the expected speed column, I've used two different forms to express the same information. Most programs using Zmodem report transfer speeds in the form of cps, while most FTP/WWW programs report transfer speeds in the form of K/sec. As a means of comparison, cps divided by 1,024 equals K/sec.

More compressible files (such as plain text files) will yield higher speeds than those listed above. So if you're pulling in speeds higher than these estimates (some text files can transfer up to four times faster), you don't need to worry at all. However, if you're pulling in speeds slower than these, you have a problem. Read on.

If you are using Zmodem, the most common causes of slow transfers are CRC errors. Skip ahead to the next problem to learn what to do. If you are using FTP or WWW, you face a potentially more confusing scenario. There are three major causes of slow transfers via FTP/WWW.

- **CRC errors.** As with Zmodem, CRC errors can be the problem with FTP/WWW transfers. Again, skip down to the next problem to learn how to banish CRC errors.

- **Poorly tuned MTU/RWIN settings in your TCP/IP software.** These settings essentially fine-tune the flow of data in and out of your computer. These are somewhat complicated settings to explain in a Quick Fix, and what's worse is that Microsoft's Dial-Up Networking makes them difficult to access. First, ask your service provider what MTU setting to use with their system. Then, if you use Trumpet Winsock, read the Trumpet Winsock documentation or the Trumpet Winsock coverage in this book to learn how to adjust these settings. If you use Windows 95, go to the Web site **http://www.windows95.com** and follow the links to information on how to modify the settings. You can also find discussions and help on these matters in the Usenet newsgroups at alt.winsock, alt.winsock.trumpet, and comp.os.ms-windows.networking.tcp-ip.

- **Heavy network traffic on the Internet.** The Internet is a place of varying busyness, and everyone has to share the same pathways. Thus, it is vulnerable to traffic jams. Even if you have the correct configurations, if you attempt to transfer large files—especially from far-away machines—across the Internet during high usage hours (business hours), you're likely to run into slowdowns. The only solutions are to try finding information on geographically closer servers or servers that are less heavily used, or to wait until off-peak hours.

My communications software is reporting many "overrun" or "CRC" errors.

This error occurs when the data flows into your PC too quickly for your PC to process it. It is, in essence, a flood. This data overrun causes the PC to have to request repeat transmission of the lost data. Repeating transmission wastes time. And because you're transferring the same data multiple times, many repeated transmissions result in a slower overall transfer speed for the data.

Overruns (which are called *CRC errors* by some software) are the result of problems unrelated to your software configurations or what protocol you are using. They represent a more fundamental problem in which your computer cannot keep up with the incoming flow of data. Although many factors influence whether your computer is able to keep up, a few specific things cause the majority of all overruns.

- **The UART** This only applies if you use an external modem. Your serial port (which is probably part of your I/O card) has a buffer on it that is intended to prevent data overruns. This buffer is called a UART chip or a FIFO. Old serial cards have a UART model 8250 or 16450. These older UARTs are generally not sufficient for today's high-speed modems of 14.4kbps and higher. Current I/O cards have model numbers of 16550A or higher (16550AFN, for example), which are capable of higher speed buffering. Thus, the first and foremost recommendation if you experience many overruns is to check your UART.

Checking your UART is simple. Whether you use Windows 3.1 or Windows 95, you must first exit to DOS; you *cannot* just open a DOS window. In Windows 3.1, then, open the **File** menu and select **Exit**; in Windows 95, click **Start**, select **Shutdown**, and click **Restart the Computer in MS-DOS Mode**. At the DOS prompt, type **msd** and press **Enter**. In that program, select **COM ports**, and it tells you what UART model you have. If it's not 16550A or higher, the simplest solution is to buy a new I/O card. (They cost around $30.) Most new PCs already have proper UARTs, but older ones may not.

The UART on this
modem's COM port

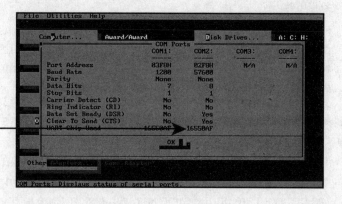

In addition, if you use Windows 3.1, you must tell it to use the UART by adding the line **COMxFIFO=1** in the [386enh] section of your windows\system.ini file. Replace *x* with the number of the COM port to which your modem is installed. Thus, if your modem is on COM 2 (which is common), the line should read **COM2FIFO=1.**

If you use Windows 95, verify that the UART is functioning by opening **My Computer** and selecting **Control Panel**, **Modems**, **Properties**, **Connection**, and **Port Settings**. Check the **Use FIFO buffers** option if it's not already enabled.

- **Old hardware drivers** Drivers for some video cards and some hard drives use nasty tricks to increase their own performance, and in doing so, they cause Windows to be susceptible to data overruns. If you are still receiving many overrun errors and you've ruled out the UART as the source of the problem, contact the manufacturers of your video card and hard drive (or ask around on the Net) for updated, current drivers. Many manufacturers now offer drivers that will behave themselves.

The modem seems to hang up randomly while connected.

Sometimes you'll be merrily Netting along, when the modem will just hang up—apparently out of the blue. Why? One common cause is call waiting, which is discussed in detail in the problem "I want to disable or enable call waiting" (page 442). Aside from that, you need to try to determine whether the culprit is on your end of the connection or at the other end. Let's do a little detective work.

Do you only connect to one phone number? Try calling other modems in the area—local BBSs, other service providers, and so forth—and see if it happens with them. This kind of experimentation helps you get an idea of whether the cause is you or your provider.

Next, ask other subscribers to your provider if they have the same problem. More often than not, random disconnects are problems on the provider's end, sometimes due to differing brands of modems. Most modems are supposed to be able to talk to one another regardless of manufacturer, but there are some exceptions. (One particular modem model may have trouble communicating with another particular model, for example.)

Finally, although random disconnects probably are not the result of a configuration problem on your end, if you aren't sure, try the factory reset command. You may have twiddled some esoteric setting that set it off. (Modern modems have hundreds of esoteric settings.)

My #!?@ roommates keep lifting the phone extension and ruining my connection.

This is not an uncommon problem in households or apartments in which multiple devices use the same phone line. Often, both a phone in the kitchen and the modem in the bedroom are on the same line. When someone in the kitchen lifts up the phone and hears the horrible screech of the modem, they have succeeded in ruining the connection. A solution? There are three possibilities.

Obviously, multiple phone lines are a solution, but not everyone can afford that. If it's not an option for you, try talking to the other people in the house to work out some system of knowing who is on the line.

If diplomacy doesn't work, try a technological solution. Most modems have a jack in the back for a phone. Some modems, if they are online, disable the phone hooked to this jack. Thus, although it's a wiring nightmare, if you can connect the aforementioned kitchen phone to the back of the modem, the phone will be disabled when the modem is in use. However, this only works with a modem that does, in fact, disable its phone jack when online.

The only other answer lies at that ubiquitous gadget store: Radio Shack. They sell a little doohickey that you can place on the phone line that disables one extension when the other is in use. That doohickey is called a "Teleprotector" (Radio Shack catalog #43-107), and it sells for approximately $10.

I want to disable or enable call waiting.

To many, the bane of telephone conversations is also the bane of modem communications. If you are using the modem when a call waiting beep comes down the lines, your connection will probably be broken. You may or may not appreciate this. Some people who are online frequently but cannot afford a second line may prefer being knocked off the line to having their callers get busy signals all day long. However, most people prefer not to be interrupted while online.

If you don't want those interruptions, you can usually disable call waiting on a per-call basis by inserting ***70** into the dial string of your communications software. For example, if you normally dial **555-1515** to access your service provider, change it so your software dials ***70,555-1515**. The *70 prefix works in most telephone regions. If it does not seem to work for you, contact the local phone company to find out how to disable call waiting. Note that this disables call waiting only during the current call; as soon as you disconnect the modem, call waiting is automatically enabled again.

When I quit my connection, the modem doesn't hang up the line.

Most communications software has some feature to "hang up." This isn't always the same as exiting. With some software, if you quit the software but do not choose to hang up the line, the modem won't disconnect.

The obvious rule is to hang up before you exit the software. However, if you forget to hang up first and the modem doesn't hang up automatically, try running the communications software again. It may hang up the line when it starts in order to clear it for use. If that doesn't work, try to run your terminal program and select **hang up**. The terminal program should pass the hang up command to the modem.

If you have an external modem, you can flip the power switch (turn it off and back on). Finally, as a last resort, reboot Windows, but only if all else fails.

E-Mail Troubles

The e-mail I sent came back to me undelivered.

This is known as *bounced* mail. It means that the mail could not be delivered to the specified recipient. A couple of things often cause mail to bounce.

- **There's no such user.** The recipient you specified doesn't exist. Either you have the wrong e-mail address, or you typed it wrong.

- **The mailbox is full.** There isn't enough room in the recipient's mailbox to hold your e-mail.

When you receive a bounced e-mail, you get your original message back along with a brief explanation of the problem. For example, you might see a message like this at the top of the bounced message:

```
----- The following addresses had delivery problems -----
<markymark@interlog.com>   (unrecoverable error)
     ----- Transcript of session follows -----
... while talking to gold.interlog.com.:
>>> RCPT To:<markymark@interlog.com>
<<< 550 <markymark@interlog.com>... User unknown
550 <markymark@interlog.com>... User unknown
```

As you can see, in this example, the error is described as "User unknown." In such a case, check your spelling to see if you made a typo in the address. Note that capitalization does not matter in an e-mail address, so that would not be the cause of a User unknown error.

My e-mail was never delivered to the other party, but it didn't bounce.

An e-mail message travels through several computers on the way to its ultimate destination. Sometimes one of these computers may be down temporarily. Or the destination computer itself might be down. In these cases, there will obviously be a delay in delivery.

There are procedures in place on the Internet that try to account for possible obstacles. If the destination computer is down, delivery will often be attempted periodically (automatically—without your assistance or knowledge) until it's successful. Sometimes, however, it does not succeed after several attempts, usually because of network problems with the destination computer or another computer near that end of the line. In some such cases, after several days you will receive a warning e-mail saying that your message could not be successfully delivered. This is not a bounce, it's a notification. The system will continue to attempt delivery for a specified period of time.

Suppose you have a persistent problem with your e-mail not reaching recipients in various locations. If your e-mail seems to have truly vanished, you need to check two possible suspects: your e-mail software and your outgoing mail server (provided by your service provider).

- Make sure your e-mail software is, in fact, sending the e-mail and not queuing it. Mail applications such as Eudora and Pegasus Mail offer you the option whether to "queue" outgoing mail or send it immediately. If you choose to queue your mail, all of your composed messages are stored on your hard drive to be sent out in one batch when you instruct the program to "send all queued mail." Of course, if you never tell it to send the queued mail, that mail will never leave your PC. Queuing is generally only useful for users who compose mail offline and then dial in to their provider when they're ready to send all their e-mail in one batch. For users who remain online while they write e-mail, it's more sensible to have the mailer actually send it out when you complete the composition.

- Your service provider's outgoing server may not be working properly or reliably. You have two options: speak to your provider or use a different outgoing server. The outgoing server is known as the SMTP server, and you can configure it via options in your e-mail application. Often, you can use any SMTP server—not just the one your provider offers. Check around to see if you can find another provider locally, such as at a nearby university. If so, find out the name of their server (often, they are named in the form *mail.providername.com* or something very similar). If you find another SMTP server that's more reliable, stick with it. However, because you are paying your ISP, it is worth talking to them about their server.

I need to send the same message to multiple people.

This is an easy one! There are two ways you can do this, depending on your needs.

- You can often include multiple e-mail addresses in the To: header, separated by commas. Perhaps more commonly, you can use the CC: header line provided by most e-mail programs to enter one or more addresses. This sends "carbon copies" of the one message to all cc recipients. Thus, you can address your message in either of the following ways:

  > To: person1@isp.com,person2@otherisp.com,
  > person3@yetanotherisp.com

  > or

  > To: person1@isp.com
  > Subject: Hello
  > CC: person2@otherisp.com,person3@yetanotherisp.com

- You can use distribution lists. Some e-mail applications enable you to create a distribution list. A distribution list contains multiple e-mail addresses that you can refer to with one label—very useful if you frequently send memos out to the same group of people. For example, you could create a list of all the people in your immediate department and name the whole group "Co-workers." Then when you compose a message in that e-mail program, you can simply address it **To: Co-workers**, and the message is sent to all the people on the list. Check to see if your e-mail program has this capability.

When I retrieve my e-mail, I keep receiving old messages along with the new.

Nowadays, many users have SLIP/PPP accounts. You dial into your provider and check e-mail with a program such as Eudora or Pegasus Mail. These programs retrieve your e-mail from a machine known as a POP server. The POP server holds all the e-mail that is sent to you.

Most e-mail programs allow you to configure at least two options related to retrieving this mail: a "delete mail from server" option and a "download only unread/new mail" option. If you choose to enable mail deletion, the program deletes each message after it is downloaded to your PC. Of course, the only copies of those messages are on your PC, and if you delete or lose them, they're gone for good. On the other hand, deleting from the server might be better, because you probably have a mailbox size limit and don't want all the mail you've ever received to keep piling up on the server.

If you turn on the mail deletion option, the "download only..." option is irrelevant. But if you prefer to leave your mail on the server instead of deleting it after retrieval, you will probably want to enable the "download only unread/new mail" option. If you don't enable this option, every time you check mail, *all* of your messages will be downloaded, including those you have downloaded in the past. If you do enable this option, only new messages will be downloaded; the rest remain on the server.

Although each e-mail application is different, these options are usually among the Network configurations settings. For Pegasus Mail users, for example, use the **File**, **Network Configuration** command to access these options.

How can I have e-mail checked automatically?

Almost all e-mail applications allow for *background polling*. This means that your program can automatically check your POP server for new e-mail periodically. In many programs, you can configure how often the program polls, setting it to check mail every 10 minutes or—if you're like me—every 45 seconds!

Some mail programs prevent you from doing other tasks while they poll, others do not. If you intend to use the background polling feature, you should consider this when deciding which e-mail program to use. When they perform the background poll, most programs will notify you of new mail by way of either a pop-up window or a sound. This quickly leads to Pavlovian conditioning; you may soon find yourself anxiously awaiting the next "You have new mail" bell to sound.

Sometimes when I check e-mail, I get an error such as "POP server timed out."

This indicates that the e-mail program could not connect to the POP server. In most cases, the POP server is temporarily inaccessible, maybe because that machine (owned by your Internet service provider) has crashed or been taken down for some reason (usually only for a short time). In addition, POP servers usually have a limit of how many people can connect and check for e-mail at one time. So if you happen to attempt a connection when the machine is at its limit, it might refuse you. That could generate this error message or a similar one.

It is possible that you have a problem with your TCP/IP software, but if this were the case, you would always get the above message. If you only get timeout errors some of the time, it's basically not your fault. Just wait a few minutes and check again. If you find that your ISP's POP server times out a lot, complain to them. If there is a problem on your end, you're likely to have problems connecting to virtually anywhere else (FTP, the Web, and so on). In this case, verify your TCP/IP software settings as described in the Quick Fixes under "Networking Niggles."

I have a slow connection, and it takes forever to retrieve very large e-mail messages.

Many people check their e-mail from several locations—perhaps from work or school during the day and from home at night. Generally, Internet connections from home are often slower than those at workplaces or school computer centers. Suppose you ask someone to e-mail you a one-megabyte file. You may not really want to download it from home, but if you check e-mail from home and the file is waiting for you, it's going to be downloaded—unless you can configure your e-mail program *not* to download files that are particularly large.

Often, you can set such an option. Some e-mail programs may have a predetermined file size limit; others will let you specify with an option such as "Don't download messages over ___ k." In Pegasus Mail, for example, choose **File**, **Network Configuration** and set the **leave mail larger than** option to whatever size you want to be the maximum. Messages larger than that will not be deleted from the server when the rest of your e-mail is delivered and deleted. You can retrieve them at a later time—perhaps from work or school.

How can I have e-mail to my old account forwarded to my new one?

Just as people move from one home to another, they sometimes move from one Internet service provider to another. And that usually means a new e-mail account. Of course, the problem is that everyone knows your old address.

First, you should tell everyone you know about your new account. In addition, check with your service provider to see if they offer some form of forwarding. If you are still paying both providers, you definitely should be able to have mail forwarded from one account to another. The exact method varies; ask the provider that you want to forward your messages what method to use. However, if you've stopped paying one service provider and signed up with a new one, you may not be able to cajole the old provider into forwarding mail. After all, you're no longer a paying customer to them. If they won't let you forward mail after leaving them, and it's important that you not miss messages, you might have to pay for both accounts until everyone you know catches up with your new address.

One way to avoid this problem is to use an e-mail forwarding service. The most popular by far is called Pobox (http://pobox.com). Although this is a for-pay service, the fees are low. When you use a forwarding service, you give out the address the forwarding service assigns you as if it were your true e-mail address. All e-mail sent to that address is then forwarded to your "real" address, which you give to the forwarding service. The nice thing about this arrangement is that if you change your "real" e-mail address, you simply reconfigure your account with the forwarding service and give them your new address. And no matter how many times you change accounts or service providers, people can always send your messages to the same address.

Help! I accidentally deleted a message.

The first question is, where did you delete it from? In most cases, deleting a message by accident is not a good thing. If you deleted it from your PC (your mailbox in your e-mail program), it may still be on the POP server if you are not configured to delete messages from the POP server upon download.

Some e-mail programs enable you to control when they actually delete messages. For example, with one possible configuration, you might be able to mark messages for deletion, but they will not be deleted for real until you exit the e-mail application. Investigate your e-mail program's settings that distinguish between immediate deletion and marking messages for later deletion.

If you really did, in fact, delete the message and it's no longer on the POP server, it's basically gone. One last resort is to contact the original sender. Many e-mail programs store copies of outgoing mail, and if the sender has a copy of the message saved, he could just resend it. You might also try asking your ISP if they keep backups of the POP server. It is highly unlikely that such a backup could help you, though, because chances would be slim that the backup was made in the time span between when the message was received and when you deleted it from the server.

People keep telling me that my e-mail has "long lines."

Not everyone uses the same size screen, fonts, and so on. You can't assume that text that fits on your screen will fit the same way on someone else's. It is generally considered proper practice to use no more than 75 characters per line in an e-mail message. This ensures that everyone will be able to read it properly, without strange linewrapping that makes the message more difficult to read.

Some e-mail programs let you set the width of a message. If yours does, set it to 75 characters per line, and you won't have to worry about taking note yourself. If you're stuck with a program that doesn't have such an option, try to keep the 75-character limit in mind and hit Enter to break to each new line ...or get a new e-mail program. If you cannot keep your line lengths to 75 characters, you may continue to hear about it from people who have a hard time reading your messages.

How can I make an e-mail signature?

A signature is a little blurb that appears at the bottom of every message. Some people use it as an opportunity to impart some clever witticism or express some personality trait. Others use it for more utilitarian purposes, such as to give their name, address, and contact information.

You do not have to have a signature at all, but if you want one, you can specify it in your e-mail program. For PC-based programs, either you can create a signature from an option directly in the program, or you can configure the program to use a pre-existing signature. Because a signature is just a text file, you can create one in any basic text editor such as WordPad or Notepad (in Windows 95) if your e-mail program doesn't enable you to create a signature. Then, at the very least, your e-mail program should let you specify which file to use as the signature.

You should follow one basic rule when creating your signature: don't let the size get out of hand. As you know, you shouldn't use more than 75 characters per line. On top of that, you should keep your signature to no more than 4 lines. A very large signature is considered obnoxious; short and tasteful is recommended.

Can I filter incoming e-mail into separate mailboxes?

Would you believe—maybe? It depends entirely on your e-mail program. First, consider what mail filtering is all about. Suppose you frequently receive messages from a few sources: a mailing list about ferrets, a mailing list about chocolate, and a best friend. Normally, upon retrieval, all these messages would appear in one new-mail folder. Some people move the messages into specific folders, such as "ferrets," "chocolate," and "bestfriend." Filtering allows for the retrieved message to be automatically sorted into their appropriate folders.

Mail filtering is a feature (or lack thereof) of each particular e-mail application. Some do not provide any mail filtering capabilities at all. Some provide moderate capabilities (defined as how complexly you can define the filtering rules), while others provide advanced filtering capabilities (the ability to create detailed filtering rules). Both popular Windows programs, Eudora Pro and Pegasus Mail, offer mail filtering, but Pegasus Mail is generally considered the most capable in this area.

How do I handle/create messages with attached files?

As e-mail programs' capabilities to deal with attached files have improved, the popularity of attaching files to messages has grown accordingly. An attached file is a file that is sent with an e-mail message. Perhaps, you want to send someone a .JPG format graphic file. You might write them a message that says "Here is that picture of my new puppy." Then you would attach the file (perhaps puppy.jpg) to the message.

"Attach" refers to an e-mail program feature usually called **attach**. All modern e-mail programs allow you to select one or more files to attach to a given message. This is normally relatively straightforward. In Eudora, you click an Attachments header line to select files to attach. In Pegasus Mail, when in the message editor, you can select an Attach button and choose the files to attach.

When you receive an e-mail message with an attachment, your e-mail program may handle it in a number of possible ways. Some programs such as Pegasus Mail will show you that the e-mail contains one message and one attachment. You then have the opportunity to select the attachment and save it to a file. Other programs such as Eudora will automatically save the attached file(s) upon receipt. From there, you can use them in whatever application they were intended. Many of the latter types allow you to configure an "attachments directory" to which all received attachments are automatically saved.

The e-mail program won't open a file mailed to me.

Sometimes you receive an attachment that doesn't seem to work properly. Perhaps the e-mail program complains that it cannot read the attachment.

Attached files must be "encoded" before being sent via e-mail. This encoding, to be brief, is used to convert a binary file (such as a document, graphic, sound, or executable program) to a text file suitable for e-mail transmission. There are several encoding schemes, and it's necessary that the encoding scheme used by the originating e-mail program be comprehensible to the receiving e-mail program.

The two major encoding schemes are UUENCODE and MIME. MIME is probably the more common scheme for attached files in e-mail. Some e-mail programs will allow you to select which scheme to use for encoding (sending) a file. Others will not and automatically use one (probably MIME). Likewise, upon receipt of an encoded file, your mail program will attempt to determine what encoding scheme was used, and then will automatically decode the file and save it to disk (or offer you the option of saving it to disk). Of course, if the sending program used a scheme that your e-mail application cannot handle, you'll run into a problem.

The safest bet for all sides is to stick with MIME encoding if you are offered such configuration choices. If you receive a file that your e-mail program cannot seem to decode, you have two options:

- Attempt to determine what encoding scheme was used. If you view the attached file as a text file somehow (perhaps by loading the message into Notepad), it might say what encoding scheme was used. There are auxiliary utilities for

Windows that can decode most encoding schemes. However, doing this is a pain. Having an e-mail program that can decode on its own is certainly much better.

- Notify the original sender that his attachment is in an unreadable format; ask him to send it again using MIME.

I want off this mailing list!

Mailing lists can be great sources of information or discussion within a particular interest area. However, they can also generate a lot of daily e-mail, and you may eventually decide that you can't deal with it anymore. Or perhaps you simply have lost interest in the discussion.

To rid yourself of a mailing list, you have to *unsubscribe*. The confusing part is that many mailing lists have their own method of unsubscribing. It usually entails sending a message to a particular address—but it's often a different address than you use to send messages to the list. This message might have various syntaxes depending on the list. Usually, you need to at least write **unsubscribe**, sometimes followed by the list name and/or your e-mail address. Because it varies, you'll have to find out the specific procedure for your own mailing list.

If at all possible, find information on how to unsubscribe to your list without asking anyone in the list. Often the list has unsubscribe info posted in its signature file and makes it available via online information as well. Asking the list members how to unsubscribe is the most common "annoying question" that pops up in mailing lists. Of course, if the list has not made the information readily available elsewhere, you have little choice but to bug the list subscribers (in which case, they're asking for it anyway).

Somebody keeps sending me abusive or harassing messages.

Unfortunately, this is not an uncommon problem. Granted, it's not a technical problem, per se, but it's frequent enough to warrant addressing. Regardless of the technologies at their disposal, people aren't always very good at behaving themselves. Especially if you get into an online argument with someone, it is possible (not likely, but possible) that you will start receiving abusive e-mail from him or her.

You can simply ignore it, but if you would prefer to take other action, there are some options at your disposal. First and foremost, save all the abusive messages, as well as copies of any replies you've sent. No matter how offensive the messages are, you shouldn't delete them; you'll be destroying your own evidence.

It's always a move in your favor to keep a cool head and not to sink to the other person's level. Let him know that you plan to contact his system administrator. If that does not stop him, go through with it: send a polite but detailed messages to his system administrator. To do this, you need to figure out what provider he uses. In many cases, this is relatively easy. It is indicated in the portion of the e-mail address following the @ sign. The rightmost two domains of the address are the best bet. Consider this address, for example.

bobjerk@horribleguy.isp.com

In this example, isp.com is most likely the provider. Every ISP has an account named **postmaster**. Thus, you would address your complaint to **postmaster@isp.com**, in this example. You needn't provide all your collected evidence in the first message to the postmaster, but let him know you have it. If he asks for the evidence, provide it. Although the postmaster of an ISP has no *obligation* to do anything to help you, most—for the sake of their own business—will reprimand and/or cut off service to users on their system who are being abusive to others.

I think someone is forging messages under my name.

A forged e-mail message occurs when someone fakes the From: address, so that it looks as if it originated from someone other than the actual source. This is very devious, but it's not terribly difficult to do. A "bad forgery" is easy to trace, because even though the From: address may have been faked, the rest of the e-mail headers give away the actual source of the message. Good forgers would cover their tracks better.

In any case, sometimes—perhaps as a twisted form of abuse, or perhaps simply to hide his own identity—someone will attack others on the Net with messages forged as if they were from you. The most probable way in which you'll learn of this abuse is through complaint letters sent to you or to your postmaster about you. Being totally innocent (presumably!), you will be bewildered as to why these accusations are being laid against you.

If messages are being forged under your name and you protest against the accusation, you shouldn't have too difficult a case. The forged messages will almost always be traceable to some origin other than you. This isn't a matter so much of what you should do if someone is forging you (he will be found out, or at the least, you will be vindicated); it's more a case of understanding why you are being accused of something that you never did.

Note that forging is different than someone breaking into your account and sending abusive e-mails from it. That's not forging because the person is, in fact, e-mailing from your account. This is a different matter, in which case, you'd need to provide evidence that your account was broken into. Still, this is often traceable as well, if your service provider is interested enough in doing so.

How can I find someone's e-mail address?

There is no central directory of all Internet users. The easiest way to find someone's e-mail address is to ask him. Obviously, this is not possible in many cases, such as if you are searching for an old friend or some person with whom you have had no other contact.

Many, if not most, colleges and universities provide online directories for their students, and sometimes for staff and faculty. The Web pages of a university is a good place to start a search, if you know the person to be so affiliated. Many businesses and commercial Internet service providers do not provide directories of their users. In these cases, there really is no sure-fire way to locate someone's address.

A number of services attempt to provide directories. A good place to browse is the Yahoo catalog (http://www.yahoo.com) in the subject area **Reference : White Pages**.

Some of these directories simply solicit users to enter their name and address, creating something of a volunteer phonebook. Other directories pull names and addresses from Usenet postings. These can be a very good way to find anyone who has ever participated in Usenet. Most directory services are a combination of these two strategies.

World Wide Web Worries

Can I change the startup page for my browser?

Yes. Most browsers come preconfigured to access their own home page upon startup. If you like that, fine. However, many people prefer to choose a different startup page, or in some cases, no startup page. One way to speed startup is to choose a startup page that is saved on your own PC. This way, the browser doesn't immediately have to connect to a remote site to retrieve the startup page, which saves a little time.

In Netscape, choose **Options**, **General Preferences**, and **Appearance**. There you'll find an entry that allows you to select either a blank startup page or a specified location. Enter the location of the page you want to use. If you have saved a page to a local .htm file on your PC, you can include its file name in the URL **file:///Cl/*yourpath*/ *filename*.htm**.

In Internet Explorer, choose **View**, **Options**, **Start and Search Pages**. Here, you can select the current page loaded as the search page by clicking the **Use Current** button. This is a slightly awkward way to select a start page, however, because it means you have to go to that page to get to the options setting.

In NCSA Mosaic 2.0, choose **Options**, **Preferences**, **Document**. You can enter a URL in the **Home Page** text box, or you can click the **Use Current** button to cause the currently loaded page to become the home page.

Netscape keeps crashing!

No surprise, it does that to everyone. Netscape is somewhat notorious for crashing, even though it is a very nice browser otherwise. Netscape can be a little finicky because it's a very complex program. Here are some things to watch for in case of crashes.

- Be sure to use the proper version and flavor of Netscape for your version of Windows. Version? Currently, there are two release versions of Netscape available: 1.22 and 2.0. The latter is the newest and most feature-filled version. Flavor? Either of those versions also comes in two "flavors"—one for 16-bit operating systems (Windows 3.1) and one for 32-bit operating systems (Windows 95). So, whichever version of Netscape you choose to use, 1.22 or 2.0, be sure to get the flavor (16- or 32-bit) appropriate for your operating system.

- I recommend that before you install a new version of Netscape, you uninstall the previous version. Doing this may prevent mysterious crashes. However, it also wipes out your existing Netscape preferences, including helper app definitions.

- If you do not choose to uninstall before upgrading, try deleting a file called **netscape.hs** from the old Netscape directory. It seems to be the cause of crashes when upgrading to a newer version.

- Are you using a Beta version of Netscape? Netscape Corporation likes to release Beta versions of their product for users to play with, and they are labeled as Betas. (A Beta is a version that is not fully tested or finished.) But remember that a Beta version is known to have bugs and, therefore, will most likely crash in certain circumstances. You use Beta software at your own risk, but it's good to report crashes to Netscape so that they can investigate. To find out whether your copy of Netscape is a Beta or final version, open the **Help** menu and choose **About Netscape**. You'll see the Netscape logo and the words **Netscape Navigator Version xx**; Beta versions will say **beta** in this message.

The graphics or colors appear all wrong.

The most common cause of messed-up graphic appearance in the Web browser is video card driver incompatibility. Because browsers and Windows 95 both are newer than many video card drivers, sometimes problems arise. One solution, then—and this applies to more than simply Web browsing—is to be sure to have the latest video card drivers for your video card. These are often made available by the manufacturers via the Web or online.

If colors appear strange, also consider double-checking that you have set your Windows to 256 colors or higher (this presumes that you have a video card capable of such as all new cards are). Many images in Web pages have more than 16 colors, and if your Windows is set to only 16 colors, the images will look freaky on-screen. In Windows 95, you can check your screen preferences by right-clicking anywhere on the desktop background. A little menu will pop up, from which you choose **Properties** and **Settings**. There you will find a selector named **Color Palette** that allows you to choose between the varying numbers of colors your video card supports.

My browser redownloads images that have already been retrieved.

Some browsers have what are known as *caches*. The cache stores the files and graphics you retrieve from the Web on your hard drive so that if you return to one of those pages, your computer can quickly load the graphics from your local storage instead of having to download them from the Net again. However, several factors can cause the ideal principle behind a cache to fall short of reality.

The first major factor is size: be sure your cache is set large enough. You should usually configure your browser's cache to 4–5 megs (4096–5000k). If the cache is too small, it won't have the room to store many graphics. If the cache is very large, it takes up a great deal of hard drive space.

Second, be sure the cache is enabled. In Mosaic, the cache options provide a specific Enable button that should be selected with a check mark.

Third, take note of how the browser is configured to operate with the cache. All three major browsers offer options similar to those listed below to increase cache-reliance. The following figure shows these typical cache settings in Netscape Navigator 2.0.

- Once per session: If you attempt to load a page you've already been to, the browser will check to see if the page has changed at all since last time. If the page has changed, it will reload the page. If not, it will use the files from the cache. With this option, it will only check for page updates one time during this session; subsequent returns to that page will be drawn from the cache automatically.

- Every time: Browser will always check the server to see if the page has been changed at all before drawing from cache.

- Never: If you've been to this page before, the browser will not even check to see if it has changed and will draw the files from the cache.

Understanding these options should help you to understand the logic behind the browser's cache behavior. To access these options in Netscape, use the **Options**, **Network Preferences**, **Cache** command sequence. In Internet Explorer, choose **View**, **Options**, **Advanced**. In NCSA Mosaic, use the **Options**, **Preferences**, **Cache** sequence.

Lastly, some browsers' cache management just doesn't work properly. Needless to say, if that's what you're up against, there's no good solution except to switch to a new browser. The browsers discussed here should work properly (although Beta versions of each release may not).

All of the letters look like Greek or something.

This is probably because you somehow managed to change the browser font to Greek. This seems to happen to people periodically, although it's not clear if the user is doing something wrong or if there are some goblins haunting the browsers. In any case, check your font settings.

Each browser allows you to configure which fonts to use to show the Web page contents. You can find the settings in Netscape by selecting **Options**, **General Preferences**, and **Fonts**. In Mosaic, select **Options**, **Preferences**, and **Fonts**. For Internet Explorer, select **View**, **Options**, and **Appearance**. In any case, simply be sure that the selected fonts are, in fact, legible fonts such as Times New Roman and Courier (popular choices). Choosing to change the font will allow you to see what the current fonts look like and help you make a proper selection.

Some Web pages never finish loading.

Isn't this frustrating? You attempt to connect to a Web page, and it starts downloading, as indicated by the spinning progress icon or the shooting stars in Netscape. But it never seems to finish. You may be left staring at a blank screen waiting for this endless page to complete.

Although several factors could be at fault here, this problem has been recognized as a particular bugaboo for Netscape users who also use Windows 95 Dial-Up Networking. In some cases, the delay may simply be justifiable network traffic. One simple solution is to hit the **STOP** button in the toolbar of the browser. This will cause it to give up and will probably show the contents that it has retrieved (which may be virtually all of the page, minus a picture or three).

Links to sounds are not playing.

That's probably because you don't have an appropriate audio player configured as a helper application. When the Web browser encounters a link to a file that is a sound, it attempts to send that sound to whichever audio player you've chosen—if you've chosen one. Upon installation, some browsers may automatically default to a certain player; others may not.

The key here is to check your viewer or *helper app's* (same thing) configurations. Netscape carries these around in **General Preferences** (shown in the following figure) and **Helpers**, while Mosaic tucks them away in **Options**, **Preferences**, and **Viewers**. Internet Explorer bases its helpers on the file associations defined in Windows 95; select **View**, **Options**, **Filetypes** to get there.

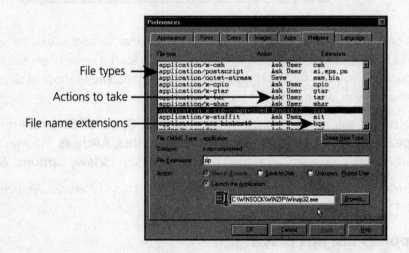

File types

Actions to take

File name extensions

Although you may encounter several types of sound files, WAV and AU files are the most common. Be sure you've configured a player for both. (You'll find entries for both in the viewer configurations previously mentioned.) You can certainly use the same player if it can play both types of files. Netscape comes with an AU player but not a WAV player. Windows 95 includes the program mplayer, which can play both types of sound files, so it is a common pick for a sound viewer.

If you want to check out others, you can find a cornucopia of helper apps at Stroud's Consummate Winsock Apps List. It's on the Web at http://www.stroud.com or http://www.cwsapps.com.

Followed links are not remembered.

When you click a link to follow it, the browser may or may not "remember" that you've visited that link before. In some browsers, the link becomes a different color after you select it so you can keep track of which links you've followed in the past and which ones you have not. The following figure shows two different links in Netscape Navigator.

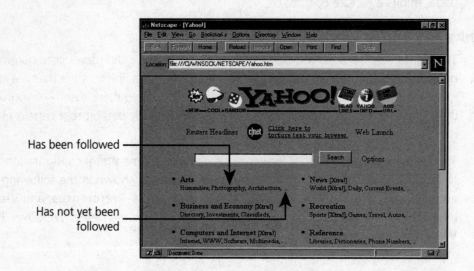

This behavior is determined completely by the browser settings. Every browser that marks followed links allows you to determine how long it remembers the followed links. If you want, you can set this history to "expire" after some number of days (that is, you tell the browser when to forget the followed links).

In Netscape, you change this behavior by selecting **Options**, **General Preferences**, **Appearance**. In Mosaic, select **Options**, **Preferences**, **Anchors**. Internet Explorer offers a slightly more limited version of these settings in **View**, **Options**, **Appearance**.

Keeping track of followed links is only to help you know where you've been. It doesn't affect the browser's functionality.

Java applets are not playing.

Java applets are little programs that can add all manner of useful and/or nifty enhancements to a Web page, such as animated text or images. An increasing number of Web pages now feature Java applets. If you find that professed Java applets are not playing on your system, consider the following factors.

- This may sound obvious, but does your browser support Java? At this point in time, most do not. In fact, only HotJava by Sun and Netscape 2.0 did at the time of writing of this book. Presumably, Internet Explorer will catch up in this regard; other browsers may not.

- Are you using a 32-bit browser? This especially applies to Netscape 2.0, which comes in a 16-bit version for Windows 3.1 users and a 32-bit version for Windows 95 users. Although the two versions are *almost* the same, the 16-bit version does not support Java because it cannot be done easily in the Windows 3.1 environment. Therefore, you will need to have a 32-bit operating system such as Windows 95 to have a chance of seeing Java applets. Macintosh versions of Netscape are intended to support Java but have lagged behind development-wise.

- If you are using 32-bit Netscape 2.0 in Windows 95 but still do not see Java applets, check to be sure Java has not been disabled in your browser. Choose **Options** and **Security Preferences**, where you will find a "disable Java" check box. Of course, it should be deselected to enable Java.

- Lastly, some TCP/IP software has had trouble playing Java applets with Netscape. At the time of this writing, released Beta versions of Trumpet Winsock 32-bit do not support playing of Java applets. Windows 95's Dial-Up Networking does work with Java.

Sending e-mail from my browser doesn't work.

Most importantly, be sure you have configured a viable SMTP server in your browser's mail preferences. Use the same one that you've configured to use in your e-mail application, if you use one. Often, this will be an address provided by your provider with a name such as mail.*yourisp*.com or smtp.*yourisp*.com.

Check your Netscape mail settings by selecting **Options**, **Mail and News Preferences**, and **Servers**. Be sure the Outgoing Mail (SMTP) Server text box contains the name of a working server. You needn't fill in the Incoming Mail (POP) Server text box unless you want to use Netscape to retrieve e-mail as well. Also be sure you choose **Options**, **Mail and News Preferences**, and **Identity** and enter your name and e-mail address.

In Mosaic, you can find this information by choosing **Options**, **Preferences**, **Services**. Internet Explorer does not have a built-in e-mail capability; instead, it uses Microsoft Exchange, which is part of Windows 95.

I cannot convince audio—or video—on-demand programs (such as RealAudio) to work.

There are several new breeds of Web applications that provide audio and video in realtime; that is, they are played while they download, rather than having to be fully downloaded first. Some popular examples include RealAudio, Internet Wave, VDO Live, and XingStreamWorks.

As part of the normal proper installation, the browser needs to be configured to use these helper apps (viewers). Often, this is done automatically by the on-demand installation programs. However, if you select, for example, a RealAudio link and are presented with a query from the browser as to what to do with this type of file, your helper app is not properly configured. In this case, go into the helper apps configuration of your browser, find the listing for the file type in question, and set the play program appropriately.

For some users the helper app *is* configured properly but the on-demand application simply doesn't work. The most common reason for this is that users are not using "real" SLIP/PPP connections. Many users nowadays use "pseudo-SLIP" connections, provided by such programs as The Internet Adaptor (TIA) and SLiRP. These programs allow users with only dial-up UNIX account to gain much SLIP/PPP functionality. While most Web browsing works fine with these sorts of connections, the multimedia on-demand programs often do not.

To be technical for a moment, the only way to possibly get these programs to work if you use TIA or SLiRP instead of a "real" SLIP/PPP account, is to use a feature called *port redirection*. Current releases of TIA do not even support port redirection, so the point is moot there. SLiRP does, but it's too complicated to explain here; if you do use SLiRP for your Net connection and want to use one of these programs, check into the newsgroup alt.dcom.slip-emulators. There you can find or initiate discussion on exact port redirection settings for each on-demand application.

This page says "wait to continue," but nothing more ever happens.

Push-pull. What? Some Web servers use something called "push"ing and "pull"ing to automatically cause events to occur on your end, such as moving to a new Web page. Only problem is, not all browsers care about the server's pushy demands. In those cases, nothing will happen; the page will simply sit there.

Wise Web authors provide an alternative for those of you whose browsers don't push or pull, such as a link to click to take you where they want you to go. Those who don't offer this alternative may simply leave you hanging without the proper browser. The three main browsers should all handle the pushy-pullies properly. If your browser does not support push-pull, and no alternative traditional link has been provided, you have no choice but to abandon the page.

I'd like to maximize the usable space in my browser window.

With all window options enabled, a fair amount of desktop space is covered up by the browser's screen elements (see the following figure). Many users—especially those who use smaller sized desktops such as 640 x 480—want all the browser space they can get. Although all those button bars and navigation icons are pretty, they take up screen space.

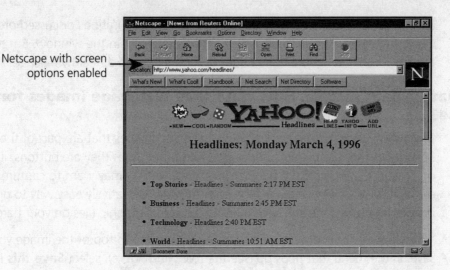

Netscape with screen options enabled

Each browser's configurations allow you to alter the appearance of the window. If you use the options right, you can maximize the window space. Here are some tips for doing so in each of our three browsers:

- In Netscape, uncheck **Options** and **Show Directory Buttons**. Select **Options**, **General Preference**, **Appearance**, and choose **Show Toolbar as Text**. You can even remove the entire toolbar (but you'll have to use the menus to navigate) and the window that shows your current location by deselecting **Options**, **Show Toolbar** and **Options**, **Show Location**. As you can see in the next figure, such judicious disabling of extra features gives you much more browser window real estate.

- In Mosaic, you can hide the toolbar, the status bar (at the bottom of the window), and the location window by deselecting the respective options in the Options menu. Permanent changes can be made via **Options**, **Preferences**, **Window**.

- Internet Explorer also lets you hide the toolbar, status bar, and location bar by deselecting those options in the **View** menu.

Netscape with the toolbar and Location bar turned off

Lastly, you can fiddle with font sizes in the font configurations discussed previously. Obviously, making fonts smaller allows more text to fit in the window. But making them too small can mean more visits to the optometrist. Find a healthy balance.

That's a neat picture. How can I save Web page images for my own use?

Many Web pages contain lots of *inline graphics* (images that are part of the page). Sometimes they are pictures or designs, and other times they are buttons, lines, and so on. You just want a picture because you like it, or you may want to capture a design element for your own use. Each browser provides a relatively easy way to grab these images from the page and save them to individual graphic files on your hard drive.

In Netscape 2.0, simply click the right mouse button on top of the image you want to save. In the menu that pops up (see the following figure), select **Save this image as**. Then you can select a location on your hard drive to which you want the image saved for your future pillaging.

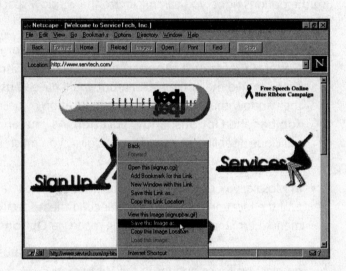

You use the same right-click technique in Mosaic. When you do, a slightly different menu pops up, giving you the option of saving the image in its original format ("Remote site format") or in a Windows .BMP format. If you plan to use the image in future Web pages, remote site format is probably the better choice for compatibility purposes.

You use much the same method for Internet Explorer. Just right-click over the image and select **Save As** from the shortcut menu. Voilà.

I'd like to access files in my private UNIX account.

If you have a UNIX account, you can access its file from within the Web browser using its FTP capabilities. To do so, you open a URL in this format:

ftp://*yourid*@*yourisp*.com

For example, if my UNIX user id were "harry99" and my account was at jimbo.jones.com, I'd open a URL to ftp://harry99@jimbo.jones.com. The Web browser would prompt me for my password (the password of my UNIX account). With that information, the Web browser would display a list of the contents of the UNIX account.

Note that while this works with Netscape and Mosaic, it does not work with the current version (as of this writing, version 2.0) of Internet Explorer. Explorer does not seem to possess a means of accessing private password-protected accounts.

A large file transfer was interrupted. Can it be salvaged?

Any number of culprits can cause an interrupted file transfer. It could be anything from a computer crash, to modem disconnects, to a user who clicked the wrong window closed and accidentally aborted the transfer in progress.

There isn't any way for the Web browser to resume an interrupted transfer. If you have a UNIX account and a terminal program, you could try re-retrieving the desired file to the UNIX account and then dialing into that account with your terminal program. Then use a Zmodem transfer, which may be able to find the semi-completed stub of the aborted transfer on your hard drive and pick up where it left off. This is a convoluted solution, but it is the only real possibility at this point in time.

One browser supports some features, another supports others. Just tell me, which browser should I use?

Okay, I admit that the information I'm about to give isn't really a "quick fix." But the question is a common and reasonable one. As each new browser is developed, it comes up with new nifty features in an attempt to win market share away from the other browsers. Netscape took the early, far lead in this regard by developing a number of "extensions" to traditional Web page design which allowed for new effects. Thus, people who wanted to design even "cooler" pages started adopting Netscape's extensions. In doing so, this meant Netscape's browser had to be used to view the page, thereby increasing Netscape's market share. At the time of this writing, Netscape is far and away the most popular browser, with some seventy percent of the browser market.

Microsoft leapt out of the woodwork to play catch-up when it introduced Internet Explorer, which is probably the closest rival to Netscape. Explorer, in turn, offered its own *extensions*. Now there are pages that are designed for Netscape and some that are designed for Explorer. Most pages can be viewed on either browser, but special features may not be, and certain design elements may appear strange or distorted in the "wrong" browser. Mosaic is not a renegade browser; it tries to stick to "official" specifications. Thus, it lacks some of the pizzazz of Netscape and Internet Explorer. There are numerous other Web browsers available, as well, but all possess fewer feature sets than the main three.

By far, Netscape is the popular choice. Many people choose to have multiple browsers; after all, Internet Explorer and NCSA Mosaic are both free products. Netscape is free for evaluation use and educational use. So, if one has the hard drive space and/or the inclination, it's not unreasonable to have multiple browsers on your PC. If not, their order of popularity is Netscape, Internet Explorer, and then Mosaic.

Networking Niggles

Windows 95 includes the necessary software for connecting to the Internet, called Dial-Up Networking (or DUN). Most home users (and readers of this book) will want to connect to the Net via SLIP or PPP accounts, which are offered by most Internet service providers. And although they achieve essentially the same functionality and performance, PPP connections are slightly easier to set up in Windows 95. Having said that, Microsoft designed DUN setup and configuration are less than obvious to a novice user.

Windows 3.1 does not include software for SLIP or PPP connections. One very popular package previously discussed in this book, which provides such access for Windows 3.1 users, is Trumpet Winsock, a shareware product. Trumpet comes with very helpful documentation and is less subject to configuration difficulties.

How do I create a SLIP or PPP connection?

It's not quite obvious upon first glance just how one connects Windows 95 to the Internet. The key is to create a Dial-Up Networking (aka "DUN") connection by opening **My Computer**, opening the **Dial-Up Networking** window, and choosing **Make New Connection** from the **Connections** menu. The details for this are somewhat lengthy and are fully explained in "Configure Your TCP/IP Software" on page 97.

Again, Windows 3.1 users with Trumpet Winsock face a less confusing situation. After Trumpet Winsock has been installed, one must launch the software, which is represented by the TCPMAN icon. Having launched the program, simply choose **Setup** from the **File** menu. Although you still need to enter several strange-looking numbers, this procedure is documented clearly both in this book (see "Configure Your TCP/IP Software" on page 97) and in the Trumpet Winsock help file.

Why is there no SLIP option in Windows 95 DUN?

If you have access to only a SLIP account from your service provider, setting up Windows 95 DUN is bit trickier. While configuring the new DUN connection, you may have noticed that there is no SLIP option for the dial-up server type. You'll first need to install the following bit of software, which will provide the option of a SLIP-style DUN connection. Once you install this software, you can then choose a SLIP connection via the **Server Type** settings available in the **Properties** of your Dial-Up Networking connection.

If you do not have the CD versions of Windows 95 or the Plus! Pack, you must first download the SLIP software from Microsoft's Web page at http://www.microsoft.com. Follow the links for Windows 95 free software. (If you cannot access this site because you don't have any way to connect to the Internet yet, then you'll have to find a connected friend—a classic catch-22.)

No matter how you go about it, the file you ultimately need is called Rnaplus.inf. Use **File Find** (available by clicking the Windows 95 **Start** button, selecting **Find**, and clicking **Files or Folders**) to locate it on your CD if necessary. Once you find this file, right-click on it and select **Install** from the shortcut menu. The SLIP support will then be installed.

DUN claims to be establishing a connection, but it never succeeds.

After DUN connects to your provider's modem, it then tries to negotiate the connection and log you in. In some cases, it claims to be **Establishing connection** but never gets past that, and eventually the modem hangs up.

This may be caused by a variety of problems. Your modem may have difficulties negotiating a speed with your provider's modem. Be sure that your baud rate is set properly for this particular DUN connection. To check or change it, right-click on the connection icon in the Dial-Up Networking window, and then select **Properties** from the shortcut menu. Once in the properties window, select **Configure** to find the baud rate selector.

Also, it may be that you are dialing the wrong phone number. Double-check that. Some providers offer multiple phone numbers for different modem speeds; consider that possibility, and be sure you are connecting to the correct one.

Finally, the most common cause of this problem is an improper login sequence on your end. Read the answer to the next question for the gory details.

How do I log in to my ISP with my user name and password?

For users of Trumpet Winsock, this is relatively straightforward: if you're not using an automatic login script, simply select **Manual Login** from the **Dialler** menu after launching Trumpet. This enables you to manually enter the commands to connect to your provider. You would use standard modem AT commands to dial up your provider (for example, **atdt 555-5555** or whatever phone number you must call). Once connected, you can log in by manually typing your user name and password at the respective prompts.

Unfortunately, as the result of a strange interface design on Microsoft's part, there is a common misunderstanding about how to log in to your provider using Windows 95's Dial-Up Networking. When you launch your DUN connection, a Connect To window appears (see the following figure).

Although this window provides a place to enter your user name and password, these are misleading entries. Most Internet providers use a system in which you must manually type your user name and password to log in upon connection. If you've been filling in these entries expecting them to work, it's no wonder you've been confused when your connection was never established. Your provider's computer was waiting for you to manually enter your login information.

DUN won't allow you this opportunity unless you've properly configured the dial-up connection. Right-click on the connection icon and choose **Properties** from the shortcut menu. In the Properties window, select the **Configure** button and the **Options** tab to access the dialog box shown in the next figure. Make sure the **Bring up terminal window after dialing** check box is enabled (contains a check mark). Then click **OK**.

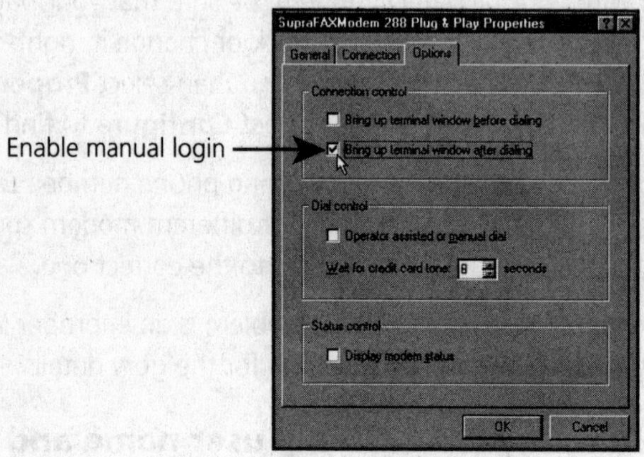

Enable manual login ⟶

From now on when you attempt to establish your connection, a window will appear after the connection is made, asking you to manually log in.

Clicking the Dial button is tedious.

It seems a repetitive task to be required to click **Dial** every time you attempt to launch a connection with DUN. While Microsoft provides no way around this, several Internauts have taken it upon themselves to circumvent this redundancy.

Three mini-utilities worth recommending are RTRevco, Dunce, and Keep going. You can find these at any Windows 95 shareware site, such as http://www.windows95.com. Each of these will, among other things, allow you to automate the pressing of the Dial button, thus saving your finger muscles many clicks over a lifetime.

Can I create login scripts with Dial-Up Networking?

Manually logging into your provider at every connection can become tedious. Fortunately, Microsoft provides a bit of add-on software that allows you to construct a *login script*. A login script is a simple mini-program you can write to manually log in for you. Follow these steps to construct your own login script:

1. First, you need to obtain and install the Dial-Up Scripting Tool software. You can get it from one of three places:

   The Windows 95 installation CD. Access it using the path Admin/Apptools/Dscript/scripter.exe.

   The Microsoft Plus! Pack. To get the Dial-Up Scripting Tool from here, you must install the Internet Jumpstart component of the Plus! Pack.

   Microsoft's Web site.

For now, open the Web page at **http://www.microsoft.com/windows/software/admintools.htm**. Then click the **Dial-Up SLIP and Scripting Support** link, and the file dscrpt.exe is downloaded to your computer. When the download is complete, run the program by clicking the **Start** button, selecting **Run**, and clicking **dscrpt.exe**.

2. Once the scripting software is installed, you can access it by clicking the **Start** button, selecting **Programs**, selecting **Accessories**, and clicking **Dial-Up Scripting Tool**. The dialog box shown in the following figure appears.

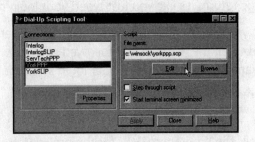

3. To automate your login, you must select which connection to script, and then assign a script file to it using the interface as pictured here.

Learning to write the script file is too involved for this Quick Fix, but the Help button in the Scripting Tool dialog box gives you access to everything you need to know. It is mostly a matter of describing which messages from the server to watch for, and what answers to supply in return. The exact format of these scripting commands is explained clearly in the associated Help topic.

My Trumpet Winsock login script isn't working.

The upside of a login script is that it allows you to automate the repetitive process of dialing and logging into your service provider. The downside is that it opens up a whole new area for things to go wrong—getting the script to work!

Trumpet's scripting language is different from Windows 95's, although they aim for the same goal. Trumpet's built-in scripting is essentially a mini-programming language. Overall, it is too detailed to go into fully here, but it was covered in detail in "Configure Your TCP/IP Software" (page 97).

If the login script is not working—that is, if it's not logging you in—consider these two questions.

1. Is it dialing your provider?

If the modem isn't even dialing and/or connecting to your provider, make sure that you're at least running the script. In Trumpet, you run the script one of two ways:

- Open the **Dialler** menu and choose **Other**. In the file dialog box, select the script file you want to run. Scripts in Trumpet usually end with the file name extension .cmd.

- Open the **Dialler** menu and choose **Login** or set up Trumpet to automatically log in upon launch (using **Dialler**, **Options**). Either way, your script *must* be named login.cmd.

2. Are your login entries followed by a carriage return?

This is another common problem in a Trumpet script. An appropriate script will, for example, wait for the provider to send the text **login:** (or something similar). When it receives the login command, the script sends your login name. However, the script must also send a carriage return after your login name. When the script doesn't send a carriage return, it's like you just typed your login name but didn't press Enter.

When you use Trumpet's **output** command to send text such as your user name back to the provider, the text must be followed by \13, which is the code for a carriage return. For example, say a portion of your login script looks like this:

```
input "Login:"
output "myusername"
```

This tells the program to wait for the provider to send the text Login: and then to reply with the text *myusername*. Without a carriage return code, you would never advance past this portion. (The provider would eventually give up on you, and the modem would disconnect.)

In reality, that section of script *should* look like this:

```
input "Login:"
output "myusername"\13
```

This is important to remember for all uses of the **output** command in your Trumpet scripts and when sending login info to the provider.

I need to use TIA or SLiRP, but how?

TIA and SLiRP are two different software packages that perform similar functions. They are designed to give SLIP or PPP access to users who have only dial-up, text-based UNIX accounts. Because these connections are not *exactly* the same as a "true" SLIP/PPP connection, they are called "SLIP emulators" or "psuedo-SLIP." In any case, they both work quite well. (TIA is a commercial product, available from http://marketplace.com, while SLiRP is freeware and available from http://blitzen.canberra.edu.au/slirp/.)

Using either of these with Windows 95 DUN is only slightly difficult. You still need to create a SLIP or PPP connection (both TIA and SLiRP support PPP emulation, so it makes the most sense to go with that) as previously explained. The documentation to TIA and SLiRP explain how to determine what your IP address and DNS server will be.

Most importantly, be sure that you have selected **Bring up terminal window after connection** in your connection properties (right-click your DUN connection icon, select **Properties**, select **Configure**, and click the **Options** tab). This way, when DUN connects to your UNIX host, you can log in to your shell account. From your UNIX prompt, you can then launch your TIA or SLiRP program (as described in their respective documentation), and then exit the terminal window (F7) to complete establishing the connection. You may also create a Dial-Up Script, which is only slightly trickier, because there may be more interaction to program as compared to a straightforward SLIP/PPP login.

For users of Trumpet Winsock and Windows 3.1, using TIA or SLiRP is no different, except that your login procedure has more steps because you first must log into the UNIX account, and then run TIA or SLiRP. This can easily be done either by going through the motions manually (with Trumpet's **Dialler**, **Manual Login** command) or by coding the appropriate interaction into a Trumpet login script.

The reported connect speed in DUN seems wrong.

Keep in mind that Windows 95 DUN reports your connect speed as the *actual* modem speed of the connection, not the baud rate. Thus, if you have a 28.8kbps modem, and your baud rate is configured (via the Modem Properties) to 57600, DUN will report the speed of the connection between the two modems. This might be 28,800 or lower, depending on the quality of your connection.

No need to worry in this scenario—everything is fine. Of course, if DUN is reporting a connection speed markedly lower than the maximum speed of your modem (for example, a 9,600 connection when you're using a 14.4kbps modem), you may be experiencing some other problems, such as those addressed in the section "Connection Frustrations."

I frequently get DNS errors when using network applications.

Most commonly, this problem occurs when you're trying to use 32-bit network applications, such as Netscape Navigator 32-bit, with Windows 95 Dial-Up Networking. The common cause of the problem is quite esoteric: Windows 95 is failing to find the wsock32.dll file.

Normally, this file should be located in your windows\system folder, on whichever hard disk Win 95 is installed (usually C). The first thing to check is your windows\system folder for the wsock32.dll file. In the current release of Windows 95, this file should have the size 66,560 bytes.

The second potential culprit lies within the messy Windows Registry. The Registry is a large database of settings that control a huge variety of Windows' characteristics. The Registry is not something to play with unknowingly, as the system could become quite damaged. To browse or edit the Registry, choose **Run** from the **Start** menu and enter **regedit** in the Run dialog box. The Registry Editor shown in this figure appears.

First, save a backup of the current Registry using the **Registry**, **Export Registry File** command. This way, if anything becomes damaged, you can simply rerun **regedit** and **Import** the backup file to restore everything to its predamaged state. Following these instructions should not yield any damage. But don't play around haphazardly.

To navigate the Registry, you click the folders (as specified) to open them into sublevels, just like navigating files in the Windows Explorer. To check the DNS problem, first open the **Hkey_local_machine** folder. From there, open the following sequence of folders: **system**, **currentcontrolset**, **services vxd**, **mstcp**, and **serviceprovider**. Once there, you will notice in the right-hand window a Registry key called ProviderPath. A *Registry key* is simply one entry in the Registry, which is basically a value assigned to some label name. Be sure that the path specified is %windir%\system\wsock32.dll. If yours does not say that, right-click **ProviderPath** and choose **Modify** from the shortcut menu. Modify the path and exit the Registry Editor to preserve the changes.

In this example, you verified a pair of problems that may or may not both exist on your system: that wsock32.dll does reside in windows\system, and that your relevant Registry key points to this location.

Running an Internet application *should* automatically run DUN, but it doesn't.

In theory, DUN features a *dial on demand* capability. This means that if you try to launch an Internet application before you've connected, the connection procedure will automatically be initiated first. Then, when you quit your Internet applications, the connection will be dropped. Again, *in theory*, all you need to do to use this feature is launch an Internet application without first having launched the Dial-Up Networking connection.

The problem: this only works with 32-bit applications. 16-bit Internet applications cannot dial on demand with Windows 95 DUN. Thus, the most likely cause of your problem is attempting to launch a 16-bit application. This is not entirely uncommon, as several high-quality Internet applications for Windows still exist only in 16-bit form—and they still run fine, but they won't dial on demand (Pegasus Mail is a good example).

Trumpet Winsock is not automatically running when I launch an Internet application.

Trumpet Winsock sports *dial on demand* capability. If you launch an Internet application such as Eudora before having run Trumpet, Trumpet should automatically run and connect (assuming your login script is named login.cmd). If this is not working, check two likely culprits.

First, be sure that you are launching a 16-bit Internet application. Many Internet programs now come in two "flavors"—16-bit and 32-bit. As a Windows 3.1 user, you should be using 16-bit software anyway. Because Trumpet Winsock for Windows 3.1 is a 16-bit program, only 16-bit Internet applications can take advantage of the dial on demand feature.

Second, be sure that Trumpet's main program, tcpman.exe, is in your Windows path. In fact, the entire Trumpet directory should be in your Windows path. The path is a list of directories on your hard drive that Windows searches for commands. This path is specified in your autoexec.bat file, probably located on the C: drive.

Open your autoexec.bat file in a text editor such as Windows Notepad. It should contain at least one line that looks something like this:

```
path C:\WINDOWS;C:\DOS
```

There may be many more directories listed in your particular autoexec.bat file. Notice that each directory is separated from the next with a semicolon. Be sure that the directory that includes Trumpet is listed on this line, preferably first. So after it's modified, the previous line should look like this:

```
path C:\TRUMPET;C:\WINDOWS;C:\DOS
```

Of course, that's assuming that Trumpet was installed to the directory c:\trumpet. Alter as necessary to conform with your particular setup.

Are there any alternatives to the DUN included with Windows 95? To Trumpet Winsock for Windows 3.1?

Dial-Up Networking is really just a name for Microsoft's stab at a 32-bit TCP/IP stack with dialer. In practice, any TCP/IP stack software for Windows will work fine. Others may have the advantage of less twisted configurations and speedier operation (Microsoft's implementation turns out to be rather slow compared to other manufacturers'). The main advantage of DUN is that it is a 32-bit stack that allows you to run all the 32-bit network applications.

Older popular TCP/IP stack such as Trumpet Winsock support only 16-bit applications. They will work fine but lose some of the efficiency of running 32-bit applications. The ultimate alternative, then, is third-party 32-bit TCP/IP stacks. Are there any? The pickings are slim at this point in time.

Without endorsing either of these, Core Systems offers their own DUN replacement called Internet Connect (http://www.win.net/~core/) and FTP Software offers their alternative called OnNet32 (http://www.ftp.com/). Finally, the ever-popular Trumpet

Winsock is slowly working toward a 32-bit version but isn't quite there yet. (There is a Beta 32-bit, which means that a 32-bit version is available for public use, even if it is unfinished and unstable.) Keep track of their progress at http://www.trumpet.com.au.

There are a number of alternative TCP/IP stacks available for Windows 3.1 besides Trumpet Winsock. Trumpet is by far the most popular, as it is widely available and relatively low-cost shareware. Trumpet's competitors are generally bundled with other off-the-shelf software such as Spry's Internet-in-a-Box, FTP software's OnNet, Netcom's Netcruiser, and others. All work similarly in Windows 3.1, as far as functionality goes.

Usenet News Jams

My news server says "You have no permission to talk. Goodbye."

Most Usenet news servers are configured to allow only certain sites to connect to them. This prevents anyone in the world from connecting and draining the resources of the server. Some servers, as just explained, allow only certain domains to connect, while others require a user name and password.

First, be sure that you are connecting from a valid domain. For example, let's say that you go to school at Kazoo University and want to connect to their news server, news.kazoo.edu. If you have a SLIP/PPP account provided by Kazoo, there should be no problem. However, let's say you are using another SLIP/PPP account, perhaps that of a local commercial Internet provider. In that case, Kazoo will not know that you have rights to their machine. So you must be sure you are connecting to the server from an account within its acceptable domain.

Second, if the server requires a user ID and password, be sure you've filled in both things in your Usenet application's configuration settings.

I'd like to post anonymously.

There are a variety of "noncriminal" reasons why someone would want to submit an anonymous post to a Usenet newsgroup. In any case, doing so simply requires that you submit your post via an anonymous posting service.

This is done by contacting any one of several anonymous remailers and following their particular instructions for submitting your post. They will then send your post to the Usenet newgroup(s) you request. Private e-mail replies to your post will come back to you, but the replier will not know who you are (and, often, you will not know who they are).

Because there are many remailers to choose from, I cannot provide step-by-step instructions here. Most remailers are designed by default to send anonymous private e-mail, and thus they take special commands in the body of the message to make a Usenet post. You can read the help instructions for the popular remailers at the Web site http://electron.rutgers.edu/~gambino/anon_servers/anon.html.

Several Web sites offer easy interfaces in which you can compose a message and select a remailer. Two worth trying are the Community ConneXion (http://www.c2.org/remail/by-www.html) and Noah's Place (http://www.lookup.com/Homepages/64499/anon.html).

I want to change my posted name and organization.

Although a non-anonymous Usenet post will always contain your e-mail address, it need not contain your real name. Some users prefer to change their listed name, either for personal or cosmetic reasons. If you are using a PC newsreader, such as Agent, Free Agent, or News Xpress, changing these settings is quite easy.

For example, in Agent (which is rapidly becoming the most popular newsreader for the PC), you simply choose **Options**, **Preferences** and click the **User** folder tab. You can enter any personal name and organization name that you want. Each of the newsreader applications has a similar capability, including Netscape Navigators built-in newsreader (accessed via **Options**, **Mail and News Preferences**, **Identity**).

After I post, I receive "Post failed" errors.

A post can fail for several reasons. One common cause of a post failing is known as *throttling*, and the error message may indicate this if it's the problem. In short, throttling occurs when your provider's news server is filled to capacity. There is nothing you can do except complain. If a provider is suffering from many throttling errors, they seriously need to upgrade their storage capacity.

Another cause of post failing errors is a server timeout. Your newsreader will attempt to contact the news server to send it your post, but the news server may not answer. This may be because the news server machine is down or is overloaded with users. The odd server timeout does occur, and you should simply wait a few minutes and then resubmit your post. Again, though, if this problem happens with some regularity, your provider is likely at fault.

Although it is possible that your TCP/IP settings are misconfigured, preventing connection to the server, if this were the case, none of your Internet applications would be connecting to anywhere.

Lastly, some newsreaders fail to post in an attempt to enforce two Usenet customs:

- Signature files longer than four lines are considered a violation of netiquette (waste of network traffic). Although many newsreaders won't object if you break this custom, a few will.

- In another attempt to conserve traffic and improve content, some newsreaders prevent you from submitting a follow-up post in which you include less new text than you quote from the previous message. This is a dubious "rule" that's intended to prevent someone from reposting an entire message and only adding "Yes I agree." Again, although most newsreaders do not enforce this rule, the custom is something to keep in mind when composing follow-up posts.

What is a moderated newsgroup? How can I post to one?

Although all Usenet newsgroups are publicly accessible, some are more democratic than others. The vast majority of newsgroups are *unmoderated*. This means that anyone can post anything to that newsgroup. Although this invites the widest possible array of discussion, it also draws a lot of garbage. Some newsgroups are *moderated*, which means that posts are submitted to a moderator, who then may accept or reject the post for the newsgroup.

Nobody is forced to use moderated newsgroups. In almost every instance, there are unmoderated alternatives in which to discuss the same subject matter. But, there are advantages to participating in moderated newsgroups—specifically, a high discussion content-to-noise ratio. Usually, a moderated newsgroup will be marked as such in the newsgroup description (although some PC newsreaders don't display the newsgroup description). In other cases, you will usually find a FAQ posted regularly within the newsgroup that explains how to submit posts to the moderator. Besides being a tip-off that this is a moderated newsgroup, it also provides the instructions you need. The basic idea is that you'll e-mail your post to the moderator, as per his guidelines outlined in the FAQ, and he will take it from there.

Attempting to post directly to a moderated newsgroup will likely result in a rejected post.

Why are there messages missing from this newsgroup?

Nothing can be more frustrating (well, not *nothing*) than discovering that desired posts are missing from the newsgroup. You may be reading an ongoing discussion and find that reference is made to a post that you don't see. Or perhaps you are attempting to decode a binary file that is posted in multiple parts, and one or more of the parts are missing. Argh!

This isn't your fault and may only indirectly be your service provider's fault. The problem partially lies in the design of Usenet. In brief, Usenet is like a large network of rivers and streams, each feeding into one another at various nodes. In theory, the water from each stream should eventually feed into every other stream, except this doesn't always happen. There are blockages and dams, and sometimes only partial feeds reach your local server. Ultimately, your service provider subscribes to a feed from another source; if that incoming feed is incomplete, yours will be, too. The only "fix" to this is to complain to your service provider and pressure them to add a new newsfeed from another source. (For example, newsfeeds provided to service providers from MCI are known for being quite complete, whereas those from Sprint are notoriously incomplete.)

Why does this group have few or no posts anymore?

If a well-trafficked group that you've been reading suddenly starts to plummet in activity, I'd suspect a newsfeed problem with your provider. Perhaps the service feeding your provider decided to cut that newsgroup from their feed, for instance.

Other newsgroups are simply low-traffic by nature; there are quite a few newsgroups, especially in the alt.* hierarchy, that are either "joke" creations or that simply appeal to an extremely limited audience.

What is the best way to practice posting?

Given how many people read Usenet, if you've never made a post before, you might want to be sure that you know how before you attempt it. Not only do you risk making a major public faux pas otherwise, but you also want to be sure that your message reaches the intended audience. In other cases, you may have plenty of Usenet experience but want to test new newsreading software to be sure you know how to post with it.

Although it is not uncommon to see messages posted in newsgroups with subject lines such as "TEST – ignore" or "Please ignore," that is not the correct way to test your posting capabilities. There are several global groups in which you can post test messages; for example, try alt.test and misc.test. Note that if you post to one of these newsgroups, you may receive a flood of e-mail messages from automated news servers, notifying you that your message was successfully received.

You can also test to a local or university test newsgroup, such as ny.test, tor.test, or cornell.test. If you do this, you won't receive a flood of e-mail from servers around the world, but if you reread the newsgroup a few minutes later, you should see whether your post appeared.

When I reply by e-mail, the other party never receives it.

To successfully reply to a poster via e-mail, your newsreader has to be properly configured for sending e-mail. Normally, this is done by at least choosing an e-mail server, known in technospeak as an SMTP server—the sort of machine which can send e-mail.

For example, in Agent or Free Agent for the PC, you would configure this setting by choosing **Options**, **Preferences** and then the **System** folder tab. Which machine should you choose as your e-mail server? Your best bet is the same one you've chosen in your e-mail program. Your Internet provider should have supplied you with the name of your SMTP server; it is often something like mail.*yourprovider*.com.

Assuming you've set the e-mail server properly, don't forget to fill in your name and return e-mail address in the newsreader's other settings. This was covered briefly in an earlier question about changing your personal name in Usenet posts.

People tell me to read some group "such.and.such," but it doesn't seem to exist.

Again, this is most likely a newsfeed-related problem. Besides the fact that not all newsfeeds provide all the available posts, many do not provide all available newsgroups. If you are interested in a newsgroup that doesn't seem to be carried by your provider, ask them to add it. Often, they will do this upon request.

Note, though, that if your provider adds a new newsgroup, it may take several days to fill up with traffic.

How do I view posted pictures, sounds, and movies?

This question opens up quite the can of worms. Usenet was not originally designed to exchange binary data, which by its nature is 8-bit. Plain text data, such as messages from one human to another, are 7-bit, and so is the nature of Usenet. Nonetheless, people have tried to devise ways to exchange binary data over this medium because it is a convenient way of exchanging files publicly.

The most common method of posting binary files to Usenet is known as Uuencoding. Uuencode is essentially a program that converts 8-bit data into 7-bit data for transport purposes. Once you retrieve this 7-bit data, it must be converted back to 8-bit data before it will be usable for its intended purpose (video, sound, and so on).

Furthermore, because binary files tend to be of large size, they are often split into several smaller sections before they are posted. That is why you will often see binary files posted with subject lines such as these:

```
homer.wav  (1/3)
homer.wav  (2/3)
homer.wav  (3/3)
```

Thus another step is added into the decoding process: each of the parts must be retrieved, combined, and then decoded back to 8-bit data. Whew! Over the years, newsreaders have grown increasingly intelligent about automating this entire process. The newest newsreaders such as Free Agent and Agent make life easy as pie. You simply select any section of the posted file, and it finds all of them, retrieves them in order, and then decodes them. You need to select **File**, **Decode Binary Attachment** after high-lighting the binary messages you want to download.

Other popular newsreaders have similar capabilities, and it is recommended that you use the latest versions of your newsreading software, such as the Agent siblings, News Xpress, and so forth. Netscape Navigator 2.0 includes a built-in newsreader that auto-matically decodes single-part binary files. However, it doesn't do such a good job with multipart binary postings, and so the above-named newsreaders are recommended if you plan to work with many binary posts in Usenet.

How do I post my own binary files?

Of course, the concepts described in the previous Quick Fix hold true in this scenario, too—they're just reversed. The same newsreaders are also capable of taking a specified binary file, chopping it into slices, encoding it, and then posting it. For example, you can configure how Agent manages this task by choosing the **Options**, **Preferences** com-mand and clicking the **Attachments** folder tab. The Preferences dialog box shown here contains options with which Agent can convert a binary file suitable for posting.

In the first half of the window, you select whether Agent should post the whole file in one large piece or chop it up into several pieces. Because some news servers will reject files larger than a certain size, you should slice files into 900-line segments. To do so, enable the **Send attachment as multiple messages** option and enter **900** in the **Lines per Message** box.

The bottom half of the settings window deals with any text you may want to include as a preface to the file (such as "This file is an MPG format video of my dog Scrappy in a compromising position"). If you select the option labeled "Send text as a preface message (0/N)," Agent will post a message numbered part 0 (which contains only the text) before the post(s) containing the Uuencoded binary file. If you choose the second option, Agent will include the text at the beginning of the first part of the binary file post. The second option is inconvenient because the user must download at least one whole chunk of the file just to read your description. The third option here tells Agent not to include any preface text at all.

Chop file or keep whole

Preface message text

Again, other newsreaders will have similar configuration capabilities. When you choose to compose a new Usenet post, there will be an Attach file option, which lets you select the particular file to post.

Someone is flaming me. What should I do?

A flame in Usenet is much like a flame in e-mail: a rude, often coarse, derogatory message directed at someone, either for his statements or beliefs. The best strategies for handling flames are those same strategies that work best in the playground: ignore them.

If you cannot ignore them or you feel that the flames are damaging to you in a public sphere, publicly ask the flamer to stop. If he does not, privately ask him the same. Remember to keep copies of all messages you send to him and those that he sends to you, in case future evidence is needed. Finally, if none of this quiets the storm, send a message to his or her service provider using the address postmaster@*isp*.com and report the person's behavior.

The last recourse you want to take is to flame back and become involved in a flame war. Besides wasting your time, it is also a waste of network traffic and is extremely tedious for everyone else to wade through.

Basic UNIX Account Snarls

Many Internet users also (or only) have text-based UNIX accounts, through which they use a command prompt to access e-mail, Usenet, and so forth. UNIX is actually an extremely complex environment (the manuals consist of dozens of volumes), but the basic user needs only to learn how to manage a tiny subset of UNIX's esoteric commands to lead a happy Net life.

The text on my screen is totally misaligned/jumbled.

This is because of a terminal emulation problem. For the purpose of formatting text on the screen and mapping the keyboard, UNIX relies on a *terminal*. There are many possible terminals UNIX can use, and they have names such as Heath-19, VT100, VT200, and many more. Once upon a time, these were all actual hardware devices—keyboards with screens—that people used to connect to mainframe computers. Nowadays, your PC acts as the terminal, and the software you use to connect to and use your UNIX account (a terminal program) has the capability to emulate some of these terminals.

Your terminal program software must be set to emulate the same terminal that your UNIX account thinks it is running on. In the great majority of cases, the preferred terminal is VT100. Your UNIX account probably assumes this by default. You can check what terminal your UNIX account is assuming by entering the following command at your UNIX account prompt:

```
echo $term
```

Most likely, it will report `vt100`. Your next step is to check your terminal software to see which emulation it is using. Be sure to set it to the same emulation that the above echo command reports, such as `vt100`. You may then need to exit your account and reconnect for the changes to take effect.

I want to use the arrow keys to see a command history.

In some UNIX command lines (aka *shells*), you can use the up and down arrow keys to scroll through a history of commands you've already entered. This makes life easier, especially if you recently typed a long command and need to run it again.

A shell is the command line in which you enter commands. In fact, there are a variety of shells that a UNIX account might use, and each sports its own special conveniences. Shells often have names such as csh, tcsh, ksh, and bash. All of those except csh support command histories as described here. Unfortunately, many UNIX accounts are created by default to use the csh shell—which does not support the arrow keys. To see which shell you are using, enter the following command at your UNIX prompt:

```
echo $SHELL
```

It might report the shell as a path name, such as /bin/csh. All you care about is the rightmost part, which is the shell name—in this case, csh. On most systems, you can change your login shell by entering the command **chsh** and selecting a new shell. On a few systems, the chsh command has been disabled for security reasons. If you run into that, e-mail your system administrator and request a different login shell such as tcsh. Make sure you get one that allows you to use command histories with the arrow keys.

I changed my password, and now it doesn't seem to work.

Changing your password is certainly a vital matter—and not being able to log back in is downright frightening! Your password may no longer work for one of two reasons.

- You're not entering the new password correctly. This sounds silly and obvious, but be sure that you are, in fact, entering the password exactly as you did when you just changed it.

- The password database has not been updated yet. Sometimes a password change does not take effect immediately. Some systems may take several minutes to distribute the new password information within the system. In these cases, you may still be able to use your old password, or you may just need to wait 5–10 minutes.

How much disk space am I eating up?

Many service providers have a restriction on the amount of disk space that your account can use. If you hog up space beyond that, they may charge you extra fees. Some quota-tracking systems keep a close eye on you and prevent you from surpassing the quota. Other systems only check your account periodically and tally up how far you've exceeded your quota.

To determine how corpulent your account has grown, first try the **quota** command at the UNIX shell prompt. On some systems, this will reveal how much space you are taking, and how much space you have left. If that command does not work on your system, this one will:

```
du -s ~userid
```

Replace *userid* with your actual login ID, but don't overlook the tilde (~) mark, which is necessary. This command will report the size of your account in kilobytes, such as 2,150. 2,150 kilobytes is about 2 megs (there are 1,024 kilobytes in 1 megabyte). If your provider has told you that your limit is 5 megs, you have about 3 megs of space left.

I've suspended a program and can't get back into it.

UNIX can run multiple programs simultaneously, but you have only one window in your account. If you are, say, running TIN to read news but would like to check your e-mail, you needn't quit TIN outright. You can simply "suspend" it in the background, run your e-mail program, and then return to TIN. You suspend a program in UNIX by pressing Ctrl+Z.

To return to a suspended program, simply type the **fg** ("foreground") command at your UNIX shell prompt . That will bring the suspended application back to your screen.

I cannot figure out how to quit this program I've run.

You've found yourself in a strange UNIX program and cannot quit. The typical keys (such as "Q") don't seem to help. You're trapped! Maybe. But one of these three recommendations might work.

- Try **Ctrl+D**, which can be used to quit some UNIX programs.

- Attempt to find some online help for the program, perhaps by pressing **H** or **Shift+H**. You may find a clue there.

- A more brutal solution is to suspend the program in question, and then once you're back at the shell prompt, to kill the program. To do this, first suspend the program with **Ctrl+Z**. Then, at the shell prompt, type **ps**. This will produce a list of current "processes" that you are running, each of which has its own ID, such as:

```
PID    TT STAT   TIME COMMAND
21535  p1 S      0:00 -tcsh (tcsh)
21545  p1 T      0:03 tin
21547  p1 R      0:00 ps
```

In this example, we suspended the program TIN, which you can see has a process ID ("PID") of 21545. The semibrutal way to quit TIN is to kill its process using the following command:

```
kill -9 21545
```

Shortly thereafter you will receive the message

```
[1]    Killed                tin
```

Finally, if none of these methods manages to exterminate your problem program, you can just abruptly disconnect from your account, by manually powering off your modem, for example, or by choosing the hang up option from your terminal program software. Wait a few minutes before reconnecting; your UNIX account will likely figure out that you were wiped out, and it'll kill your leftover processes. Even if it fails to kill them, when you log back in, you'll be at a shell prompt, and you can use the **ps** command to kill them.

My witty .plan file is not being seen by people who finger me.

If you have a UNIX account, people around the world may be able to *finger* you to learn more about you. Many users create what is known as a "plan" file: a text file that contains information about you that you want others to see when they finger your UNIX account.

Creating a plan file is simple. You create a file named **.plan** (note the preceeding decimal point) and include any text information you want. The problem many people run into, though, is that when people finger them they don't get the plan file.

When you create the .plan file, it is viewable by you only—not the outside world. Why? Every file in UNIX has *permissions* that define who can access it. If you're facing this problem, you need to change the permission for your file to make it "readable" to others. So, after you've created your .plan file, type this command:

```
chmod 775 .plan
```

That enables anyone who fingers you to see your plan—and after all, isn't that the whole point?

I want my own signature for e-mail and Usenet news.

Creating a signature—a bit of text that appears at the end of every e-mail message or Usenet post you send—is quite simple. Just as with the plan, simply create a file named **.signature** and enter whatever text you like.

Creating a new text file in UNIX is also relatively easy. Of the many text editors in UNIX, one of the most common and popular is called Pico. So, to create a .signature file, type this command (be sure to use lowercase):

```
pico .signature
```

Then type out your text. Pico provides a small guide to its functions at the bottom of the screen (see the following figure). As you can see, you can press Ctrl+X to exit and save the file.

The files that I ftp to my UNIX account wind up corrupted.

There are two common FTP programs available in many UNIX accounts: standard FTP and NcFTP. The latter is preferred because it is quite easy for a new user to use, and it automatically takes care of little details that might be overlooked otherwise. To see if your UNIX account has NcFTP available, simply type **ncftp** at the UNIX shell prompt. If that doesn't yield anything, you'll have to use the standard UNIX FTP program, simply called FTP, which is what you type to launch it.

The most common reason ftp'd files become corrupted is that the user makes an ASCII mode text transfer when he or she needs to make a binary mode transfer. You can prevent this from happening to you. After you connect to the FTP site but before you begin a transfer, type the FTP command **asc** to use ASCII mode, or type the command **bin** to use binary mode. The majority of files you will be transferring are binary, including all graphics, sounds, and compressed archives (such as .ZIP files). So you will use the **bin** command in the FTP program before beginning most transfers. Note that NcFTP defaults to bin mode when launched, saving you from needing to remember this step. However, the standard FTP program defaults to ASCII transfer mode, unfortunately.

Some user keeps causing messages to pop up on my screen.

There are two invasive ways for another user to attempt to grab your attention. One is to send you a talk request with the command **talk *you@your.provider*.com**. The other is with the write command, which allows a user on your same service provider to pop messages onto your screen.

If you'd like to be left alone from such intrusions, enter the following command at your shell prompt:

```
mesg n
```

You may want to add this command at the bottom of the file named .cshrc in your account, which contains all the commands to execute automatically upon login. Note, though, that refusing messages (which is what **mesg n** does) refuses both talk requests and write messages. To re-enable message accepting, use **mesg y**.

FTP Hangups

How do I log in using anonymous FTP?

Anonymous FTP is a phrase that pops up repeatedly in Internet circles (and books, articles, and posts). FTP, or File Transfer Protocol, is a common method for transferring files from one computer on the Internet to another. For authorization purposes, passwords are implemented to control who can access the files on each computer.

Anonymous FTP is used for public archives: file storage that may be accessed by anyone in the public. To access such archives, you connect to the site and log in with the user ID **anonymous**, and at the password prompt, you enter your e-mail address. For example, if someone told you to ftp some files from ftp.site.com via anonymous FTP, you would do the following (the parts in bold text are what you would type):

```
ftp> open ftp.gated.cornell.edu
Connected to GATED.CORNELL.EDU.
220 comet.cit.cornell.edu FTP server Wed Jun 7 17:22:02
995) ready.
Name: anonymous
331 Guest login ok, send your complete e-mail address
Password: dog@woof.woof.com
230-Please read the file README
230-  it was last modified on Fri Jan 26 09:52:01 1996
230 Guest login ok, access restrictions apply.
```

The estimated time of transfer is inaccurate.

Some FTP programs, such as NcFTP, attempt to estimate how long the transfer will take. When looking at file transfer time estimates—FTP or anywhere else—take them with several grains of salt. An estimated time of transfer necessarily assumes consistent transfer speed. This rarely happens, especially when using FTP. Network traffic and bottlenecks anywhere between you and the remote computer can alter the speed of the transfer. So these time estimates are quite like their brethren in the auto repair world: *estimates*.

Can I salvage an interrupted transfer?

Recall that in the UNIX account scenario, downloading a file from the Internet to your PC is a two-step process. First, you must retrieve the file into your UNIX account, using a method such as FTP. Then you must download the file from UNIX to your PC, using a method such as Zmodem. For this question, we are considering the first step only: retrieving the file from the Internet to your UNIX account.

Although you can retrieve files to your account with FTP, Gopher, or the World Wide Web (with the program Lynx, for instance), none of these commonly support *resumed transfers*. Resuming transfer is the capability to start a transfer at some mid-way point, picking up where a previously interrupted transfer left off. It's a very convenient feature, but it has not yet been implemented widely enough to be feasible.

Therefore, the short answer is "no." You basically cannot salvage an interrupted transfer from the Internet to your UNIX account. The only real solution is to simply transfer the file again from scratch.

But my FTP program has a "resume transfer" option. Why doesn't it work?

The truth is that FTP *can* support resuming transfers. Some FTP programs have implemented support for the reget command, which is the FTP command that can be used to resume a transfer. However, both the FTP program *and* the FTP server must support reget for it to work, and very few FTP servers do.

Because few FTP servers and FTP programs support reget, it is not a very commonly available feature. So even if your FTP program does support resume transfer, it'll work only if you've connected to one of the FTP servers that support it.

I'm trying to access my UNIX account at ftp.*myprovider*.com, but it denies me access.

This is a common error users make. Let's say that your UNIX account is on the *provider*.com machine. You want to FTP some files from your UNIX account to some other machine. Naturally, you attempt to connect to **ftp.*provider*.com**, but when you log in with your account user ID and password, access is denied. Why?

Because ftp.*provider*.com is probably not the machine you need to be connecting to. That is your provider's "public" FTP server, meant to serve files for public availability. Your UNIX account resides on *provider*.com, so you, in fact, want to open your FTP connection to *provider*.com. Then your user id and password will work, and you'll have access to the contents of your account.

Downloading Difficulties

My download was interrupted partway through!

Recall the doom and gloom in the two earlier problems about resume transfer? Now you are considering the second step of the UNIX two-step: transferring the file from your UNIX account to your PC. In this case, you have the benefit of the magical Zmodem.

Zmodem fully supports resuming transfers, but it calls the process *crash recovery*—different words, same meaning. Be sure that you have Zmodem crash recovery enabled; check the Zmodem settings in your particular terminal program.

Assuming that it is enabled, if a Zmodem download dies partway through, you can simply begin the download again. Zmodem will automatically recognize that a portion of the file has already been downloaded, and it will pick up from where it left off. Nice!

I try to download the file, but nothing seems to happen.

Now you run into some of Zmodem's other settings. Not all terminal programs allow you to configure all possible Zmodem settings, but we'll assume that yours does.

In many terminal programs, you can determine exactly how crash recovery will behave. For instance, if you attempt to download a file that already exists on your PC, Zmodem can compare the two files. Suppose that both have the same time and date—which they would if you were attempting to resume a file transfer that was previously interrupted. Upon realizing this, Zmodem can begin crash recovery, start over from scratch for that file, or skip transferring that file altogether. Your terminal may allow you to select these behaviors from its Zmodem configuration screen, but this varies from product to product.

If you attempt to Zmodem download a file and nothing happens, the problem might be that you already have a file with the same name in your download path on your PC. Your terminal program is probably configured to skip transfers instead of resuming or overwriting them. This is one of those "easily forgotten" settings.

Strange text started spewing all over my screen.

Ugh! The transfer seemed to be motoring along just fine, and then suddenly the progress window disappeared and illegible goop started being output to the screen. This is a Zmodem transfer problem that happens from time to time when the connection between you and your provider burps.

There isn't any notable way to prevent this from occurring. After it does, the file is no longer being properly transferred, so you can simply hang up the modem. Wait a few minutes and reconnect to your UNIX account, and then you should be able to resume the transfer with Zmodem.

Why do some files download much faster than others?

Your terminal program probably displays a progress window while a transfer is in progress. The following figure shows a transfer progress meter from HyperTerminal, the terminal program included with Windows 95.

Speed of transfer is often measured in "characters per second" (cps) or "bytes per second" (bps), which mean the same thing. If, for example, you have a 14.4kbps modem, you may have noticed that many files download at around 1600–1650cps. Owners of 28.8kbps modems will generally achieve twice that speed.

However, some files seem to transfer much faster—at perhaps 3000cps on a 14.4 modem or 5000cps on a 28.8 modem. What's going on? Compression. Your modem always attempts to compress the data that is being transferred. Doing so cuts down the amount of data to transfer and the transfer time, and results in a faster perceived transfer rate.

Many binary file types, such as .ZIP files, are already compressed. Thus, your modem can do no more to help them, and you see the typical speeds of 1650cps. Other files that are not compressed (such as ASCII text files) benefit from your modem's built-in compression, and they appear to transfer much faster.

In the end, it makes little difference where the compression takes place. If you compressed the text file in UNIX before transferring it, the cps rate would drop back to 1650, but the file would be a smaller size. After the smoke is cleared, the total amount of time it takes to download the file is no different whether it was compressed before transfer or during.

I downloaded a text file to my PC, and it looks messed up.

The ASCII versus binary mix-up claims another victim. Don't be a statistic!

The reason the file appears all screwy is that it has improper end-of-line (EOL) markers. These are special characters that tell the computer where the end of a line of text is. The classic problem is that UNIX uses a different EOL than does MS-DOS/Windows. There are two feasible solutions to this:

- When downloading a file from UNIX to your PC, you are most likely using Zmodem, with the UNIX sz command. In this case, if you are going to transfer a plain text (ASCII) file, use the sz -a command instead; that will automatically convert the UNIX EOLs into PC-compatible EOLs.

- If you've already downloaded the file with improper EOLs, all is not lost. There are many tiny utilities available for the PC that can convert the file into correct form for you. All are available at major PC archive sites, such as http://www.winsite.com. One I especially recommend is the shareware product UltraEdit, also available at any major site for Windows software. UltraEdit is a versatile text editor that includes a built-in option for converting EOLs from UNIX to PC and vice versa.

The program I downloaded to my PC claims to be corrupted.

Suppose you ftp'd a file that was not corrupted to your UNIX account, but you were told that it was corrupted when you attempted to download the file to your PC. Where is the culprit in this scenario?

First, you have to consider whether this is, in fact, true. If you mistakenly ftp'd a binary file in ASCII mode, for instance, it has been corrupted already. But if you did not make this error, what might corrupt a perfectly good file on its way from your UNIX account to your PC?

In my experience, the most common answer to this question, strangely enough is "nothing." That is, I almost bet that if you investigate, you will find that the file was, in fact, corrupted in its original location. That is, the file you ftp'd was *already* corrupted before you even came around. Of course, this means there is nothing you can do about it, except perhaps notify the administrator of the site from which you ftp'd the file.

If you find that's not the case, though, be sure that you are using a robust transfer protocol between your UNIX account and your PC. By far, the recommended choice is Zmodem, which any good terminal program supports. The sz *filenames* command is used in UNIX to initiate a Zmodem download. A protocol such as Zmodem will not corrupt your files, but you should use **sz -a** *filenames* if you're downloading an ASCII text file.

Miscellaneous Lukewarm Leftover Grumbles

My ISP does not offer an IRC server. How can I connect?

The many available public IRC servers should more than fulfill your global chatting needs. However, because the list changes often, listing particular servers here would be fruitless. Instead, I can recommend some reliable sources for current information on public IRC servers:

- On Usenet, check the newsgroup alt.irc. It contains periodic posts of public servers, or you can post a request.

- On the World Wide Web, go to the Yahoo catalog (**http://www.yahoo.com**). Enter **IRC** in the search box, and it will bring up a list of IRC-related Web sites, some of which contain lists of public servers. Even these Web sites change, which is why they are not listed here. This method will definitley lead you to a list though.

When choosing a public IRC server, try your best to use one as geographically close to you as possible. Not only will it reduce network traffic for everyone, but you will get speedier response times as well.

While I was on IRC, somebody asked me to DCC a file. What is that?

DCC is a form of file transfer for use within the IRC public chat system. Using DCC, users can exchange files with one another. It is quite simple to use; recall that all IRC commands begin with a slash (/).

In your IRC program, to send a file to someone via DCC, enter this command:

```
/dcc send theirnick fullfilename
```

For example, to send the file beagle.jpg to the IRC user whose nickname is harry, you would type the following:

```
/dcc send harry c:\pix\beagle.jpg
```

If someone attempts to DCC a file to you, your IRC program will notify you. Some IRC programs will automatically accept the file and begin receiving it. If yours does not, simply use the command **/dcc get *theirnick***. You can enter the command **/dcc** without any other parameters to see the current progress of the transfer.

Do those "Internet telephone" programs really work?

Admittedly, the answer to this question is not a Quick Fix, but the question is asked often. Internet telephony has become a hot market in the past year, as several products are competing for your voice (Internet Phone, WebPhone, and DigiPhone to name a few). The main attraction of these products is that you can speak to anyone on the Internet, anywhere in the world, without having to place a traditional long-distance phone call.

But are they as good as a real phone call? Not really—at least at this point in time. It takes a great deal of compression technology to push your voice through a typical 14.4 or 28.8kbps modem. In addition, the Internet is a vast network of shared pathways, wherein data cannot travel at a consistent speed from point A to point B. The result of these factors is that Internet telephone programs tend to produce speech that is slightly fuzzy and noticeably choppy.

Certainly, the closer the two speaking parties are to one another on the Internet, the more fluidly these programs will work (that is, if both users are on the same service provider, speech will work far better than if one is in New York and the other in Melbourne or even Los Angeles). All is not lost forever, though. As home connections speed up and the Internet itself becomes more robust, these sorts of "telephones" will become much more feasible to use.

This is costing me. How can I keep track of my online time?

This is an important consideration for many Internet users who are charged by the hour. Most terminal programs have built-in online time displays, which are often located on a status line like the one shown in the following figure.

The status line shows how long you've been connected. →

However, this is of no help to SLIP/PPP users, who don't use a terminal program. Fortunately, Windows 95 provided a built-in solution for those who use its Dial-Up Networking. After your connection is established, a small window (shown in the next figure) displays the connection speed and online duration. This window remains on the screen unless you choose to minimize it to the taskbar.

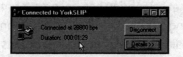

My connection disconnects if I am idle for too long.

To prevent users from leaving their modems connected and hogging up the modem resources, some service providers institute an idle-time rule. If you remain connected but don't engage in any activity for longer than, say, 30 minutes, you are automatically disconnected. While this is a reasonable practice, it may be a problem under certain circumstances, such as if you are awaiting an important e-mail message or chat request. As you might expect, there are ways around it.

One little utility program written to work around this idle time disconnect is called Keep Alive. You can find Keep Alive at many major software sites, such as Winsite (http://www.winsite.com) or Stroud's Consummate Winsock Apps (http://www.cwsapps.com). Keep Alive simply sends a bit of data (known as a *ping*) every so often to keep your connection from being completely idle.

PART 4

Handy Reference

I n this final part of the book, you'll find a handy reference section of items to help you use the Internet. For example, if you need help looking for an IRC chat server to access Internet chat, turn to "IRC Chat Servers" on page 489. You'll also find tables in this part of the book that list Internet service providers and their phone numbers, the top World Wide Web pages to view, famous Internet addresses, and more.

You can use this reference section when you need to look up a particular item, or when you need to find out what a specific Internet emoticon means.

Service Providers

The first step to accessing the Internet is finding a connection. Unless you're directly connected, you'll need to use a service provider for Internet access. There are thousands of companies across the country that will sell you access to the information superhighway using their own Internet connections—for a small fee, of course. Look in computer magazines and your local yellow pages for a service provider near you.

To help you begin, the following list displays the names of a few vendors you can contact for more information about Internet accounts. Many of them also offer local access numbers you can use to connect to the Internet so you won't have to pay long-distance charges.

Service Provider	Phone Number
ANS	313-663-2482
Arrownet	517-371-7100
BBN Planet Corporation	800-472-4565
CICNet, Inc.	313-998-6104
Delphi	800-695-4005
free.org	715-743-1700
Greenlake Communications	810-540-9380
HoloNet	510-704-0160
Hypercon	800-652-2590
ICNet	313-998-0090
IDS World Network	401-885-6855
Imagine Communications Corp.	800-542-4499
Institute for Global Communications	415-442-0220
Internet Access Houston	713-526-3425
IPSnet	407-426-8782
LogicalNET Corporation	518-452-9090
MV Communications, Inc.	603-429-2223
netILLINOIS	708-866-1825
NetManage	408-973-7171
Northwest Internet Services, Inc.	503-342-8322
NovaLink Interactive Networks	800-274-2814
NTC's Earthlink.net	800-359-8425
PANIX	718-865-3768

Service Provider	Phone Number
Portal Information Network	408-973-9111
PSInet	703-620-6651
Questar Microsystems, Inc.	800-925-2140
The Well	415-332-4335
The World	617-739-0202
Traders Connection	800-753-4223
Village Group	800-225-0750

IRC Chat Servers

In order to use IRC chat, you must first log onto an IRC chat server. IRC servers are connected to form a network that allows various users from all over the world to log on and carry on conversations. There are several IRC networks you can connect to, as well as a variety of servers. The following list includes chat servers from different IRC networks. Keep in mind that not all servers will accept everyone who tries to log on. Sometimes there are restrictions, such as number of users or specific domains that are allowed to connect.

IRC Chat Servers in the U.S.	
irc.escape.com	irc-2.mit.edu
irc.texas.net	anarchy.tamu.edu
irc-2.texas.net	eff.org
irc.colorado.edu	irc.cerf.net
irc.ilstu.edu	irc.gate.net
irc.iastate.edu	irc.catt.ncsu.edu
irc.harvard.edu	irc.eskimo.com
droopy.colorado.edu	bazooka.rutgers.edu
cs-pub.bu.edu	azure.acsu.buffalo.edu
backer1.u.washington.edu	dewey.cc.utexas.edu
irc.ecn.uoknor.edu	irc.digex.net
irc.cs.rpi.edu	irc.caltech.edu
irc.bridge.net	irc.apk.net
irc.indiana.edu	irc.ksu.edu

(continues)

(continued)

IRC Chat Servers in the U.S.	
copper.ucs.indiana.edu	irc.uiuc.edu
irc.ecn.bgu.edu	t8.mscf.uky.edu
world.std.com	pegasus.ccs.itd.umich.edu
irc.ucsd.edu	irc.ucdavis.edu
B-w6yx.stanford.edu	w6yx.stanford.edu
harp.aix.calpoly.edu	irc.netcom.com
irc.primenet.com	irc.HACKS.Arizona.EDU
merlin.acf-lab.alaska.edu	irc.tc.umn.edu
sluaxa.slu.edu	hertz.njit.edu
irc.rutgers.edu	organ.ctr.columbia.edu
red-dwarf.cit.cornell.edu	alfred1.u.washington.edu
irc02.irc.aol.com	poe.acc.Virginia.EDU
irc.math.byu.edu	acme.etsu.edu
irc.pitt.edu	chestnut.chem.upenn.edu
mcnet02.med.nyu.edu	norman.ok.us.undernet.org
austin.tx.us.undernet.org	davis.ca.us.undernet.org
milwaukee.wi.us.undernet.org	boston.ma.us.undernet.org
manhattan.ks.us.undernet.org	washington.dc.us.undernet.org
sanjose.ca.us.undernet.org	stgeorge.ut.us.undernet.org
rochester.mi.us.undernet.org	tampa.fl.us.undernet.org
jive.rahul.net	irc.ucdavis.edu
groucho.sonoma.edu	blackstone-36.rh.uchicago.edu
moe.bu.edu	irc-gw.xgw.fi
unccsun.uncc.edu	ca.us.iao.net
de.eu.iao.net	tn.us.iao.net
fl.us.iao.net	mi.us.iao.net
ny.us.iao.net	va.sura.ideal.net
tx.sprint.ideal.net	nd.nw.ideal.net
il.ans.ideal.net	ca.barr.ideal.net
ny.sprint.ideal.net	ca2.barr.ideal.net
ny2.sprint.ideal.net	tn.surs.ideal.net
nasa.ideal.net	tn2.sura.ideal.net

IRC Chat Servers Outside the U.S.	
United Kingdom	coanwood.ncl.ac.uk
	stork.doc.ic.ac.uk
	dismayl.demon.co.uk
	serv.cs.man.ac.uk
	serv.eng.abdn.ac.uk
	sun4.bham.ac.uk
	supercomputer.swan.ac.uk
	fennel.compnews.co.uk
Australia	skylark.qabc.uq.oz.au
	troll.elec.uow.edu.au
	yoyo.cc.monash.edu.au
	edna.cc.swin.edu.au
	irchat.utas.edu.au
	ircserver.cltr.uq.oz.au
	notjules.itd.uts.edu.au
	yamabico.cs.uow.edu.au
Canada	aahz.magic.mb.ca
	cythera.unb.ca
	elk.nstn.ca
	services.ca
	sifon.cc.mcgill.ca
	irc.cs.mun.ca
	irc.pangea.ca
	irc.polymtl.ca
	irc.unb.ca
	irc.yorku.ca
Austria	irc.studorg.tuwien.ac.at
	irc.wu-wien.ac.at
	uni-linz.ac.at
	itc.univie.ac.at
Belgium	irc.belnet.be
	othello.ulb.ac.be
	is1.bfu.vub.ac.be
Finland	irc.nokia.com
	ircd.funet.fi
	mato.funet.fi
	irc.cs.hut.fi
France	Eurecom8.Cica.FR
	irc.enst.fr
	irc.univ-lyon1.fr
	irc.labri.u-bordeaux.fr

(continues)

(continued)

IRC Chat Servers Outside the U.S.	
Germany	uni-stuttgart.de
	uni-karlsruhe.de
	fu-berlin.de
	Uni-KL.de
Hungary	irc.bme.hu
	darmol.elte.hu
	irc.sch.bme.hu
Iceland	isgate.is
Israel	irc.tau.ac.il
	irc.biu.ac.il
	irc.technion.ac.il
Italy	irc.cdc.polimi.it
	irc.ccii.unipi.it
Japan	endo.wide.ad.jp
	dec504.aist-nara.ac.jp
	irc.ube-c.ac.jp
	scslwide.sony.co.jp
Mexico	hp9k.lag.itesm.mx
	next00.mty.itesm.mx
	mexico.sprint.ideal.net
Norway	icr.hitos.no
	irc.pvv.unit.no
	irc.uib.no
	irc.ifi.uio.no
Poland	irc.lublin.pl
	irc.agh.edu.pl
	irc.put.poznan.pl
Spain	krilin.upc.es
	scott.uab.es
Sweden	irc.dd.chalmers.se
	irc.ludd.luth.se
	irc.nada.kth.se
Switzerland	irc.ethz.ch
Taiwan	irc.csie.nctu.edu.tw
	irc.ntu.edu.tw
	irc.seed.net.tw
The Netherlands	irc.nijenrode.nl
	irc.xs4all.nl
	irc.sci.kun.nl

Internet Emoticons and Acronyms

Emoticons, or smileys, are symbols used in Internet communications to express emotions or convey facial expressions. Emoticons are often used on the IRC chat channels, in newsgroup messages, and in Internet e-mail. Emoticons are created using symbols on your keyboard keys. For example, a simple smiley :) consists of a colon and a right parenthesis. To read an emoticon, tilt your head to the left. The following table shows emoticons you can use in your own Internet messages.

Emoticons	
Emoticon	*Meaning*
:)	a smile, happy
:-)	a smiley with a nose (nose dash is optional for any smiley symbol)
;)	a wink
:(	a frown
:-<	really sad
:->	devious smile
>:-(	mad or annoyed
:-c	bummed out, pouting
:-I	grim
:-/	skeptical
:-o	shouting
:-O	shouting loudly
:-D	laughing
:-p	sticking out tongue
:-&	tongue-tied
:-*	puckering for a kiss
:-x	my lips are sealed
I-o	yawning
I^o	snoring
I-I	asleep
X-(	dead
:*)	drunk

(continues)

Emoticon	Meaning
#-(	hung over
:-()	big mouth
:-)~~~	drooling
:~(	crying
8-)	wearing glasses
B-)	wearing cool shades
%-)	I've been staring at this screen too long
:-()	I have a mustache
{(:-)	wearing a toupée
=l:-)	wearing a top hat
*<:-()	Santa Claus
C=:-)	a chef
0:-)	an angel
xxooxxoo	love, or hugs and kisses
@>--,--'--	a rose
<g>	grin

In addition to emoticons, Internet communications include acronyms and abbreviations that work like online shorthand. They're used to speed up typing time, and you'll find them sprinkled throughout Internet e-mail, newsgroups, and chat channels. They can be used with all capital letters or all lowercase letters.

Acronyms

Acronym	Meaning
AAMOF	as a matter of fact
AFAIK	as far as I know
AKA	also known as
AOL	America Online
AFK	away from keyboard
BAK	back at keyboard
BBS	bulletin board system
BBL	be back later
BIF	basis in fact

Acronym	Meaning
BRB	be right back
BTW	by the way
CIS	CompuServe Information Service
CU	see you
CUL	see you later
DIIK	darned if I know
DL	download
FAQ	frequently asked question
FOAF	friend of a friend
FOTCL	falling off the chair laughing
FWIW	for what it's worth
FTF	face to face
FYA	for your amusement
FYI	for your information
GMTA	great minds think alike
GR&D	grinning, running, and ducking
HHOJ	ha ha, only joking
HHOK	ha ha, only kidding
HHOS	ha ha, only serious
IAC	in any case
IAE	in any event
IANAL	I am not a lawyer
IMO	in my opinion
IMHO	in my humble opinion
IMNSHO	in my not-so-humble opinion
IMAO	in my arrogant opinion
IOW	in other words
LOL	laughing out loud
LOLSCOK	laughing out loud, spitting coffee on keyboard
LTNS	long time no see
LTNT	long time no type
L8R	later

(continues)

Acronyms *Continued*

Acronym	Meaning
MEGO	my eyes glaze over
MOTAS	member of the appropriate sex
MOTD	message of the day
MOTOS	member of the opposite sex
MOTSS	member of the same sex
NBIF	no basis in fact
NBD	no big deal
NRN	no response necessary
OIC	oh, I see
OTB	off to bed
OTOH	on the other hand
OTW	on the way
PITA	pain in the a**
PMJI	pardon my jumping in
PC	politically correct, or personal computer
PI or PIC	politically incorrect
POV	point of view
RL	real life
ROFL	rolling on the floor laughing
ROFLOLPIMP	rolling on the floor, laughing out loud, peeing in my pants
RSN	real soon now
RTM	read the manual
RTFM	read the #*@!#@* manual
SIFOTCN	sitting in front of the computer naked
SITD	still in the dark
SO	significant other
SOS	same old stuff
SYSOP	system operator
TANSTAAFL	there ain't no such thing as a free lunch
TIA	thanks in advance
TIC	tongue in cheek
TM	trademark

Acronym	Meaning
TPTB	the powers that be
TTFN	ta-ta for now
TTYL	talk to you later
UL	upload
unPC	politically incorrect
WB	welcome back
WTG	way to go
WTH	what the heck (or h***)
YMMV	your mileage may vary

Common UNIX Commands

From time to time, your Internet journeys may take you to places that require you to use UNIX commands. Don't panic when faced with a UNIX prompt; just flip back to this table for some help. The following list of most-used UNIX commands can assist you.

Command	Function
Backspace	Backspaces on the command line
Ctrl+C	Cancels an operation
cd /directoryname	Changes to the designated directory
cd ..	Changes back to the previous directory
cd	Changes to the home directory
Ctrl+U	Clears the command line
cp oldname newname	Copies a file
cp oldname directoryname	Copies a file to another directory
rm filename	Deletes a file
ls -al	Lists everything in a directory, including hidden files
ls -l	Lists the contents of a directory
ls	Lists directory files
ls -x	Lists the contents of a directory in column format
Ctrl-d	Logs off

(continues)

(continued)

Command	Function
mv *filename directoryname*	Moves a file to the specified directory
cat *filename*	Reads a text file
more *filename*	Reads each page of a text file, page by page
mv *oldname newname*	Renames a file
r	Repeats a command
rm *filename*	Removes and deletes a file
cp *filename filename2*	Copies a file and gives it a new name
mkdir *directory*	Creates a new directory of your designation
finger *username*	Finds out basic information about another Internet user (only works while the person is logged onto the Internet)
grep *"text" filename*	Searches for specific text in a specified file

Interesting Internet Addresses

With the potential to send e-mail messages all over the globe, it's sometimes fun to target specific people and places. The following table lists some of the more interesting ways you can use e-mail on the Internet, as well as some very important people you can contact electronically.

Service/Person	Address/Details
To contact the President of the United States of America, use this address	**president@whitehouse.gov** and fill in your e-mail message
To contact the Vice President of the United States of America, use this address	**vice.president@whitehouse.gov** and fill in your e-mail message
To find your congressman's e-mail address, use this address to receive a list of all congressional e-mail addresses	**congress@hr.house.gov** and leave the subject line and message body blank
To find White House-related documents, use this address	**publications@whitehouse.gov**, leave the subject line blank, and type **help** in the message body
To have a WWW page sent to your electronic mailbox, try this address and procedure	**listproc@www0.cern.ch** and leave the subject line blank, but specify the page's URL in the message body (for example, **send http://www.netwave.net/wave_reviews/**)
To have David Letterman's latest Top Ten list e-mailed to you, use this address	**infobot@infomania.com** and type **topten** in the subject line

Service/Person	Address/Details
To look up word definitions, use this address	**infobot@infomania.com**, type **webster** and the word you're looking up, and leave the message body blank
E-mail yourself a word puzzle from the WordSmith wordserver at Case Western Reserve University	**wsmith@wordsmith.org**, type **rhyme-n-reason** in the subject line, and leave the message body blank
To subscribe to the WordSmith's A.Word.A. Day mailing list, use this address	**wsmith@wordsmith.org**, type **subscribe** *yourname* in the subject line, and leave the message body blank
For a quick quote from a famous person, contact the Almanac Information Server at this address	**almanac@oes.orst.edu**, leave the subject line blank, and type **send quote** in the message body
To find out how you can tap into the Movie Database Mail Server to look for movie information, use this address	**movie@ibmpcug.co.uk**, leave the subject line blank, and type **help** in the message body
To e-mail yourself recent stock quotes from QuoteCom, use this address	**services@quote.com**, type **help** in the subject line, and leave the message body blank
For a list of electronic magazines on the Net, use this address to get a copy of The Internet Press	**ipress-request@northcoast.com**, type **archive** in the subject line, and type **send ipress** in the message body
For a list of wacky weekly news stories, contact Randy Cassingham's weekly newsletter at this address	**listserv@netcom.com**, leave the subject line blank, and type **subscribe this-just-in** in the message body

FTP Servers

When searching for information and files on the Internet, you'll need to know some FTP servers to start out with. The table below lists 14 popular FTP sites that you can try. For each site listed, log on as an anonymous user and use your own e-mail address.

Site	FTP Address
University of Michigan's Electronic Texts Archive	etext.archive.umich.edu
Washington University's Archives	wuarchive.wustl.edu
Rutgers University's FTP Archives	quartz.rutgers.edu
The Bloom-Picayune FTP Server at MIT	rtfm.mit.edu
Library of Congress Archives	seq1.loc.gov

(continues)

(continued)

Site	FTP Address
UUNET Archives	ftp.uu.net
Princeton University's FTP Server	princeton.edu
University of Michigan's Software Archives	archive.umich.edu
The Typhoon FTP Server at Berkeley	ocf.berkeley.edu
Sunsite's FTP Server	sunsite.unc.edu
Netcom FTP Server	ftp.netcom.com
Mississippi State Archives	ra.msstate.edu
The Gatekeeper Archives	gatekeeper.dec.com
The Oak Software Repository	oak.oakland.edu

HTML Codes

If you want to build your own Web page, you'll need to know a few HTML codes. You'll find such codes and other HTML-related topics readily available on the Internet. (Use a search engine, as covered in "Search for Information on the Web" on page 180, to locate HTML-related topics.) This table lists some common HTML codes you can use.

Code Name	HTML Code	Function
Anchor code	<A>	Used to define a section of text as a hyperlink or target of another hyperlink
Blockquote	<blockquote>	Defines text as quoted material; often italicized or indented
Body	<BODY>	Defines the main part of the HTML page
Boldface	<B>	Makes text bold
Comment	<!—comment— >	Prevents text from appearing in browser display window; useful for author comments
Emphasis	<EM>	Makes text appear to be emphasized; usually in italics
Header	<HEAD>	Defines a title or header elements on a page
Headings	<H1> - <H6>	Causes text to appear separated from other text and in a different style
Horizontal Rule	<HR>	Creates a rule line that runs the length of the display window
HTML	<HTML>	Signifies an HTML page or document
Italics	<I>	Italicizes text

Code Name	HTML Code	Function
Line Break	 	Causes a line break in the text
List Item	<LI>	Displays the element as an ordered or unordered list
Unordered List	<UL>	Defines item as a bulleted item in an unordered list
Ordered List	<OL>	Defines item with a sequential number in an ordered list
Paragraph	<P>	Starts a new paragraph of text
Strong	<STRON>	Strongly emphasizes text; usually in bold type
Title	<TITLE>	Signifies the title text of the document
Typewriter text	<TT>	Text appears in a monospace font (similar to that of a typewriter)
Underline	<U>	Text appears underlined

101 Best Places to Visit on the Internet

The Internet is chock-full of interesting places to visit, and the following list describes a few that you might try. They range in interest and in seriousness, so you can have some fun, too.

Description	Site
Microsoft junkies will find lots to appease them at Microsoft's WWW site, including technical support, product information, freeware, and even Bill Gates' keynote speeches.	http://www.microsoft.com
To keep on top of the latest Internet browser programs, tap into the BrowserWatch site for an up-to-date look at the major browsers, sites where you can get the programs, and news about up-and-coming browsers.	http://www.browserwatch.com/
The Netscape home page is full of information, including the latest versions of Netscape Navigator, lists of other cool sites, and Internet directories.	http://home.netscape.com
If you're interested in all things Web-related, you should definitely check out the Silicon Graphics page. It has dazzling art, along with Web authoring and serving software (including freeware).	http://www.sgi.com

(continues)

(continued)

Description	Site
You'll find some interesting photography on Quang-Tuan Luong's Web page, plus photo tips for photography enthusiasts.	http://robotics.eecs.berkeley.edu/~qtluong/photography/index.html
To find your favorite music CD or the latest music industry gossip, turn to CDNow. It offers over 165,000 CD titles you can purchase, plus music news.	http://cdnow.com
Post free classified ads on the Web at Fun City Classifieds. If you're looking to buy or looking to sell, you'll find plenty of ads for all kinds of items. It's tons of fun for bargain and treasure hunters.	http://www.funcity.com/classifieds/browse.html
Shopaholics will find all kinds of thrills with the Internet Shopping Network. Like the home shopping shows on cable TV, the Internet Shopping Network lets you buy everything from flowers and jewelry to computer software and hardware.	http://www.internet.net
If you're at all curious about the CIA, check out the Central Intelligence Agency site, which includes a virtual tour of the facility in Washington D.C., collections of maps, and CIA publications.	http://www.odci.gov/cia
Business entrepreneurs can get a free trial copy of *Innovation*, a publication about business innovations, trends, and strategies.	innovation-request@NewsScan.com (Send e-mail, leave the subject line blank, and type **subscribe** in the message body)
NASA fans can find the latest information about shuttle flights, video and sound files, and even a real-time Mercator tracking map to view the mission.	http://shuttle.nasa.gov
If you like MTV's *Real World* soap opera show, you'll love *The Spot* on the Internet. It's an episodic virtual soap opera following the lives of six inhabitants of a Santa Monica beach house.	http://www.thespot.com/
If you don't like *The Spot*, visit its evil twin, *The Squat*. It's a parody of the MTV-like phenomenon, except it takes place in a trailer park instead of a hip California beach house.	http://theory.physics.missouri.edu/~georges/Josh/squat/
For something a little different, stop by My Dog Ate the Internet, which contains 31 links hidden in the fur of a pug.	http://fish.lanl.gov/dog.html

Description	Site
If you're trying to figure out what Web sites to visit, you might want to stop at Point Communication's Top Sites page. It lists ratings of Web sites, based on content, presentation, and number of visits (popularity).	http://www.pointcom.com/gifs/topsites/
If you subscribe to cable TV's Discovery Channel, you already know what a great source it is for nature and science programs, among others. Tune in to the Discovery site for the same great information.	http://www.discovery.com
Another great TV-related Web page to see is the Sci-Fi Channel's Dominion page. You'll find video and sound clips, information about programming, and even interactive polling.	http://www.scifi.com/
The Wild Wilde Web site is an excellent resource for those looking for information about the career of British playwright Oscar Wilde.	http://www.anomtec.com:8001/oscarwilde/
Kids going to college soon? Visit the Financial Aid Information page for some tips and links to useful information about college loans, scholarships, and more.	http://www.cs.cmu.edu/afs/cs.cmu.edu/user/mkant/ Public/FinAid/finaid.html
For the hippest fashions, surf over to the Product page. You'll find a collection of wild New York and L.A. fashion items, ranging from python leather to Mongolian faux fur.	http://www.ProductNet.com
If you need the complete works of Shakespeare, this Web page should be your first stop. It includes a hypertext glossary for looking up those old-fashioned Elizabethan words.	http://the-tech.mit.edu/Shakespeare/works.html
The renowned Old Sturbridge Village Museum in Massachusetts now offers a virtual tour of the facility, including a gift shop.	http://www.osv.org
Ever wonder what's in a Hostess Twinkie? You're not alone, and you can find out the latest test results (including how the cream-filled snacks hold up under radiation tests) on The T.W.I.N.K.I.E.S. Project page .	http://www.rice.edu/~gouge/twinkies.html
Learn how to prepare for emergencies on the Epicenter: Emergency Preparedness Information Center page. It includes tips for dealing with emergencies such as earthquakes and bombings, plus dozens of links to related sites.	http://nwlink.com/epicenter/links.html

(continues)

(continued)

Description	Site
Wired magazine has a great Web site to explore, called HotWired. You'll find back issues of the magazine and all kinds of hip computer information.	http://www.hotwired.com/
Another great electronic zine (magazine) to check out is *Urban Desires*, a collection of metropolitan passions such as book reviews, art, and interviews with celebrities.	http://desires.com/issues.html
Learn everything you want to know about wolves on the Wolf Haven Web site. You can even "adopt" a wolf on the preserve.	http://www.teleport.com/~wnorton/wolf.html
You don't have to be a kid to enjoy The Looney Tunes Home Page. It has all your favorite Looney Tunes characters and more.	http://www.usyd.edu.au/~swishart/looney.html
The world's most famous art museum is now accessible through the Internet. Stop and stroll through the galleries of The Louvre in Paris, France. The site offers pictures of the greatest works of art, museum history, and even a floor plan of the museum.	http://www.paris.org/Musees/Louvre
If it's heavy sarcasm you're looking for, you'll find it in the electronic magazine *Suck*. It's devoted to Web sarcasm and the online phenomena.	http://www.suck.com
For American art, visit The National Museum of American Art site. It has over 1,000 pieces of art to view, plus video tours of the museum.	http://www.nmaa.si.edu:80
For help guiding your children on the Internet, turn to the Interesting Places for Kids site. It has a list of fun and entertaining Net sites for kids, as well as educational stops.	http://www.crc.ricoh.com/people/steve/kids.html
Beatles fans will rejoice at the detailed Beatlemania information on The Internet Beatles Album. It includes a photo gallery of the Fab Four and a screen saver you can download.	http://www.primenet.com/~dhaber/beatles.html
The Dilbert cartoon strip, a long-time favorite of Internet users, can be found on The Dilbert Zone Web page. It offers a daily dose of Dilbert, plus other Dilbert and Dogbert fun.	http://www.unitedmedia.com/comics/dilbert
USA Today has a Web page that equals this daily newspaper publication, complete with colorful graphics and zippy photographs.	http://www.usatoday.com

Description	Site
Here's an online version of the ESPN Sports Network, in the form of the ESPNet Sportzone site. It's a great source of sports-related information, team schedules, game recaps, and more.	http://espnet.sportszone.com/
If you're looking for newspapers and news sites around the nation, stop by the NewsLink site for directions. You'll find over 2,000 links to news sites ranging from national newspapers to college campus papers.	http://www.newslink.org
You can find London's renowned *The Telegraph* newspaper on the Electronic Telegraph Web page. You'll find the standard news, weather, and sports, plus international stories.	http://www.telegraph.co.uk/
Pick up your electronic copy of *Time* magazine at the Time Magazine site. You'll find the latest editions, plus late-breaking news.	http://www.pathfinder.com/time
If it's documents you want, The Library of Congress site is the place to be. It contains more than 70 million documents, so you can spend hours wading through text on American history, politics, or any other subject that interests you.	http://www.loc.gov
Tour the U.N. building without leaving your chair. Access The United Nations site to learn about U.N. activities and events.	http://www.un.org
If you're shopping for something a little different, try out the Speak To Me! site. It's full of products that use audio, such as talking clocks or teddy bears. You can even sample the sounds before you buy.	http://clickshop.com
If you're really into news, you won't want to miss a daily visit to CNN Interactive. The site lets you view the latest stories, search for archived stories, and view videos from the video vault.	Http://www.cnn.com
Looking for the latest stock market news? Check out The Wall Street Journal Money and Investing Update site. It has corporate and market news, including information about mutual funds.	http://update.wsj.com/

(continues)

(continued)

Description	Site
Good consumers can find information on a variety of topics using the Web site Consumer Information Catalog. You can download all kinds of brochures, and many are free.	http://www.gsa.gov/staff/pa/cic/ cic.htm
If you need to e-mail the FBI, you can do so on The United States Department of Justice site. Here you'll find information about law enforcement agencies and organizations, and a list of the ten most wanted criminals.	http://www.usdoj.gov/
If you're looking for a city map, try the City Net page. It includes detailed maps and information about cities all over the world. It's a great place for vacation planning.	http://www.city.net
To find a good quote, there's no better place to look than Bartlett's Familiar Quotations. You can use keywords or search for quotes from specific authors.	http://www.cc.columbia.edu/acis/bartleby/bartlett
Look at the online magazine *Hype* for amazing graphics. You'll also find sound files, links to other graphical sites, and more.	http://www.phantom.com/~giant/hype.html
Computer art lovers should stop by Joseph Squier's Web site and browse the electronic art gallery. The art here has been created just for the Web.	http://gertrude.art.uiuc.edu/ludgate/the/place/ place2.thml
For even more culture, stop by Salvador Dali's Home Page. It's worth the visit.	http://wildsau.idv.uni-linz.ac.at/~chris/Dali/
If fine art isn't for you, perhaps you'll be interested in something less serious, such as Big Dave's Cow Page. You'll find a tribute to cows of all sorts.	http://www.gl.umbc.edu/~dschmi1/links/cow.html
Crayola Kids magazine has a Web page that's tons of fun. It also sponsors contests, so drop in and see what you can win.	http://www.crayola.com/crayola/crayolakids/ home.html
Anyone interested in kids books and the people who author them will find The Big Busy House site (created by HarperCollins Children's Books) very educational. Children can log on and meet illustrators and authors, plus learn how books are published.	http://www.harpercollins.com/kids/
Fans of Nickelodeon's *Rugrats* cartoon will find lots to interest them on The Rugrats Home Page.	http://www.gti.net/azog/rugrats/

Description	Site
If you want to fall in love, you might try posting an ad on the Web Personals. It has worked for some people, and they've even gone on to marry.	http://www.webpersonals.com/date/
If it's games you want, check out the Fun and Games at VirtuMall, an online game room for people who like crossword puzzles, Concentration, and other games.	http://virtumall.com/fast/fun_games.html
Open the Crossword Crossroads Web page and print out a crossword puzzle to do. If it's a tough one and you need help, the Web site has links to help you find the answers.	http://www.polar7.com/cc/default.html
If live-action role-playing games are more your style, try the Nero Ashbury LARP site. Its role-playing game combines King Arthur-like legends with a Tolkien's Lord of the Rings environment.	http://world.std.com/~Gadlen/nero.html
The Digital Nostalgia Web site has over 30 vintage video games you can play (IBM format).	http://www.umich.edu/~sloane/games.html
Stellar Crisis is another strategy game worth checking out. It allows multiple players (12 hours per turn) to compete for control of a fictional galaxy.	http://www.liberty.netorg.8080/sc
Kids will enjoy *Sports Illustrated for Kids* online page. It's an electronic version of the magazine.	http://www.pathfinder.com/SIFK/
The Bible Gateway site lets you view several translations of the Bible, in seven languages. Much like an electronic concordance, the Web page lets you search for words and verses.	http://www.gospelcom.net/bible
For a real taste of global sights and sounds, turn to the RootsWorld page and explore "Real Music for the Real World," which includes everything from bagpipes to drums from India.	http://www.rootsworld.com/rw/
Did you know you can visit the Rock and Roll Hall of Fame on the Internet? You can, and it lets you access information about each inductee, as well as sound files.	http://www.rockhall.com

(continues)

(continued)

Description	Site
For a variety of online items, stop by The Gigaplex page. This site has a Filmplex, Bookplex, Artplex, and many other "plexes" you can enjoy. Each plex has all kinds of information about the topic, plus video and sound clips.	http://www.directnet.com/wow
For the latest scoop about the entertainment business, visit the Mr. Showbiz page. You'll find juicy gossip, news, and reviews about your favorite stars. It's also a good place for celebrity photos.	http://Web3.starwave.com/showbiz
S.P.Q.R.: The Virtual Rome offers visitors something a little unusual—an interactive Web game that taps into ancient Rome, complete with famous Roman architecture. It takes a while to get used to playing, but it's well worth the effort.	http://www.pathfinder.com/ @@PhaM2uHPFgAAQJ18/twep/rome/
There are over 130 government-related electronic bulletin boards you can tap into with the FedWorld Information Network, including boards focusing on space, health care, natural resources, and more.	http://www.fedworld.gov/
For the latest stats on U.S. populations in cities and towns across the country, open The U.S. Census Bureau Web page. You'll also find all kinds of demographics on such topics as leading economic indicators.	http://www.census.gov
There's a digital version of *Roget's Thesaurus*, and you'll find it at the ARTFL Project: ROGET'S Form site. You can look up words and find out what they mean before you use them.	http://humanities.uchicago.edu/forms_unrest/ ROGET.html
Gumby is on the Net, and you can visit his home page to learn about his upcoming movie.	http://www.xnet.com/~gumby/gumby.html
If you're looking for literature, start with a search of the Internet Public Library Web site. You'll find reference materials, children's books, and even reading rooms.	http://ipl.sils.umich.edu/
Whether you're a hypochondriac or a medical student, you'll find something of interest at The Global Health Network, which has a wonderful collection of health-related sites to explore.	http://www.pitt.edu/HOME/GHNet/GHNet.html

Description	Site
Need to look up a translation of Homer's *Odyssey*? The Tech Classics Archive can help. With over 375 translations of Italian, Greek, and Roman classics, it's a great place to search for ancient works.	http://the-tech.mit.edu/Classics
One of the best Web search tools you can use is the Yahoo Search site. Simply type in the topic you're looking for, and it compiles a list of related Web sites.	http://yahoo.com/search.html
The World Wide Web Worm is another search engine you can use to find Web pages of interest. It lets you look for specific hypertext links, and it's easy to use.	http://www.cs.colorado.edu/home/mcbryan/WWWW.html
To quickly track down businesses that maintain and use Web pages, let the NetSearch site help you.	http://www.netmail.com/
Want to learn to speak Italian? There's a Web site sponsored by Ragu that can help you.	http://www.eat.com/learn-italian.html
Having trouble with your grammar? English teacher Jack Lynch has a Web site for all manner of grammar and style notes.	http://www.english.upenn.edu/~jlynch/grammar.html
Music fans can find a compendium of music information, bibliographies, and more at The MIT Music Library. There's also an index of over 17,000 musical recordings.	http://web.mit.edu/afs/athena/dept/libdata/applications/www/depts/music/music-top.html
Memorabilia collectors will find plenty to interest them at the collectible.com site, including old movie posters and celebrity photos.	http://www.collectible.com/
L.L. Bean has a great online catalog to browse, complete with color photos and even a Park Search tool to help you look up information about 900 national parks and forests.	http://www.llbean.com/
Mystery book lovers will enjoy book reviews and author interviews on The Mystery Zone page.	http://www.mindspring.com/~walter/mystzone.html
If you're looking for recipes, subscribe to the alt.food.recipes newsgroup and swap proven recipes with your fellow Internet travelers.	Usenet: alt.food.recipes
If seafood's your passion, you'll want to sample the catch on The Alaska Seafood Cookbook site. It includes recipes, tips, and more.	http://www.state.ak.us/local/akpages/COMMERCE/ascmain.htm

(continues)

(continued)

Description	Site
Chocolate lovers will find the scoop on chocolate facts and fiction on the I Need My Chocolate page. It even includes mouth-watering recipes.	http://www.qrc.com/~sholubek/choco/start.htm
For even more chocolate focus, stop by the Chocolate Town U.S.A. page for a visit to Hershey's chocolate company. It's packed with chocolate recipes the entire family will drool over.	http://www.hersheys.com/~hershey/
Geologists and map lovers will enjoy the U.S. Geological Survey National Mapping Information site, complete with earth science information, educational information, and many maps.	http://www-nmd.usgs.gov/
Do you watch the popular television show, *Friends*? If you do, you'll definitely want to visit The Friends Official Web Page. If you ever miss an episode, you can catch up here.	http://www.nbc.com/entertainment/shows/friends/index.html
World famous secret agent 007 has a hit Web site that you must see at least once. It contains great photos, sound files, and even James Bond trivia.	http://www.mcs.net/~klast/www/bond.html
If you're ready to explore the realm of classical music, Classical Net is the place to start. Here, you'll find information about all the world's great classical composers, plus links to other musical sites.	http://www.classical.net/music/
A dazzling page for sports fans, the NBA.com page is not only a clever promotional tool, but it's full of videos and sound files of basketball's finest players and games.	http://www.nba.com/
Create your own hometown newspaper on the CRAYON page. It's fun and easy.	http://crayon.net/
If you're interested in travel, don't pack your bags until you check out the Travel Channel on the Internet. It's a great source of travel information, and includes pictures from vacation sites around the world.	http://www.travelchannel.com/
If it's e-mail you want, then it's e-mail you shall have, if you search the LISTSERV Archives. You can look for topics alphabetically and learn how to launch your own listserv database.	Internet: gopher sjuvm.stjohns.edu; select disabled; listserv

Description	Site
America's Job Bank site offers access to thousands of jobs across the country. If you're serious about a new job or career change, this is the place to start looking.	http://www.ajb.dni.us/index.html
CareerWEB offers another database source for job opportunities, allowing you to search by job type, company, or location.	http://www.cweb.com/
Crashsite is one of those odd but interesting Web sites you just have to stop and see for yourself. It has quicktime movies, animation, and more.	http://www.crashsite.com/Crash

Index

X

Y

Z

A VIACOM SERVICE

The Information SuperLibrary™

Bookstore   **Search**   **What's New**   **Reference**   **Software**   **Newsletter**   **Company Overviews**

Yellow Pages   **Internet Starter Kit**   **HTML Workshop**   **Win a Free T-Shirt!**   **Macmillan Computer Publishing**   **Site Map**   **Talk to Us**

CHECK OUT THE BOOKS IN THIS LIBRARY.

Complete and Return this Card
for a *FREE* Computer Book Catalog

Thank you for purchasing this book! You have purchased a superior computer book written expressly for your needs. To continue to provide the kind of up-to-date, pertinent coverage you've come to expect from us, we need to hear from you. Please take a minute to complete and return this self-addressed, postage-paid form. In return, we'll send you a free catalog of all our computer books on topics ranging from word processing to programming and the internet.

Mr. ☐   Mrs. ☐   Ms. ☐   Dr. ☐

Name (first) ☐☐☐☐☐☐☐☐☐☐ (M.I.) ☐   (last) ☐☐☐☐☐☐☐☐☐☐☐☐☐☐☐

Address ☐☐☐☐☐☐☐☐☐☐☐☐☐☐☐☐☐☐☐☐☐☐☐☐☐☐☐☐

☐☐☐☐☐☐☐☐☐☐☐☐☐☐☐☐☐☐☐☐☐☐☐☐☐☐☐☐

City ☐☐☐☐☐☐☐☐☐☐☐☐   State ☐☐   Zip ☐☐☐☐☐ ☐☐☐☐

Phone ☐☐☐ ☐☐☐ ☐☐☐☐   Fax ☐☐☐ ☐☐☐ ☐☐☐☐

Company Name ☐☐☐☐☐☐☐☐☐☐☐☐☐☐☐☐☐☐☐☐☐☐☐

E-mail address ☐☐☐☐☐☐☐☐☐☐☐☐☐☐☐☐☐☐☐☐☐☐☐

1. Please check at least (3) influencing factors for purchasing this book.

Front or back cover information on book .... ☐
Special approach to the content .... ☐
Completeness of content .... ☐
Author's reputation .... ☐
Publisher's reputation .... ☐
Book cover design or layout .... ☐
Index or table of contents of book .... ☐
Price of book .... ☐
Special effects, graphics, illustrations .... ☐
Other (Please specify): _____ ☐

2. How did you first learn about this book?

Saw in Macmillan Computer Publishing catalog .... ☐
Recommended by store personnel .... ☐
Saw the book on bookshelf at store .... ☐
Recommended by a friend .... ☐
Received advertisement in the mail .... ☐
Saw an advertisement in: _____ ☐
Read book review in: _____ ☐
Other (Please specify): _____ ☐

3. How many computer books have you purchased in the last six months?

This book only .... ☐   3 to 5 books .... ☐
2 books .... ☐   More than 5 .... ☐

4. Where did you purchase this book?

Bookstore .... ☐
Computer Store .... ☐
Consumer Electronics Store .... ☐
Department Store .... ☐
Office Club .... ☐
Warehouse Club .... ☐
Mail Order .... ☐
Direct from Publisher .... ☐
Internet site .... ☐
Other (Please specify): _____ ☐

5. How long have you been using a computer?

☐ Less than 6 months   ☐ 6 months to a year
☐ 1 to 3 years   ☐ More than 3 years

6. What is your level of experience with personal computers and with the subject of this book?

	With PCs	With subject of book
New	☐	☐
Casual	☐	☐
Accomplished	☐	☐
Expert	☐	☐

Source Code ISBN: 0-7897-0753-5

7. Which of the following best describes your job title?

Administrative Assistant .... ☐
Coordinator .... ☐
Manager/Supervisor .... ☐
Director .... ☐
Vice President .... ☐
President/CEO/COO .... ☐
Lawyer/Doctor/Medical Professional .... ☐
Teacher/Educator/Trainer .... ☐
Engineer/Technician .... ☐
Consultant .... ☐
Not employed/Student/Retired .... ☐
Other (Please specify): _____ ☐

8. Which of the following best describes the area of the company your job title falls under?

Accounting .... ☐
Engineering .... ☐
Manufacturing .... ☐
Operations .... ☐
Marketing .... ☐
Sales .... ☐
Other (Please specify): _____ ☐

Comments: _____
_____
_____

9. What is your age?

Under 20 .... ☐
21-29 .... ☐
30-39 .... ☐
40-49 .... ☐
50-59 .... ☐
60-over .... ☐

10. Are you:

Male .... ☐
Female .... ☐

11. Which computer publications do you read regularly? (Please list)

_____
_____
_____
_____
_____
_____
_____
_____
_____
_____

Fold here and scotch-tape to mail.